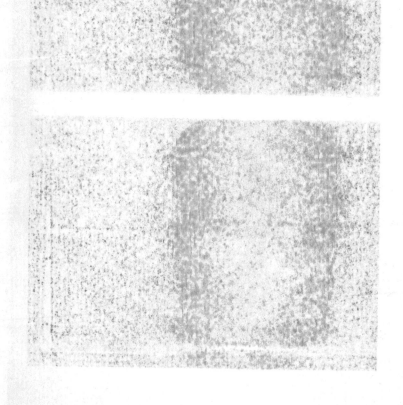

ENGLISH RECUSANT LITERATURE
1558—1640

Selected and Edited by
D. M. ROGERS

Volume 196

RICHARD BROUGHTON
The Judgement of the Apostles
1632

RICHARD BROUGHTON
The Judgement of the Apostles
1632

The Scolar Press

1974

ISBN o 85967 173 9

Published and printed in Great Britain by
The Scolar Press Limited, 59-61 East Parade,
Ilkley, Yorkshire and
39 Great Russell Street,
London WC1

1810344

NOTE

Reproduced (original size) from a copy in the library of Ushaw College, by permission of the President.
References: Allison and Rogers 163; STC 3898.

THE
IVDGEMENT
OF THE
APOSTLES.

*

THE
IVDGEME·NT
OF THE
APOSTLES:
AND OF THOSE OF THE
FIRST AGE, IN ALL POINTS
of doctrine queſtioned betweene the
Catholikes and Proteſtants of England,
as they are ſet downe in the 39. Articles
of their Religion.

By an old ſtudent in Diuinitie.

AT DOWAY,
By the widdow of MARK WYON,
at the ſigne of the golden Phœnix.

M. DC. XXXII.

TO HER MOST
EXCELLENT MAIESTY
MARIE
BY THE GRACE OF GOD
QVEENE
OF GREAT BRITTANY,
FRANCE AND IRELAND.

ALL dignities (Most Gratious Queene) haue assembled themselues in your Maiestie, striuing (as it were) to make you Great and Glorious: Whether we respect that great Monarchie of Fraunce, whose Iewell & darling you are, or that great Monarch HENRY the fourth your no-

* 3   ble

ble Father, surnamed GREAT for his
MARTIALL CHIVALRIE, or your
Most Illustrious Mother descended
of the howse of the great Duke of
Florence , or your most Christian
brother King of Fraunce surnamed
I V S T E, or your noble Sisters, the one
married to the great and CATHOLIKE
King of Spaine , the other to the
potent and warlike Duke of Sauoye.
And although your Maiestie may
seeme to haue left all these dignities
in leauing Fraunce, & transporting
your selfe to Inglãd : Yet they follow
you as inseparable attendants on
your royall vertues ; yea now there is
a new dignitie accrewed vnto your
Maiestie greater then all the rest, to
wit, Your mariage with our great
King CHARLES, his great Crowne
and Kingdome:because by your former dignities, you were only daughter and Sister to Kings and Queenes;
by

by this you art a greate Queene, and
Spouſe to the mighty Prince and
greate King of the great Brittanie:
and by him, you haue all the greatneſſe alſo which the Royall bloud
of him and his Anceſtours can adde
vnto yours. I may adde to all this
another thing which doth agrandize
your greatneſſe more thē all the reſt:
to wit, your Maieſties Conſtancie in
Religiō amidſt ſo many diuers ſectes
of hereſie, your zeale towards the Catholike cauſe, your compaſſion of
your Catholike Subiectes, for whom
you are often ſuppliant to our noble
Souueraigne in all their diſtreſſes; &
laſtlie your manie pretious and rare
indowmentes of nature & grace, for
which our noble King loueth you
dearely, your ſubiectes admire you,
and God hath bleſſed you with a
Royall and hopefull iſſue. When I
caſt mine eyes on the reſplendent

beames

beames & luftre of this your Greatneffe, I confeffe I was daunted, and
feared to approach to fo Great maieftie, efpeciallie with fo litle a prefent,
as I had prepared, to wit, this litle pam-
phlet rudelie compiled, and in ref-
pect of it felfe and the Authour, nothing befeeming, becaufe nothing
proportionate, to your greatneffe.
But becaufe great Princes, who cannot be Higher or greater in Temporall dignitie, difdaine not, yea take
pleafure, to bowe euen to their loweft
Subiectes, and doe willinglie accept
of their loyall duties and refpectes,
be they expreffed by neuer fo litle
prefentes, I aduentured (prefuming
on your Maiefties great and gratious
Goodneffe) to dedicate this my
booke vnto your Royall Maieftie, &
my felfe and humble feruice with it:
hoping that although in other refpectes, it be too litle a prefent for fo

great

great a Queene, yet in that it containeth the Iudgement of the great A-
poftles and Apoftolicall Doctours of
the firft age after Chrift, concerning
the Proteftant Religion conteined
in the articles authorized by Parlament, it will not be flighted nor light-
lie efteemed by your moft Excellent
Maieftie: It will rather confirme and
comfort your Maieftie in the Catholike faith, when by this booke you
shall perceaue, that you profeffe the
fame religion which the Apoftles and
Apoftolicall Doctours preached and
deliuered ; which S. PETER taught
in our countrie; which S. IOSEPH of
Arimathie (who buried CHRIST
and was at his mothers death and Affumption) taught and practifed at
Glaftenburie, where he and his companions fixed their aboade, and paf-
fed their life in faftinges, watchinges
and prayers, as our Annalles doe teftifie,

ſtifie : Which not onelie the noble Kings of France, from CLODO-VEVS the firſt Chriſtian King, to King LEWIS the IVST who now raigneth, imbraced; but alſo our firſt Chriſtian King LVCIVS re-ceiued from that holy Pope ELEV-THERIVS, who ſent him not onely preachers to inſtruct him and his people, but alſo, as our Annales re-corde vnto vs, *ſent vnto him an hal-lowed crowne, and extended the limits of his Kingdome to Norwaye and Den-marke*: Which faith all our firſt Chri-ſtian Kinges who were alſo Saintes mantained by ſword and Scepter : as Sainct LVCIVS our firſt Chri-ſtian King, S. LVCIVS or LVCIAN Apoſtle to the BAVARIANS, S. CONSTANTINE Emperour amongſt the Grecians, S. CONSTANTINE King, S. THEODRICKE, the two SS. ETHELBERTES, the two SS.

ETHEL-

ETHELDREDS, S. GVNDLEVS, S.
OSWALD, S. OSWIN, S. SEBBE,
S. CEADWALL, S. INAS, S. SIGE-
BERT, S. RICHAD, the twoe SS.
ALFREDS, S. CEOLNVLPHE, S.
FREMVND, S. KENELME, S. E-
THELNVPH, SS. EDGAR, S. ED-
MVND, the two S. EDWARDS, and
S. MALCOLME, and their holie
Queenes also imbraced: as S. HELEN
Queene and Emperesse mother to
CONSTANTINE the great, S. AV-
DRIE or ETHELDRED, S. CHIN-
NEBVRGE, S. EANFLED, S. ER-
MEMBVRGE, S. ETHELBVRG; S.
ERMVILD, S. HERESWIDE, S.
BVTHILDIS, S. SEXBVRGE, S.
WILFRED, S. EADGITH, S. AL-
GVIE, S. AGATHE, S. MARGARET,
S. MAVDE. To which I willinglie
adde our holie Queene S. BERTH,
as whom your Maieſtie ſo much re-
preſenteth and reſembleth. She was
daugh-

daughter to a King of France, so is
your Maiestie : She was married to
King ETHELBERT who then was of
a contrarie religion to her; so is your
Maiestie despoused to our King
CHARLES the GREAT, different as
yet from your Maiestie in Religion:
She was allowed a Bishop and others
to be about hee, who were of her religion; so is your Maiestie: She by her
prayers and good examples together
with some religious preachers sent
by S. GREGORIE the great, procured the conuersion of her HVS-
BAND and his people vnto the Christian and Catholike faith and religion; so we hope that your Maiestie
shall by your holie prayers and examples, for which our soueraigne loueth
you dearely, be a cause of his conuersion to the Catholique Faith; at least,
we hope your Maiestie shall worke in
him such a liking of the Catholike
Faith,

Faith, that he shall neuer permitte that faith to be perfecuted, for the defence whereof againft Luther, King HENRY the eight, his great vncle, was the firft who by Pope LEO the Tenthe, was Honoured with the glorious title of DEFENDOVR OF THE FAITH, which with the crowne and Kingdome is lineallie defcended vnto his Maieftie. Certes, his morall life free from all note of vice, in which he yeeldeth to no Chriftian Prince in Europe, feemeth to promife noe leffe. This our Kingdome (moft noble Queene) is ftiled in auncient hiftories THE DOWRIE OF MARIE the mother of God : Which perchaûce is the caufe why it hath beene fo fortunate in Queene MARIES, as in Queene MARIE who reftored the Catholike Religion after the death of her brother King EDWARD

the

the fixt: and in Queene MARIE
our Souueraignes grand-mother, who
sanctified our Land with her bloud
shed for defence of the Catholike
Faith : and laftlie by your Maieftie
our laft Queene MARIE, by whom
this land is bleffed by a royall iffue,
and as we hope shall in time be made
happie by reftitution of the Catholike Religion, ether in your owne, or
your childrens dayes. And the rather
when England shall fee by the Iudgement of the Apoftles, that the Catholike religiō aggreeth in all points
with the religion taught & deliuered
by the Apoftles and firft Apoftolicall
preachers, and that the Proteftant religiō is difcoūtenaunced, difcarded,
condemned by them. This shall appeare by this booke, which I, your
Maiefties moft humble fubiect, an
old ftudent in holie learning, doe in
all dutifull manner prefent vnto you;
wish-

wishing to your Gracious Maieſtie, and to our noble Souueraigne,
your deare Spouſe, a long and happie
raigne in our great Brittainie, & ſuch
a temporall raigne amongſt your
ſubieƈtes, as you may both raigne in
heauen eternallie with God, his
Saintes, and Angelles.

Your Maieſties

moſt humble

and deuoted ſubieƈt

R.   B.

APPROBATIO.

CVm mihi conftiterit ex teftimonio fide digni S. Theol. Doctoris, in hoc libro, cui titulus *Apoftolorum iudicium &c.* nihil inueniri Catholicæ fidei aut bonis moribus contrarium, fed multa quæ oftendunt religionem Catholicorum effe Apoftolicam, hæreticorum verò Apoftaticam, cenfui vtiliter prælo committi poffe. Actum Duaci die 23. Iunij 1632.

GEORGIVS COLVENERIVS *S. Theol. Doctor & Regius ordinariufque Profeffor, Collegiatæ Ecclefiæ S. Petri Præpofitus, Duacenfis Academiæ Cancellarius, & librorum Cenfor.*

THE FIRST CHAPTER:

CONCERNINGE THE FIRST 5. PRO-
teſtants Articles, not differinge from the Apoſtles Religion, and the Roman Church.

B EINGE to enter into the Examen, and compariſon of the parlament proteſtant Articled Religion
of England, with the Religion of
the preſent Church, of Rome, and
the whole Chriſtian world, named Catholike,
(for profeſſion whereof, the Catholiks of England,
by the proteſtants thereof, haue longe tyme ſuffered, and ſtill moſt conſtantly endure, moſt bitter
perſecutions) by the firſt knowne and confeſſed
true Chriſtian, Catholike, Apoſtolike, Religion,
of the Apoſtles, and that their happy age; wee finde
not in the firſt fiue Articles of this new Religion,
any difference or difficulty, *to be thus decided*, both
Catholicks and parlamētary proteſtants agreeing,
in them all, *and they all beeing ordeyned by theſe proteſtants, againſt other Sectaries ſo ſoone within 4.
yeares of the beginning of Q. Elizabeth her Reigne, re-
uiueing old condemned hereſies, amongſt them, as their
hiſtories, and regiſters remember: and therefore*, it will
here ſuffice, onely to recite the Titles of theſe articles to giue notice thereof. The contents and title
of the firſt article are. *Of faith in the holy Trinity.*
The ſecond : *of the word or ſonne of God which was*

A

made

made very mā. The 3. *Of the going downe of Christ into hell*. The 4. *Of the Resurrection of Christ*. The 5. *Of the Holy Ghost*. The whole Article (the Title being subiect to doubt) is *The holy Ghost*, *proceeding from the Father and the sonne, is of one substance, Maiesty, and glory, with the Father, and the Sonne, very and eternall God*. Hitherto wee finde nothing against the doctrine of the Catholike Church. Which not vnlikely these men did rather to winne some credit at their entrance to be thought louers of truth, then that they hated the enemies of these articles, not yet suppressed among them.

THE SECOND CHAPTER.

*Examining their 6. Article about Scriptures and tra-
ditions, and condemning it, by the Apostles,
and Apostolike men, and doctrine
of their age.*

THEIR next sixt Article intituled, *of the suf-
ficiency of the holy Scriptures for Saluation*: is thus: *holy Scripture containeth all things necessary to saluation: Soe that whatsoeuer is not read therein, nor may be proued thereby is not to be required of any man, that it should be beleeued as an article of faith, or be thought requisite or necessary to saluation. By the name of holy Scripture, wee doe vnderstand those canonicall bookes of the old and new testament, of whose authority was neuer any doubt in the Church*. And from the number of those bookes which there they allowe to be canonicall, They doe in expresse words, and tearmes reiect. *The booke of Tobias, the booke of Iudith, the rest of the booke of Esther, the booke of wisdome,*

Iesus

Iesus the sonne of Sirach, Baruch the Prophet, the songe. of the three children, the story of Susanna, of Bel and. the Dragon, the prayer of Manasses, the first and second Bookes of the Machabees. Concerning the new testament thus they adde: *all the bookes of the new testament, as they are commonly receiued, wee doe receiue and accompte them for canonicall.* This their Article is in their proceedings, as the grounde worke and foundation, whereupon their Religion is wholy framed, and builded; and yet so weake, Feeble, totteringe ruinous arid deceitefull, that not any one true certaine and infallible point of doctrine (as euery Article in true religion is) can be framed vpō it, or from it 'so deduced, by the expresse graunt of this article it selfe, and of all English Protestants, professed, and sworne maintainers of it.

For whereas they sentence and define : *In the name of holy Scripture, wee doe vnderstand those canonicall bookes of the old and new testament, of whose authority was neuer any doubt in the Church :* They plainely make the Iudgment of the Church, to be the highest tribunall in spirituall questions, euen of the scriptures themselues. And thus their best and cheife writers, published by authority doe glosse and expound this article.; And of necessity so they must say, except at their first entrance they will plainely confesse their religion, and congregation, their Church of England (as they terme it,) to be erroneous or hereticall, and to haue noe power or warrant at all to doubt deny or determine, and propose what bookes be, or be not Scriptures canonicall, either of the old or new testament. Or what one chapter, or sentence in them is part or not part of such canonicall and vndoubted holy

Art. 6. supr.

Field Booke
of the Church
lib. 4. cap. 5.
Wotton def. of
perk.pa.442.
Couell. ag.
Burg. pag.60.
def. of Hooker pag. 31.
32.33.protest.
glosse on the
6. art. Tho.
Rogers ibid.

Scriptures: for this power and prerogatiue being onely committed to the true Church by their Article, and profeffors before, if thefe men doubt, or Iudge otherwife in this cafe, then the true confeffed Church hath hitherto done, They can be noe part, or members of that true Church. And whatfoeuer is read, or may be deduced from vntrue or doubted Scriptures, cannot be poffibly any certaine, and vndoubted article of faith, and religion. For noe conclufion can be more certaine and vndoubted, then the Maximes and authorities from which it is concluded, but as the light of nature, & common law and vndeniable Maxime of true reafoning teacheth all men, and all men truely acknowledge for a verity moft certaine, it euer followeth the weaker part; euer erroneous, doubtfull, vncertaine or falfe, if both, or any of the propofitions from which it is deduced, be or is of that nature. Nothing can giue that to an other, which it felfe wanteth, and by noe meanes hath to giue. A lying falfe or vncertaine humane witneffe or affertion, can by no meanes poffible make a conftant and certainely true probation in any thing whatfoeuer, much leffe in fupernaturall matters, articles of faith aboue mans capacity, and therefore to be proued by diuine teftimony, which poffibly cannot deceaue vs.

And in this miferable and defolate eftate and condition, is the Proteftant congregation of England, in, and for euery article pretended by them to be of faith which they hold againft the Roman Church at this day, and fo they cenfure themfelues by their owne definitiue fentence, in this their owne cheefeft Article, and publikely authorized

gloffe

gloſſe thereof, with diuers others of their Religion, allowed and recommended writers among them, In their Article receauing onely for canonicall bookes, neuer doubted of in the Church, and in the others (to vſe their owne authorizing words) *peruſed, and by the lawfull authority of the Church of England, allowed to be publike,* plainely & manifeſtly deliuering from all kinde of Authors, Greeke and Latine, old and late, Catholike and Proteſtant, That euery booke in particular, not one excepted, which they allowe for canonicall Scripture, either in the old or new teſtament, haue both beene doubted of, and by their owne, men, Proteſtants, denied for ſuch.

Therefore it remaineth without queſtion contrary to this Proteſtante Article, euen by themſelues and their beſt authority, that neither all nor any one of thoſe bookes which vpon this vayne pretence they haue blotted forth from the Canon of holy Scripture, and the Roman Church ſtill receaueth, may be denyed by that Title of ſometimes being doubted of: for wee ſhould haue noe Scripture canonicall at all, all bookes thereof hauing beene thus doubted of. By that colour wee might deny all Articles of faith, which ſometimes doubted of, haue beene concluded and agreed vpon againſt the vileſt heretiks that euer were, and all their hereſies both might and ought to be reuiued againe. Sainct Paul and Sainct Thomas Apoſtles were thus to be denied Apoſtles, and thruſt out of heauen, becauſe they had doubted; wee might and ought to ſay, that no conuerted Chriſtian firſt doubting, was a true Chriſtian, neither our firſt brittiſh Chriſtian Kinge Sainct Lucius, nor Kinge Ethelbert among

A 3 our

Margin notes:

Artic.6. ſupr. Confeſsio Wirtemberg. cap. de Scriptura. Proteſt. gloſſe in art.6. & p. 1. Willet Synop. quæſt. 1. of ſcriptnre. pag.2.5. edit. an.1594. holniſh. chron. f. 1299. Stowe hiſt. an. 1579. in Q. Elizabeth, Io. Brét. Apolog. contfeſſ. Wittemberg. hiſtor. Dauidis Georg. Diſplay Art.6. Magdeburg. hiſt. cent.3. ca. 11.

our Saxons, nor any of their first doubting and afterward conuerted Subiects, and soe of the whole Christian world doubting or denying before it receaued the law of Christ. All Courts, Consistories, Tribunals, and Seates of Iustice and Iudgment ecclesiasticall, and ciuil, to decide and determine must be ouerthrowne, no sentence or decision though of Kings, Parlaments, or any community is to be obeyed, no doubt, no Controuersie, hitherto euer was, or hereafter can or may be finally determined; nothing but doubtes, quarrels, Controuersies, and contentions, as wee see among Protestants, no peace, quiet or vnion must be left vnto vs. Therefore this Protestant paradoxe and presumption in reiecting so many bookes of holy Scripture againtt both the Latine and Greeke Church, onely vnder colour of being sometime, and by some doubted of, being thus grosse and absurd by their owne Iudgments, and proceedings, let vs examine what this first pure and Apostolike age did Iudge of thē.

The new testament by Protest. trāsl. published by King Iames authority.
Matth. 6.
2. Cor. 9.
Luc. 14.
Ioan 9.
Hebr. 5.
1. Cor. 1.
Hebr. 1.

Rom. 11.

And first to begin with the scripture it selfe of the new Testament euen as our Protestants receaue and translate it. King Iames his new testament in the 6. chapter of Sainct Matthew his ghospell, and the 9. chapter 2. Corinth. citeth Ecclesiasticus in two seuerall places. In the 14. chapter of Sainct Luke the 4. chapter of Tobias is cited. And in the 10. chapter of Sainct Ihon the 4. chapter of the first booke of Machabees. And in the 5. chapter to the Hebrewes the second booke. And 7. chapter of the Machabees. In the 1. chapter 1. Corinth. The first chapter of the booke of wisdome is cited. 1. chapter to the Hebrewes citeth the 7. chapter of wisdome. And the 9. chapter thereof is cited Rom.

cap.11. And yet wee shall scarcely finde any Text of diuers bookes of the old Testament, which our Protestants allowe for canonicall, to be cited at any time or place of their new testament, as the 4. Booke of the Kings, the 1. and 2. of Paralip. the booke of the Iudges, Ruth, Esdras 1. and 2. Esther, Ecclesiastes, Cantica canticorum, Abdias, Sophonias, Therefore wee are as well warranted by this argument of concordance of Scriptures, and that holy authority to receaue for canonicall Scriptures of the old Testament, all those bookes which our Protestants haue excluded, as those they haue receaued. The Canons ascribed to the Apostles, and published by Sainct Clement *per me Clementem* Successour to S. Peter in this age, are plainely acknowledged by the sixt generall Councell to haue beene receaued by the holy Fathers before them as deliuered from God, *firmi stabilesque maneant, qui à sanctis patribus qui nos precesserunt, suscepti ac confirmati sunt, atque à Deo nobis etiam traditi sunt, sanctorum Apostolorum nomine* 85. *Canones,* These doe in the last Canon expressely receaue the books of the Machabees, Esther, and the booke of Ecclesiasticus for holy Scriptures of the old testament. *Venerandi ac sacri libri veteris Testamenti.* In the very same maner as they doe the others which our Protestants allowe for such. Sainct Clement often citeth, and alloweth for bookes and parts of the old Testament, Baruch, Ecclesiasticus, Sapientia, Tobias, The prayer of Manasses, the history of Susanna, the booke of Esther, those parts of Daniel which our Protestants reiect, the bookes of Machabees and others. Sainct Ignatius receaueth the booke of Daniel which our Protestants deny, Ecclesia-

Concil gener. 6. cap. 2.

Canon. Apostolor. can. 85. vlt.

Clem.epist.1. 2.Apostolic. constitut.li.2. c.4. cap 22.c. 49.51.cap 63. l.3. cap 3. l.6. c.19. 23. 29. l. 8. l.7.

A 4

Ignat.epiſt.ad
Philadelph.e-
piſt. ad may-
neſian epiſt.
ad Heron.Po-
lycarp.epiſt.
ad Philippen.
Dioniſ.l.de
diu.nom. cap.
4.Eccleſiaſt.
Hier. c.2.de
diu.nom. c.7.

Eleuther.ep.
ad Lucium
Reg.Rritan.
apud Gal.
Lambrrt. 1 de
leg.S.Eduardi
Stowe hiſt.
fore tom. 1.
Godwin. Cō-
uerſ. of Brit.
Hollinsh hiſt.
of Eng.Speed.
Theat. of Bit.
Matth.park.
antiq. Britan.

Matth.park.
antiq. Brit. p.
6.9.10. Goſc.
hiſt.Eccl.Da-
uid.poiuel. in
Annot. in l.2.
c.1.Girald.
Cābr.Itiner.
Cābr. Bal.1 1.
Script.Brit.
cent.1. in Au-
guſt.Rom.l.2.
de Act. Pon-
tif. Rom.in
Greg. 1.

cleſiaſticus. Sainct Policarpus approueth Tobias. Sainct Denys the Areopagite conuerted by Sainct Paul alloweth the booke of wiſdome, calleth the part of Daniel excluded by our Proteſtants, diuine Scripture. *Diuina ſcripta.* Theſe be all, or the chiefeſt writers eſpecially by Proteſtants allowance in this firſt age, and conſideringe how few of their works are preſerued to poſterity, and how briefe they are: It is rather to be wondred, that they should cite and allow ſo many of thoſe books, of the old teſtament, and parts of them, ſo often as they doe, then that they should omit any.

And although wee doe not finde any Antiquity of Britaine which in this age entreateth of ſuch things, yet the moſt auncient which our Proteſtants will graunte vnto vs beinge the Epiſtle of Pope Eleutherius to Kinge Lucius, wee finde therein, that he makinge mention, that Britaine had receaued both the Teſtaments of holy Scripture, although in particular he citeth ſo few bookes of them, that out of the new teſtament he citeth no more then onely the 23.chapter of S. Matthew, & from the old teſtamēt, but three texts, two of them beinge out of the Pſalmes 45. 55. the third is the booke of wiſdome, diſallowed by theſe Proteſtāts in this Article, but allowed by him and our primatiue Chriſtian Britans of that time, and ſo from our firſt receauing of holy Scriptures. And if I may but write what all our Proteſtant Antiquaries generally affirme for a conſtant, and vndoubted truth, that our Chriſtian Britans did neuer vntill Sainct Auguſtines coming hither change or alter any on materiall point in the holy Religiō which they receaued in the Apoſtles time, I muſt needs auouch,

that

that those Scriptures of the old testament which
this Article refuseth Were receaued both in Britaine, and in other nations, as Italy and Rome,
whence our conuersion came, with other contries
in that happy Time, for Sainct Gildas our most
auncient, and allowed Historian, both in many manuscripts, and bookes published by Protestants &
their warrant, for his wisdome Surnamed, *Sapiens,*
the wise, doth very often in one short worke allowe
and cite for holy Scriptures diuers of those bookes,
especially Ecclesiasticus, many times, and the
booke of wisdome vsinge the authority thereof 8.
times in one page and lesse. And vnto what time,
persons, or place soeuer wee will appeale for Triall,
wee shall in noe age, contry, councell or auncient
particular writer finde, any one person which a-
greeth with this Protestant Article in the nuber &
bookes of canonicall Scripture. It citeth S. Hierome but both hee himselfe and these Protestants,
Kinge Iames his Protestant Bishops in their publik
dispute at Hampton Court with others, proue that
S. Hierome spake onely againſt the bookes which
these Protestants reiect, not in his owne opinion,
but what the Iewes obiected. *Moſt of the obiections*
made againſt thoſe bookes were the old cauils of the
Iewes, renewed by S. Hierome in his time, who was the
firſt that gaue them that name of Apochryphe: which
opinion vpon Ruffinus his challendge, hee after a ſort
diſclaymed: and the rather becauſe a generall offence
was taken at his ſpeaches in that kinde. They are moſt
true, and might haue the reconcilement of other Scrip-
tures. If Ruffinus be not deceaued, they were approued
as parts of the old teſtament, by the Apoſtles. S. Hie-
rome pretendeth, that what hee had ſpoken, was not his
owne

Godwyn Cô-
uerſ. of Brit.
pag. 43. 44.
fore pag. 463.
edit. an. 1576.
Holinsh. hiſt.
of Engl. cap.
21. l. 4. fulke
anſw. to a
coûterf. cath.
pag. 40. harr.
deſcript. Brit.
c. 9 Gild. ep.
de ex cid. &
conq Britan.

Conference
at Hampton
Court pag.
60. Couel ag.
Burges pag.
87. 8. 86. 88.
89. 90. 91.

owne opinion, but what the Iewes obiected. *And for his paines in tranſlating the booke of Iudith (which this ar-ticle reiecteth) he giueth this reaſon: becauſe wee reade, that the Councell of Nyce did reckon it in the number of holy Scriptures.* And Sainct Hierome is plaine, both for this booke of Iudith, and the reſt, that he did not deny them; for firſt, of Iudith hee ſaith the Nicen Councell which he and all Catholiks euer honored, receaued it: *Hunc librum Synodus Nicæna in numero ſanctarum Scripturarum legitur computaſſe.* And for the other books beinge chardged by Ruf-finus, to ſpeake in his owne words, to be the onely man, *qui præſumpſerit ſacras Sancti Spiritus voces & diuina volumina temerare. Diuino muneri & Apoſto-lorum hæreditati manus Intulerit. Auſus eſt Inſtru-mentum diuinum quod Apoſtoli Eccleſijs tradiderunt, & depoſitum Sancti Spiritus compilare.* To haue herein abuſed the words of the holy Ghoſt and diuine volumes. To haue offered violence to the diuine office and Inheri-tance of the Apoſtles. And (to ſpeake in Proteſtants tranſlation) to haue robbed the Treaſure of the holy Ghoſt, and diuine Inſtrument, which the Apoſtles deli-uered to the Churches. Sainct Hierome neuer denieth any of thoſe things for true which Ruffinus ſpake of the authority of thoſe books of Scriptures, that the Apoſtles deliuered thē for ſuch to the Churches, and no learned man euer denied it, and that S. Peter at Rome deliuered them to the Church, *Petrus Ro-manæ Eccleſiæ per viginti & quatuor annos præfuit. Quid ergo? decepit Petrus Apoſtolus Chriſti Eccleſiam, & libros ei falſos tradidit?* But onely denieth that he wrote in his owne, but in our Enemies the Iewes opinion: *non enim quid ipſe ſentirem: ſed quid illi contra nos dicere ſoleant, explicaui.* And writinge

to

Hieron. Tom. 3. oper. præf. in Iudith.
Ruffin. inue-ctit. 2. in Hieronym.

Couel. ſup. pag 87.

Ruffin. ſupr.

Hier. Apol. 2. aduerſ. Ruffin. Tom. 4 oper. præf. in libros Ma-chul.

to Pope Damaſus plainely teſtifieth, that he ioyned with the Catholike Church in this buſines: *nouum & vetus teſtamentum recipimus, in eo librorum numero quem ſanctæ Catholicæ Eccleſiæ tradit authoritas.* And our Proteſtants from Antiquities acknowledge thus: *The Iewes at the cominge of Chriſt were of two ſorts, ſome named Hebrews commorant at Hieruſalem and in the holy land, properly named Hebrewes: others named Helleniſt, that is Iewes of diſperſion, mingled with the Greeks, theſe had written certaine bookes in Greeke, which they made vſe of, together with other parts of the old Teſtament, which they had of the tranſlation of the Septuagint. But the Hebrews receaued onely, the 22. bookes before mentioned. Hence it came, that the Iewes deliuered a double Canon of the Scripture, to the Chriſtian Churches.* And in this ſecond Canon of the Iewes, as theſe men write, were thoſe bookes of the old Teſtament which this article denieth. And whereas ſome Proteſtants would excuſe this Article by ſome old Authorities, of Melito, Sardenſis, Origen, the Councell of Laodicia, S. Cyrill of Hieruſalem, Sainct Gregory Nazianzen, and Amphilochius. There is not any one of them which ioyneth with this Article, but they all differ from it in the very places which they cite. *Melito Sardenſis* receaueth the booke of wiſdome, which this Article reiecteth, and omitteth Iudith. Origen onely citeth the books of the old teſtament according to the firſt Canon of the Hebrews, *ſicut Hebræi tradunt,* And yet in the end addeth the books of Machabees: *præter iſtos ſunt libri Machabæorum, qui Inſcribuntur Sarbet Sarbaneel.* And doth not agree with them in the books of the new teſtamēt. The Councell of Laodicia differreth from this article, in omittinge

Feild l. 4. of the Church. cap. 23. pag. 245. Act. 6. Gloſſ. ordin. & Lyra. in eund. locum.

Melito Sard. apud Euſeb. hiſt. Eccl. l. 4. cap. 25. Origen. in pſ. 1. Euſeb. hiſt. Eccl. li. 6. cap. 24.

Conc. Laodic. can. 60.

Greg. Naziáz. tinge Eſther in the old, and Apocalips in the new
de vir. & Teſtament, otherwiſe then this article doth. S. Gre-
Gorm. ſacræ gory Nazianzen ſo likewiſe numbreth as Amphi-
Scrip. l. 6. Am-
phil. l. ad Se- lochius alſo. Sainct Cyrill omitteth the Apocalips.
lēcum. Cyrill. So this Article hath no authority from any old
Hieroſolim. writer, Iew or Chriſtian, Greeke or Latin in this ſo
Catech. 4.
Tho. Rogers greate, and with them moſt important Queſtion,
vpon this 6. whereupon they grounde all Religion.

Art. Confeſſ.   And as litle concordance amonge themſelues:
Gallic. c 3. 4. for amonge 13. or 14. Confeſſions of Proteſtant
Confeſſ. Belg. Religion, they onely cite, and haue noe more then
c. 4. 5.
two of France and Belgia Rebels and Traytors to
their temporall Kings in ciuill matters, as they are
in ſpirituall to God and his holy Church, and theſe
for want of other authority founde this their error,
as the reſt vpon the hereticall conceipt of internall
reuelation, and their ſpirit ſo tellinge them, *ex te-*
ſtimonio, & intrinſeca Spiritus Sancti reuelatione. By
the one and the other: *quod Spiritus ſanctus noſtris*
conſcientijs teſtetur illos à Deo emanaſſe. And by this
Spirit they are at ſuch harmony, and agreement
amonge themſelues, as in other places, ſo in Englād
as I haue related, none of them agreeinge together
herein. But by the ſuggeſtion of this falſe ſpirit, and
their exploded doubt of Scriptures doe leaue all
Scriptures and queſtions of Religion to be deduced
Bilſō Suruey from them, doubtfull, which Bilſon a Proteſtant
pag. 664. Biſhop of wincheſter, one of the beſt learned they
euer had, thus proueth: *The Scriptures themſelues*
were not fully receaued in all places, no not in Euſebius
time. He ſaith the Epiſtle of Iames, of Iude, the ſecond
of Peter, he ſecond and third of Iohn are contradicted.
The epiſtle to the Hebrews was cōtradicted: The Church
of Syria did not receaue the ſecond epiſtle of Peter, nor
the

the second and third of Ihon, nor the Epistle of Iude, nor the Apocalipse: the like might be said for the Churches of Arabie. Will you hence conclude, that these parts of Scripture were not Apostolike, or that wee neede not receaue them, because they were formerly doubted of? The same reason is of all the books of the old testament which this Article reiecteth vpon the same surmise for Eusebius ouerliuinge Constantine, and writinge his life and deathe, deliueringe this doubt of so many bookes of new Testament liued neere the time of the Councell Chartage of 428. Bishops in which both these bookes of the new Testament contradicted in his dayes, but receaued by our Protestants, and all those bookes of the old Testament which in this Article they disable, are by all those Bishops in one and the same tenor of words with the rest decreed to be, *Canonicæ scripturæ* canonicall Scriptures. This Canon and Catologe of Canonicall bookes is confirmed by the Pope of Rome, then beinge, and other Bishops absent as appeareth by the same Councell. Pope Innocentius deliuereth the same Canon of holy Scriptures *Canonem sacrarum Scripturarum.* S. Augustine hath the same, as receaued by all Churches, *Scripturæ Canonicæ quæ ab omnibus accipiuntur Ecclesijs Catholicis.* And saith that all which feare God receaue them, *in his omnibus libris timentes Deum & pietate mansueti quærunt voluntatem Dei.* Pope Gelasius with a Councell of 70. Bishops declareth that to be the Canon which the holy & Catholike Roman Church receaueth, and reuerenceth, *quem Sancta & Catholica Romana suscipit & veneratur Ecclesia.* So hath Alcimus Auitus, Cassiodorus and others.

And this may suffice for this place of this Question.

Marginal notes:

Euseb. de vit. Const. lib. 3. hist. c. 22. l. 3. cap 3.
Concil. Cart. 3. can. 47.

Concil. Cart. 3. supr.

Innoc. 1. epist. ad Exuperiú Tholosanum
Episc. August. lib. 2. doctr. Christ. c. 8. & in speculo.

Gelas. Tom. Concil.

Alcim. Auit. l. ad Soror. de consol. Cassiodor. lib. 1. diu. Inst. c. 13.

ſtion. And it further proueth how feeble and weake the reſt of this Proteſtant Article of the ſufficiency & allowance of onely Scripture and diſableinge Traditions is, for if ſo many Canonicall bookes of Scripture in both teſtaments were doubted of, vntill ſo greate a time aboue 300. yeares in the lawe of Chriſt were paſſed, and Religion generally, and in all queſtions neceſſary to ſaluation planted, and receaued, how were or poſſibly could all theſe neceſſary things be reade in Scripture or proued thereby (which is the rule of this Article) when ſo many bookes were not then receaued for certaine and vndoubted holy Scriptures? Things and euidences doubtfull and vncertaine can make nothinge certaine in morall certainty, much leſſe with certainty of true and infallible faith, which aboue all others is and muſt needs be moſt certaine. Secōdly as Sainct Ireneus diſputeth,

Ireneus l. 3. cap. 4.

and proueth vpon his certaine knowledge and experience, That many nations which had not receaued the Scriptures, or any part of thē did truely beleeue in Chriſt, by vnwritten traditions, which the Apoſtles deliuered to the Churches. *Quid ſi neque Apoſtoli ſcripturas reliquiſſent nobis, nonne oportebat ordinem ſequi traditionis quam tradiderunt ijs, quibus committebant Eccleſias? cui ordinationi aſſentiunt multæ gentes barbarorum, eorum qui in Chriſtum credunt ſine charta & atramento, veterem traditionem diligenter cuſtodientes.* This he writeth both of this firſt age, and the ſecond in which he died by martyrdome. And it is moſt euident both by holy Scriptures and other antiquities, that many nations, not onely of the barbarous, which were without learninge, but of the learned did thus beleeue before

fore any Scriptures of the new Testament, in which and by which Protestants necessitate vs to reade and proue our Religion, were written.

This is manifestly proued by all the epistles of Sainct Peter, Sainct Paul, and the rest of the Apostles written vnto such places, and persons, as had before beleeued, and receaued the Religion of Christ, as is in euery of them plainely expressed. And yet as is shewed before diuers of these were doubted of, and not generally receaued for holy Scripture vntill 300. yeares after they were writtē. The not receauers or doubters of them being faithfull & true Christians in all points. S. Matthew the first of the Euangelists which wrote, writinge for the conuerted Iewes in Hebrew, could not thereby profit any but Hebrews, And yet Sainct Ireneus witnesseth he did not write, vntill both Sainct Peter and Sainct Paul were come to Rome. *Matthæus in Hebræis ipsorum lingua scriptura tradidit Euangelij, cum Petrus & Paulus Romæ Euangelizarent, & fundarent Ecclesiam.* And onely for the Iewes before conuerted without scripture. *Propter eos qui ex circumcisione crediderunt.* And taught them by tradition, not writinge, vntill he was to depart from them, to preache vnto others in other places, And so was vrged by a kinde of necessity, as S. Iohn, also to write a Ghospell. *Ex omnibus Domini discipulis commentarios nobis soli Matthæus, & Ioannes reliquerunt, quos etiam necessitate ad scribendum esse adactos ferunt ; Matthæus enim quum primum Hebræis prædicasset, etiam ad alios quoque transiturus esset, Euangeliū suum patrio sermone literis tradidit , & quod subtracta præsentia sua desiderabatur, illis à quibus discedebat, per literas adimplent.*

Rom. 1. 1.
Cor. 1. 2. Cor.
1. Gal. 1. Ephes.
1. Phil. 1. Colloss. 1. Thess. 1.
& 2. 1. Tim. 1.
2. Tim. 1. Tit.
1. Epist. ad
Philem. Hebr.
1. Iacob. 1. 1.
Petr. 1. 2. Pet.
2. Ioh. 1. Io. 2.
& 3. Iud. 1.

Irenæus lib. 3.
aduer. hereses
cap. 1.
Hieron. catal.
Script. Eccl. in
S. Matthæo.
Euseb. hist.
Eccl. l. 3. c. 21.
Iren. supr.

Sainct

Sainct Marke placed in order to be the second
Euangelist, he beinge none of those Apostles and
immediate Schollers of Christ, but disciple of Sainct
Peter the Apostle, as he could not receaue his learninge in Christian Religion, from the Scriptures
but from his Master, and Tutor in Christ S. Peter,
noe writer of any Ghospell, but of one onely short
epistle at that time, if the first was then written, the
last & second being written a litle before his death,
as the same Scripture withnesseth: *certus quod velox
est depositio tabernaculi mei secundum quod & Dominus noster Iesus Christus significauit mihi.* So followinge Sainct Peter, and learninge his Ghospell from
him, he writ it by Sainct Peters warrant, and order
at the entreaty of the Christians at Rome. This for
whome hee wrote it being conuerted before without Scripture, *Marcus discipulus & Interpres Petri,
iuxta quod Petrum referentem andiuerat, Rogatus Romæ à fratribus breue scripsit Euangelium. Quod cum
Petrus audisset, probauit, & Ecclesiæ legendum sua authoritate edidit, sicut Clemens in sixto Hypotyposeon libro scribit.*

The case of Sainct Luke was the like with S.
Marke, but that Sainct Luke cheifely followed S.
Paul, which was not of the 12. Apostles which conuersed with Christ, wryting his Ghospell, after S.
Marke, & the Acts of the Apostles being writtē in
Rome, in or after the 4. yeare of New the 57. or 58.
of Christ, both the Bookes were writtē by traditiō
and after the faith of Christ receaued, as he himselfe witnesseth of the first : *sicut tradiderunt nobis
qui ab initio ipsi viderunt, & ministri fuerunt Sermo-
nis.* His Acts of the Apostles is an history of things
done, and encrease of Christians by tradition.

By

---

2. Petr. 1.

Clem. lib. 6.
hypot. Hier.
l. de Script.
Eccl. in Marc.
Euseb. hist. l. 3.
c. 21. l. 2. cap
15 Matth.
Westin. chr.
an. 42. Flor.
Wigorn. chr.
an 45. & 67.
Marian. Scot.
an. 47. Ma-
rian. Scot. an.
47. Martin.
Polon. an. 44.
Hier. lib de sc.
in Luc. Act. 1.
Luc. c. 1.

By all Antiquities S. Iohn was the laſt, which
wrote his Ghoſpell, at the entreaty of the Bishops
of Aſia, againſt Cerinthus, and other heretiks, and
cheifely the Ebionites, denying the diuinity of
Chriſt : *Ioannes nouißimus omnium ſcripſit Euange-*
lium, rogatus ab Aſiæ Epiſcopis, aduerſus Cerinthum
alioſque hæreticos, & maximè Ebionitarum domga
conſurgens, qui aſſerunt Chriſtum ante Mariam non
fuiſſe. And neuer wrote before, but onely by word
preached vnto the people, conuertinge them by
vnwritten tradition. *Ioannem aiunt, qui toto tempore*
Euangelici curſus prædicatione ſine literis vſus fuerat,
tandem ad ſcribendum hiſce de cauſis eſſe permotum.
Whereby wee alſo ſee, that his Epiſtles were not
written vntill his later time, and the two laſt, longe
time doubted of, as his Apocalipſe alſo was, and
yet neither written, nor reueaeled vntill his bannish-
ment into Pathmos in the 14. yeare of Domitian
the yeare of Chriſts Natiuity 97. or 98. And the
common opinion in antiquity is, that he did not
write his Ghoſpell vntill his returne to Epheſus,
after the death of Domitian. Matthew of weſt-
miſter with others ſaith, that he firſt by worde condemned thoſe heretiks Cerinthus and Ebion affir-
minge the world was made by the Angels, that Chriſt
Ieſus was onely man, and denying the reſurrection
of the deade, and after by entreaty or compulſion
rather of the Chriſtians, wrote his Ghoſpell to the
ſame end. *Ioannes Apoſtolus Epheſum redijt. Et quia*
concuſſam ſe abſente, per hæreticos vidit Eccleſiæ fi-
dem, Cerinthi & Ebionis hæreſim, ibidem damnauit.
Aſtruunt enim mundum ab Angelis factum, & Ieſum
hominem fuiſſe tantum, nec reſurrexiſſe, reſurrectio-
nem quoque mortuorum non credebant. Contra hanc hæ-

Hieron. lib. de Script. Eccl. in Ioanne A-poſt. Euſeb. hiſt. Eccl. l. 3. cap. 21.

Euſeb. ſupr. l. 2. & 3. hiſt. Hier. libr. de Scriptor. Ecc. in Ioanne.

Athanaſ. Sy-nopſi Crdren. in nerua. Epi-phan. Hier. 51. Iren l. 3. ca. 1. & apud Euſ. l. 5 hiſt. cap. 8. flor. Wigorn. chron. an. 81. 103. Mat. weſtin. chron. an. 98.

B *reſim*

resim à fratribus compulsus Apostolus Euangeliũ scripsit, ostendens in exordio eius, in principio fuisse verbum, & ipsum esse Deum, per quem omnia facta sunt.

Therefore it is thus made euident, that the world was not conuerted to Christ, nor his doctrine, and Religion receaued and established first by scriptures, but vnwritten tradition. As to exemplifie in this our Kingdome of Britaine, whose history I write, one of the remotest then knowne nations from Hierusalem, and apply the rest to the same being in like estate with it, for these things. It is proued both by old and late, Greeke and Latine, domesticall and forreyne, Catholike & Protestant writers, that it receaued the faith of Christ, longe before any part of the new testament was written. And it is euident in Antiquities that none of the Ghospels except that of Sainct Marke, was written in this parte of the world, or in any language which the Britans vnderstood. And that was, but *breue Euangelium*, a short Ghospell, and so short as being assisted both with the Ghospell of Sainct Matthew and Sainct Luke they were not all thought able to condemne those named hereticks, which S. Ihon confounded. Amonge the Epistles onely that of S. Paul to the Romans, was sent into these parts, It was in a language wee did not vnderstand, and written after the faith of the Romans was spredd both in Britaine, and all the world, as Sainct Paul witnesseth : *fides vestra annuntiatur in vniuerso mundo.* The two Epistles of Sainct Peter according to antiquity were written in Rome, and after Britaine had receaued the faith, especially the last; and the first being longe doubted of, was sent quite con-

trary

Hier. in Marco supr. & Io. an Euseb. li. 3. hist.

Rom. 1.

trary from Britayne vnto the contries of *Pōtus, Galatia, Capadocia, Aſia, and Bithynia* in the eaſterne parts. Wee finde no memory after of Scripture receaued here vntill longe time after in the ſecond age, expreſſed in Pope Eleutherius his Epiſtle to our King Lucius. And yet all our Proteſtāt antiquaries haue before aſſured vs, that Britaine had in the Apoſtles time and longe before any Scripture came hither, or probably was written, and poſſibly in morall Iudgment could come hither ; receaued the faith of Chriſt, ſo fully) purely, and ſincerely that it neuer changed it in any materiall point, after the Scriptures were receaued here, nor diuers hundreds of yeares after.

And if wee will be directed by Scriptures in this point, thoſe which our Proteſtants allowe for ſuch, giue teſtimony to vnwritten Traditions in many places. To exemplifie onely in Sainct Paul which wrote moſt in the new Teſtament, hee chargeth S. 1. Tim. 6. Timothy, and all others in him, to keepe & obſerue things ſo deliuered without writing. *O Timothee,* 2. Tim. 2. *depoſitum cuſtodi.* This in his firſt Epiſtle, not hauinge written vnto him before. And in his ſecond epiſtle hee giueth him commaund, that the things which he had heard frō Sainct Paul, he ſhould deliuer vnto others fit to teach them. *Quæ audiſti a me per multos teſtes, hæc commenda fidelibus hominibus, qui idonei erunt & alios docere.* And expreſſely com-2. Theſſal. 2. maundeth the Theſſalonians, and in them all, in his ſecond epiſtle to them, to obſerue and keepe the Traditions, which they had learned either by word or writinge. *State & tenete traditiones, quas didiciſtis, ſiue per ſermonem, ſiue per epiſtolam noſtram.* Which the Fathers expound of the neceſſity of

kee-

keepinge vnwritten traditions, as Catholiks now

Chrisost.in 2.
Thess. orat. 4.

doe. *Hinc est perspicuum, quòd non omnia per epistolam tradiderunt, sed multa etiam sine scriptis: & ea quoque sunt fide digna. Quamobrem Ecclesiæ quoque traditionem censeamus esse fide dignam. Est traditio, nihil quæras amplius.* And expoundinge that of S. Paul in his first epistle to the Corinthians, how they kept his commaundements by word before he wrote vnto them, *sicut tradidi vobis præcepta mea tenetis,* he doth inferre the doctrine of Traditions: *ergo sine literis multa tradiderat, quod alibi sæpe meminit.* And Sainct Hierome vpon the same words:

Hier. in ea-
dem Verba.
Tom. 9.
Ambros. in
1.Cor.Epiph.
hæresi 69.

quasi legem præcepta mea tenetis, scientes illum in me spiritum loqui, qui in lege locutus est, & prophetis. The like hath S. Ambrose vpon the same, and S. Epiphanius: *oportet & traditione vti non enim omnia à diuina Scriptura possunt accipi: Quapropter aliqua in traditione Sancti Apostoli tradiderunt : Quemadmodum dicit Sanctus Apostolus: Sicut tradidi vobis. Et alibi, sic doceo sic tradidi in Ecclesijs.*

Thus the best learned both Greeke and Latine Fathers expounded these, to inferre a necessity of Traditions, and their equality with Scriptures. Which our best Protestant writters with their

Feild. l. 4. c.
20. pag 238.

common allowance thus confirme. *Our aduersaries, meaninge Catholiks, make traditions equall with the words, preecepts, and doctrines of Christ, the Apostles, and Pastors of the Church, left vnto vs in writinge, neither is there any reason, why they should not so doe, if they could proue any such vnwritten verities, for it is not the writinge that giueth things their authority, but the worth and credit of him that deliuereth them, though by word and liuely voyce onely.* Thus they confesse, and the reason which they giue, so enfor-

ceth

ceth them, the worth and credit of the reuealer and deliuerer or propoſer of holy miſteries ſupernaturall being the motiue and cauſe of mans aſſent, ſo firme and vnmoueable, in articles of faith, not to be proued by humane reaſon, and not the writinge or not writing being fallible and ſubiect to many caſualties, corruptions, and vncertainties, which we are ſure are not to be found in Chriſt the reuealer, nor his holy Church the vndoubted true propoſer of his myſteries and reuelations. And both theſe are the ſame, and as certaine in traditions not written, ſuch as Catholiks maintaine, as in the written Scriptures. For wee doe not defend any one vnwritten tradition, that it ſhould be *beleeued as an Article of faith, or to be thought requiſite neceſſary to ſaluation*, which be the very words of this Proteſtant Article of Religion, but wee produce, the higheſt authority in their owne publike Iudgment alſo in theſe their Articles, the true primatiue Church of Chriſt to warrant it, *The which Church hath power and authority in controuerſies of faith.* That euery tradition came from Chriſt and his Apoſtles to be receaued & profeſſed in Chriſtian Religion. 　　*Artic. of Proteſt. Relig. 20.*

As, to inſtance in ſome, and thoſe which moſt concerne, euen in our Proteſtants proceedings, and by their owne confeſſions, and teſtimonies, vnwritten Traditions are neceſſary. For firſt in this very article they haue giuen their finall ſentence, in the very firſt words thereof that the holy Scriptures are of this nature. *Holy Scripture containeth all things neceſſary for ſaluation: So that whatſoeuer is not read therein, nor may be proued thereby, is not to be required of any man, that it ſhould be beleeued, as an Article of faith, or to be thought requiſite neceſſary to ſal-* 　　*Engl. Proteſt. Rel. artic. 6.*

*uation.*And yet in the immediatly following words, they plainely declare, and professe, that wee haue noe warrant in Scripture, for any booke, chapter, or sentence of Scripture to be such holy Scripture, but for euery least percell thereof wee must resort to Tradition, and the Churches Iudgment. *In the name of holy Scripture, wee doe vnderstand those canonicall bookes of the old, and new testament, of whose authority was neuer any doubt in the Church.* Where wee are assured from these men, that the Church, and Tradition vnwritten is supreme Iudge of all questions in Religion, euen of the Scriptures themselues. And so necessarily they must say, & confesse, or els leaue no Religion, or Scripture at all, to be proued, or proue vnto vs. For it is vnquestionable that no part of Scripture doth propose vnto vs, any Catalogue or Canon of Scriptures. Which they thus further testifie in their publikely approued writers: *much contention there hath beene, about traditions, some vrginge the necessity of them, and others reiectinge them. For the clearinge whereof, wee must obserue, that wee reiect not all: for first wee receaue the number and names of the Authors of bookes diuine, and canonicall, as deliuered by tradition. This tradition wee admit. The number, Authors, and Integrity of the partes of these bookes, wee receaue as deliuered by tradition. The Church of Christ according to her authority, receaued frō him, hath warrant to approue the Scriptures, to acknowledge, to receaue, to publish, and commaunde vnto her children. The Church of Rome teacheth noe badde opinion, to affirme, that the Scriptures are holy, and diuine in themselues; but so esteemed by vs, for the authority of the Church. That the Scriptures ar true wee haue it from the Church. Wee say that wee are taught to receaue the*

Feild.l. 4. pa.
238. c. 20.

Couell cont.
Burg pag. 60.
Whitaker ib.
Wotton def.
of Perk. pag.
442. Couell.
def. of hook.
pag. 31. 34 32.
33. feild l. 4.
c. 5. pag. 203.
Ormer.pict.
Pap. pag. 93.
Sutcliffeag.
the 3. conu.
pag. 79.

word

*word of God, from the authoritie of the Church: wee see
her Iudgment, wee heare her voyce: and in humility
subscribe unto all this. The Church hath fower singular
offices towards the Scripture. First to be of them, as it
were, a faithfull register. Secondly to discerne and Iudge
betweene false and adulterate, and that which is true
and perfect. The third to publish and diuulge, to pro-
claime as a Crier, the true Edict of our Lord himselfe.
The last is, to be an Interpreter: and in that followinge
the safest rule, to be a most faithfull Expositor of his owne
meaninge. Wee thinke that particular men and Churches
may erre damnably: But that the whole Church at one
time cannot so erre: for that the Church should cease ut-
terly for a time, and so not be Catholike, beinge not at all
times: & Christ should sometimes be without a Church.
The Church is called a pillar, because it is like unto a
pillar. For as a pillar doth support, and underproppe a
buildinge, and maketh it more stable, firme, and stronge:
So the Church doth sustaine and supporte the truth: for
the truth is no where preserued, but in the Church.
Christs true Church is a diligent and wary keeper of doctrines committed to her, and changeth nothinge, at any
time, diminisheth nothinge, addeth nothinge super-
fluous, looseth not her owne, nor usurpeth things belon-
ginge to others.* And this is publikely warranted in
these their Articles and Rule of their Religion,
where thus they define the Church: *The visible
Church of Christ is a congregation of faithfull men, in the
which the pure word of God is preached. And the Sacraments be duely ministred, accordinge to Christs ordinance, in all those things that of necessity are requisite
to the same.*

Secondly those men in their Rules of Religion,
and their priuate writers affirme, that the Apostles

B 4   Creede,

Protest. Reli.
of Engl. Art.
19.

Art. 8. Catech.
com. Booke.
Iniunct. Ca-
nons feild l.
4. c. 20. pag.
238. 239.

Creede, which by all Antiquity, was by them deliuered to the Church, and by thefe Proteftants, *as a*
Rule of faith, before the Scriptures of the new Teftament were written, is an vnwritten Tradition,
yet by their words, *a fummary comprehenfion of the*
cheife heades of Chriftian Religion, a Rule of the
Churches faith. And yet it is conftantly maintained
by many Proteftants, that diuers articles thereof,
as our Ladies perpetuall virginity, *natus ex Maria*
Virgine, Chrifts defcending into hell, *defcendit ad*
inferos, The communion of Sainčts, and forgiue-
neffe of finnes, *Sanctorum communionem Remiffionem*
peccatorum, and others by diuers others Proteftants,
are not contained in any Scripture written before
or after. And this Creede deliuered by word, and
tradition onely by the Apoftles before the new teftament written, this Scripture could not poffibly
be a rule or direčtion vnto it, but rather otherwife
for euery rule hath priority to the thinge ruled, and
the things ruled pofterity to their rule. Matters are
done without rule, when there is no rule vntill after
they be ačted.

Feild fupr.
pag. 239.
Thefe Parlament Proteftants proceede further
in this queftion, and plainely fay, with greate allowance : *The third kind of Tradition is that fomme of*
Chriftian doctrine, and explication of the feuerall parts
thereof, which the firft Chriftians receauinge of the fame
Apoftles, that deliuered to them the Scriptures, com-
mended to pofteritie. This may rightly be named a tradi-
tion, for that wee neede a plaine and diftinct explication
of things, which are fomewhat obfcurely contained in
the Scripture. The fourth kinde of tradition, is the conti-
nued practife of fuch, as neither are contained in the
Scripture expreffely, nor the example of fuch practife
expref-

expressely there deliuered of this sorte is the Baptisme of
Infants, which is therefore named a traditon, because it
is not expressely deliuered in the Scripture, that the A-
postles did baptize infants, nor any expresse precept there
founde, that they should doe it. Which their rule of
Religion in these Articles thus further iustifieth:
The Baptisme of yonge children is in any wise to be re-
tained in the Church, as most agreable with the institu-
tion of Chrift. Where they plainely in their publike
rule of Religion make it a tradition, and no Scripture article. And by the cōmon practicall of their religion, their communion booke, so they practise,
baptizinge all infants, and sayinge, *all Chriftian*
Churches allowe of the baptifme of infants. And these
Proteftants are onely baptized when they are infants, and not after, and yet confesse it is most necessary to faluation.

And whereas they reiect all other Sacraments besides this, and the Euchariſt, or the Cōmunion, as
they terme it, confessing that these Sacraments be
neceffary to faluation, And yet denyinge the Eu-
charift to be, as Catholiks profesfe, the true body
and blood of Chrift, and facrifice for the lyuinge
and deade, they contradict themfelues, for that they
confesse that in this finfe it was generally vfed in
primitiue Church, that the Apoftles so deliuered it
by tradition, all Churches so obferued it, and it was
herefie to deny it. Their words be: *The facrifice of*
the altar, and vnbloody facrifice were vfed in the pri-
mitiue Church. The primatiue Church did offer facrifice
at the altar for the deade, facrifice for the deade was a
tradition of the Apoftles, and the auncient Fathers.
Aerius condemned the cuftome of the Church, in naming
the deade at the altar, and offeringe the facrifice of Eu-
charift,

Art. of Engl.
Prote.Relig.
Art. 17.Com-
muniō Booke
Tit.Baptifme.
The. Rog. in
Art. 27. Q.
Elizab. and k.
K. Iames In-
iunct.and Ca-
nons.

Art. of Relig.
art. 25.

Kinge Iames
and Cafaub.
refp ad Card.
per. pa. 51. 52.
20.Middlet.
Papiftom.20.
p.92. 113.49.
137. 138.47.
45. Feild l. 3.
cap 29.p 138.
Couell, Exa.
pag. 114.

charist, from them: and for this his rash and inconsiderate boldenesse, and presumption, in condemninge the
vniuersall Church of Christ, he was iustly condemned.

King Iames, Prot. Lords, Bish. & Doct. in Confer. at Hapt. Court. p. 13. 18. 35. 36 10. 11. Couell. ag. the plea. of the Innoc. p. 104. Barlow Serm. before the K. Sept. 21 an. 1607. part. 3. cap. 2.

Their whole congregation, Kinge Iames, his councell, Protestant Bishops, and best learned Doctors
assembled in publike conferēce, haue left thus concluded: *The particular and personall absolution from
sinne after confession is apostolicall and a very Godly ordinance. That baptisme is to be ministred by priuate persons in time of necessity, is an holy Tradition. Bishops
and Archbishops be diuine ordinations, confirmation is
an apostolicall traditiō.* And in their publike Rituall,
their communion booke, they testifie that confir-

Communion booke of Engl. Protest. Titul. Confir- mation. §. Al- mighty. Prot. of Religion art. 25.

mation was a Tradition of the Apostles, hath an externall signe also, vsed by them, and giueth grace,
which by the 25. Article of their religion maketh it
a Sacrament. So that to insist onely vpon these
graunted Traditions, not contained in Scripture,
by these Protestants, and yet so necessary to saluation as they by their greatest allowance and authority deliuer, wee may not say as this Article doth:
*Holy Scripture containeth all things necessary for salua-
tion.*

Articul. 6. supr.

These men also deliuer vnto vs, with greate approbation (makinge the Author of that worke, and
for the same, a Bishop) certaine sure rules to
knowe such true Thraditions by, in these words:

Feild. Books of the Church l. 4. pag. 242. August. l. 4. contr. Donat. c. 23.

*Rules by which wee may Iudge which are true and In-
dubitate Traditions. The first rule is deliuered by Sainct
Augustine. Quod vniuersa tenet Ecclesia, nec Concilijs
Institutum, sed semper retentum est, non nisi authoritate apostolica traditum rectissimè creditur. Whatsoeuer
the whole Church holdeth, not ordained by Councels; but
beinge euer holden, it is most rightly belieued to haue
beene*

beene deliuered by Apostolike authority. The second rule is, whatsoeuer all or the most famous, and renowned in all ages, haue constantly deliuered, as receaued from them, that went before them, no man contradictinge, or doubting of it, may be thought to be an Apostolicall Tradition. The third rule, is the constat Testimony, of the Pastors of an Apostolike Church, successiuely deliuered. Amongst Apostolike Churches the Church of Rome is more specially to be obeyed, reuerenced, and respected. The Church of Rome is our mother Church, it was a rule to all both in doctrine and ceremonies when it was in her florishinge and best estate. The Church of Rome was the cheife and onely Church. It was a note of a good Christiā to cleaue vnto the Romane Apostolicall Church. Euery Church ought to haue respect to the Church of Rome, for her eminent principality. And our English Protestant antiquaries and Diuines, haue generally giuen their allowance, that the Church of Rome both in this and the next age, when Britayne did receaue the most pure Religion of Christ, from thence, was most holy and vnspotted free from all error. Therefore whatsoeuer wee doe, or may bringe in generall, or particular, for vnwritten traditions, either from this so renowned Apostolike Church in this time, from the whole Church, or the most famous and renowned in this age, beinge our Protestants owne allowed rules, and to be denied by none, must needs be euidence and testimony vndeniable, in this, and all others their questioned Articles. Frst I exemplifie in the Apostles Creede stiled by our Protestants before, *a sundry comprehension of the cheife heads of Christian Religion, a rule of the Churches faith,* This was deliuered by the Apostles, by tradition, not by Scripture, but before

Feild. supr. l. 4
c. 21. p. 242. c.
5. pag. 202.
Kinge Iames
and Confer.
at Hampton.
Couel. def of
Hooker. Ormer. pict pap.
p. 184. Down.
l. 2. Antichr.
pag. 105. Sutcliffe Suberf. pag. 57.

Protest. supr.
Ruffin in exposit. Symboli & alij.

fore the Scriptures of the new Testament, were
written, as both they and the auncient Fathers by
common consent of the whole Church of Christ
are witnesses. And the same consent of Christs
Church with these our Protestants, in these their
Art. 8. of prot. Religion. Articles so conclude, of Sainct Athanasius, and the
Nicen Creede, in these words: *The three Creeds, Ni-*
cen Creede, Athanasius Creede, and that which is com-
monly called the Apostles Creede, ought throughly to be
receaued & beleeued. And so generally they obserue,
although the reason which they immediatly yeeld
thereof, *for they may be proued by most certaine war-*
rants of holy Scripture, is childish and impertinent:
for being confessed that the Apostles Creede was
deliuered onely by tradition of the Apostles and by
that authoritie receaued before the Scriptures either receaued or written, this Creede could not possibly be receaued by the written warrant of Scriptures but vnwritten tradition and warrant of the
Apostles. And although the Nicen and S. Athanasius Creeds were written longe after this time, yet
they were both written & receaued in the Church
before the Scriptures were generally allowed and
receaued, as both the auncent Fathers, and Protestants haue acknowledged before, and it is testified
Prot. Glosse by authority of Church of Engl. in Art. 8. by the publike warranted Protestant glosse vpon
these their Articles, that very many both old and
late writers, euen whole sects and professions,
namely (to vse their owne words, *Ebionites, Tre-*
theits, Antitrinitarians, Apollinarians, Arians, Ma-
nichies, Nestorians, Origenians, Familists, and Ana-
baptists with others) are Aduersaries vnto, and de-
niers that these Creeds, may be proued by holy
Scripture. Much more doe they, and many others
                                                       both

both Catholiks and Proteſtants themſelues deny, that all and ſingular their articles neceſſary to ſaluation, may ſo be proued.

And to come to the holy and happy Apoſtolike writers, and Saincts which liued, and wrote in this firſt age, and firſt hundred of yeares, to wit S. Linus Sainct Clement, Sainct Denys the Areopagite, S. Martial, Sainct Ignatius, Sainct Policarpus, or any other of whom any worke is extant: I shall make it euident that in euery Article in this Proteſtant Religion contained in their booke of the Articles thereof, they diſſented from theſe Proteſtants, and they and the Apoſtolike Church then vniuerſally agreed in, and profeſſed the ſame doctrine, which the preſent Roman Church doth at this day in all points. This will plainely appeare in euery Article hereafter, and therefore in this place I will onely cite Sainct Ignatius, as a ſufficient pawne or pledge for the reſt, vntill I come to them in the Articles followinge. He had perſonally ſeene our Sauiour, was an eyewitneſſe of his reſurrection, had written vnto, viſited, was inſtructed and confirmed in Chriſtian Religion, both by the words and writinge of the bleſſed Virgin Mary Mother of Chriſt. Hee was diſciple to Sainct Ihon the Euangeliſt, diſciple and immediate Succeſſor, of Sainct Peter the Apoſtle at Antioch, conſecrated there Biſhop by him, as Sainct Chryſoſtome Patriarke there, Sainct Felix Pope of Rome and Theodoret teſtifie : *S. Ignatius dextera Petri ordinatus Epiſcopus Eccleſiæ Antiochenæ, per magni Petri dexteram Pontificatum ſuſcepit.* And ſo conſecrated Biſhop, was taught himſelfe, and taught others before either the Ghoſpels, or other parts of the new Teſtament were written.

S. Ignat. epiſt.
ad Smyrn.
Theod. dialo.
Euſeb. l. 3. c. 31.
Hierar. lib. de
vir. Illuſt. S.
Bern. Serm. 7.
in pſ. 9. Marc.
Michal Carnoten. lib. de
vir. illuſtr.
Dion. Carth.
ad l. Areop. de
diuin. nom.
Sint. Sin. lib. 2.
Ignat. ep. ad
S. Ioh. 1. 2. ad
B. Mar. Virg.
B. Mar. epiſt.
ad Ignat. S.
Ignat epiſt. ad
Smyrnen. Euſeb. hiſt. l. 3. ca.
33. S. Chriſoſt.
orat. de traſl.
S. Ignatij. Fœlix Rom. ep.
ad Zenon. Imperat. ſynod.
S. Conſtant.
Theodoret.
Immutabil.
dialog. 1.

Hee

Hee liued longe Patriarke of Antioch the cheife
and Apostolike See of the Greeke Church, he died
a blessed Martyr at Rome, the greatest of all
Churches, he ioyned in Religion with the most renowned Churches, and Prelates, Apostles, and o-
thers of the Christian world, as the very Titles of
his extant epistles to the Romans, Philippians, E-
phesians, Smyrnians, Philadelphians, Magnesians,
Trallians and others. To Sainct Ihon the Apostle,
Sainct Policarpe, with others most famous amonge
Christians, and all auncient writers, Sainct Hierome, Eusebius, Ireneus make him a most glorious
learned man and Sainct Eusebius testifieth that he
wrote a particular worke of the Apostles traditios.
But those few and short Epistles which he wrote &
receaued, as all, Greekes, Latines, and amonge our
primatiue Britans, the most auncient historian S.
Gildas is an ample witnesse, will sufficiently proue
vnto vs. That very many things euen necessary in
Christian Religion and to saluation in our Protestants Iudgment, and in their opinion not contained
in Scripture, were then taught, practised and generally receaued in the Church of Christ in the Apostles time. Concerninge the Church of Rome he
thus stileth it: *misericordiam in magnificentia altissimi*
Dei Patris, & Iesu Christi vnigeniti filij, Ecclesia san-
ctificata & illuminata per voluntatem Dei (qui fecit
omnia, quæ pertinent ad fidem & charitatem Iesu Chri-
sti Dei & Saluatoris nostri) quæ & in Loco Romanæ re-
gionis, Deo digna, decentissima, beatificanda, laudanda,
digna qua quis potiatur, castissima, & eximiæ charitatis,
Christi & Patris nomine fruens, spirituque plena. The
Rulinge Roman Church, sanctified, Illuminated, worthy
of God, most decent, blessed, to be praised, worthy to be
attained

Euseb l. 3. hist.
cap. 32.
Euseb. hist. l 3.
c. 33. Hieron.
l. de Scriptor.
in S. Ignat.
Gildas epist.
de excid. &
conquest. Bri-
tan.

S. Ignatius
epist. ad Ro-
manos in ini-
tio.

attained vnto, *most chaste, of excellent charity enioyinge the name of Christ and his Father, and full of the holy Ghost:* With other Titles of dignity and priuiledge, more then he giueth to any, or all, those principall Churches of Greece to which he wrote, and as greate and ample as any learned Catholike now yeeldeth to the Church of Rome at this time, or heretofore, since then. Hee remembreth the same Ecclesiasticall Orders in the Church then, which Catholiks now and euer since obserue, as in the Church of Antioch founded by Sainct Peter and Sainct Paul and their tradition there, *Pauli & Petri fuistis discipuli ne perdatis depositum.* Hee himselfe was there Bishop, besides whome it had Preists, Deacons, Subdeacons, Exorcists, Readers, Ianitors. *Saluto sanctum Presbyterorum Collegium, saluto sacros Diaconos. Saluto Hypodiaconos, Lectores, Ianitores Exorcistas.* And him that was to be Bishop after his martyrdome, as it was reuealed vnto him: *optabile illud nomen eius quem video in spiritu locū meum tenere, vbi Christum nactus fuero.* Hee giueth them the same honor preeminence worth office and dignity which the Church of Rome now yeeldeth to them. All must honor and obey the Bishops. *Omnes Episcopum sequimini vt Christus Patrem.* Kings and Rulers must be ruled by him being greatest in the Church. *Honora Deum vt omnium Authorem & Dominum : Episcopum verò vt Principem Sacerdotum, Imaginem Dei referentem : Dei quidem, propter principatum : Christi verò propter Sacerdotium. Honorare oportet & Regem : nec enim Rege quisquam præstantior, aut quisquam similis ei in rebus creatis : nec Episcopo qui Deo consecratus est pro totius mundi salute, quicquam maius in Ecclesia. Nec inter principes quisquam*

Epist. ad Antiochen.

Epistol. ad Symrnen.

quàm similis Regi, qui in pace & optimis legibus subdi-
tos moderatur. Qui honorat Episcopum à Deo honorabi-
tur: sicut qui ignominia afficit illum à Deo punietur. Si
enim Iure censebitur pæna dignus, qui aduersus Regem
insurgit, vt qui violet bonas legum constitutiones:
quanto putatis grauiori subiacebit supplicio, qui sine E-
piscopo aliquid egerit, concordiam rumpens, & decentem
rerum ordinem confundens? Sacerdotium enim est om-
nium bonorum, quæ in hominibus sunt Apex: qui ad-
uersus illud furit, non hominem ignominia afficit sed
Deum, & Christum Iesum primogenitum. Laici Dia-
conis subijciantur, Diaconi Presbyteris, Presbyteri Epis-

Epist. ad Phi-
ladelphienses.
copo, Episcopus Christo. Principes subditi estote Cæsari,
milites principibus, Diaconi Presbyteris, Presbyteri verò
& Diaconi atque omnis clerus simul cùm omni populo &
militibus atque principibus sed & Cæsare obediant Epis-
copo, Episcopus vero Christo, sicut Patri Christus, & ita
vnitas per omnia seruatur. Where wee plainely see
there was no Princes supremacy in spirituall things
in those happy times, but Princes kings and Empe-
rors, as those of the cleargy and all others were subiect and ought obedience to the Bishop, and preisthood was the highest and most honorable dignity
in the world. And the honor which was due to
Kings themselues was inferior to that of Bishops.

Epistol. ad
Smyren.
Ego dico honorate Deum, vt authorem omnium & Do-
minum, Episcopum autem tanquam Principem Sacer-
dotum, Imaginem Dei ferentem, principatum quidem
secundum Deum, Sacerdotium vero secũdum Christum,
& post hunc honorare oportet etiam Regem. Nemo enim
potior est Deo, neque similis illi, neque Episcopo honora-
bilior, in Ecclesia Sacerdotium Deo gerenti pro mundi
salute, neque Regi quis similis in exercitu, pacem & be-
neuolentiam omnibus principibus cogitanti. Where he
giueth

giueth an vnanswerable reason of the preeminence
of Episcopall dignity before the Regall, though in
a good Kinge, because this ruleth onely in martiall
and temporall affaires, the Bishop in spirituall, the
Church of God, his howse and Kingdome. And he
chargeth all without exception to be subiect, not
onely to the Bishop, but to Preists and Deacons
euen vnder paine of eternall damnation. *Enitimini* S. Ignatius
subiecti esse Episcopo, & Presbyteris & Diaconis, qui epist. ad E-
enim his obedit, obedit Christo qui hos constituit. Qui phesios.
verò his reluctatur, reluctatur Christo Iesu : qui autem
non obedit filio, non videbit vitam, sed ira Dei manet
super eum. Præfractus enim contentiosus, & superbus
est qui non obtemperat præstantioribus. And by that
reading which the Canon law vseth, euen Princes
and all not obeying their Bishops are excluded both
from the society of the faithfull on earth and the
Kingdome of heauen. *Si vobis Episcopi, non obedie-* S. Ignat. citat.
rint omnes clerici, omnesque Principes, atque reliqui po- C. Si autem.
puli, non solùm infames, sed etiam extorres à Regno 11. quæst. 3.
Dei, & consortio fidelium, ac à limitibus sanctæ Eccle- Iacob. Siman-
siæ alieni erunt : eorum est enim vobis obedire, vt Deo, cha l. de digni-
cuius legatione fungimini. And he plainely confineth pali.
obedience to temporall Princes, that it be not with
preiudice of the spirituall, and danger of the soule.
Cæsari subiecti estote in ijs in quibus subdi, nullum ani- S. Ignat. Epist.
mæ periculum est. And saith plainely that a Bishop is ad Antioc.
aboueall other principality and power. *Quid aliud* I. Ignat. Epist.
est Episcopus, quàm is qui omni Principatu & potestate ad Trallia-
superior est? And to expresse the lamentable estate
of them which want true Bishops, Preists, and
Deacons, concludeth, there neither is nor can be
any true Church, nor communion of Saints without them. *Sine his Ecclesia electa non est, nulla sine his*

San-

Sanctorum congregatio, nulla Sanctorum collectio. And setteth downe their holy functions and offices to be such, that noe Protestants can possibly clayme to haue either Bishop, Preist, Deacō, or other Cleargy

Epist. ad Magnesian. & ad Philadelph. Epist. ad Heronem.

man amonge them. *Sine Episcopo, nec Presbyter, nec Diaconus, nec Laicus quicquam facit.* The Bishops, saith he, doe baptize, offer sacrifice, giue orders, & vse Imposition of hands. *Baptizant, sacrificāt, eligunt ordinant, manus imponunt.* Nothing is to be done in the Church without their allowāce, no Sacrament

Epist. ad Smyrn.

ministred, he is dispenser of all spirituall busines, it is not lawfull for the Preists without his approbation, to baptize, to offer, to sacrifice, to say Masse. *Sine Episcopo nemo quicquam faciat eorum quæ ad Ecclesiam spectant. Rata Eucharistia habeatur illa quæ sub Episcopo fuerit, vel cui ipse concesserit. Non licet sine Episcopo baptizare, neque offerre, neque sacrificium immolare, neque dochen celebrare* others reade, *neque Missas celebrare,* which is sufficiently expressed and approued in *offerre,* and *sacrificium immolare,* before. The Bishops did consecrate Virgins, and

Epist. ad Polycarp.

Mariages made by their warrant. *Si quis potest in castitate permanere, ad honorem carnis Dominicæ, vitet iactantiam: & si idipsum statuatur sine Episcopo corruptum est. Decet vero, vt & ducentes vxores, & nu-*

Epist. ad Smyrn. & ad Heronem.

bentes, cum Episcopi arbitrio coniungantur. The Preists. besides their preaching, and ministring of Sacraments, did offer sacrfice, and say Masse, as is before expressed. And the Deacons ministred vnto the Bishops, and Preists in their holy sacrifice. *Diaconus Sacerdotum minister. Sacerdotes sacrificant.* And writinge to Sainct Heron a Deacon of the Church of Antioch hauing immediately spoken before how the Preists did offer sacrifice, he saith, that he did

minister

miniſter to them in the holy Sacrifice, as Sainct
Stephen did to Sainct Iames the Apoſtle, & Preiſts
in Hieruſalem, prouing that they there ſaid Maſſe,
as the Preiſts of Antioch and other Churches did.
Tu illis miniſtras, vt Sanctus ille Stephanus Iacobo &
Presbyteris qui erant Hieroſolimis. And in an other e-
piſtle ſaith plainely, that Deacõs ought to doeſuch
duty in thoſe miſteries to Preiſts, as Sainct Stephen did to Sainct Iames, Sainct Timothy and S.
Lucius, to Sainct Paul, Sainct Anacletus and Sainct
Clement, to Sainct Peter. *Purum & inculpatum mi-*
niſterium illis exhibent, vt S. Stephanus Beato Iacobo:
Timotheus & Linus, Paulo : Anacletus & Clemens
Petro. And expreſſeth this their office in theſe plaine
termes. *Oportet Diaconis myſteriorum Chriſti, per omnia*
placere; nec enim ciborum & potuum miniſtri ſunt, ſed
Eccleſiæ Dei adminiſtratores. The Geeke readinge
cheifely ſignifieth miniſtring in the holy ſacrifice of
Maſſe, and ſo expreſſeth it ſelfe in this matter. Λει-
τȣργȣντες λειτουργίαν καθαράν καὶ ἄμωμον. He remembreth both altar and ſacrifice, θοϐία, θοϐιαϛέ-
ριον in as plaine termes, as any preſent writers of
the Roman Church now doth; and to manifeſt he
doth not meane ſuch acts as Proteſtants terme ſacrifice, and are ſo many as the different kindes of
deuotion, but onely the externall common ſacrifice, he ſaith, there is but one ſacrifice and this ſacrifice the onely fleſh and blood of Chriſt. *Vna eſt*
caro Chriſti Ieſu Domini noſtri, vnus illius ſanguis qui
pro nobis effuſus eſt, vnus panis omnibus confractus, &
vnus calix, qui omnibus diſtributus eſt; vnum altare
omni Eccleſiæ. The prayer and words of a Preiſts, are
of ſuch force, that they place Chriſt among vs. *V-*
nius ſiue alterius precatio tātarum virium eſt, vt Chri-

Epiſtol. ad
Trallian.

Epiſtol. ad
Philadelp.

Epiſtol. ad
Epheſ.

C 2   *ſtum*

stum inter illos statuat. It is a preparatiue of eternity, a preseruatiue against death, procuring life in God, and a medicine expelling all euill. *Pharmacum im-*

Epis.ad Rom. *mortalitatis, mortis antidotum, vitamque in Deo con-cilians per Iesum Christum, & medicamentum, omnia expellens mala.* The breade or foode of God, heauen-

Ignat. apud Theodoret. Dialog. 3. ly breade, the flesh of Christ the sonne of God, the blood of Christ. *Panis Dei, panis cælestis qui est caro Christi filij Dei, & potus sanguis illius.* The Eucharist which is the flesh of our Sauiour, which suffered for our sinnes, which his Father raised againe. *Eucharistia est caro Saluatoris quæ pro peccatis nostris passa est, quam pater sua benignitate suscitauit.* These holy sacrificing Bishops and Preists, and Deacons ministring vnto them, in those sacred misteries, as they were farre from the pretended Protestant cleargy, which haue to their vttermost endeauour euer afflicted such holy Functions, especially in England with most bitter edicts and persecutions, and the sacred Priests of that, & for that onely pro-fession, with most barbarous and cruell deathes: So seing by the most constant Testimony and practise of this blessed Apostolike age, no true Church was, or could be without them, no Protestant company or congregation, all of them wantinge such duely consecrated Bishops, Preists, and Ecclesiasticall persons, and Professors, can possibly haue the name and Title of a true Church and religion : And con-tending (as they doe, that these sacrificing holy Or-ders, without which no true Church can be, are not contained in Scripture, They must needs yeeld, They were deliuered vnto the Church, and so the Church well founded in these so essentiall things, by Tradition. Which they must needs likewise

graunt

graunt of these ensuing doctrines and practises in Religion vsed in the same time, and remembred by this and other Apostolike writers of that first age.

First whereas Protestants ascribe iustification to onely Faith, being a cheife foundation of their new religion: Sainct Ignatius and this happy age knew no such doctrine, but the contrary, That faith was onely to begin Iustification, but it was perfected by charity and good deeds. *Non vos lædet aliqua diabolica cogitatio, si vt Paulus perfectam habueritis in Christum & fidem & charitatem, quæ initium vitæ & finis est. Principium vitæ fides: finis eiusdem charitas. Hæc autem duo quoties in vnum coeunt, Dei hominem perficiunt.* And againe: *Eleemosyna & fide expiantur peccata. Præsens labor modicus, multa quæ hinc expectatur merces. Nihili pendo supplicia hæc, neque tanti facio vitam meam, vt eam plus amem quam Dominum. Quare paratum me offero igni, feris, gladijs, cruci, dummodo Christum videam Saluatorem & Deum meum. Obsecro vos, quotquot pænitentia ductire dierint ad vnitatem Ecclesiæ, suscipite illos cum omni mansuetudine, vt per bonitatem & patientiam resipiscentes ex diaboli laqueis, dignii am Christo facti salutem consequantur æternam in regno Christi. Illibatum mihi est archiuum Crux Christi, mors & resurrectio eius, & fides, per quæ cupio iustificari precibus vestris. Qui honorat Prophetum in nomine Prophetæ, mercedem Prophetæ accipiet, nimirum qui honorat vinctum Iesu Christi, Martyrum accipiet mercedem. Nihil vobis apud Deum peribit eorum, quæ in illos contulistis: det vobis Dominus vt inueniatis misericordiam à Domino in illa die. Vtinam meus spiritus cum vestro commutari possit, & vincula hæc mea, quæ non fastidistis, nec ob ea erubui-*

Epistol. ad Ephesios.

Epist. ad Heronem.
Epist. ad Mar. Cassobolit.
Epist. ad Tarsen. ad Rom.
Epist. ad Philadelphenses.

Epistol. ad Smyrnenses.

C 3 *stis.*

stis. Quare nec de vobis erubescet consummata spes Ie-
sus Christus. Precationes vestræ appropinquarunt ad

Epist. ad Po-
licarpum.

Antiochenam Ecclesiam, & pacem habet. Deposita ve-
stra, sunt opera vestra, vt quæ accepistis, eadem digna
Deo reportetis. Antiochena Ecclesia pacem est nacta per
orationes vestras, & ego tranquilliori animo factus sum,
in securitate Dei, si per passionem Deum assecutus fuero,

Epist. ad He-
ron.

discipulus inueniar per orationes vestras. Quibus det
Deus inuenire misericordiam à Domino in illa die prop-

Epistol. ad
Trallianos.

ter officium & ministerium erga nos. Orate pro me, qui
in Dei misericordiä charitate vestra indigeo, vt dignus
fiam sorte ad quam assequendam iam destinor, ne repro-
bus inueniar. Where wee euidently see, by many testimonies, that the Imagined Protestant faith neither doth, nor possibly can iustifie any man; but
charity, almes, pennance, praier and other holy
works, and deeds of Christians, are meritorious and
iustifie them.

And that Protestants paradoxe of the certainty
of Saluation is most certainely false. Which he
confirmeth also in other places, as where he taketh
vpon him the knowledge of the celestiall spirits,
their orders, and dignities, yet he plainely maketh

Epistol. ad
Trall. supr.

himselfe ignorant of his owne saluation, much
more not certaine thereof. Our Protestants
pretend for themselues. *Angelicos ordines, Archan-*
gelorum militiarumque differentias, thronorum pote-
testatumque distantias, principatuum magnificentias,
Cherubim Seraphimque excellentias, spiritus sublimi-
tatem & Domini regnum, & incomparabilem Dei Pa-
tris omnipotentis diuinitatem; hæc cum nouerim, non
continuo perfectus prorsus ego sum, multa desunt ne à
Deo derelinquar. Where wee see him further to haue
described the heauenly hierarchy and orders in
heauen

heauen as Catholiks now doe and Protestants take
no notice of them.

And he doth not onely thus describe them, but
assureth vs, they know the things on earth, and so
by protestant allowance may be praied vnto, as Catholiks vse, and they condemne. *Pracipio tibi coram* Epistol. ad
Deo vniuersorum, & coram Christo prasente, & San- Heron.
cto Spiritu & administratorys Angelorum ordinibus,
custodi depositum meum, quod ego & Christus tibi com-
mendauimus. Where the holy Angels doe not onely
knowe our actions as Christ and the blessed Trinity doth, but assist and minister vnto vs. And is
so farre from denying this knowledge, to Saints, &
Angels in heauen, that he yeeldeth knowledge of
affayres on earth namely of the Passion of Christ Epistol. ad
euen to the soules which were in *Limbus patrum,* or Trallian.
Purgatory at that time. *Verè crucifixus & mortuus*
videntibus cælestibus, terrenis & ijs qui sub terra
detinebantur : cælestibus quidem inspicientibus, ni-
mirum incorporeis naturis : terrenis verò, vt Iudæis
& Romanis, & cæteris qui tunc temporis crucifixo
Domino aderant : subterraneis autem, ijs videlicet,
qui plurimi cum Domino resurrexerunt, multa enim,
inquit, corpora Sanctorum, qui dormierant, cum Matth. 27.
Domino resurrexerunt, monumentis apertis. Descen-
dit ad infernum solus, regressus est cum multitudi-
ne, & septum illud æternum rupit, & medium parie-
tem illius destruxit. By this wee finde, as Catholicks
hold, and Protestants deny, a place where soules
were, and whence there is deliuery and redemption, and not euerduring Torment, and despera-
tion, of the reprobate, and damned in their hell; and
place of eternall punishmēt, of which there is no end
or freedome to be had, or hoped for. And therefore
C 4 it a

a place from whence a Ranſome will make deliuery, and there is no merit or deſeruing after this life, as our Proteſtants moſt freely graunt.

This freedome of ſoules from that place of puniſhment, purgatory, or howſoeuer wee ſhall name it, is principally to be procured, and effected, by the ſacrifices, prayers, almes and other meritorious deeds, and workes of holy Chriſtians ſtill liuing in the eſtate and condition of deſeruinge. Such as S. Ignatius hath before remembred. And other Apoſtolike writers of this age, as Sainct Denis the Areopagite, and Sainct Clement Schollers of the two greate Apoſtles Sainct Peter and Sainct Paul, to be cited with others in this particular queſtion in the proper place thereof, beinge of the ſame religion in all points with Sainct Ignatius, & the holy Church of Chriſt, doe as plainely expreſſe, and deliuer for the conſtant cuſtome practiſe, and doctrine of, that time, to offer ſacrifice, pray, and doe other holy workes, for faithfull people departed out of this life, as any learned writer of the preſent Roman Church doth in theſe dayes. And Sainct Ignatius with much honor remembreth them, eſpecially S. Clement Scholler to Sainct Peter and Paul and Pope of Rome *Papa beatiſſimus Clemens Petri & Pauli Auditor,* and teſtifieth, that he liued in perpetuall chaſtity, *in caſtitate exegit hanc vitam.* Which he affirmeth of other Apoſtolike Preiſts and Biſhops of that age Sainct Timothy Sainct Titus S. Euodius his predeceſſor at Antioche, & of himſelfe in diuers places; So that then neither the Preiſts of the Latine or Greeke Church, Antioche beinge the cheifeſt, and where the name of Chriſtians firſt began, were maried, but continually liued all

their

Epiſtol. ad
Mar. Caſſob.

Epiſt. ad Philadelph.

their life time in chastity, *in castitate exegerunt hanc vitam.*

And therefore they were honored in those dayes, and the holy Maydens which had professed virginity, were compared to the Preists in this point of perfection, and for it honored as they were. *Eas quæ in virginitate degunt in pretio habete, velut Christi Sacerdotes.* It is manifest, their were Colledges or Nunneries of such vowed and professed virgins and Nonnes then. *Saluto Collegium virginum.* And they liued in perpetuall virginity. *Saluto eas quæ in perpetua degunt virginitate.* They were professed by the Bishop, whether men or women: *Si quis potest in castitate permanere, ad honorem carnis dominicæ, sine iactantia permaneat: si idipsum statuatur sine Episcopo corruptum est.* And of this profession & consecration of virgins, he further putteth them, and all in memory in this manner: *virgines agnoscant, cui seipsas consecrarunt.*

And he proueth, That it is in the power and free will of man, to doe these, and all holy duties in a Christian life, by the grace of Christ, and noe man necessitated to sinne, heauen and hell good and bad in the free will and election of man. *Decet non modo vocari Christianos, sed esse, nec enim dici, sed esse, beatos facit. Obseruationi proponitur vita, mors inobedientia, & singuli, qui hoc aut illud elegerunt, in eius quod inuenerint locum abituri sunt, fugiamus mortem, & eligamus vitam. In hominibus enim geminas notas inuenirt dico, & hanc esse veri numismatis, illam vero adulterimi. Pius homo numisma est à Deo excusum: impius ementitum, adulterinum, & illegitimum, non à Deo, sed à diabolo effectum. Non quòd velim dicere duas esse hominis naturas, sed vnum esse hominem, qui*

iam

Epistol. ad
Tarsens.

Epistol. ad
Philippen.
Epistol. ad
Smyrn.
Epistol. ad
Polycarp.

Epistol. ad
Antiochen.

Epistol. ad
Magnes.

Epiſt. ad E-phesios.

iam Dei, iam diaboli ſit. Si quis pietati ſtudet, Dei homo eſt; ſi impiè agat, diaboli eſt: non id factus per naturam, ſed animi arbitrium. He proueth that concupiſcence without conſent, condemneth not nor is ſinne as proteſtants hold. Cum nulla in vobis ſit conſcupiſcentia, quæ vos inquinet, & ſupplicium adferat, ſecundum Deum viuite. Non vos lædet aliqua diabolica cogitatio, ſi vt Paulus perfectam habueritis in Chriſtu, & ſidem, & charitatem: He hath before in one place ſpoken of foure Sacraments, Baptiſme, the Sacrament of Chriſts bleſſed body and blood, Orders, and Con-

Epiſtol. ad Heron.

firmation, by al expoſitors: Baptizant, Sacrificant, Eligunt, manus imponunt. He hath aſcribed iuſtification vnto pennance, and ſo allowed it in that degree, and although he hath ſo dignified the virgi-

Epiſt. ad Philadelph.

nall life, and ſaith it is better præſtantius, κρεῖttον, then wedlocke, he giueth ſo much honor vnto Marriage, that it was not to be performed without

Epiſt. ad Polycarpum.

the Biſhops aſſent and allowance. Decet verò vt & ducentes vxores, & nubentes, cum Epiſcopi arbitrio coniugantur, vt nuptiæ iuxta Domini præceptum ſint, non autem ad concupiſcentiam.

Our proteſtants generally and abſolutely deny theſe holy Chriſtian doctrines, and practiſes, to be contained in Scriptures, or to be proued by them; Therefore they muſt needs yeeld that that primatiue and Apoſtolike Church by ſo greate and liuing-then witneſſe, held and profeſſed them by tradition, and certaine it is, that many bookes of Scripture were neither generally receaued, nor written, when the things were ſo generally vſed, and profeſſed, not onely in the commaundinge Greeke Church of Antioch, where Saint Peter, S. Paul, S. Euodius and Saint Ignatius profeſſed, and practized

&tized them: *Pauli & Petri fuistis discipuli, ne perda-* Epist. ad An-
tis depositum.Mementote Euodij beatißimi Pastoris ve- tiochen.
stri, qui primus vobis ordinatus est ab Apostolis Anti-
stes. Where the disciples were first called Christias,
when Sainct Peter and Sainct Paul came thither, Epist. ad Ma-
and there founded the Church: *Antiochiæ primum* gnesian.
discipuli appellati sunt Christiani cum Petrus & Pau-
lus fundarent Ecclesiam : But in all the renowned
Churches before remembred, and in all the whole
Christian world, at that time, by the preachinge
and tradition of the holy Apostles,as the same Apostolike man thus witnesseth : *Scribo ad vos, monco-* Epist. ad Phi-
que vt vna prædicatione, vna Eucharistia vtamini. ladelph.
Vna enim est caro Domini nostri Iesu Christi, vnus il-
lius sanguis, qui pro nobis effusus est, vnus item panis
omnibus confractus,& vnus calix qui omnibus tributus
est : vnum altare omni Ecclesiæ, & vnus Episcopus
cum presbyterorum collegio, & diaconis. Quandoquidem
est vnus est ingenitus Deus & Pater, & vnus vnige-
nitus Filius Deus, verbum & homo, vnus Paracletus
Spiritus veritatis, & vna prædicatio & fides vna, &
vnum baptisma,& vna Ecclesia, quam suis sudoribus
& laboribus fundarunt Sancti Apostoli à finibus terræ
vsque ad fines, in sanguine Christi. Vos itaque oportet
vt populum peculiarem, & gentem sanctam omnia per-
ficere concordibus animis in Christo. And directly Epistol. ad
concludeth, that whosoeuer shall teach otherwise, Heron.
then the Traditions of the Church be, he is to be
accompted a wolfe amonge sheepe, though he be
otherwise, a man of credit, fasteth, liueth chastely,
doth miracles, and prophecieth: *Quicumque dixerit*
quippiam præter ea quæ constituta sunt, παρα τα δια-
τεταγμένα, tametsi fide dignus sit, quamuis signa edat,
quamuis prophetet, pro lupo illum habeas qui sub ouina
pelle

pelle exitium peſtemque adfert ouibus. Wee may adde vnto theſe greateſt ſolemnities, and feſtiuall dayes of the Criſtians, receaued in the Church in this time by tradition, and not Scripture, and by the ſame authority of tradition without Scripture, the feaſts & higheſt feſtiuities of the Iewes euen thoſe which were ſolemnely ſet downe and commaūded in Scripture to be religiouſly obſerued, quite eua-cuated and vtterly reiected.

The Sabbath which is now our ſaterday, was with greate ceremony and ſolemnity deliuered in Scripture to be kept euery weeke, and that which wee call ſonday was commaunded to be a working day. Yet all Chriſtians in this time, by tradition did celebrate that old working day next after the old Sabbath, for our Lords day, conſecrated to Chriſts resurrection as the cheifeſt of all dayes. *Poſt Sabbatum omnis Chriſti amator Dominicum celebret diem, reſurrectioni conſecratam Dominicæ, Reginam & principem omnium dierum, in qua, & vita noſtra exorta eſt, & per Chriſtum mors deuicta:* as all Chriſtians now alſo doe. The feaſt of Easter was alſo chaūged, with other ſolemnities, and they were accompted as curſed perſecutors of Chriſt, and his Apoſtles, which obſerued otherwiſe, or kept any feſtiuity of the Iewes, although before commaunded in Scriptures. *Si quis cum Iudæis celebrat Paſcha, aut Symbola feſtiuitatis eorum recipit, particeps eſt eorum, qui Dominum occiderunt, & Apoſtolos eius.* He proueth plainely, that both the principall feaſts and faſts alſo of the Church, as Lent and others were then in vſe, by this authority of Tradition: *Feſtiuitates ne dehoneſtetis, quadrageſimale iciunium ne ſpernatis, continet enim imitationem conuerſationis Dominicæ. Poſt Paſsio-*

nis

Epiſtol. ad Magneſianos. & epiſt. ad Trallian.

Epiſt. ad Philadelphenſes.

Epiſtol. ad Philippen.

*nis Dominicæ hebdomadam ieiunare quartis & fextis
ferijs ne negligatis. Si quis Dominicam diem ieiunarit,
hic Chrifti interfector eft.* He often there remembreth
the perpetuall virginity of the Bleſſed Virgin
Mary: *Mariæ Virginitas & admirandus ille partus:
Virginem eſſe quæ parit.* The forme and manner of
offering the holy Sacrifice of Chriſts body and
blood, of conſecrating Biſhops, Preiſts, and other
Clergy men, of miniſtringe ſo many Sacraments, as
he hath remembred, the publike Church ſeruice,
to which he bindeth all, the order of receauing penitents, the cuſtome and limitation of their vſed
faſts, and whatſoeuer almoſt appertaining to the
holy vſe and exerciſe of Chriſtian Religion in that
Apoſtolike age, was knowne, and practized by this
bleſſed diſciple and all Apoſtolike men which was
deliuered and vſed onely by tradition, and ſo deſ-
cended to later ages and poſterities, no Scripture
preſcribing Chriſtians, any ſuch requiſite inſtruction, in ſo neceſſary and eſſentiall parts of Religion or the true practiſe and profeſſion thereof, to
which all true Chriſtians vnder paine, and daunger
of euerlaſting damnation were bound.

And as Sainct Ignatius, ſo alſo teſtifie the other
holy and Apoſtolike writers of this age as I ſhall
moſt clearely proue and cite them in euery particular article, queſtioned by theſe Teachers. For
this preſent it will be more then needfull to remember what they write hereof in generall termes.
Sainct Denis the Areopagite conuerted by Sainct
Paul the Apoſtle, writinge of Chriſtian neceſſary
doctrines, ſaith plainely that the Apoſtles deliuered
ſome of them by tradition onely without writinge,
as they did ſome by writinge: *partim ſcriptis partim
non*

Dionysius A-
reopag. l. Ec-
clef. Hierarc.
c. 1.

non scriptis suis institutionibus ex Sacrosanctis legibus nobis tradiderunt. And proueth that in this Aposto-like time, the Christiã mysteries were neither com-municated by writing nor word for their greate re-uerence, but to holy and perfect Christians. *Vide ne Sancta Sanctorum enunties, sed reuerceberis ea potius, & quæ occulti Dei sunt, cognitione mentis & animi in honore habebis ac pretio: ita tamen vt ea & minus per-fectis non tradas, & cum ys solis, qui Sancti erunt, cum Sancta illustratione, pro sacrarum rerum dignitate com-munices.* And setteth downe expressely. That the Apostolike Church then did not permit Catechu-mens, Energumens, or penitents to be present at the the holy misteries. *Catechumenos, & Energumenos, quique in pœnitentia sunt, Sanctæ Hiererchiæ mos pati-tur quidem audire sacram psalmorum modulationem, diuinamque sacrarum Scripturarum recitationem: ad sacra autem opera quæ deinceps sequuntur, atque myste-ria spectanda, non eos conuocat, sed perfectos oculos eorum qui digni sunt.* And testifieth what greate care the Christians then had, to conceale their ce-remonies.

Cap. 5.

Cap.

Dionyf. supr.
c. 1.
S.Dionyf.l.de
diuin. nomin.
cap.3.
Clem. Rom.
ep. 1.2.3 4.5
l. Recog.l.cõ
stitut Apost.
Chrif. hom.
49. in Matth.
Eufeb. histor.
Eccl. Cedren.
Nicephor.
Callist. hist.l.

Sainct Timothy also, as this holy writer proueth, was of this opinion and practise. S. Hierotheus also Tutor to Sainct Denis did write a booke of Christians holy traditions. *Hierotheus clarißimus præceptor noster elementa Theologica magna cum laude collegerit.* And this before S. Denis write.

The Apostolike Traditions collected together, and committed to writinge by Sainct Clement Successor to Sainct Peter at Rome, as both he him-selfe, with other auncient and approued Authors, Greeke and Latine and generall councels witnesse, are so many that a short volume containeth them
not,

not, yet in all things condemne Protestant Religió, not approuing it in any one Article, wherein it differreth from Catholiks and the doctrine of the present Roman Church, as will be made euident in the particular articles hereafter, manifestly knowne and confessed by Ruffinus his translation and testimony, to haue bene then, and from the beginninge contained in his workes, and aggreable both with the Apostolike doctrine of this age, and other confessed vnspotted times after, as in the fourth hundred yeare of Christ, wherein Ruffinus liued, & the Church of Rome at this time, wherein wee now liue. I will onely in this place exemplifie in the publike liturgy, Masse, or Church sacrifice published by him vnto the Church of Christ. Greeks Latines, French, and our old brittesh antiquities & our Protestants theselues confesse, That as Peter at Antioch, S. Marke at Alexandria, Sainct Iohn and S. Andrew in Asia, So Sainct Clement wrote and published a forme of Masse, and generally all Churches embraced it : *Omnesque vniuersæ Ecclesiæ vbicumque sint, per eam quam Sanctus Clemens conscripsit liturgiam tradiderunt.* In this so old, so vniuersall, so approued, wee finde protection of the Angels, *Angelorum tutelas,* honor to all Saincts, Patriarks, Prophets, Apostles, Martyrs, Confessors &c. *Sanctis, Patriarchis, Prophetis, Iustis, Apostolis, Martyribus, Confessoribus. Sanctorum martyrum memoriam colamus.* Prayer for the faithfull deceased. *Pro ijs, qui in fide quieuerunt, oremus.* The Ecclesiasticall orders which I haue before remembred from Sainct Ignatius. That the holy sacrifice was offered for all Seruants of God. *Offerimus tibi pro omnibus qui à sæculo placuerunt tibi.* Wee finde virgins, and liuers

2. Epiphan. in panar. Ruffin. præf. in Clem. Bed. in cap. S. Luc. Freculp. Lerouien. Chron. lib. 2. Synod. Sext. in Trullo. Ruffin. præf. & translat. oper. S. Clement.

S. Proclus Patriarch. Constant. l. de tradit. diuinæ Liturg. Nichol. Episcopus Methonen. l. de vero Christi corp. in Eucharist. Marcus Ephes. l. de corpore & sang. Christi. Bessar. l. de Sacr. Eucharist. Manuscript. Gallic. antiq. an. D. in S. Clem. Manuscript. Brit. antiquis. Protest. Collectió of priuate prayers. An. 1627. p. 147. 125. 107. 87. 35. Mat. Park. antiquit. Brit. pag. 47.

liuers in professed chastity. *Pro virginibus & castitatē seruātibus.* The sacrifice of breade & wine made the body & blood of Christ. *Corpus Christi, Sanguis Christi. Episcopus det oblationē dicens, corpus Christi, & sumens dicat Amen. Diaconus teneat calicem, & quando tradit, dicat. Sanguis Christi, calix vitæ, & bibens dicat Amen.* And this very body and blood of Christ were receaued by the Cōmunicants, those kept thē in godlinesse, procured remission of their sinnes. *percepto pretioso corpore, & pretioso sanguine Christi, gratias agamus ei, qui dignos nos reddidit percipiendi Sancta eius mysteria, & rogemus vt non in Iudicium, sed in salutem nobis fiant in vtilitatem animæ, & corporis, in custodiam pietatis, in remißionem peccatorum, in vitam futuri sæculi.* The Preists which said Masse, were adorned with a sacrificing vestiment, signed themselues with the signe of the crosse, and so came to the altar. *Orans pontifex vna cum Sacerdotibus; induensque vestem splendidam, & stans ad altare, trophæo crucis se consignans infronte.*

S. Procl. supr.
S. Isod. l. 1. de
off. ca. 15. Al-
bin. lib. diuin.
offic. c. de ce-
lebrat. Missæ.
Egbert. Serm.
de increment.
& manif. cath.
fidei. Steph.
Edu. l. Sacr.
altat. Paschas.
Rathert. l. de
corpore &
sang. Christi.
Mich. Singel.
in vit. S. Dion
Areopag. E-
piph. l. de her.
in Andian. &
Messal. Nice-
phor. l. 3. c. 18.

That the holy traditions could not but be from the Apostles, from whom Sainct Clement receaued them, both Sainct Proclus and other witnesses without exception giue vs able testimony: *multi diuini Pastores, qui Apostolis successerunt sacrorum diuinæ liturgiæ misteriorum rationem explicantes, scriptis mandatam Ecclesiæ tradiderunt, in quibus primi & clarißimi sunt S. Clemens, summi illius Apostolorum discipulus, & successor, qui sacrosancta illa mysteria, à sanctis Apostolis sibi reuelata in lucem edidit.*

Our old brittish manuscript of the first institution of the Ecclesiasticall office especially in Frauce and Britaine most concerninge vs euen as our Protestant

testât Antiquaries intitle it, *prima Institutio & varie-* Manuscript.
tas Ecclesiastici scruity, præcipue in Britannia & Gal- Brit.antiq. de
lia, doth also assure vs, That S. Trophimus, Sainct prima Insti-
Photinus, and others, disciples of the Apostles, tutione Eccl.
(which Antiquaries agree, Sainct Clement sent into officij,
Fraunce and these parts) did vse this Romane forme
of Masse, digested by Sainct Clement, and in the
French persecution it was carried to him againe at
Rome to be perused. *Beatus Trophimus Episcopus*
Arelatensis, & Sanctus Photinus Martyr & Episcopus
Lugdunensis, discipulus S. Petri Apostoli cursum Ro-
manum in Gallijs tradiderunt. Inde postea relatione beati
Photini Martyris cum quadraginta & octo Martyribus
retrusi in ergastulum, ad beatum Clementem quartum
loci, successorem beati Petri Apostoli deportauerunt.
Where it hath the warrant and testimony of the
most glorious Apostolike men and Martyrs in
this part of the world. All the formes and Orders
of Masse, ascribed to the Apostles, to Sainct Basil,
Sainct Chrysostome, and whosoeuer Greeke or
Latine, conspire and agree with this of Sainct Clement in all and euery tradition denied by our Protestants, and vsed by him. Sainct Denis the Areopagite, and Sainct Martiall whom with others he
sent into Fraunce renowned among the Apostolike
writers of this time, haue the same and more. I haue
already spoken of Sainct Denis, and shall more specially hereafter. Sainct Martiall, who saith he was
present at Christs Ascension in heauen : *Testes su-* Martial.epist.
mus, quia eum ascendere in cœlum vidimus, He testi- ad Burdegal.
fieth that the Priests then ministred life in their cap. 1.
holy sacrifice, *Sacerdotes Dei omnipotentis vitam tri-* Martial.supr.
buunt in calice & viuo pane. Sacrificium Deo Creatori cap. 3.
offertur in ara. Sacrifice on the Altar. The Altar de-

dicated

dicated to God and Sainct Stephen. *Dedicata in nomine Domini Dei Israel & ipsius testis Stephani.* This sacrifice was the body and blood of Christ offered by the Masse: *cuius* (Christ) *corpus & sanguinem in vitam æternam offerimus,* for obtaining life. The same body of Christ which the Iewes crucified was offered in Masse, and for to obtaine eternall life, and Christ so ordained and Instituted. *Quod Iudæi per inuidiam immolauerunt, nos causa salutis nostræ in ara sanctificata proponimus, scientes hoc solo remedio nobis vitam præstandam, & mortem effugandam. Hoc enim ipse Dominus noster iußit nos agere in sui commemorationem.*

Cap. 8. He giueth as much power and reuerence to the crosse of Christ, signe, and vse thereof as S. Clement did, or any learned Catholike now doth. *Cruce Domini semper in mente, in ore, in signo tenete. Crux enim Domini armatura vestra inuicta contra Sathanam, galea custodiens caput, lorica protegens pectus, clypeus tela maligni repellens, gladius iniquitatem & angelicas insidias peruersæ potestatis sibi propinquare nullo modo sinens. Hoc solo signo cælestis victoria data est nobis; & per crucem baptisma Dei sanctificatum est.*

Cap. 11. He teacheth that the Church of Christ shall neuer fayle: *firma Ecclesia Dei & Christi, nec cadere, nec disrumpi poterit vnquam.*

Martial. epist. ad Tolosanos. cap. 8. 9. He affirmeth, Christ cõstituted three degrees, the married, widowhood, better, *viduitatem in præmio maiori,* virginity the third, most excellent, and angelike, *tertium excellentem gradum honestatis in virginitate demonstrate nobis perfectum, & per omnia simile angelicæ dignitati.* And that it was then vowed, euen by such as were espoused, as namely by S. Valeria Virgin and Martyr, spouse of the King then called Stephen by S. Martial his preaching : *Virgo Va-*

Valeria sponsa Regis terrestris, sed melius sponsa Regis cœlestis, quæ per meam prædicationem, virginitatem mentis & corporis Deo deuouerat, gladio decollata.

That S. Lazarus whom Christ raised from death, Bishop of Marsiles, said Masse in the same manner, as S. Maximus also, both the French Antiquities, & their sacrifying or massing vestures still reserued in the Cathedrall Church there, are sufficient testimonys: *in cathedrali Basilica, & caput, & vestes in quibus Missas celebrabat adhuc hodie conseruantur & monstrantur.* S. Martha Sister of S. Mary Magdalen had many Virgins and Nunnes with her, and S. Fronto 70. Monkes in one place, in an other 300. So in all other Apostolike Persons in Fraunce aggreeing in the same onely true profession of Religion. For Britaine it is euident before, it receaued Christianity before the Scripture of the new Testament was either receaued, knowne of, or for the most part written. And yet the Christians here praied vnto Saints, and Angels, for the dead, reuerenced the signe of the crosse, & other holy Images, and sacred Reliks, said, or heard Masse, and practized other Christian rites and duties, which protestants deny to be contained in, or proued by Scripture.

Tertullian lyuing and writing as many testifie, euen Protestants, before Pope Eleutherius time, and witnessing Britayne had in his dayes receaued the faith of Christ euen in those parts thereof whether the Pagan Romans could neuer come, *loca Romanis inaccessa,* speaketh of the traditions before remembred, as both his owne works, Catholiks and Protestants proue in these words : *Tertullianus in genere de doctrina suæ ætatis inquit eam consentire*

cum

Demochar. ll
2. Petr. de Natal. l. 1. Bed.
16 cal Ian.
Anton. pact.
1 cap. 19. Guliel. Eisengrencent. 1.
part. 5. Mant.
fast. l. 8. Antonin. part. 1.
Petr. de natal.
l. 9. Bed. 8. cal.
nou. Ado.
Treu. ib. Volater. l. 3. 16.

Tertull. l. de præscription.
Magdeburg.
Centur. 3. col.
34. c. 4. col.
240. 241.
Sutcl. subu.
p. 4. Whitg.
def. Respon.
pag. 96.

cum Ecclesijs Apostolicis, eamque consensum & concordiam communem esse omniū Ecclesiarum in Europa, in Asia, & in Africa testatur: That this the doctrine of his time did agree with all *Apostolike* Churches : that it was the common consent and concordance of all the Churches in Europe, in *Asia* & in *Afrike*. And though wee assigne a somewhat later time to Tertullian, as others doe in the later end of the second age, yet when he so confidently and generally assigneth this common consent of all Churches of Britaine, Fraunce, Spaine Italy all Europe Asia and Afrike in these holy Christian doctrines thus impugned by Protestants, hauing therein the consent of all Apostolik Churches, wee must needs say, whether they were receaued, and professed from Scriptures, or Traditions, being longe before any generall Councels kept, by the generall confessed rule of the Fathers and Protestants before, they must needs be deliuered by authority of the Apostles : *non nisi authoritate Apostolica traditum certissimè creditur.*

And the first receauing of the holy Scriptures in Britayne which wee finde in Antiquities, was in the time of Pope Eleutherius, and from the Church of Rome, the same Catalogue of Scriptures it then vsed and still vseth, as wee finde in the epistle of that holy Pope to Kinge Lucius : *suscepistis nuper miseratione diuina in Regno Britaniæ legem & fidem Christi.* Habetis penes vos in Regno vtramque paginam. You haue there in your Kingdome both testaments. So our Protestants translate it, or, both parts of Scripture.

Eleuth. Pap. epist. ad Lucium Regem Britan. Godwin. Cōuerf. of Brit. in epist. Eleuther. Stow. hist. Romans.

THE

THE THIRD CHAPTER.

The 7.8.9.10. Articles examined; and wherein they differ from the present Romane Church, condemned by this first Apostolike age.

HAVING thus absolutely, and at large confuted and ouerthrowne by the Apostolike age, the last Article, the erroneous ground of all Protestant Religion, wee may be more breife in the rest, being all at the least generally confuted and ouerthrowne in their false foundation, so destroyed. And vntill wee come to their 11. Article intituled: *of the Iustification of man* : It may be questioned, whether any of them doth in common, and probable construction, and meaninge, oppose the Roman Church or no. And for the two next, the 7. and 8. Articles, it is most certaine and euident, the first of them being intituled: *of the old testament,* only teacheth, *The old Testament is not contrary to the new.* And the other stiled, *of the three Creeds,* is in the same condition, onely affirming, *The three Creedes, Nicene Creede, Athanasius Creede, and that which is commonly called the Apostles Creede, ought throughly to be receaued and beleeued.* But the reason hereof, which thus they yeeld: *for they may be proued by most certaine warrantes of holy Scripture* , is both before confuted, & very friuolous, for neither is the Scripture the compleate Rule of Religion, neither was the Scriptures of the new testament written, when the Apostles deliuered their Creede, to the Church, nor the Scriptures agreed vpon, vntill after both the Creedes of the Nicene Councell, and Sainct

Atha-

Athanasius were generally receaued and professed by all Catholiks, as is already made manifest, euen by Protestants themselues aswell as other Authors of more worthy credit. The next Article is intituled: *of Originall or birth sinne.* And was expressely concluded by them against the Pelagians, denying originall sinne in man, as they expoūd themselues, naming the Pelagians, and their heresie there, with a confutation of it in their proceedings, holding that Originall sinne in those that be not baptized, *deserueth Gods wrath and damnation.* Yet in the last and concluding words of the Article, their phrase of speach hath perhaps giuen occasion to some puritane Nouelists, to thinke they held as these men Caluin and such doe, that concupiscence without assent is sinne, The words be : *Although there is no condemnation for them that beleeue, and are baptized: yet the Apostle doth confesse, that concupiscence & lust hath of it selfe the nature of sinne.*

A Puritane glosser vpon this place saith : *Concupiscence, euen in the regenerate, is sinne.* Among fourteene Protestant Confessions he citeth but two for his opinion by his owne exposition, And so seauen to one by his owne argument of Protestant authority, he is deceaued. And the Puritan Heluetian assembly ruled by Caluine, holdeth this besides their other errour, which our English Protestants deny, in ther next article, that man hath not free will to doe well, or fly sinne. And he plainely confesseth, that all the primatiue Fathers, sufficient for this purpose, are against him, holding concupiscence without assent to be no sinne. *Omnium sententias.* So do our English Puritans also, which hold that errour, acknowledge, and it is apparant euen by the

Artic. 9. supr.

Thomas Rogers in Articul. 9.
Confes. Helu. 2. c 9. Saxon. ar. 2. 20.

Protest. Engl. Art. art. 10.
Caluin. lib. 1. Instit. c. 5. l. 2. c. 2. & 3. & à lib. l. 3. c. 3.
Ant. Wotton. against D. Bish. pa. 112.

the words of this article before related, that the English Protestants doe no otherwise terme cōcupiscence sinne, then materially as the Apostle doth, whose onely authority they vse in that matter, and not properly and formally, as sinne is truely and in right sense vsed, and taken, hauing liberty and consent of minde annexed vntoit; otherwise Infants, Ideots, frantike madde men without iudgment, and men sleepinge, doinge the materiall part of things sinfull, should also sinne: or if the flesh of it selfe, the vegetatiue or sensitiue power abstracting from reason could sinne, creatures onely hauing beeing, vegetation, and sense might and should sinne, equally, as those that be reasonable: Beasts, fishes, fowles, plants, herbes and trees would be both capable and guilty of sinne,

And our English Protestants in their communion booke of as greate credit, and approued by as greate authority with them, and their Religion, as these articles, *acknowledge that the baptized are deade to sinne. And the whole body of sinne is vtterly abolished in them. They promise and vowe to forsake the deuill, and all his workes, the carnall desires of the flesh, and not to followe, and be ledde by them, obediently to keepe Gods commaundements,*

Communion Booke Titul. ministrat. of publike Baptisme. And Catechisme.

Therefore I dare not say, that the Parlament Protestants of England doe, or by their religion should professe, that condemned errour, which holdeth concupiscence without assent to be truely sinne. And all auncient expositors of holy Scripture both of the Greeke, and Latine Church, doe expounde the Apostle in the place insinuated in this Article, to speake of sinne onely materially, & not properly when he termeth concupiscence by that name. D 4 This

This is confessed by the professors of this error before, and the name of the Fathers are needlesse, and too many to be cited in a confessed cause. And wee haue the Catholike doctrine in this point deliuered and taught by Apostolike men of this age. Sainct Ignatius proueth, that concupiscence without assent defileth not: *cum nulla in vobis sit concupiscentia, quæ vos inquinet, & supplicium adferat, profectò secundum Deum viuitis.* And Rabbi Moses Hadarsan proueth the same, for the true beleeuing Iewes: *& quod iam scriptum est: & ad te concupiscentia peccati, scilicet, quod est figmentum malum iugiter concupiscens, & affectans, & tu dominaberis illius, hoc est, si volueris præualebis aduersus eum.* And all the holy writers of this time affirme the same, when they teach, that free will is in man, & sinne is not contradicted without it, nor can be, where, & when it doth not consent. Which cannot possibly be in the first motions of concupiscence, by common experience, Iudgment and agreement of all, arisinge both without and against the will and liberty of man.

First Sainct Ignatius who hath so plainely testified before, that concupiscence not consented vnto, doth not defile, and so cannot be sinne, proueth also, *obseruationi proponitur vita, mors obedientiæ: & singuli qui hoc aut illud elegerint in eius quod inuenerint locum abituri sunt: fugiamus mortem, & eligamus vitam,* That to sinne or not sinne, to haue life or death, is in the power and will of Christians. And againe, most plainely that sinne is not without free will. *Si quis pietati studet, Dei homo est;, si impiè agat, diaboli est : non id factus per naturam, sed animi arbitrium.* ἀπὸ τῆς ἑαυτῇ γνώμης γινόμεν⊙.

Sainct

Ignat. epist. ad Ephes.

Rabbi Mos. Hadar. ad ca. 4. Gen.

Ignat. epist. ad Magnesian.

Sainct Clement disciple and Successor to Sainct
Peter the Apostle speaketh as plainely , or rather
more,both in Sainct Peters and his owne words &
opinion and all true beleeuers : *liberi sumus arbitrij,* Clem. Rom.
quia liberum est animo, in quam velit partem declinare epist 3.
iudicium suum, & quam probauerit, eligere viam,con-
stat euidenter inesse hominibus arbitrij libertatem. And Recognit. l.3.
affirmeth plainely , that they which should deny
Free-will in man , consequently should say that
God could not iudge aud condemne men for any
thing termed sinnes : all ciuill courts, lawes , and
Iustice should cease , there should be no goodnesse:
no wickednesse no sinne, no vertue, nor God at all.
Quomodo Deus iudicat secundum veritatem vnum in-
quemque pro actibus suis , si agere aliquid in potestate
non habuit? Hoc si teneatur, conuulsa sunt omnia ; fru-
stra erit studium sectandi meliora: sed & Iudices saeculi
frustra legibus praesunt, & puniunt eos qui male agunt:
non enim in sua potestate habuerunt vt non peccarent.
Vana erunt & Iura populorum,quae malis actibus poenas
statuunt : miseri erunt & qui seruant cum labore iusti-
tiam: beati verò illi qui in delicijs positi cum luxuria &
scelere viuentes tyrannidem tenent. Secundum haec er-
go nec iustitia erit, nec bonitas, nec vlla virtus, &, vt
vis, nec Deus.Est ergo in potestate vniuscuiusque,quia Lib. 4.
liberi arbitrij factus est homo, vtrum nobis velit audire
*ad vitã,an dæmonibus ad interitũ.*And defineth free-
will to be an essentiall and vnseparable power of
the soule of man,to yeeld to whatsoeuer acts it
will : *Arbitrij potestas est sensus animae habens* Lib. 3.
virtutem quam possit ad quos velit actus incli- Dionis.Areo-
nari. pag.. Eccles.
   Sainct Denis the Arepagite is plaine of the same Hierar.cap.2.
opinion , and calleth that which wee commonly l.de diuu.nom.
                                        terme cap. 4.

terme freewill, *electualibertas*, electiue liberty, and
that man hath such power in himselfe. αὐτερού-
σιꝏ.

Rab. Moses
Hadarf. ad c.
4. Gen. Rab.
Akiba in ca-
pitul patrum.
Philo. l. quod
Deus fit im-
mutabilis.
Rab. Moses
Fil. Maim. e-
pistola adu.
Astrologos.
Ioseph. Alb.
fund. tract. 1.
c. 9. Rab. Iu-
das in capi-
tul. pa. Clem.
Rom. l. 3. Re-
cognit. Iof.
lib. 13. Antiq.
c. 4. Epiph. l. 1.
Tom. 1. cont.
hær. c. 16. de
pharifæis.
Plutarch. l. 1.
de placitis
Philofopho-
rum cap. 27.
Clem. Alex.
l. 5. stromat.
part. ante fin.

This was the constant and receaued opinion, &
doctrine both of Iewes and gentiles also: for the
first, their Rabbines, Rabbi Moses Hadarsan,
Rabbi Akiba, Philo, Rabbi Moses ben-Maimon,
Iosephus, Rabbi Iudas with others doe aboundantly proue it. So doth Sainct Clement reciting the testimony of *Simon Magus*, professor of the aduerse
errour, confessing it was the receaued doctrine of
the Iewes, though he singularly denied it. *Simon
Magus inquit ad Petrum: quoniam Hebræis ista man-
dantur, velut recte scientibus Deum, & opinantibus
quod vnusquisque in suo arbitrio habeat agere ea,
de quibus iudicandus est; mihi autem ab illis discrepat
sententia.*

Iosephus, Sainct Epiphanius and others proue
the same, and put such Iewes as held otherwise in
the number of heretiks. So Plutarch, Clemens A-
lexandrinus and others proue of the Gentiles testifying how Heraclitus was singular among them,
for the contrary errour, & Plato proued inuincibly
the truth of the Christian Catholike doctrine in
this point, otherwise, God should be cause of sinne,
which he possibly could not be. *Liberum autem arbitrium Plato per hæc ostendit: virtus autem non paret
alterius dominio, quam prout vnusquisque vel hono-
rauerit, vel despexerit, erit eius particeps. Eius qui ele-
gerit, culpæ non potest in Deum causa conferri: Deus
enim nunquam est causa malorum.*

Thus generally and confidently the doctrine of
free will was receaued and professed in this first age
in the same manner as the present Roman Church

now

now doth, approuing and requiring alſo the neceſſity of grace, and not excluding it, as the Pelagian
heretiks firſt did, ſome hundreds of yeares after, and
not makinge mens actions meritorious, but as they
were aſſiſted by grace. *Nihil meritis veſtris aſcriba-*
tis, quaſi non egentes Dei gratia: quia ſine Deo nihil po-
teſtis facere.

Martial. Epiſ.
ad Toloſan.
cap.22.

And in this ſenſe the Proteſtant Article of free-
will receaueth this doctrine, & their writers admit
it in theſe Termes: *wee deny not, that it is in the power*
of man, to make choyce of life, wee ackowledge, that the
fault is in euery mā, that is not ſaued. Wee ſay with Au-
ſtin both in words & meaning that true Religion neither
denies free will, either to a good or badd life. As S. Ber-
nard ſaith, there is a threefold freedome, from neceſsity
from ſinne, from miſery. The firſt of nature, the ſeconde
of grace, the third of glory. In the firſt from the bondage
of coaction, the will is free in its owne nature, and hath
power ouer it ſelfe. That freedome by which the will of
man is named free is the firſt. And thereof wee dare ſay,
that the wicked want not the freedome of will.

Wotton de-
fence of
Perk. pa. 67.
68.65.88.90.
Couel.def. of
Hooker.p.35.

Thus they write publish and approue with their
authority to be the doctrine and allowed opinion
of English Proteſtants in this matter. Our primatiue Chriſtian Britans of this firſt age could neither
learne of their firſt Apoſtles, and Fathers in Chriſt,
nor profeſſe any other doctrine, or opinion in this
point: for Sainct Peter being the firſt founder of
their Church, and faith, could deliuer no other in
this matter to them, then he had taught at Antioch, and Rome, and recommended to his two
glorious Succeſſors S. Ignatius and S. Clement in
thoſe two higheſt Apoſtolike Sees.

And Sainct Clement either preached here in
Britaine,

Britaine, or as he expreſſely deliuereth, by charge
giuen, and committed to him by Sainct Peter, did
ſend learned Biſhops into all theſe weſterne parts,
where Sainct Peter had not ordained ſuch before.
And for Sainct Ioſeph of Aramathia and his holy
company, who made free choyce and election, for
the loue of Chriſt, to forſake contry, kindred and
all temporall goods, and trauayle ſo many thouſands of myles into the end of the knowne world,
to liue and dye there, in ſuch auſterity and Sanctity of life as they practized lyuing here, they muſt
of neceſſity, be profeſſours, as they were renowned

Tertul.l.de a-
nima c 20.
21.l.2. aduerſ.
Murc.c.5.6.8.
de epiph. or-
tat.de conſtit.
cap.2.

Examplars in this buſineſſe. And that the Britans
then generally that were conuerted, ſo profeſſed,
with the whole Chriſtian world, Tertullian an vndeniable teacher of this doctrine in many places, teſtifieth of it, as of others before, that all Apoſtolike
Churches, Europe, Aſie, and Afrike agreed therein. And it ſo continued euer in Britaine in ſuch
manner that afterwards Pelagius the heretike ex-
tolled it to much, and was therefore both by Britans and all other Catholiks condemned and de-
teſted for an heretike, for ſo enabling it, without aſ-
ſiſtance of grace. All writers, Catholike and Proteſtants thus agreeing.

THE FOVRTH CHAPTER.

The 11. *Article*, of the Iuſtification of man, *examined, and condemned by the Apoſtolike
Fathers of this firſt age.*

THEIR next 11. Article is intituled : *of the iuſtification of man:* and expreſſed in theſe words.

Wee

Wee are accompted righteous before God, onely for the merit of our Lord, and Sauiour Iesus Christ, by faith, and not for our owne workes, or deseruings. Wherefore that wee are iustified by faith onely, is a most wholesome doctrine, and very full of comfort, as more largely is expressed in the homily of Iustification.

This is the whole article, and the doctrine thereof, that wee are iustified by faith onely, is before condemned by Sainct Ignatius and the Apostolike S. Ignatius e-doctrine of this first age, affirming, that faith is pist.ad Ephes. onely the beginninge of mans perfection or iustice, and charity doth perfect it, without which a man is not iustified. *Principium vitæ fides: finis eius charitas: hæc autem duo quoties in vnum coeunt, Dei hominem perficiunt.* He saith also, that sinnes be taken away by almes, and faith, and not by faith onely, as this article speakes. *Eleemosina & fide expiantur peccata.* And though a man be otherwise faithfull, Ignat.epist. fasteth, liueth in virginity, worketh wonders, and ad Heron. prophecieth, yet if he keepe not the constitutions of the Church, he is to be esteemed as a wolfe among sheepe. *Quicunque dixerit quippiam præter ea quæ constituta sunt: tametsi fide dignus sit, quamuis ieiunat, quāuis in virginitate degat, quamuis signa edat, quamuis prophetet, pro lupo illum habeas qui sub ouina pelle exitium pestemque adfert ouibus.* All men agree, Sainct Ignatius was a true beleeuer, yet writing to Ignat. epist. the Philadelphians, he confesseth he was not there- ad Philadelp. by sure of his saluation, as Protestants say they are, but desired to be perfected by their prayers. *In Domino Iesu vinctus, necdum perfectus sum, sed precatio vestra ad Deum me perficiet, vt id consequar, ad quod vocatus sum.* He professeth that he beleeued in Christ, as he ought to doe, yet desired to be iustified

by

by others prayers. *Iesus mihi pro Archiuis est; quem nolle audire, manifesta pernicies est. Illibatum mihi est archiuū, crux eius, & mors, & resurrectio eius, & fides horum, per quæ cupio iustificari precationibus vestris.*

True it is Sainct Ignatius citeth and approueth that saying of scripture, *Iustus ex fide viuit,* the iust man liueth by faith, which the Protestants make as a ground of their errour, in this question, but he giueth not that prerogatiue vnto it, which they doe, either to iustifie onely, or at all, but to be necessary to iustification, as all true Catholiks cōfesse, & that no man can be iustified without it, neither doth he meane the Protestants pretended presumptious faith, or such as is singular to any sect, but the common faith of the vniuersall Church of God; yet in the same place ascribeth iustificatiō to constancy in goodnesse, doing and suffering for the loue of God, and louinge him aboue our selues and all other things. *Nihili pendo supplicia hæc, neque tanti facio vitam meam, vt eam plus amem quam Dominum.*

Epist. ad Tarsenses.

Quare paratum me offero igni, feris, gladijs, cruci, dummodo Christū videam, Saluatorem & Deum meum, qui propter me mortuus est, obsecro vos ego vinctus Christi state in fide; este constantes, quia iustus ex fide viuit, estote immobiles, quia Dominus habitare facit vnius moris in Domino.

That faith where there is but one preaching thereof, one Church founded by the Apostles in all the world, where the professours liue in one vnity, haue one altare, one sacrifice: *vna prædicatio, & vna fides, & vnum baptisma, & vna Ecclesia quam suis sudoribus & laboribus fundarunt Sancti Apostoli à finibus terræ vsque ad fines in sanguine Christi: vos oportet vt populum peculiarem & gentem Sanctam, omnia*

Epist. ad Philadelph.

nia

nia perficere concordibus animis in Christo. Vna est caro Domini nostri Iesu Christi, vnus illius sanguis, vnum altare omni Ecclesiæ. And yet the true vniuersall, and Catholike faith which all Protestants and particular sectaries doe want, though it is so necessary to saluation, that no King, Prince, Prelate, Potentate or whosoeuer can be iustified and saued without it, yet of it selfe, without hope, charity, and loue of God and our neighbour, which bringeth all good vnto vs, and the keeping of Gods commaundements, such faith, neither saueth, nor iustifieth. *Nemo erret, nisi crediderit Iesum Christum in carne conuersatum, & crucem illius confessus fuerit, & pas-* Epistol. ad *sionem & sanguinem quem effudit pro mundi salute,* Smyrnen. *non assequetur vitam æternam, siue Rex fuerit, siue Sacerdos, siue princeps, siue priuatus homo, siue Dominus, siue seruus, siue vir, siue fœmina. Qui capit, capiat, qui audit, audiat. Locus, dignitas, diuitiæ neminem efferant, ignobilitas & paupertas neminem deyciant. Totum namque & præcipuum, est fides in Deum, & spes in Christum, & fruitio eorum quæ expectamus bonorum charitas in Deum & proximum. Diliges enim Dominum Deum tuum ex toto corde tuo, & proximum tuum sicut teipsum. Et Dominus inquit: hæc est vita æterna, vt cognoscant te solum verum Deum, & quem misisti Iesum Christum. Et mandatum nouum do vobis, vt diligatis vos mutuo. In his duobus mandatis pendet tota lex & Prophetæ.* Sainct Clement teacheth the same doctrine, assuring vs, that Christ was so farre from teaching, that man is to be iustified onely by faith, in the lawe of the ghospell, that he tyeth vs to more strict lawes, and commaundements then vnder the lawe of Moyses. *Qui tunc homicidium interdixit, nunc etiam iram tenere concitatam: qui tunc adulterium,*

nunc

Clem.Rom.l. 6.conftit. A-poft. cap. 23. *nunc prauam quoque cupiditatem: legem naturalem non suftulit, sed confirmauit. Qui dixit diliges proximum tuum, idem in Euangelio ait renouandi gratia, mandatum nouum do vobis, vt diligatis inuicem.* And teaching the way and meanes, how wee should be made friends with God, and so be iustified, he telleth vs, that this friendship is to be procured by liuing well, and obaying his will, which is the law of

Clem.Rom,l. 1.recognit. all liuing men. *vt tendamus ad amicitiam Conditoris, amicitia autem efficitur bene viuendo, & voluntati eius obediendo, quæ voluntas omnium viuentium lex est.*

The like hath Sainct Martiall, vtterly condemning all such presumption as is in the pretended Proteftant iuftifying faith, teaching, and directing to obay the will of God, in holy words, and good

S.Martial.ep. ad Tolofan. cap. 17. workes. *Vobis est testis scutator renum & cordium. In eius obedientia nihil arroganter, nihil superbè, nihil temerè præsumere, sed tanquam pusillus grex Dei voluntatem eius adimplere studete, in verbis Sanctis, & operibus bonis.* Where wee euidently see that the will of God is not fulfilled, nor iustice wrought, by onely faith, but holy speaking, and doing good workes.

Sainct Denis the Areopagite saith, that he knew well, and therein agreed with the diuine Scriptures, that euery one was to be rewarded ac-

Dionyf.Areo. Eccl. Hierar. cap. 12. cording to his worthinesse, or deseruing. *Probè scio scriptis diuinis assentiens, vnumquemque præmium accepturum pro dignitate.* And addeth, that euery Bishop or learned Preift being the Interpretor of diuine things, doth learne from holy Scriptures, that euerlasting life and happenesse is with most iust measure giuen vnto men according to their deseruings,

uings, and merits. *Diuinus Antistes, interpres diuinorum iudiciorum, didicit à scriptis quæ diuinitùs prodita sunt, clarißimam diuinamque vitam pro dignitate ac meritis, iustißimis lancibus tribui.*

Sainct Polycarpe in his Epistle, which Sainct Ireneus, Eusebius, and others cite and approue, doth distinguish faith and iustice, in Christians, and sheweth that holy men that are saued, obtayned glory, by such distinct iustice and sufferings for Christ. *Hi omnes qui non in vacuum cucurrerunt, sed in fide & iustitia, & ad debitum sibi locum cum Domino, cui & compaßi sunt, abierunt.* And this glory was due vnto them, for such iustice, and sufferings.

Irenæus l 3. c. 3. Euseb. l. 3. hist. c 36. Polycarp. epist. ad Philipp.

Sainct Iustine in his publike Apologie, for all Christians to the Emperour, protesteth, that all good Christians euer from the beginning so held, liued and practised, that men were punished or rewarded, according to the worth and dignity of their deeds, and the Prophets before the Apostles so taught. *Hoc etiam explicamus, nos supplicia & pœnas, atque præmia pro dignitate actionum redditum iri, à Prophetis didicisse, idque verè enuntiamus.*

Iustin. Apol. 2 pro Christianis ad Anton. Pium Imper. post med.

That this article of Catholike Religion was professed and practiezed here also, it is euident, being the vniuersall doctrine and profession of the whole Catholike Church, as before appeareth. And for that this Kingdome being so remote a nation from Hierusalem, Rome, Antioch, and other cheife places, where Christian Religion then most florished, and those glories of the world whose authorities I haue cited, and such others as then florished, must needs receaue their faith from them, and thence, and be of the same minde and opinion with them herein.

E   And

And to examplifie onely in particular in them which our Proteſtant antiquaries confeſſe to haue beene Chriſtians of or in this nation in this age, Sainct Beatus a noble Britan, Sainct Ioſeph of Aromathia who buried Chriſt, and his holy companions, which conuerſed with the Apoſtles, and the Apoſtolike Doctors remembred they thought not faith onely to be it by which men were iuſtified as theſe Proteſtants hold, but liued in moſt ſtrict & penitentiall life, all their dayes, in watchings, faſtings and prayers, ſo ſeruing God, the bleſſed Virgin Mary, with other Saincts, and Angels. *Vigilijs Ieiunijs & orationibus vacantes, Deo & Beatæ Virgini deuota exhibentes obſequia.* Their reuerence which they vſed to the holy reliks, which they brought with them, ſpoken of before, and to the croſſe and other Chriſtian Images, ther building a chappell in honour of the bleſſed Virgin Mary, by the admoniſhment of S. Gabriell the Archangell, *Archangeli Gabrielis admonitu*, their poore, chaſte, and obedient religious life, foreſaking all, euen their wiues, Sainct Ioſeph bringing his wife into Britaine as theſe antiquities ſay, and leauing her and all wordly comforts for the loue of Chriſt, proue ſufficiently vnto vs, they were not of our Proteſtant profeſſion, that onely faith did iuſtifie, and that there was no Iuſtice, merit, or reward by and for good workes, holyneſſe and perfection in lyuinge well.

Speed Theater of greate Britaine li.6. Pantal.de vir. Illuſtrib.German. Antiquitat. Glaſt. tabulis affir. Guliel.Makn. l.de antiq. cæn. Glaſton. Cupgr.in S. IoſephArom.

THE

THE V. CHAPTER.

The 12. *Article examined , and in whatsoever dif-
fering from the present Romane Church, condemned by the Apostolike age. So of the
13. and* 14. *Articles.*

AN D by this, their next article also is plainely
confuted: the title thereof is : *of good workes;*
and the whole article as followeth,: *Albeit that
good works , which are the fruites of faith, and follow
after iustification, cannot put away our sinnes, and endure
the seuerity of Gods Iudgment : yet are they pleasing &
acceptable to God in Christ, and doe springe out necessarily of a true and liuely faith, in so much that by them a
liuely faith may be as euidently knowne, as a tree dis-
cerned by the fruite.* For it is euidently proued. before, that good workes done in grace, doe iustifie,
by the common doctrine and practise of this Apostolike time, or else man could not possibly be iustified at all, but notwithstanding the incarnation,
labours, and passion of Christ, man should still be
without iustification and remaine in sinne, and vn-
iustice: for all haue agreed, that faith alone or onely,
doth not iustifie: then if wee take iustificatiō away
from our holy Christian Sacraments, which be
good workes, and from all other good workes, as
this article doth, and the other before likewise did,
Christians haue no meanes to be iustified, either by
good workes, or without good workes.

And besides that which is said already, in this
matter, and reason conuinceth so, Sainct Peter the
Apostle in his publike sermon, and Sainct Clement

Petrus con-
cion. apud S.
Clement. l.6.
Recog. & l.1,
Recognit.

E 2   the

the Regifter and publisher thereof, doe proue it in his manner: *confertur meritum homini pro bonis geftis; fed fi ita gerantur, ficut Deus iubet. Deus autem iuſſit omnem colentem ſe, baptiſmo conſignari.* And otherwife a man cannot be faued, neither iuſtified, for the iuſt ſhall be ſaued: *ita peruenire poteris and ſalutem: aliter verò impoſsibile eſt. Sic enim nobis cum Sacramento, verus Propheta teſtatus eſt dicens: Amen dico vobis, niſi quis denuò renatus fuerit ex aqua, non introibit in regna cælorum. Eſt in aquis iſtis miſericordiæ vis quædam, quæ ex initio ferebatur ſuper eos, & agnoſcit eos, qui baptizantur ſub appellatione triplicis Sacramenti, & eripuit eos de ſupplicys futuris: quaſi donum quoddam offerens Deo, animas per baptiſmum conſecratas. Confugite ad aquas iſtas, ſolæ ſunt enim quæ poſsint vim futuri ignis extinguere Baptiſmus per omnia neceſſarius eſt: Iniuſto, vt peccatorum que geſſit in ignorantia remiſsio concedatur. Cum regeneratus fueris per aquam, ex operibus bonis oſtende te in ſimilitudinem eius qui te genuit patris. Agnouiſti enim Deum, honora patrem: honor autem eius eſt, vt ita viuas, ſicut ipſe vult. Vult autem ita viuere vt homicidium, adulterium neſcias: odium, auaritiam fugias: iram ſuperbiam, iactantiam reſpuas, & execreris, inuidiam cæteraque his ſimilia, penitus à te ducas aliena. Eſt ſane propria quædam noſtræ religionis obſeruantia, quæ non tam imponitur hominibus, quam propriè ab vnoquoque Deum colente cauſa puritatis expetitur.* Where wee finde that man is iuſtified by ſacramentall & other good workes, keeping Gods cõmaundemts, auoyding all mortall finne, and embracing vertue, and this obligation is impoſed vpon all Chriſtians, and by them to be effected, and performed, and without ſuch perfermance they are not iuſtified.

And

And Chrift will giue to euery one according as
they haue deferued or merited. *Mortuos eft excitatu-*
rus, mundo finem impofiturus, & vnicuique pro meritis
tributurus.

Clem. l. 6.
conft. Apoft.
c. 30.

Sainct Denis the Areopagite, befides that which
he hath teftified before, proueth the different degrees of glory in heauen, fome more glorious then
others, as the Scriptures are plentifull in the fame,
becaufe the good workes and merits of fome, in
this life are greater and more then others. *Oftendit*
cunctos in regeneratione illas confequuturos fortes, ad
quas hîc vitam propriam direxerunt: puta, fi deiformem
quis hic & fanctiſsimam egerit vitam, quantum viro
poſsibile eft Deum imitari, diuina in feculo futuro, &
beata donabitur requie: Sin autem fummâ illa deiformi
vita inferiorem egerit, factam tamen, conformia & ifte
recipient facra præmia. And by this their 14. Article
intituled : *of workes of fupererogation*, is alfo confuted; their next and 13. Article ftiled, *of workes be-*
fore Iuftification, being rather a queftion in naturall
or morall Philofophy, then Theologicall, and to be
handled in Chriftian Religion, and fo more fit to
be omitted then handled in this treatife of religious
Controuerfies, though it be not wholy founde in
Philofophicall proceedings. That the 14. Article is
already condemned, will be plaine by the recitall of
it in thefe words: *voluntarie workes, befides ouer and*
aboue Gods commaundement, which they call workes of
fupererogation, cannot be taught without arrogancy, &
impiety.

Dionyfius A-
reop. Ecclef.
Hierarch. c.3.

This is euidently contradicted and condemned
by Sainct Denis, Sainct Clement, and Sainct Ignatius before, prouinge different degrees of glory in
heauen, and wearing the diuerfities of mens merits

on

on earth, assuring, that they which haue not liued
in such perfection as others haue, and they also
might haue done, yet keeping the precepts, and
doing things commaunded shall be saued, and so
are iustified, though they haue not wrought such
workes of counsaile onely and perfection, as many
more holy haue done, and therefore are rewarded
with greater ioyes and honour, as both the Scriptures & Apostolike Fathers of this age are plaine in
many places. And the pretended reason which they
onely yeeld in this article in maintenance of their
errour, is both ridiculous, and hereticall, being this:
for by them men doe declare, that they not onely render
vnto God as much as they are bound to doe, but that they
doe more for his sake, then of bound duty is required:
whereas Christ saith plainely, when you haue done all
that are commaunded to you, say, wee be vnprofitable
seruants.

This first is ridiculous, and proueth nothing to
the question of workes of perfection, not commaunded, and their eminent and singular reward
but onely of the commaundements, and things of
duty, which Catholiks say (more then Protestants
ordinarily doe) are to be done and performed vnder
paine of eternall damnation. It contradicteth their
owne doctrine, which vsually graunteth there are
both precepts, and counsailes in Scripture, as of
voluntary pouerty, chastity, obedience and such
others, which no sect of Protestants performeth,
and yet they speake much of their Iustification or
righteousnesse in this life, and saluation after. That
it is hereticall and condemned the old *Apostolici*,
heretiks, some Pelagians and others, and their condemnation for it, will witnesse from the beginning,

as

as both Sainct Ireneus, Sainct Epiphanius, Sainct Auguftine with fuch renowned writers and our Proteftants themfelues doe proue. *Apoftoli affirmabant non poffe faluari eos, qui non viuerent in cælibatu, ac paupertate more Apoftolorum.*

The heretiks called Apoftoliks did affirme that thofe which liued not vnmarried and in pouerty after the manner of the Apoftles, could not be faued. The Eucratitæ Schollers to Tatianus were drowned in the like herefie: *docuerunt omnes Chriftianos debere à nuptijs abftinere, & cælibes viuere, & fic continentiam volebant effe præcepti & non confily.* Hierax and his Hieracitæ maintained the like, excluding all married Chriftians from the Kingdome of heauen. *Non admittit nuptias, conceffum eft ait, in veteri teftamento, nuptias contrahere, verum à Chrifti aduentu, non amplius nuptias admitti, neque poffe ipfos poffidere regnum cælorum.* Some of the Pelagians alfo held, that no man could be faued, except he fold all he had, and gaue it to the poore: *neminem faluum effe poffe, nifi omnia venderet & daret pauperibus, quafi non confilium, fed præceptum hoc effet. As if this were not a counfaile, but a commaundement.* Which the Proteftants thus alfo plainely confeffe: *in thefe points all haue not holden the fame opinions; fome thought the counfailes to be of the fame neceffity with precepts: as thofe heretiks called Apoftolici.* Thus with publike approbation, And yet this article in the reafon it would make, falleth into the fame herefie, plainely affirming that whatfoeuer worke of piety or perfection is, or may be wrought, or done in this life, virginity, chaftity, voluntary pouerty, obedience, or what fuch foeuer, none excepted, in this their doctrinall decree, *all men are bounde to doe,*

th'y

Epiph. hęref.
61. Auguftin,
hęref. 40.

Irenęus. l.1.c.
10. Epiph. l. 1.
Tom. 3. hær.
in Tatian. c.
46. vlt.
Epiphan. l. 2
Tom. 2. hær.
cap 67. cont.
Hieracit.

Auguft. epift.
89.

Concl. def. of
Hook. p. 52.

they be bound in duty, they are commaunded. And so no married men or women, none that be rich, none that be in authority, and rule spirituall, or temporall, Kinge, Prince, Prelate or whofoeuer, that liue not in virginity, and chaftity, forfake not all for Chrifts fake, and followe him, as the Apoftles and fuch did, or liue not in profeffed obedience, which no Proteftants doe, or euer did, can poffibly be faued by the expreffe conclufion of this article, leauing no place or hope of faluation for any of that religion, which hath vtterly to their power abandoned all fuch holy eftates and conditions of perfection. When Chrift himfelfe and his Apoftles, and the Apoftolike writers of this age haue taught vs otherwife, that the keepinge of the commaundements is fufficient to bringe men to faluation, and there be other perfections of counfaill, and not neceffity, bringing greater glory, and reward in

Matth. c. 19. heauen. *Si vis ad vitam ingredi ferua mandata. Ait illi Iefus, fi vis perfectus effe, vade, vende omnia quæ habes, & da pauperibus, & habebis thefaurum in cœlo,*

1. Cor. cap. 7. *& veni fequere me. De virginibus præceptum Domini*

Matth. 19. *non habeo, confilium autem do. Qui matrimonio iungit virginem fuam, bene facit, & qui non iungit melius facit. Sût eunuchi qui feipfos caftrauerunt propter regnum cælorum, qui poteft capere capiat*

That thefe holy eftates of perfection befides the

Ignat. epift. ad
Philippen. ep.
ad Philadelp.
epift. ad Smy.
epift. ad Polycarp. Dion.
Areop fupr.
Ignatius ep.
ad Heron.

keepinge of the commaundements, were profeffed, exercifed and honored in this age, I haue proued before, by the Apoftolike writers then, Sainct Ignatius, Sainct Denis, and others. And in his epiftle to Sainct Hero thefe holy virgins are ftiled *the pretious Iewels of honor vnto Chrift. Virgines ferua vt pretiofa Chrifti monilia.* Sainct Iames in his liturgy makerh

maketh honorable mention of the liuers in mona- Dionysius A-
steries in such condition. *Pro ijs qui in virginitate &* reop. Eccl.
castitate in monasterijs degunt, Dominum oremus. S. Hierarc.c,6.
Dionisius giueth vnto them the greatest titles of
honour perfection & holinesse, which this life can
haue, and next to God himselfe. *Ordo monachorum*
ad exactißimam perfectionem diuina ratione subuehi-
tur.Vnde sancti patres nostri diuinis eos appellationibus
sunt prosecuti, partim Therapentas, id est, cultores à
sincero Dei famulatu, atque cultu: partim monachos, ab
indiuidua & singulari vita appellantes, vt quæ illos
sanctis diuisibilium complicationibus in diuinam &
Deo gratam monadem perfectionemque promoueat. The
order of monkes by a diuine manner is exalted to the most
exact perfection. Whereupon our holy predecessors called
them by diuine names, partly Therapents, that is wor--
shippers, for their sincere seruinge and worshippinge of
God, partly also naming thē monkes for their indiuiduall
and singular life, exalting them to an heauenly perfe-
ction and acceptable vnto God.

Antiquaries recken Sainct Iohn Baptist, greater
then whome by the testimony of Christ himselfe
the best witnesse, no man was who was onely man,
inter natos mulierum non surrexit maior Ioanne Bap-
tista, his chastity, contempt of the world, pouerty,
and austerity of life was a profession, lesson, and paterne of this perfection. We may recken such both
by Scriptures, and histories, all the Apostles, which
for the loue of Christ forsook all, and followed
him in holy chastity, paines, pennance and austerity of life, so longe as they liued. And this was not
singular and peculiar vnto them, but a thinge almost common to very many Christians besides the
Apostles, and properly named disciples, selling their
pos-

possessions and giuing away their wealth,& Riches of this world, to serue God in more perfection, and to be made rich in heauen, and were honored more for so doing, as the holy Scriptures and the most worthy writers proue. So at Hierusalem : *omnes qui credebant, habebant omnia communia. Possessione & substantias vendebant, & diuidebant illa omnibus, prout cuique opus erat. Habentes gratiam ad omnem plebem.* So at Alexandria vnder Sainct Marke, as Philo then liuing & seeing it, Sainct Hierome and others witnesse. *Philo disertissimus Iudæorum, videns Alexandriæ primam Ecclesiam adhuc Iudaizantem, quasi in laudem gentis suæ librum super eorum conuersatione scripsit. Et quomodo Lucas narrat Ierosolymæ credentes omnia habuisse communia: sic & ille, quod Alexandriæ sub Marco fieri Doctore cernebat, memoriæ tradidit.* So it was also in the Church of Rome vntill Pope Vrbanus time, as Sainct Clement and Sainct Vrbanus write, and after as others proue. And our Protestant antiquaries consent, affirming that Pope Vrban so concluded and decreed in his time: *fundos vltrò Ecclesiæ oblatos, accipiendos esse: prædia debere esse communia, prouentus vero viritim inter clericos distribuendos esse iussit.* S. Ignatius speaking of the honour and noblenesse of chastity, and how it was kept by cleargy men, exemplifieth in the Church of Rome, Antioch, Ephesus, of Creete: and instanceth in their Apostolike Bishop, Sainct Timothy, Sainct Titus, Sainct Euodius, and Sainct Clement, ioyning them therefore in dignity with Iesus the sonne of Naue Melchisedech, Heliseus, Ieremias, and Sainct Ihon Baptist the most renowned, and greatest Saincts. *Vtinam fruar vestra sanctimonia, vt Iesu filij Naue, vt Melchisedech, vt Helisæi, vt Ieremiæ vt Baptistæ Ioannis,*

Act. c. 2.

Philo l. de vita contempl.
Hieron. l. de Script. Eccl. in Marco E-uangel.
Clem. l. 1. re-cogn. & in ep. presertim. S. vita communi. Vrban. Papa ep. de-cret. Robert. Barnes. in vit. Pontif. Rom. in Vrban. 1.
Ignat. Epistol. ad Philadelp.

Ioannis, vt Timothei, vt Titi, vt Euodij, vt Clementis, qui in castitate exegerunt hanc vitam.

That this holy chaste and religious conuersation was also vsed amonge the Philadelphians to whom he thus wrote, is plaine in the first cited words, *vtinam fruar vestra sanctimonia, vt Iesu filij Naue:* comparing them in this point to those glorious Saincts of the old and new testament, among whom S. Ihon Chrysostome and S. Hierome stile S. Ihon Baptist the most holy, *monachorum principem* the prince of monkes. S. Gaius, or Caius called also in the 10. chapter of the Acts of the Apostles Derbeus, was a monke, as Sainct Denis in his Epistle to him, and others testifie. So was Sainct Demophilus as the same S. Denis is witnesse.

The auncient and renowned monastery *monasterium nouietense*, now named Ebershaime in Germany as the Antiquities of that contry proue, was first founded by Sainct Maternus and Sainct Valerius sent into those parts by S. Peter the Apostle. So likewise was the monastery at Treuers by S. Eucharius directed thither by Sainct Peter with the same Saints. S. Fronto disciple of S. Peter also liued with. To others religious in a most desart wildernesse. S. Amator Scholler to S. Martiall liued in a rocke in Fraunce still called by his name. Neither were many holy virgins and chast women wantinge in this sacred state of life in this age remembred in Antiquities and diuers of them set downe by Gulielmus Eisengrenius and others, euen our most auncient Martyrologes.

Sainct Ignatius hath told vs before that this sacred state of perfection was euer professed by the Bishops admittance and benediction. So hath S.

Denys:

Chrys. in
Mar. homil. 1.
& homil. de
Ioan. Baptist.
Hier. epis. 22.
ad Eustach.
Dion. Areop.
ep. ad Gaium.
Maxim. in
Dion. Grat.
dist. 93. Dion.
ep. 8. Vuolfg.
Laz. geneal.
Austriac. l. 1.
Annal. Abbat.
Ebershaym.
Annal. Treu.
Petr. de Nat.
l. 9. Vincent. l.
9. Ant. part. 1.
Ant. sup. Tit.
6.
Guliel. Eisen.
centenar. 1.
part 3. Martyrol. Rom.
Bed. vsuard.
Menolog.
Græc. Ignat.
Epist. ad Polycarp. Dion.
Areop. lib. de
Eccl. Hier. c. 6

Denys: *diuina ſanctio eos conſecrante quadam inuoca-*
tione dignata eſt, ſaying the diuine decree was ſo.
And ſetteth downe at large the manner and Order,
how they publikly renowned the world, profeſſed
perfection, were ſigned with the ſigne of the holy
Croſſe, their hayre ſhaued, their cloathes chaůged,
they communicated. This Kingdome of Britaine
was now renowned with this holy ſtate of perfection, and the profeſſours thereof here for their excellent piety, and worſhippe towards God called in
the old language, *Culdeis*, *Dei cultores*, renowned
worſhippers of God, as all Antiquaries euen Proteſtants themſelues acknowledge, continuing here
from the beginning vntill the yeare of Chriſt as
they ſay 943. It was firſt founded and ſettled here
by Sainct Ioſeph of Aramathia, who buried our
bleſſed Sauiour, and his holy Aſſociats many
in number at Glaſtenbury, in the 63. yeare of
Chriſt.

Georg. Buch.
rer. Scoticar.
l.4.c.35.& l.6
c.75.Hollin.
hiſt. of Engl.
and Scotl in
fin.com. Hect.
Boeth.hiſt.
Scot.l.6.
Antiq. Glaſt.
Guliel.Malin.
l.de antiq.cæ-
nob. Glaſten.
Capg. in S.
Ioſeph. & S.

Their regular obedience is ſufficiětly teſtified by
all antiquities making S. Ioſeph their Superiour,
cheife or Abbot, prouing a regular order and diſcipline among them; ſo doth the manner of their liuing in ſeperated cels, yet often euery day at appointed times aſſembling together in their poore
Church to performe their diuine office. *In diuerſis*
locis ſicut Anachoritæ primi duodecim primitus habita-
runt, in vetuſtam tamen Eccleſiam ad diuina obſequia
deuotius complendacrebò conuenerunt quotidiè.

Their continued longe life there in ſolitary and
eremiticall manner, without any woman with or
neare them, leauing noe child or poſterity, nothing
but deſart and deſolate cells with ſignes of their
perfect profeſſion of Chriſtian Religion behinde
them

them is sufficient argument of their perpetuall chastity in that place and state.

Their forsaking all they had, riches, contry,
frends, and cominge so many thousand myles for
the loue of Christ, into an outward Iland of the
world, and here to finde no other patrimony or
temporall preferment, then a little out cast Ile
neuer before Inhabited, and hauing nothing fit for
the life of man, compassed about with woods, bu-
shes, and fennes, *Insula syluis, rubis atque paludibus
circundata*, and their Church their greatest riches
& honour onely builded by their owne labours, of
writhen wands, call vs sufficiently to minde how
greate their voluntary pouerty was. And they
which next succeeded ,them in place, succeeded
them also in the same state and condition of perfection and contempt of this world by all Antiquities
in diuers ages.

Our Protestants themselues with common consent of all of them, which they take to be of sound
Iudgment, are as they write with publik allowance in these words, of this opinion: *There is none of*
any sound Iudgment, in our (Protestant) *Church,*
which doth not thinke, that willinge pouerty, humble
obedience, and true chastity, are things very commen-
dable, and bringe with them greate aduantage, to the
true perfection of a Christian life. By these wee doe more,
then without these wee should. Precepts and counsailes.
Haue this difference, that the one is of absolute necessity.
The other left vnto our free election.

To cast away wholly the things of the world, is
no precept of necessity, but an aduise of greater perfection. Hee that obeyeth not a precept, is guilty of deserued
punishment: but he that faileth of those counsailes, only

Prot. of Engl.
apud Couel.
def. of Hoo-
ker pa. 51. 52.
50.

wanteth

wanteth without ſinne, that meaſure of perfection. For it is not a faulte, not to vow, but to vowe and performe is praiſe. He that performes the one, ſhall haue greater glory, but hee that faileth of the other, (without repetance) ſhall haue certaine puniſhmet. Neither is it ſaid, ſaith S. Auguſtine, *as thou ſhalt not committ adultery, thou ſhalt not kill: So thou ſhalt not marrie, for thoſe are exacted, theſe are offered. This if it be done, is praiſed: thoſe vnleſſe they be done, are puniſhed.* For ſaith S. Hierome, *where it is but aduiſe, there is left a freedome, but where there is a precept, there is a neceſſity.* Precepts are common to all: counſailes to the perfections of ſome few.

The precept being obſerued, hath a reward, being not obſerued a puniſhmet: But a couſaile or aduiſe, not obſerued hath no puniſhment; & being obſerued hath a greater reward, all our Proteſtant Antiquaries remeber with greateſt honour, all of this nation, which profeſſed the holy ſtate of life in this age, making the ſingularly renowned on earth and glorious in heauen. So they teſtifie of our noble Britan Suetonius both in name & deed called for his extraordinary Sanctity, *Beatus, bleſſed.*

Theater of great Britaine l.6 §.9. Beat. Rhen. hiſt. germ. Pantal. l. de Vir. Illuſtr. Stumph. l. 7. de S. Ioan. Leland. in Arthur. ſtowe hiſt. Drayton polcolb. Georg. Buchan. rerum Scoticar. l 5. c. 65. Holinsh. hiſt. of Engl.

They ſtile the remembred Eremites of Glaſtenbury, the Sainctes of that place, and the place of their buriall in honour of them and ſuch others buried there, *Tumulus Sanctorum,* the graue of Saints, and holy Church yard *cæmeterium Sanctum* to this day. So they teſtifie of their Succeſſors in that Eremitage, and order, and in other places euen vnto, and after the time of Charles the greate Emperour one of them Sainct Albinus, or Alcuinus, his Tutor, *Caroli præceptor,* a man moſt renowned in that age. And others both for learning and ſanctity illuſtrious: *multi erant monachi, vetere diſciplina nondum extincta*

extincta literis & pietate insignes, founders of the schoole of Paris in Fraunce, & both with learning and piety especially euangelicall perfection, making both Britaine Ireland, Fraunce and Germany renowned. All their writers and allowed publike kalenders keepe memory of such, for most holy and worthy Saincts. Their perpetuall and vowed estate in such holy perfection, is sufficiently before remembred by S. Ignatius, and S. Martial with others who giue confirmation vnto it.

But of all others that diuine man S. Denis in his booke of the ecclesiasticall Hierarchy or holy order of the true Apostolike Church of Christ, speaketh of the worthinesse and dignity thereof, aboue all others, preistly order excepted, with the solemne manner of their profession: *initiandorum* Dion areop. *omnium excellentior ac sublimior ordo monachorum est* l. de Ecclef. *sancta distinctio, expiatione omni, tota virtute, atque* Hirarc. c.6. *exactissima suarum operatione mundata, omnis item (quantam sibi licet imspicere) sacræ operationis spiritualiter speculatrix & princeps facta, pontificumque consummantibus virtutibus tradita.*

This he further deliuereth, both by the words of the Bishop which professeth him, and vowe of him that is professed, with all the significatiue ceremonies in that holy admittance. *Stat Sacerdos ante sacrum altare, monasticam imprecationem psallens, ea finita, Sacerdos ad eum accedens interrogat primum, an renuntiet diuisibilibus omnibus, non solum vitijs, verum imaginibus quoque ac phantasijs. Deinde, exponit illi perfectissimam vitam, illud apertè contestans, oportere illum medio longe antecellere. Vbi vero ille ista omnia intentè promiserit, consignans eum crucis signo sacerdos, tondet, trinas diuinæ beatitudinis perso-*

nas

nas inclamãs: Exutumq; veste omni, aliã induit, & cum sanctis alijs, qui astant, viris ipsum salutans, diuinorum mysteriorum participem efficit. And deliuereth the particular and religious signification of euery one of those sacred significant ceremonies, to shew the perfection of that holy state, their cominge to the altar, next behinde the Bishop, and Preist, their perfection nearest and next vnto them, and aboue all others. Their vowed abrenuntiation of worldly things, signifying, and binding them to that perfection, from which others without offence are free. Their signing with the crosse, protesting mortification of all carnall and other not good desires. Their Tonsure declareth their most pure life. Their putting of their old, and putting on a new garment, is a testimony of their passing from the middle order of life, though holy, vnto a more perfect. As the white vesture in baptisme was the signe of sacred Innocency. *Diuisibilium non modo vitarum, verum Imaginationum quoque abrenuntiatio supremam illam monachorum philosophiam indicat, dum in scientia operatur viuentium mandatorum. Est enim (vt dixi) non medij ordinis, sed omnibus celsioris Idcirco plurima quæ impunè à medio geruntur ordine, monachis omnino interdicuntur: quippe qui vnum ipsum ambire debent, & ad sacram monadem cogi, itaque ad sacerdotalem (quantum fas est) formari vitam, & vt in plurimis illi congruentem. Nullus quippe ex ordinibus reliquis illi propinquat magis. At vero crucis sanctæ signaculum, vt iam dictum est, mortificationem omnium simul carnalium cupiditatum signat. Porrò tonsura crinium vitam mundißimam indicat, & nulla figura fucatam, & quæ nullis fictis coloribus animi deformitatem exornat: sed ipsa in seipsa non humanis venustatibus, sed singulari-*
bus.

bus & vnicis ad Dei exactißimam similitudinem pro-
peret. Prioris autem vestis positio, alteriusque assump-
tio, migrationem illam à media vita (sacra scilicet) ad
perfectiorem significat: sicut in diuina generatione, pro-
motionem indicabat a purgata vita ad contemplantem,
illuminantemque habitum illa vestis candentis immu-
tatio. And saith plainely that this profession, and
consecration, giueth them perfecting grace: *porfi-*
cientem eis indulsit gratiam. Which hee doth not
meane, in such manner as Sacraments doe *ex opere*
operato, by their owne efficacy from their diuine institution, but rather the merit and worthinesse of
the estate so professed, and the forsaking of all
worldly things for the loue and perfect seruing of
God, which is the greatest loue wee can shew vnto
him in this life, and so perfecteth man towards
him, and consequently the grace and loue of God
to man so duely louing & seruing him is shewed in
the measure, accordingly as is intreated of merit before, which good works done in grace do carry
with them. As Christ himselfe is best witnesse, Matth. ca 19.
when he saith: *Omnis qui reliquerit domum, vel fra-* Marc. cap. 10.
tres, aut sorores, aut patrem, aut matrem, aut vxorem,
aut filios, aut agros propter nomen meum, centuplum ac-
cipiet & vitam æternam possidebit. Euery one which
forsaketh house, or brethren, or sisters, or father, or mo-
ther, or wife or children, or possessions for my name,
shall receaue an hundred fold more, and possesse eternall
life. If such perfection and reward is due for leauing any of those things for God, They which by
his grace, vowe, and performe the foresaking of
them all, and all earthly things, for his loue and
seruice, must needs be endued with perfect grace,
merit, and haue reward accordingly.

F THE

THE VI. CHAPTER.

*The 15. 16. 17. 18. Articles so examined: and where-
soeuer repugnant to the Roman Church,
likewise condemned.*

THE next & 15. in number English Protestant
Article being intituled: *of Christ alone without
sinne*, seemeth by their glosse vpon it to haue beene
agreed vpon, to condemne the old heresies of *Ma-
nichees, Catharans, Donatists, Pelagians, Marcionites,
Adamites, and Carpocratians*, reuiued among them,
and especially their new sect called the family of
loue. For to speake in their owne words: *Some
were of opinion, as the Pelagians, and family of loue,
that they were so free from sinne, as they needed not to
say, forgiue vs our trespasses. Which family also teacheth, how there be men liuing, as good, and as holy, as
euer Christ was. An errour of Christopher vitels, a
cheife elder in the saide family: and that he which is
a familist, is either as perfect as Christ, or els a very
deuill.*

Protestant
publ.glosse
vpon Articl.
is Conc. Mi-
len.c 8. Dis-
play tit. 6.
Answ to the
fam. libera.li.
3. Display. R.
6.

These things cannot be applied to any opinion
held by Catholiks about the immaculate inno-
centy & freedome of the blessed Virgin, both from
originall and other sinne. And neither this article
nor any other Protestant confession once nameth
her, when they treate of this subiect, but they
plainely speake of the ordinary sorte and condition
of people, especially lyuing in these dayes, to proue
vnto vs, that they herein contradicted the named
heresies then raigning among them, as these their
article words be cleare: *All wee the rest, although
baptized,*

baptized, *and borne againe in Christ, yet offend in many things, and if wee say,* (as those named heretiks did, and doe) *wee haue no sinne, wee deceaue ourselues and the truth is not in vs.* Where they speake plainely of the baptized;and actuall sinne,& sinnes:whereas Catholiks ascribe that purity of our lady, euē from originall sinne, and before any were baptized, or the Sacrament of Baptisme instituted.

And our English Protestants by their best pub- Engl.Prote-
like warrant and authority expressed and set forth stantcommu-
in their communion bookes,doe celebrate the feast Calendar.8.
of her conception as immaculate from all cōtagion Decemb.
of sinne; so likewise they doe concerning the natiuity of Sainct Iohn Baptist keeping and making Iane 24 supr.
it a greate holy day, and the euen fasted. Which loge of holy
they could not doe without greate contradictory daies in cōm.
absurdity, except thereby they professed they hold booke confir,
that our lady was preserued from originall sinne, by Parlam.
& Sainct Ihon sanctified before he was borne into
the world. For opinion of either sinfull conception
or natiuity rather requireth greife and sorrowe,
then ioye and festiuity, which may not be made
for sinne, which is to be lamented and sorrowed
for, and farre from being reioyced at, with any
signe or shewe of gladnesse, much lesse with cele-
bration of publike festiuities and such solemnities.

And in the authenticall decree of their holy
dayes,where they thus set downe for holy day the
birth day of Sainct Iohn Baptist:*The day of the natiuity of S. Iohn Baptist,* they diuers times call and declare our lady in their opinion and practise. *The
blessed Virgin.* Which they neuer so singularly
giue to any other man, or woman. And euer to be
blessed,euer excludeth the misery which is in all
sinne,

sinne, no such lamentable estate being able to consist with the least degree of blessednesse. Therefore if any Protestant will oppose against this her immaculate perfection, wee haue the Angell from heauen, testifying shee was full of grace and most blessed of all women, *gratia plena, benedicta in mulieribus* before she conceaued Christ. Sainct Ignatius is witnesse, she was a wonder of perfection, and often pilgrimage vsed by holy Christians to visit and honour her when she was yet liuing. *Sunt hic multa de mulieribus nostris Mariam Iesu videre cupientes, & quotidie à nobis ad vos discurrere volentes, vt eam contingant, & vbera eius tractent, quæ Dominum Iesum aluerunt. Et quædam eius secretiora percunctentur ipsam Mariam Iesu.* And not finding any like vnto her on earth for immunity from all sinne, and fulnesse of perfection, calleth her singularly *cæleste prodigium, & sacratissimum spectaculum.* The heauenly wonder, and most sacred spectacle.

That she abounded with all graces full of all vertues and grace. That it was the common opinion of credible good Christians, that the nature of Angelicall innocency and sanctity was ioyned to humane nature in her. *Notificauere eandem Matrem Dei omnium gratiarum esse abundantem, & gratiæ fæcundam. A fide dignis narratur, in Maria Iesu humanæ naturæ, natura sanctitatis Angelicæ sociatur.* And as she testified of herselfe, that all generations especially of the good, should call her blessed, *beatam me dicent omnes generationes,* so it was performed in this first generation of Christians, *ab omnibus magnificatur.* In the Masse ascribed to Sainct Iames the Apostle she is stiled, *Sanctissima, immaculata, gloriosissima, Domina nostra, Mater Dei & semper Virgo*

Ignat. epist. ad S. Ioan.

Missa S. Iacobi.

Virgo Maria· the most holy, Immaculate. Our most glorious lady Mother of God, and euer a Virgin Mary. In the Masse of Sainct Marke the Euangelist vsed aunciently in this Kingdome, she is called full of grace, blessed among all women, the excellently most holy vnspotted, our blessed lady, Mother of God, and euer Virgin Mary *gratia plena, benedicta in mulieribus, in primis sanctissima, intemerata, & benedicta Domina semper nostra Dei genetrix, & semper Virgo Maria.* *Missa S. Marci. Manuscr. antiquum Britan.*

The old tradition of the Church from the time of her death as Sainct Damascen and others deliuer, *ex antiqua accepimus traditione.* That all the Apostles wheresoeuer then dispersed were miraculously assembled together, to worshippe her holy body, *quod Deum susceperat corpus adorare.* S. Timothy, and Sainct Denis the Areopagite, with others, besides the Apostles, as he himselfe is a good witnesse, were then present. And by all their Iudgments, her holy body after three dayes of continuall angelicall musike in the place of her departure, out of this life, was assumpted into heauen, the place where her sacred body lay, filling their senses with an vnspeakeable sweetnesse: *ea tantum inuenerunt in quibus fuerat compositum, & ineffabili, qui ex ijs proficiscebatur essent odore repleti.* *Damasc. orat. 2. de dormitione Deiparæ. Breuiar. Rom. die 18. Augusti. Dionis. Areo. ad Doroth.*

Wee need not appeale any further to our primatiue Christians and frends: for Mahomet and his Turkes, and Tartars, our greatest enemies, in their Alcoran the rule of their Religion, doe plainely, to the euerlasting shame of such Protestants or others which maligne the Blessednesse of this most blessed virgin, confesse, that our blessed lady Mary was more resplendant pure and vnspotted, then any other *Mahomet. in Alcoran. Azoar. 5.*

F 3   ther

ther weere earthly creature continually ſerueing
God. *D.Maria omnibus viris & mulieribus ſplēdidior,
& mundior, atque lotior, ſoli Deo perſeueranter ſtu-
dens.* And further adde : there is none borne of the
children of Adam , whom Sathan did not touche,
*beſides Mary and her ſonne. No woman was euer perfect
but Mary the Mother of Iſa.* (So they call Ieſus) *nullus
naſcitur de filijs Adam, quem non tangat Sathan, præter Mariam, & eius filium. Nulla vnquam perfecta ex
mulieribus, niſi Maria Mater Iſa.*

Azoar. 75.

Martin. Luth.
in Euang. l. de
Concept.
Mariæ.

The Father of Proteſtants Religion Martin
Luther deliuered the ſame doctrine for all them
that would be children to ſuch a Father : ſaying it
is piouſly beleeued that the conception of Mary
was without originall ſinne, & in the firſt moment
when ſhe began to liue, ſhe was without all ſinne.
*Mariæ conceptio piè creditur ſine originali peccato facta
eſſe. Atque ita in primo momento cum viuere inciperet, omnis peccati expers erat.* And ſaith, that euen
from her conception ſhe was full of grace, and ſo

In Euang. de
Annunt. Mar.

hauing no place for any ſinne. *Maria Virgo iuxta
animā plena gratia concepta eſt. Gratia Dei ipſam omnis
boni abundantem facit. Et ab omni malo liberat. Deus
cum ea eſt, hoc eſt, omne quod facit, aut omittit, diuinum
eſt, & in eo a Deo perficitur : ad hæc tutatur eam, & de-*

Antiquitat.
Glaſton. ma-
nuſcrip tabul.
lign. fixe. Io.
Capgrau. in
vit. S. Ioſephi
ab Arama-
thia. Guliel.
Malmesbur. l.
de an iq. cœ-
nob.
Glaſtonien.

*fendit ab omni, quod obnoxium & incommodum eſſe po-
teſt.* That from her conception ſhe was full of grace, &
whatſoeuer ſhe did, or omitted was holy and diuine,
ſhe was free from all thing ill or ſinfull. Her honour
here in Britaine was ſo greate and timely, *that within* 31. *yeares of the paſſion of Chriſt, and* 15. *of the bleſſed
Virgins Aſſumption, anno poſt Paſſionem Domini tri-
ceſſimo primo, ab Aſſumptione vero Virginis glorioſæ
quinto decimo,* S. Ioſeph and his holy company, by admonition of the holy Angel Gabriel and diuine warning

*builded here a Chapell vnto her honour. It is accompted
the first Church of Britaine dedicated miraculously by
Christ in honour of his Mother, The Christiā builders in
greate deuotion, watching, and fastings and prayers,
there serued God, and the blessed Virgin, and by the
helpe of the blessed Virgin were releiued in their necef-
sities. Prædicti sancti per Archangelum Gabrielem in
visione admoniti sunt, Ecclesiam in honore sanctæ Dei
genetricis & perpetuæ Virginis Mariæ in loco cælitùs
demonstrato cōstruere. Qui diuinis admonitionibus obe-
dientes capellam consummauerunt. Et cum hæc in hac
regione prima fuerit Ecclesia, ampliori eam dignitate
Dei filiusinsigniuit, ipsamin honore suæ matris dedicando. Duodecim sancti prædicti in eodem loco Deo &
Beatæ Virgini deuota exhibentes obsequia vigilijs ieiunijs & orationibus vacantes, eiusdem Virginis,Dei
genetricis auxilio, in necessitatibus suis refocillabantur.*
Thus haue our most auncient antiquities, both by
Catholiks and Protestants testimonies.

The three next articles being thus intuled : *The
16. of sinne after Baptisme: the 17. of predestination,and
Election: and 18. of obtaining eternall saluation, onely
by the name of Christ,* doe not seeme in equall and
morall construction, euen as they expound themselues, to haue opposition, to any Catholike doctrine,but to haue beene receaued by them to condemne newly risen vp heresies among them, as li-
bertines, denyers of saluation to penitent sinners,
predestinaries not respecting to liue well, vpon
wicked presumption of their predestination, and
such as affirmed *that euery man shall be* saued,Iew,
Turke, Pagan, or whatsoeuer Infidell, or heretike
*shall be saued by the law or sect, which he professeth,
so that he be diligent to frame his life according to that*

F 4

law,

law, and the light of nature, as is plainely regiſtred and ſet downe in thoſe Articles.

The VII. Chapter.

The 19. Article examined, and condemned by the ſame authority.

THEIR next and 19. Article intituled, *of the Church, is this: The viſible Church of Chriſt, is a congregation of faithfull men, in which the pure word of God is preached, and the Sacraments be duely miniſtred, according to Chriſts ordinance in all thoſe things, that of neceſſity are requiſite to the ſame. As the Church of Hieruſalem, Alexandria, and Antioche haue erred: ſo alſo the Church of Rome hath erred, not onely in their liuing and manner of ceremonies, but alſo in matters of faith.* Hitherto this article. Whoſe definition or deſcription of the Church, if wee should allowe, wee are ſufficiently inſtructed by that is ſaid before, that the Proteſtants new congregation cannot be this true viſible Church of Chriſt, erring from the truth in ſo many neceſſary, and requiſite things, as hath beene proued in all Articles before, wherein it oppoſeth the receaued doctrine of this primatiue Apoſtolike age, and the preſent Church of Rome as the like demonſtration shall be made againſt them, in all their contradictory Articles following, in their due place, And ſo is alſo and will be moſt manifeſt, that the preſent Roman Church agreeing in all thoſe Articles both already, & hereafter to be examined, with the vndoubted true Church of the Apoſtles, and this their age, is, and muſt needs be the true Church of Chriſt: And

their

their affertion in the fecond parte of this Article,
*That the Church of Rome hath erred not onely in their
liuing and manner of ceremonies, but alfo in matters of
faith,* is moft euidently falfe and impudently flaun-
derous: And the open dore to infidelity. For if all
the commaunding Churches in the world, *Hieru-*
falem, Alexandria, Antioche and Rome, as they are
fet downe in the firft greate Councell of Nice, and
approued by the Parlaments and Parlament Re-
ligions of Queene Elizabeth, King Iames, & King
Charles, haue erred in matters of faith, as this Article affirmeth, then all other Churches, all being
fubiect vnto them, haue likewife erred. And this
new Proteftant pretended Church not being then
fprünge vp, being noe congregation of faithfull
men in that time, nor any congregation, or men at
all, and fo neither hauing the pure word of God
preached, nor Sacraments duely miniftred, nor any
one point of doctrine yet preached, or Sacrament
miniftred, nor man to preach or minifter any fuch,
could not, nor can poffibly by their owne rule and
Iudgment be the true vifible Church, or any
member, peece, or part thereof. That true primatiue and Apoftolike Church teaching by all Preifts
and Cleargy men, it had, both to the congregation
of faithfull men (to vfe thefe mens phrafe) conuerted, and to others yet not Chriftians, all thofe
neceffary articles, hitherto examined, contrary to
Proteftant Religion, when the onely want of any
one of fuch neceffary things, by their owne definitiue fentence before, taketh away the name and
title, to be the true Church, at this prefent, any
time paft, or to come, the preaching of the pure
word of God, & due miniftring of the Sacraments

*Nicen. Con-
cil.Can.
Parlament. 1.
of Queene
Eliz. Parl.1.
Iacob. & 1.
Caroli.*

in

in all things of necessity being one and the same to all persons, in all times and places.

And to be of any other minde quite crosseth with Chrifts Inftitution, and the continuance, and vifibility of his Church, which both that article of their Creede, *I beleeue the holy Catholike Church*, and this their article and confeffion of an euerduring vifible Church doth proue. For if at any time after Chrifts founding his Church, either in this Apoftolike, or any age after, it had generally erred, in matters of faith, that it retained not the name and truth of the true Church, there was then by this article no true Church in the world. For whofoeuer it was whom wee will dreame to haue beene the firft finder out of this generall errour and fuppofed Apoftafie. Martine Luther, Iohn Caluine, Thomas Cranmar or whofoeuer in any time or place, and preacher of the cótrary truth as Proteftants would haue it, yet this man being but one, could not make a congregation of faithfull men, which muft needs be a number, nor preach the pure word of God, *in a congregation of faithfull men, nor duely minifter the the Sairaments, according to Chrifts ordinance*, no fuch faithfull men or congregation yet being to preach, and minifter them vnto, which is a generall and vnanfwearable demonftration, by this Proteftant article it felfe, that the Church could neuer fo generally erre, nor their new pretended congregation be any part, or parcell of the true Church. Which is alfo manifeft by their fourteene fifteene or more feuerall Proteftant confeffions and pretended congregations, euery on of them different from other, and with it felfe alfo, as here in England the new Church of Kinge Henry VIII. King Eduard VI,

Proteft. Côf. Helu. Gallic. Angl. Scotic. Belg. Polonû. Argent. Anguftan. Saxonic. Wittemb. Palatin. Bohemich. Parliament. Henric. 8. Edw 6 Eliz. Can. Comm. bookes Iniunct. Canôs.

VI. Queene Elizabeth, King Iames and King Charles at open warrs with themselues, both in doctrine and Sacraments, as their seuerall approued lawes, Parlaments, proclamations, Synods, Canons, Iniunctions, Litanies, communion bookes, authorized Orders of prayer, conferences, and decrees are too great witnesses. And to quench the firey, malice of the Protestāts against the Church of Rome our Mother Church (as lately King Iames stiled it) they saying in this article, the Church of Rome hath erred in matters of faith. The Apostolike men which liued this age, will teach the contrary.

First whereas all agree that Sainct Peter was Bishop, liued and died there, Sainct Dionisius the Areopagite saith, hee was the most auncient and cheifest head of diuines. *Petrus maximum antiquißimumque Theologorum columen.* And testifieth plainely, that without doubt he was Prince or cheifest of the Apostles. *Ipse discipulorum facile princeps.*

Sainct Ignatius proueth the Roman Church was the sanctified and ruling Church. *Ecclesia sanctificata quæ præsidet in loco Regionis Romanorum.*

That it was the Church which was sanctified illuminated by the will of God who created all things which belong to the faith & loue of Christ Iesus God our Sauiour, the Church worthy of God, most decent, to be blessed, praysed, worthy to be obtained, most chast, and of excellent charity enioying the name of Christ and his father, and replenished with the holy Ghost. *Ecclesia sanctificata, & illuminata per voluntatem Dei, qui omnia creauit, quæ pertinent ad fidem & charitatem Iesu Christi, Deo digna, decentißima, beatificanda, laudanda, digna qua quis*

Dionis. Areopag. l. de diu. nom. cap. 3. Ecclef. Hierarch. c. 9. Ignat. ep. ad Rom. in titul

quis potiatur, castissima, & eximiæ charitatis, Christi & patris nomine fruens, spirituque plena. And plainely of the Christians of Rome, that they were ioined in body and soule to all the commaundements of Chrifts, and replenished with all grace. *Spiritu & corpore coniunctos omnibus mandatis Iesu Christi, repletos omni gratia Dei absque hæsitatione, & repugnatos ab omni alieno colore.* Without all doubting, freed from all errour. Sainct Clement is witneſſe, that Sainct Peter was made the foundation of the Church. *Simon Petrus veræ fidei merito & integræ præcicationis obtentu, fundamentum esse Ecclesiæ definitus est.* And was cheifeſt ruler among the Apoſtles. *Nec inter ipsos Apostolos par institutio fuit, sed vnus omnibus præfuit.* And calleth him the Father of all the Apoſtles, and that he receaued the keyes of the Kingdome of heauen. *Beatum Petrum Apostolum, omnium Apostolorum patrem, qui claues regni cælestis accepit.* And relating, how Sainct Peter a litle before his conſtituting him his ſucceſſour in the preſence of the whole Church, *in auribus totius Ecclesiæ, committed his chaire and Apostolike supreame power vnto him alone, as it was by Christ communicated and giuen vnto him. In auribus totius Ecclesiæ hæc protulit verba : Clementem hunc Episcopum vobis ordino, cui soli meæ prædicationis & doctrinæ cathedram trado. Ipsi trado à Domino mihi traditam potestatem ligandi & soluendi, vt de omnibus, quibuscumque decreuerit in terris, hoc decretum sit & in cœlis.*

Clem. Rom. epiſt. 1.

Clem. Rom. epiſt. 2.

Robert. Barnes lib. de vit. Pontif. Rom. in Clement. 1.

And this is not denied by our Proteſtant Antiquaries, but affirmed from the ſame authority: *Clemens Romanus, à Petro apprehensâ manu institutus est Romanus Pontifex, si Epistolis Clementis credendum est.* Acknowledging thoſe epiſtles to be the works

of

of Sainct Clement, which so testifie. In which and diuers other bookes he giueth lawes for the whole Church, which he himselfe sufficiently often witnesseth writing and sending his decrees to be kept and obserued to, and by all Bishops, Preifts, all Clergy men, and all Princes greater or lesse, and generally vnto all beleeuers: *Clemens vrbis Romæ Episcopus, omnibus Coepiscopis, Presbyteris, Diaconis ac reliquis Clericis, & cunctis Principibus, maioribus minoribufуè omnibus generaliter fidelibus.* This epistle traslated by Ruffinus is intituled of the *office & and duty of Preifts & Clergie men, de officio Sacerdotis & Clericorum,* for the whole Church of Christ. The like commaunde and generall authority of his Sea Apostolike he hath in diuers other bookes. Sainct Anacletus also is so cleare for this primacy, and infallibility of the Church of Rome, that our Protestants confesse it thus as plainely: *To proue that the Church of Rome hath the preeminence ouer all Churches, alleadgeth math. 16. verf. 18. vpon this rocke will I builde my Church, and he expoundeth it thus: super hanc Petram, id eft, super Ecclesiam Romanam, vpon this rocke, that is, vpon the Church of Rome, will I build my Church.*

Anacletus writeth, that the primacy of the Church of Rome ouer all Churches, and ouer all Christian people was graunted by our Lord himselfe, becaufe, faith he, he faid to Peter liuing at Rome, vpon this rocke will I build my Church. Ab ipfo Domino primatum Romanæ Ecclesiæ super omnes Ecclesias, vniuerfumque Chriftiani nominis populum conceffum effe afferuit: quia (inquit) Petro agenti & morieti Romæ dixit: tu es Petrus, & super hanc petram ædificabo Ecclesiam meam.

Sainct Euariftus writeth the like, calling the Church

Clem. epift. 3. de offic. Sacerd. & Clericor.

Anaclet. epift. 1. 2. 3. l

Ormer. pict. Pap. p. 78. Robert. Bern. l. de vit. pont. Rom. in Anacleto.

Euarift. ep. 1.

Alex. 1. ep.1. Church of Rome the head, _caput_, of Churches. S. A-
lexander affirmeth that Christ committed the dif-
posing of the greatest causes and busines of all
Churches to Sainct Peter Prince of the Apostles
Middleton.
Papist.p.200. and to the Apostolike Roman Sea as head of them.
Cui sancta & Apostolica sedi summarum dispositione
causarum, & omnium negotia Ecclesiarum ab ipso Do-
mino tradita sunt; quasi ad caput, ipso dicente principi
Apostolorum Petro:Tu es Petrus & super hanc Petram
adificabo Ecclesiam meam. Sainct Papias also , as our
Protestants confesse (to speake in their owne
words,) _taught Peters primacy, and Romish Episco-_
Martial. ep.
ad Burdegal.
cap.11.
Hier.l. de vir.
Illust.in Iren.
epist.29.ad
Theod.Tert.
l. contra Va-
lent. Marty-
rol. Rom. die
28. Iunij. _pality._ Sainct Martial a disciple of Sainct Peters and
sent into Fraunce by the Apostolike Roman
Church, and a member thereof, teacheth that the
Church of Christ is firme, and can neuer be ouerthrowne or dissolued. _Firma Ecclesia Dei & Christi,_
nec cadere, nec disrumpi poterit vnquam.

Sainct Ireneus being by Sainct Hierome, the old
Romane Martyrologe , and others, scholler to S.
Polycarpus and Papias , and neare the Apostles
time _Apostolorum temporum vicimus,_ must needs liue
and be learned in this age , and both knowe and
followe the approued doctrine thereof; being a
Iren.l.3. c.3. most Catholike holy learned Sainct, Martyr and
Doctour, yet he witnesseth of the Roman Church
that it hath principality ouer all others, and therefore euery Church & all true beleeuers must haue
concordance with it , euer keeping the truth of
Christian Religion, which the Apostles deliuered.
Ad hanc Ecclesiam propter potentiorem principalitatem,
necesse est omnem conuenire Ecclesiam, hoc est, eos, qui
sunt vndique fideles , in qua semper ab his, qui sint vn-
dique, conseruata est ea, quae est ab Apostolis traditio.

He

He faith this Church is the greateft, moft auncient, knowne to all, founded by the two moft glorious Apoftles Sainct Peter, and S. Paul keeping inuiolable the faith they taught, and confounding all that erre. *Maximæ & antiquiſſimæ, & omnibus cognitæ à glorioſiſſimis duobus Apoſtolis Petro & Paulo Romæ fundatæ, & conſtitutæ Eccleſiæ, eam, quam habet ab Apoſtolis traditionem, & annunciatam hominibus fidem, per ſucceſſiones Epiſcoporum peruenientem vſque ad nos indicantes, confundimus omnes eos, qui quoquo modo, vel per ſui placentiam malam, vel vanam gloriam, vel per cæcitatem, & malam ſententiam, præterquam oportet, colligunt.* Where this Church of Rome is euer pure and vnfpotted, free from errour, the Iudge and confounder of all, wherefoeuer or howfoeuer erring and falling from the true Apoftolike doctrine.

And particularly concerning Britaine, (So it was euer adiudged here) wee receaued our firft faith from Sainct Peter and the Roman Church, Sainct Peter ftayed longe in Britaine, conuerted many, founded here Churches, ordained Bishops, Preifts, and Deacons: *venit in Britanniam, quo in loco longo tempore fuit moratus, verbo gratiæ multos illuminauit, Ecclefias conſtituit, Epiſcopoſque & Preſbyteros, & Diaconos ordinauit.*

And all our Proteftant Antiquaries confeffe, that wee receaued this holy Apoftolike faith, and and at this time, and in euery age had Bishops and preachers fent hither from Rome, as Sainct Damianus and Faganus with others from Pope Eleutherius in the fecond age, from Pope Victor wee had many in the third age, and Sainct Mellonius or

S. Simeon Metaphraftes die 29. Iunij.
Leland. in Arthurio. Harrifon defcr. of Britaine Stow hift. of Engl. Hollinsh. hif. of Engl. Theater of greate Brit. L. 6. Caius antiquit. Cautab. Godwin. Cóuerf of Brit. and Catal. of Bish. Io. Goffcelin. hift. Manufcript. Mat. parker. Antiquit. Brit.

or Mello from Pope Stephen and S. Amphibalus
with others from the same Romes authority in the
same age. In the fourth age one holy Emperesse &
Emperour, Queene and King, S. Helen with our
whole Cleargy agreed with Sainct Syluester and
others Popes there, and Sainct Ninian with others
of ours, which where there consecrated, and sent
hither by that power Apostolike, and many of
our Bishops were then at diuers Councels as Arles
in Fraunce, Sardyce and others both ioyning with
the Roman Church, and acknowledging the supreame spirituall power thereof. In the next and
fift age, Pope Celestine and other holy Popes sent
hither S. Palladius, Sainct Germanus, S. Lupus,
Sainct Seuerus, S. Patricius, S. Dubricius. Coelius
Sedulius with others renowned in all the world.

In the sixt age the Sea of Rome sent hither and
approued here, Sainct Iuo, Sainct Ethelardus, S.
Dauid, Sainct Kentegern, Sainct Asaph, Sainct
Molochus, Sainct Augustine, Mellitus Iustus with
all that holy company sent hither by Sainct Gregory Pope then, especially to the Pagan and not
yet beleeuing Saxons. Now that our Christian
Britains neuer forsooke or chaunged in any one
materiall point their first receaued Apostolike faith,
wherein they were assisted by the Popes, and Sea
of Rome, all this while to the cominge of S. Augustine in the end of the sixt hundred of yeares, our
most esteemed Protestant Antiquaries directly testifie from Antiquities.

Two of them speake in these very same words:
apud Britannos vigebat veritatis prædicatio, doctrina
sincera, & purus Dei cultus qualis ab ipsis Apostolis
mandato diuino, Christianorum Ecclesijs traditus erat.

At

Sardice
councel.

Jo. Balæus l.2.
de Act. Rom.
Pontif. in
Greg.1.& l.de
scrip. Centur.
1. in August.
Dauid powel.
Annotat. in l.
1. Girald.
Cambren.
Haier. Camb.
cap. 1.

At the comminge of Augustine hither, here florished a-mong the Britans the preaching of the truth, sincere do-ctrine, and the pure worship of God, which by the A-postles themselues by Gods commandement was deliuered to the Churches of Christians. One of thē saith, their doctrine was most sincere. *Doctrina sincerissi-ma.* Both of them cite the brittish history, so they might haue cited the old manuscript history of Rochester with diuers others. Two other princi-pall Protestant Antiquaries, the one an Archbi-shop with them, say: *Euangelium quod primis Apo-stolorum temporibus in Britannia nuntiatum non modo semper retentum firmiter, sed singulis saeculis auctum & dilatatum creuisse. The Ghospell which was preached in Britaine in the first times of the Apostles, was both euer firmely retained, and encreased in euery age.*

Mat. Parker Antiq. Brit. p. 6. 8. 9 45. & alijs. Io. Gos-celin hist. Ec-clef. manuscr. c. Brit. nunq. prolaff. à fide. GodWin. con-uerf. of Brit. p. 43.

An other, a Bishop in their congregation wri-teth: *The Britans continued still in the same tenour of pure doctrine, which they had receaued in the first in-fancy of the Church. The doctrine and discipline of their Church they had receaued from the Apostles of Christ.* An other hath thus: *among the Britains or welchmen Christianity as yet remained in force, which from the Apostles time had neuer failed in that nation.* An other hath thus: *The Britains after the receauing of the Faith, neuer forsooke it, for any manner of false preachinge of others.* An other thus witnesseth: *The Britains be-fore Augustines cominge, continued in the faith of Christ, euen from the Apostles time.* The like haue many others, to many to be cited, not any of them contradicting it. And by this they haue euidently proued against this their Article, that the Church of Rome, in euery age, as they haue before declared assisting and directing the Christian Britans here,

Hollinsh. hist. of Engl. c. 21. p. 102. Foxe Act and mo-num. pa. 463. edit. an 1576. Fulke Answ. to a counterf. Cathol p. 40. Middleton. Papistomast. p. 202. Thea-rer of greate Brit. l. 6.

and concurring and agreeing with them in euery point and article of Religion, neither did, nor could be ſaid to haue *erred in matters of faith*. And this theſe Proteſtants expreſſely confeſſe, when they generally acknowledge, (as all Antiquities doe) that there was then no materiall or eſſentiall difference, in matters of faith, betweene the Chriſtian Britains (except ſome Pelagian heretiks among them) and Sainct Auguſtine with his company being ſent from the Church of Rome, the Pope then being a greate S. Gregory the moſt learned and holy Pope that euer was by theſe mens Teſtimony: *Gregorius magnus omnium Pōtificum Romanorum doctrina & vita præſtantiſſimus*. And therefore by them and all holy writers ſtiled *Gregory the greate*. And wherein ſoeuer any difference though ceremoniall obſeruing of Eaſter, any ceremony about the miniſtering of Baptiſme, or giuing holy Orders, was betweene the Roman Church and the Britains, all writers both Catholiks and Proteſtāts proue, the Roman Church profeſſed the truth.

And the Britains were in the errour, and ſo they freely and publikely in their firſt meeting cōfeſſed, as Sainct Bede and our Proteſtants themſelues with others acknowledge: *Tum Britones confitentur quidem intellexiſſe ſe, veram eſſe viam iuſtitiæ, quam prædicaret Auguſtinus;*and this was inuincibly proued vnto them both by vnanſwearably humane arguments, and diuine teſtimony and miracle. And they afterward generally corrected and conformed themſelues to the Romane Church in all things formerly queſtioned betweene them, as all Antiquaries Brittiſh, Engliſh, Forreine, domeſticall, Catholiks, and Proteſtants agree, neuer contending

Baleus l. 2. de Act. Rom. Pontif. in Gregorio Magno.

Bed. hiſt. Eccleſ. l. 2. c. 2.

ding about any question moued by Protestants a-
gainst the present Roman Church, but both the
Romane Church then, and our Britains, as the
whole Christian world also, iointly agreing in
euery article against this new Protestant Religion.
And this is manifestly proued, particularly already
in all articles yet examined, and so will be in all
that followe. Therefore it is manifestly false, by all
testimonies auncient, later, forreine, domesticall,
Catholikes and Protestants euen in their publike
decrees, and Confessions, that which this Article
so desperately, hath deliuered : *The Church of Rome
hath erred in matters of faith:* and the contradictory,
that it hath not so erred, nor shall at any time so
erre, is euidently true, by all witnesses. This will
be yet more euidently manifested, in the two next
following examinations, and others.

THE VIII. CHAPTER.

*The 20. Article thus examined, and in whatsoeuer
contrary to the Church of Rome, thus
condemned.*

THEIR 20. and next article intituled : *of the
authority of the Church* : is this. *It is not lawfull
for the Church to ordaine any thinge contrary to Gods
word written, neither may it so expound one place of
Scripture, that it be repugnant to another. Wherefore
although the Church be a witnesse and a keeper of holy
writ; yet, as it ought not to decree any thing against the
same, so besides the same, ought it not to enforce any
thing to be beleeued for necessity of saluation.*

In

In this article no thing needeth other anſweare or confutation then is made before in their article of Scriptures, and traditions, where the pretended ſole neceſſity of the written Scriptures, heretikely inſinuated, is moſt plainely confuted, both by the Apoſtolike doctrine and practiſe of this age, and otherwiſe. And the ſupreame power and authority which here they giue vnto the Church to be a witneſſe and keeper of holy writ, and the cheifeſt expoſitour thereof, and as their common gloſſe on this article is, *the Church hath authority to Iudge and determine in controuerſies of faith,* doth vtterly diſable and condemne thoſe Proteſtants to haue any colour or pretence to hold the truth in any one article they maintaine, againſt the Roman Church, either concerning, Scriptures, Church, or any thing elſe: for the Church which onely was, and is viſible, as they haue deſcribed the true Church before, hath in all and euery article condemned all ſuch Proteſtant Innouation.

And for theſe men to ſay, as they haue done, in their 19. Article, that the Church is *a congregation of faithfull men, in which the pure word of God is preached, and the Sacraments be duely miniſtred,* and to make it an article of faith, as they doe in their publike profeſſion of the Creede, that this Church, one holy and Catholike, doth ſo continue for euer without interruption, or corruption in miniſtring Sacraments, and preaching doctrine, and theſe things are in their cenſure ſhould onely be taken from the written word and Scriptures, It is vnpoſſible in ſuch proceedings, that the Church ſhould ordaine any thing contrary to Gods word written, or ſo expound on place of Scripture, that it be repugnant

pugnant to an other. For otherwise it should neither be *one*, *holie*, or *Catholike*, but diuers different, vnholy, particular, no pillar of truth, but a
forge of falsehood, no howse of God, no spouse of
Christ, no saluation to be had, or hoped for, in any
Iudgment Catholike or Protestant, but in the true
Church of Christ.

To this, the Apostolike men of this age giue
euident testimony. Sainct Ignatius doth make the
Iudgment of the Church both supreame, and certaine, and receauing penitents, and saith *Christ hath*
firmely builded his Church vpon a hile by spirituall
building without help of mans hands, against which the
floods dashing, and windes puffing could not ouer-
throwe it; nor any spirituall wickednesses shall euer be
able to doe it, but they shall be weakened by the power of
our Lord Iesus Christ. Iesus Christus secundum pro-
priam voluntatem suam, firmauit Ecclesiam super Pe-
tram, ædificatione spirituali, citra humanarum ma-
nuum operam, in quam collisa flumina & venti non po-
tuerunt eam subuertere: nec id valeant vnquam spiri-
tuales nequitiæ, sed infirmentur virtute Domini nostri
Iesu Christi. And saith plainely, as there is but one flesh
and blood of Christ shedd for our sinnes, one Euchariste,
one Altare, one Priestly order, one God the Father, one
God the sonne, one holy Ghost, so there is but one prea-
ching, and one faith, and one baptisme, and one Church,
which with their sweate and labours the holy Apostles
haue founded in the blood of Christ, from the one end of
the earth to the other: vna prædicatio, & fides vna, &
vnum baptisma, & vna Ecclesia quam suis sudori-
bus & laboribus fundarunt sancti Apostoli, à finibus
terræ, vsque ad fines, in sanguine Christi. Sainct Clement saith, the Catholike Church, is the planta-

Ignat. epist.
ad Philadelp.
Ephes. Trall.
Magn. An-
tiochen.
Ignat. ep. ad
Philadelp.

Clem. Rom.
Const. Apost.
l. 1. c. 1.

tion

tion of God, and his chosen vineyard, which cannot be digged vp, or destroied. *Dei plantatio est Ca-*
tholica Ecclesia, & vinea eius electa. So that no other
can be planted or chosen by Christ, but this one
alone.

Christ did purchase but one militant Church
with his pretious blood, he hath no more but one
such daughter, nor true Christians more then one
such mother, which the same Sainct Clement likewise proueth thus: *conuenite ad Ecclesiam Domini,*
quam acquisiuit sanguine Christi, dilecti primogeniti
omnis creaturæ. Ea est enim altissimi filia, quæ partu-
rijt nos per verbum gratiæ. He copareth this Church
also, to one greate shippe. Carrying passengers
from all contryes to the desired hauen and harbour,
saying, that God is alwayes the Lord and owner
of it, Christ the Master or Gouernour, the Bishop
cheife ruler vnder him, Preists Deacons and other
Clergy men euer supply their places and offices
therein. *Similis est omnis status Ecclesiæ magnæ naui,*
quæ per vndosum Pelagus, diuersis è locis & regionibus
viros portat, ad vnam potentis regni vrbem properare
cupientes. Sit ergo nauis huius Dominus, ipse omnipo-
tens Deus, gubernator verò sit Christus. Tum demum
proretæ officium Episcopus impleat, Presbyteri nauta-
rum, Diaconi dispensatorum locum teneant, hi qui ca-
techizant nautologis conferantur. He giueth also to
lay persons their place in this shippe, saying the
world is the Sea it passeth, and witnesseth that this
shippe, notwithstanding all stormes and tempests,
persecutions, tribulations, daungers, false Prophets,
seducers, persecuting potentates, hypocrites, and
whatsoeuer enemies, aduersaries and aduersities,
euer is safe, and neuer maketh shipwrake, for
Christ

Const. Apost.
l. 2. c. 65.

Clem. epist. 1.

Chriſt euer gouerneth it, and the whole Church
muſt endeuour to ſerue and obey him and his com-
maundes. *Saluator Dominus, gubernator Eccleſiæ ſuæ* — Martial. ep.
diligatur ab omnibus, & ipſius ſolius præceptis ac iuſsis — ad Burdegal.
credat, & obediat omnis Eccleſia. Thus Saint Cle- — cap. 11.
ment from the Apoſtles themſelues. And Saint
Martial alſo teacheth, that the Church of Chriſt is
ſo firme, it can neuer fall, nor be broken. And yet
in the ſame place he teacheth that the deuill and heretiks his vaſſals and inſtruments ſhall neuer ceaſe
to labour and fight againſt it: *Inimicus venturus eſt*
vt ſuperſeminet in populo Dei grana errorum. Sed fir-
ma Eccleſia Dei & Chriſti, nec cadere, nec diſrumpi po-
terit vnquam. Venient præſumptores abſque gratia Dei
loquentes, quorum gloria labiorum procedit ex ſuperbia,
ſimiles illi qui ſuperbia cælum præſumens habitare, mox
de cælo cum Angelis ſuis ſequacibus ruit in æternam
voraginem. Hi docebunt aliam doctrinam quæ aliena
eſt à Deo, amica autem diabolo, per quam ipſe ſpiritus
erroris, animas poſt ſe trahere feſtinabit. Which cannot
more properly be applyed to any ſects of hereſies,
then the libertine Proteſtants ſo firſt ariſing, en-
creaſing and ſubſiſting by wanton and lewde li-
centiouſneſſe.

S. Dionyſius Areopagita wrote a whole booke — Dion. Areop.
in Greeke yet euery where extant *de Eccleſiaſtica* — l. de Eccleſ.
Hierarchia of the Eccleſiaſticall Hierarchy, or holy — Hierarch.
order, which was in his time, and to continue euer
in the neuer fayling or ceaſing Church of Chriſt.
All the Apoſtles ſo firmely and vniformely be- — Clem. Rom.
leeued, and profeſſed this doctrine, as a neceſſary — epiſt 1. Ruff.
article of faith, for all Chriſtians, and to obtaine — in expoſit.
ſaluation by as the reſt, and ſo propoſed it vnto all, — Symbol Leo
in their *Symbolum* as Saint Clement then liuing — i i multis lo-
                                                     cis.

Ruf-

Ruffinus, S. Leo and all Chriſtians acknowlegde, *Credo Sanctam Eccleſiam Catholicam*, euer to be an Article of faith as the others, which poſſible could not be true, if at any time Chriſt ſhould want a Church holy and Catholike. And our Proteſtants of England in theſe their articles doe twiſe in one article before, intituled *of the three Creeds*, make and receaue it with the other articles of their Creede, an article of faith throughly to be receaued

Proteſt. artic. of Relig. art. 8.

and beleeued. For So they define: *The three Creeds, Nicene Creede, Athanaſius Creede, and that which is commonly called the Apoſtles Creede ought throughly to be receaued, and beleeued, affirming further, they may be proued by moſt certaine warrants of holy Scripture.* And both in the Apoſtles and Nicen Creede this article is contained with the reſt.

Engl. Proteſt. com. booke tit. Catechiſme.

This is alſo confirmed in their publike communion booke, vſed in their Churches, and allowed by their Parlaments, where beſides the Article of the Apoſtles Creede, *I beleeue in the holy Ghoſt, the holy Catholike Church,* they ſay vnto God, in the can-

Tit. morning prayer.

ticle *Te Deum,* as they tranſlate it: *The holy Church through all the world, doth knowledge thee.*

Nicen Creede

And in their Creede of the Nicen Councell they plainely profeſſe and beleeue, that from the Apoſtles till now, and euer after, there is and ſhal be one holy, *Catholike and Apoſtolike Church: vnam ſanctam Catholicam & Apoſtolicam Eccleſiam.* Where the Church is euer *one, holy, Catholike,* and the ſame in all matters of faith it was in the Apoſtles

Art. 19. ſupr.

time. And in this ſenſe and no other they haue in their 19. article before deſcribed or defined the Church *of Chriſt to be one congregation of faithfull men, with true preaching, and due miniſtration of Sa-*

cramentſ

craments in all things necessary and requisite according
as Christ ordained. And their publike glosse vpon
this 19. article diuiding it into diuers propositions,
and making this the second proposition : *There is* Thomas Ro-
but one Church : When wee doe say that the Church is gers in art.
visible and that there is a westerne, East, Greeke, Latine : 19. proposit.
English Church, wee meane not that there be diuers 2.
Churches of Christ, but that one and the same Church
is diuersely taken and vnderstood, and also hath many
particular Churches, as the Sea many Riuers and armes,
branching from it. For the visible Church is not many
congregations, but one company of the faithfull. For
proofe of this out of Scriptures, they cite diuers
texts Rom. 12. 5. 1. Cor. 10. 17. 1. Corint. 12. 13. 27.
Gal. 3. 28. and conclude thus: *all Gods people* (meaning Protestants) *agree with vs in this point.* And
particularly cite Confess. Heluet. 2. cap. 17. Bohe.
cap. 8. Gal. art. 26. Belg. art. 27. August. art. 27.
Wittemb. art. 32. Sueu. art. 15. and these Protestant Confessions so agree. I will onely cite two
for the rest, one of Heluetia, for the Caluinists, and
for the Lutherans that of Wittemberge where
Luther liued, as Caluine in Heluetia.

The Heluetian confession saith : *Cum semper v-* Confessio
nus modo sit Deus, vnus mediator Dei & hominum Ie- Heluet. c. 17.
sus Messias, vnus item gregis vniuersi Pastor, vnum
huius corporis caput, vnus denique spiritus, vna salus,
vna fides, vnum testamentum vel fœdus, necessariò
consequitur, vnam duntaxat esse Ecclesiam: quam prop-
terea Catholicam nuncupamus, quod sit vniuersalis, &
diffundatur per omnes mundi partes, & ad omnia se
tempora extendat, nullis vel locis inclusa vel tem-
poribus. Seing alwayes there is onely one God, one
mediatour of God and men Iesus the Messias, also one

Shee-

Sheepheard of the vniuersall flocke, one heade of this body, to conclude one holy Ghost, one saluation, one faith, one testament or league, it necessarily followeth, that there onely is one Church: Which therefore wee name Catholike, because it is Vniuersall, and diffused through all parts of the world, and extendeth it selfe to all times, not concluded within any places or times.

This holy Church of God, is called the house of the liueinge God, builded of liuely and spirituall stones, and seated vpon an vnmoueable rocke, and vpon a foundation, on which no other thing can be placed, and therefore it is called the pillar and supporter of truth. Hæc Ecclesia Dei sancta, vocatur domus Dei viuentis, extructa ex lapidibus viuis & spiritualibus, & imposita super petrã immotã, super fundamentũ, quo aliud locari nõ potest: & ideo nuncupatur etiam colũna & basis veritatis.

1. Tim; 3.

Confess. Wirtemberg. cap. de Eccl.

The Lutheran Religion or confession of Wittemberge saith: credimus & confitemur, quod vna sit sancta Catholica & Apostolica Ecclesia, iuxta Symbolum Apostolorum & Nicænum. Quod hæc Ecclesia à Spiritu sancto, ita gubernetur, vt conseruet eum perpetuo, ne vel erroribus vel peccatis pereat. Quod in hac Ecclesia sit vera peccatorum remissio. Quod hæc Ecclesia habeat ius iudicandi de omnibus doctrinis. Quod hæc Ecclesia habeat ius interpretandæ scripturæ. Ecclesia habet certam promissionem perpetuæ præsentiæ Christi; & gubernatur à Spiritu sancto.

Cap. de Consilijs.

Wee beleeue & cõfesse, that there is one holy Catholike and Apostolike Church according to the Creede of the Apostles and Nicen Councell.

That this Church is so gouerned by the holy Ghost, that he preserueth it for euer, that it perish not, either by errours or sinnes.

That in this Church there is true remissiõ of sinnes, that

this

this Church hath authority to Iudge of all doctrines.
That this Church hath authority to interpret the Scrip-
ture.The Church hath certaine promise of the perpetuall
presence of Christ, and is gouerned by the holy Ghost.

By this it is euident by all Testimonies of this
Apostolike age, and these Protestants themselues
that the true Church of Christ neuer did, shall, or
can erre in any Iudgment, decree, sentence, or profession in matters of faith, but is pure Catholike
and Apostolike in all such, in all times, and places,
And this article either denying or doubting of such
power, and prerogatiue in the true Church, is very
Idle or Antichristian, taking away all certaine and
holy Religion of Christ. As also that the Church
which was when these heresies began, euen Catholike and vniuersall in all places, and had beene
so in all times before, hath beene so euer since, and
still so continueth, and florisheth, is that true holy
Catholike & Apostolike Church which the holy
Scriptures, Fathers of this age, and the Article of
our Creede, giue testimony vnto, And the Protestant particular Confessions and congregations of
Heluetia, Fraunce, England, Scotland, Belgia, Po-
land, Argentine, Ausburgh, Saxony, Wittemberge,
the Palatine of Rheine, Boheme, and perhaps some
others, (being onely of particular Contryes or
Townes, and onely of some and not all persons of
them) cannot be possibly Catholike for place, and
as vnpossibly for time, the eldest of them, by their
owne testimony, and confession, vnknowne vntill
the yeare of Christ 1530. the Confession of Au-
sburge first began, not printed vntill the yeare
1540. the Confession of Boheme 1532. Heluetia
1536. Saxony 1551. England 1562. Scotland. 1581.
the

the like of the reſt. Theſe nor any of them by the ſame reaſon can be Apoſtolike, ariſing ſo many hundreds of yeares after the Apoſtles time. None of all theſe can be, that one Church, which was euer, thoſe being diuers from that, & among themſelues at warres, both for Sacraments, diſcipline & doctrine. None of their cōgregations or cōfeſſions yet hath brought forth any one man or woman knowne, which in their owne Iudgment or ſentēce is honoured, or calendred for a Saint, though their calenders, chronicles, and hiſtories be full of Saints, which were of the Roman Church, and Religion.

They haue taken away and ouerthrowne many thouſand foundations of holyneſſe ánd piety, their owne firſt foundation in ſuch kinde is yet to begin, this cannot be the one, holy, Catholike, and Apoſtolike Church of Chriſt, which our Creeds doe teach vs; being in all reſpects diametrically oppoſite, or rather contradictory to whatſoeuer is, or can be defined, or deſcribed, as they themſelues define the true Church, by thoſe attributes, properties, or diſtinctiue differences, to be *one*, to be *holy*, to be *Catholike*, and vniuerſall in all times, places, and points of doctrine, and Sacraments, and to be *Apoſtolicall*, continued without intermiſſion from the Apoſtles, in ſound and Apoſtolicall Chriſtian Religion, in all articles and matters of faith. And thus it was confeſſed, and profeſſed by our Chriſtian Britains, from their firſt couerſion, in the Apoſtles time, as theſe men themſelues haue before deliuered.

The IX. Chapter.

The 21. Article so examined, and condemned.

THE Article which followeth 21. in number, is intituled: *of the authority of generall Councels.* And in these their words. *Generall Councels may not be gathered together without the commaundement and will of Princes. And when they be gathered, for asmuch as they be an assembly of mē, whereof all be not gouerned with the spirit, and word of God, they may erre, and some time haue erred, euen in thinges pertaining vnto God. Wherefore, things ordained by them as necessary to saluation, haue neither strength, nor authority, vnlesse it may be declared that they be taken out of holy Scripture.* Hitherto this English Protestant Article. The first part of it requiring of necessity the commaundement and will of Princes, for the validity of Councels is singular, not onely against Catholiks but all Confessions of Protestants, not any one consenting in this matter with our English Protestants, as is euident in those confessions. Neither doe the Protestants of Britaine agree herein, but all they, whom they terme Puritans or Disciplinarians are quite of an other opinion. And the Parlament Protestants themselues of best Iudgment doe euen with publike allowance condemne it. Thus with such approbation they write of themselues.

The Protestants are seuered bandes, or rather scattered troopes, each drawing diuers wayes without any meanes to pacifie their quarrels, to take vp their controuersies. No Prince with any preeminence of Iurisdiction aboue

Protestant relation of Religion, cap. 47.

aboue the rest: no Patriarcke one or more, to haue a common superintendance of care, of their Churches, for correspondancy and vnity: no ordinary way to assemble a generall Councell, the onely hope remaining euer to assuage their contention. The other haue the Pope as a common Father, aduiser and conductor to all, to reconcile their Iarres, to appease their displeasures, to decide their difference, aboue all things to drawe their religion by consent of councels, to vnity.

And this is euidently and experimétally knowne to be true, by all men, no Prince or Potentate spirituall or temporall except the Pope of Rome, either hauing, or pretending to haue, any such power, as is necessary to call & assemble a generall Councell. And for Protestant Princes, none clayming such prerogatiue, but onely in his owne temporall dominions, it is absolutely vnpossible that any such assembly of Bishops, which could deserue the name of one halfe or third or lesse part of a generall Coũcell, from all Christian Kingdomes, and contries, should at any time, or place, be called, and gathered together, by any such pretended power. And if wee

The Subscriptiõs of these Protestants confessions.

should allowe meere lay and prophane men, Souldiars, Captaines, Rebels, and heretikes without knowledge in diuinity, or humane duty, to haue decisiue voyces in Ecclesiasticall matters, and to offord to euery common Artizan, the place and office of holy and learned Bishops, in such assemblies, & Iudgméts it were a thing most ridiculous, And further to say, that all the Bishops and Catholike Cleargy men in all those contries, where Protestant confession haue beene kept were present, and consented vnto them, all those assemblies and conuenticles could not come to be the halfe of a fourth

part

part of a Councell generall, out of the whole Christian world.

There was not in any of the forreine conuenticles and conciables, any one man bearing the name of a Bishop, which inuented them, or subscribed vnto them, as is euident in their subscriptions, neither any one such at this day amõg them except in Scotland, whether some of King Iames his bastard Bishops haue crept, sent, or appointed by his regall supremacy from the newly hatched broode of England, which neither now hath, or had any one true and lawfull Bishop, at the enacting and first shaping of these articles called forsooth, *Anglica confeßio, the confeßion of England,* and now scarcely a man to be founde in England, Scotland, Fraunce or other contry, where those confeßions were first vented, which consenteth vnto them. Diuers of them of late as of Bohemia, the Palatinate of Rhyne, and others in Germany wholly ouerthrowne, and all returned to the Catholike faith, and the rest so farre at variance and distastes with their confeßions, as wee see in England the late bookes of Doctor Montague, and, him that gathered the booke of prayers priuiledged by the present Protestant Bishop George of London, both them iustifiable by this booke of articles, their communion booke, and other allowed rules of their religion, are esteemed and accompted for strauge wonders among the present called Protestants. And to shew of what validity these pretended peeces of Protestants Councels and confeßions were from the beginning in their owne Iudgment, disablinge all such, as be not *gathered together by the commaundement and will of Princes,* except
here

here in England, where a woman was head in all
things both temporall and spirituall, there was not
either the commaundement, will, or assent of any
true lawfull, and cheife Prince to those confessions,
but the contrary, those assemblies and Confessions
being gathered and concluded by refractory, diso-
bedient, and vndutifull people, as is euident in the
very Protestant proceedings and histories of them
all. In the confession of Ausburg the Protestant publishers of it say, that Ihon Duke of Saxony Ele-
ctour, George Marquesse of Brandeburge, Erne-
stus Duke of Luneburge, Philip Lansgraue of
Hesse, Ihon Frederike Duke of Saxony, Francis
Duke of Luneburge, Walfangus Prince of Anhalt
the Senats of Nurnberge and Reutling subscribed,
but by their owne confession they subscribed as
subiects to the Emperour and protesting their fide-
lity vnto him. *Cæsareæ maiestatis vestræ fideles &*
subditi. And the Emperour their Supreame Lord,
and Prince, neuer consented vnto it. No Prince or
Potentate Protestant that consented vnto any of
these confessions, neuer had, or claymed any Iurisdiction or power spirituall, or temporall ouer all
other, or any one other Prince or contry, and so noe
generall Councell euer was, or can be called, by
any right, or title claymed or pretended in their religion; all Protestants agree the true Church euer
had, hath, and shall haue true discipline, Sacraments, and due ministration of them, and true doctrine in all things necessary: none of these confessions thus agree together, And the Protestants
of England with their temporall Princes spirituall
Supremacy with two onely Sacraments, and di-
uerse points of necessary doctrine differ from them
all.

Subscriptio
confessionis
Augustanæ.

all. Neither euer was there any Christian, temporall prince, King, or Emperour, or euer like to be, that did or shall Reigne ouer all prouinces, and contries, where Christians, did, doe, and are to liue hereafter, yet councels haue beene kept, and lawfully called, euen such as be named generall, from the beginning, and before any Christian King was in the world, and were lawfully kept and called, contrary vnto, and against the temporall Princes will and commaundement.

The Apostles themselues kept diuers councels in such manner; The Scripture witnesseth, that S. Peter and the Apostles assembled in Councell to be called generall for that time, consisting of all the Apostles, *hi omnes erant perseuerantes vnanimiter,* Act. cap 1. and almost 120. *Petrus in medio fratrum dixit, erat autem turba hominum simul fere centum viginti,* when Sainct Matthias was chosen in the place of Iudas.

It was a generall Councell also for that time Act. cap. 6. which was called and kept by the Apostles. When Sainct Stephen and the other 6. Deacons with him were chosen, remembred in the 6. chapter of the Acts of the Apostles. For both all the Apostles, and disciples being then very many, *crescente numero* Act. cap. 6. *discipulorum,* were present at it, called thither by Apostolike authority, both without and against the consent, will, or liking of any temporall Prince. It was also a generall Councell, for that time, when S. Paul, S. Barnabas with others, *Paulus & Barnabas* Act. cap. 18. *& quidam alij,* went a long Iorney to the rest of the Clem. Rom. Apostles and disciples at Hierusalem, about the const. Apost. question then moued concerninge circumcision. *l. 6. cap. 12.* For these were receaued by the Church, Apostles and others of the Clergy there. *Suscepti sunt ab Ec-*

H *clesia,*

clesia, & ab Apostolis, & senioribus. And the Apoſtles with the diſciples and rulers of the repreſentatiue Church gaue reſolution and ſentence vpon that doubt. *Placuit Apostolis & senioribus cum omni Ecclesia.*

Canones Apoſtol. Conſt. Apoſt. l.6. c. 12.

So wee may ſay of the councels, wherein the Canons of the Apoſtles, and their conſtitutions regiſtred by S. Clement, and remembred in many auncient writers Greeke and Latine were made.

Clemens recognit. l. 1.

The like is alſo ſet downe by S. Clement, when he relateth it in the name of the Apoſtles, a Councell which they kept at a feaſte of Eaſter. *Cum nos duodecim Apostoli ad diem Paschæ cum ingenti multitudine conuenissemus, ingressi Ecclesiam fratrum, quæ à nobis per loca singula gesta sint, breuiter exponimus.* So of that their holy Councell, wherein they decreed and compoſed the Creede, which the Church euer ſince profeſſeth, and our Proteſtants before receaue, as compoſed by them; the hiſtory of it is expreſſely ſet downe by Sainct Clement, Ruffinus

Clem. epiſt. 1. Ruffin. l. de expoſ. Symb.

and others. *Christo resurgente & ascendente in cœlum misso sancto Spiritu, collata Apostolis scientia linguarum, adhuc in vno positi, Symbolum quod fidelis nunc tenet Ecclesia, vnusquisque quod sensit, dicendo, condiderunt, vt discedentes ab inuicem, hanc regulam per omnes gentes prædicarent.* And reciting the contents thereof, concludeth, that the Apoſtles penned it by inſtinct of the holy Ghoſt. *Hoc prædicti sancti Apostoli inter se, per Spiritum sanctum salubriter, vt dictum est, condiderunt.* Diuers other ſuch ſacred

Clem. Conſt. Apoſt. l. 6. c. 14. 15. 16. 17. &c.

Councels of the Apoſtles, and Diſciples of Chriſt, wee might recite from approued writers, and yet none of them was by the commaūde or allowance of any temporall Prince, or Potentate, but otherwiſe.

wise. And to make it manifeſt to all poſterity that Princes tēporall were not to haue any commaunde in ſuch affaires, as Proteſtants in this article pretend, the ſame holy Apoſtles in their Canons, by ſome readings in the 36. by others, the 37. and by others 38. do thus decree, that *Biſhops ſhould twiſe in the yeare keepe councels and among themſelues examine the decrees of religion, and compoſe ſuch Eccleſiaſticall Controuerſies as ſhould ariſe, firſt in the fourth weeke after Pentecoſt ; and the ſecond the 12. day of October. Bis in anno fiat Epiſcoporum Synodus , & inter ſe examinent decreta religionis, & incidentes Eccleſiaſticas controuerſias componant : ſemel quidem quarta hebdomade Pentecoſtes : iterum autem Hyperberetæi, duodecimo.*

Canon. Apoſtol. can. 36. 37. vel 38.

And S. Clement from the ſame Apoſtles teacheth further, that Epiſcopall power and dignity was the greateſt on earth, Biſhops were Mediatours betweene God and men, in things belonging to diuine worſhip. The Biſhop is the Maſter of piety and Religion, the Father of Chriſtians vnder God, their Prince, their Leader, their King, their Ruler. After God, the earthly God who ought to enioy honour, the Biſhop muſt gouerne being adorned with the dignity of God, whereby he hath power ouer the Cleargy , and ruleth all the people. *Qui Epiſcopus eſt, hic eſt miniſter verbi , ſcientia cuſtos, Mediator inter Deum & homines , in ijs, quæ ad eum colendum pertinent : hic eſt magiſter pietatis & religionis: hic eſt ſecundum Deum pater veſter: hic Princeps, & Dux veſter: hic veſter Rex, & præfectus : hic poſt Deum terreus Deus, qui honore veſtro frui debet. Epiſcopus vobis præſideat , vt dignitate Dei cohoneſtatus, qua clerum ſub poteſtate ſua tenet, & toti populo præ-*

Clem. Apoſt. conſtit. l. 2. c. 30 c. 26 in al. exempl.

est. He telleth vs againe by the same Apostolike war-rant, that a Bishop representeth the example of God to men, and ruleth all men, Preists, Kings, Magistrats, pa-rents, children, and all subiects. Stude Episcope, vt mundus purusque sis, locum tuum, dignitatemque tuam actionibus declara; vt pote qui exemplar Dei repræsen-tas, præsidendo omnibus hominibus, Sacerdotibus, regi-bus, Magistratibus, parentibus, filijs, & pariter cunctis subditis. And iudgeth with power as God doth: *Iu-dica Episcope potestate fretus, tanquam Deus.*

And as Moses by God was called a God; so a Bishop is to be honoured as God. By how much the soule is more excellent then a Kingdome. Wee must loue a Bishop as a Father, feare hym as a King, honour him as Lord. It is graunted onely to Preists, to Iudge in spirituall causes. Lay men must obey, the Bishop is Steward and dispenser of Ecclesiasticall things. Wee must not aske an accompt of him, nor obserue how he performeth his dispensation, when, with whom, where, well or ill or conueniently. He hath God his Iudge, who hath committed this dis-pensation into his hands. Without a Bishop wee must do nothing. If any man doth any thing without the Bishop, he doth it in vaine. A Bishop is the heade, and must not obey the foote, a lay man, but onely God. He must rule his subiects, not obey them. The sonne doth not rule the Fa-ther, nor the Seruant his Lord, nor the Scholler his ma-stor, nor the Souldier the King, so the lay man must not commaund the Bishop. Si de parentibus secundum car-nem lex diuina inquit honora patrem tuum & matrem tuam quanto magis de spiritualibus parentibus vobis præceptum est, vt eos honoretis, & diligatis tanquam beneficos ligatosque ad Deum. Hos venerabiliter colite varijs honoribus. Hos Principes & Reges vestros pu-tatote, & tributa tanquam Regibus penditote. Si ali-*

quid

Cap. 11.

Cap. 12.

Cap. 30. c. 34.
37. 1.

Cap. 40. 39.

Cap. 31.

Cap. 17.

quid orationi addendum eſt, plura hic Episcopus, quam ille, Rex, olim. Ille enim rem militarem tantum adminiſtrabat, belli paciſque moderator, ad tuenda corpora, hic verò Dei Sacerdotium adminiſtrans; corpus & animam periculis liberat. Quanto igitur corpore eſt excellentior, tanto Sacerdotium Regno præſtat. Ligat enim id & ſoluit ſupplicio, vel indulgentia dignos. Ideo Epiſcopum diligere debetis, vt patrem, timere vt Regem, honorare vt Dominum. Non eſt æquum, caput cum ſis, ô Episcope, caudæ obſequi, hoc eſt, laico homini ſeditioſo in alterius perniciem, ſed ſoli Deo. Imperare enim debes ſubditis non parere: nam neque filius imperat patri ſecundum originis rationem, neque ſeruus Domino ſecundum poteſtatis rationem, neque diſcipulus magiſtro, neque miles Regi, ita neque laïcus Epiſcopo.

The like he hath in diuers other places, and in ample manner. S. Ignatius is as plaine in this point. He telleth vs, that all, without exception of any, muſt followe the Bishop, as Chriſt his Father. And none muſt doe any thing in matters belonging to the Church without the Bishop. *Omnes Episcopum ſiquimini, vt Chriſtus patrem. Sine Episcopo nemo quicquam faciat eorum, quæ ad Eccleſiam ſpectant.* He manifeſtly maketh the Authority of Bishops, greater then any regall, or other, on earth in theſe matters, the Princes of Preiſts repreſenting the Image of God, and next to him to be honoured and obeyed, and declareth it for a greater treaſon and diſobedience to reſiſt the Bishop, then the King, and the Epiſcopall office more honourable, then the Regall, this conſiſting onely in the inferiour temporall affaires, the Epiſcopall in ſuperiour Eccleſiaſticall and diuine. *Honora Deum vt omnium authorem & Dominum, Episcopum verò vt Principem*

S. Ignat. epiſt. ad Smyrnen.

H 3   *Sa*

Sacerdotum, Imaginem Dei referentem, Dei quidem propter principatum, Christi vero propter Sacerdotium. Honorare oportet & Regem, nec enim Deo quisquam potior est, aut ei similis in rebus omnibus creatis: nec Episcopo qui Deo consecratus est pro totius mundi salute, quicquam maius in Ecclesia: nec inter principes quisquam similis Regi, pacem & æquitatem subditis procuranti. Qui honorat Episcopum, à Deo honorabitur, sicut qui ignominia afficit illum, à Deo punictur. Si enim Iure censebitur pæna dignus, qui aduersus Regem insurgit, vt qui violet bonas legum constitutiones, quanto putatis grauiori subiacebit supplicio, qui sine Episcopo quid volet agere, concordiam rumpens, & decentem rerum ordinem confundens? And immediatly he further addeth this reason: becaufe preifthood is the heade, and cheifeft of all good things among men. And fo he that oppofeth or rageth againft it, doth not offer reproch to man, but to God and Chrift Iefus by nature the high Preift of his Father. *Sacerdotium enim est omnium bonorum, quæ in hominibus funt, Apex, qui aduersus illud furit, non hominem ignominia afficit, sed Deum, & Christum Iesum primogenitum, qui natura solus est summus Sacerdos Patris.* And teftifieth, that the Apoftles left this cũmaundement of honouring Bifhops. And faith, that a Bifhop is aboue & higher then any, or all principality and power on earth, and to be reuerenced as Chrift. *Reueremini Episcopum vestrum sicut Christum, quemadmodum beati nobis præceperunt Apostoli. Quid enim aliud est Episcopus, quam is qui omni principatu & potestate superior est: & quoad homini licet, pro viribus Imitator Christi Dei factus?* And therefore it is needfull that whatfoeuer wee doe, wee attempt nothing without the Bifhop. But wee muft alfo obey Preifts

Ignat. epift. ad Trallian.

                                                                    as the

as the Apostles of Christ. Episcopo subiecti estote velut Domino: ipse enim vigilat pro animabus vestris, vt qui rationem Deo redditurus sit. Necesse est itaque quicquid facitis, vt sine Episcopo nihil tentetis. Sed & Presbyteris subiecti estote, vt Christi Apostolis. What soeuer Bishop is placed to gouerne the Church of Christ, wee must receaue him, as him that sent him. Wee must regard our Bishop as our Lord himselfe. *Quemcunque Episcopum paterfamilias mittit ad gubernandam familiam, hunc ita accipere debetis, vt illum ipsum qui mittit. Episcopum igitur profecto aspicere oportet vt ipsum Dominum.* Wee must be subiect both to the Bishop and Preists and Deacons. He that obeyeth them, obeyeth Christ. He that resisteth them, resisteth Christ Iesus. He is peruerse contentions and proud, that obeyeth not Superiours. *Enitimini subiecti esse Episcopo, & Presbyteris & Diaconis. Qui enim his obedit, obedit Christo, qui hos constituit. Qui verò his reluctatur, reluctatur Christo Iesu. Præfractus, contentiosus, & superbus est, qui non obtemperat Superioribus.* Sainct Euaristus Pope liuing in this age writeth, as Sainct Ignatius also in diuers places doth, which I haue not cited, that preists are legates in the Church in the place of Christ: & as the Church his spouse is ioyned to him: So Bishops are ioyned to their Churches, by proportion. And the Church ought to obey the Bishop in all things. *Sacerdotes vico Christi legatione funguntur in Ecclesia. Et sicut ei sua coniuncta est sponsa, id est, Ecclesia: sic Episcopi iunguntur Ecclesiæ vnicuique proportione sua. Et Ecclesia Episcopo in omnibus obedire debet.* So our Protestants also testifie of him: *Ecclesiam debere Episcopo suo in omnibus obedire præcepit.*

And that Sainct Anacletus his predecessour decreed, that Ecclesiasticall causes should be hard

Ignat. epist. ad Ephes.

Euarist. epist. 2.

Rob. Barnes.l. de vit. Pontif. Rom. in Euarist.

Barnes sup. in Anacleto.

onely

onely before Ecclesiasticall Iudges, the greater to
be brought to the primate, the lesser to the Metropolitane Bishop, and onely temporall matters to be
tryed before temporall Iudges. *In Ecclesiasticis ne-*
gotijs, grauiores causas ad primatem, leuiores ad Metro-
politanum Episcopum referendas, secularia negotia ad
prophanos Iudices agenda esse iussit. And that all might
appeale to the Ecclesiasticall Court *Omnibus oppres-*
sis licere appellare Ecclesiasticum forum.

That he was an enemy to Christ whosoeuer
should call Preists before temporall Iudges. And
reputed them as Murtherers, which should take
away the riches & right of Christ & his Church:
because, saith he, the Apostles by the commaunde-
of our Sauiour did commaund, that the priuiledges
of the Church and Preists should be kept inuiolate. *Christo alienos esse iudicabat, qui Sacerdotes in ius*
vocarent. Christi vel Ecclesiæ pecunias auferentes, ho-
micidas iudicari debere censuit: quia inquit priuilegia
Ecclesiæ & Sacerdotum, Apostoli Saluatoris iussu in-
violata esse debere iusserunt. And yet the holy Apostolike writers being thus farre from allowing
Kings, to haue any power to commaund councels
of Bishops, or any one Bishop in such busines, doe
giue vs assurance, and some of them also commaundement, that councels were to be assembled, and
kept, euen in those times when there was no King
Christian to call, will, or commaunde them, and
in all ages to succeede without any such commaunde, or will of them. Which our Protestants
themselues plainely acknowledge, and first in this
last mentioned Pope Sainct Anacletus, who as
they confesse decreed, that councels should be kept
twise in the yeare. And such causes as could not
other-

otherwife be determined fhould be decyded in them. *Statuit congregationem virorum Ecclefiaftici ordinis bis in anno habendam: & caufas quæ apud primarios Ecclefiaftici ordinis componi non poffent in quarto concilio finiendas effe.* In the place which thefe men cite that holy Pope faith, that fuch councels were vfed, and ought to be kept twife in the yeare. *Summorum congregata congregatio per fingulos annos bis fieri folet & debet.* And the Apoftles themfelues, as Sainct Clement and others witneffe, made that decree, that councels of Bifhops fhould be kept twife in the yeare, to determine Controuerfies in religion, and Ecclefiafticall contentions, and expreffely fet downe the times of their affembling. *Bis in anno Epifcoporum celebratur Synodus, & pietatis inter fe dogmata in difpofitionem vocanto, nec non in Ecclefijs incidentes contradictiones dirimunto, femel quidem quarta feria Pentecoftes, fecundò duodecima hyperberetæi.* Which is receaued not onely in our moft auncient Popes and writers, as Sainct Anacletus before, but in firft and generall Councels themfelues. Sainct Ignatius teftifieth it was the order in his time, and giueth that order, that fuch councels fhould be often kept. *Crebrius celebrentur conuentus, fynodique.* And euident it is by all antiquities, that many fuch Councels and Synods were kept, longe before, and when and where there was not any Chriftian Prince or King to giue his will, commaund; or confent vnto them. Diuers fuch are yet extant, & Tertullian lyuing long before any fuch Chriftian King was either in Britaine which had the firft, or els where, is an ample witneffe, that in diuers places, and from all Churches councels were affembled, about affaires in religion, and

with

Robert. Barn. in Anacleto fupr.
Anacletus ep-
I.
Canon. Apo-
ftol. can. 36.
Clem. ib. con-
cil. Chalced.
act. 15. can. 19.

Concil. in
cen. I. cen. I.
can. 5. Concil.
Antioch c. 20
Ignat. epift.
Polycarp.

Tertullian.
aduerſ. Pſy-
chicos cap.13.

with greate reuerence, and ſuch as repreſented all
that were Chriſtians. *Aguntur præcepta per Gracias
illas certis in locis concilia ex vniuerſis Eccleſijs, per
quæ & altiora quæque in communi tractantur, & ipſa
repreſentatio totius nominis Chriſtiani magna veneratione celebratur.* And if wee ſhould follow the will,

Conc. Arelat.
to.1.Conc. in
Subſcript. Io.
Bal.l. de Scri-
ptor.Brit.
cent.1.Stowe
hiſt. Romans.
Godwine
conuerſ. of
Britaine Con-
cil. Suneſſan.
to.1. Concil.
in. 3. examp.
Act. antiq. S.
Marcellin.
Robert. Bar-
neſſe l. de vit.
Pontif. Rom.
in Marcellin.

and Rule of Proteſtants, to accompt them generall
councels, where the moſt Biſhops and from moſt
prouinces in greateſt number be aſſembled, wee
may relate for ſuch the Councels of Arles where
our Archbiſhop of London Reſtitutes was preſent,
gathered forth of aboue 30. Kingdomes and contries, and that of *Suneſſanum* hauing 300. Biſhops
preſent at it in ſuch time, when the King of the
Contry and Emperour of the world Diocletian
reigned and raged, the greateſt perſecutour of Chriſtians that euer was, & they aſſembled themſelues
againſt his will, and to keepe their meetinge vnknowne to him, kept their coucell in a ſecret Caue
of the earth, and thither entered not aboue 50. at
one time, it not able to receaue more together, at
one meetinge: theſe things thus agreed vpon, both
by Catholike and Proteſtant antiquaries, muſt
needs make vs all Catholiks in this point. As alſo
to ſee the firſt Chriſtian Kings and Emperours, ſo to
haue behaued themſelues in this matter, as Catholiks now profeſſe.

Britaine was made happy with the firſt Chriſtian
King, & holy S. King Lucius, who neuer tooke
vpon him any ſuch pretended ſpirituall power, but
ſo much honoured that true power in the Pope of
Rome, that by all antiquities, he ſent humble Am-
baſſadge and ſuppliant letters to the then Pope S.
Eleutherius to haue his Kingdome conuerted, and
Chri-

Chriſtian Religion ſetled here by his meanes, and
authority, and by him and his holy legates all ſuch
buſines was here eſtablished, ratified, & confirmed,
all hiſtorians forreine domeſticall, Catholike and
Proteſtāt ſo conſenting. Philipp was the firſt Chriſtian Emperour though a short time he was ſo
farre from arregating any ſuch power to him ſelfe,
or denying it to the Pope of Rome, that as Euſebius and others teſtifie, he did publike pennance,
euen among the common penitents at the Popes
enioyning it vnto him. *De Philippo fertur, quod cum*
Chriſtianus eſſet, & in die qua vltimæ Paſchatis vigi-
liæ ſeruabantur, in precationibus multitudini Eccleſia-
ſticæ tanquam conſors coniungi vellet, ab eo qui tum
Eccleſiæ præerat, admiſſum non eſſe niſi primum confite-
retur, & ijs ſe, qui propter peccata inquirebantur, & in
pœnitentiæ loco conſtituti erant, coniugeret. Alioqui
niſi hoc faceret, non fore ipſum admittendum, propterea
quòd in multis culpabilis eſſet: fertur itaque promptè
obediuiſſe, ſincerumque ac religioſum animum erga
Deum ipſis operibus declaraſſe.

This Pope as Nicephorus with others writeth
was Sainct Fabian, which ſo commaundeth the
firſt Chriſtian Emperour, and hee Chriſtianly and
dutifully obeyed him. When the firſt Nicen Councell againſt Arius, which is commonly reputed
for the firſt generall Councell, was called. That
greate glory of this Kingdome, borne here, Conſtantine the greate was Emperour, and although
he was the greateſt benefactour to the Church of
God, founder and dilatour of the honour and re-
nowne thereof, that enioyed the Empire, and hauing onely in his power then to permit ſo greate
aſſemblies of learned and holy Chriſtians Biſhops

Euſeb Eccl.
hiſt. l 6 ca. 33.
Nicephoras
Calliſt. l. 5. ca.
25.

Euſeb.lib.3.de
vit. Conſtan-
tini cap. 6.
as were preſent there, yet as Euſebius then liuing writeth, he called not the Biſhops together by his commaunde, as this article giueth to Kings, but wrote honorable letters vnto them to ſuch pur-
Ruffin. lib.1.
hiſt.cap.1.
poſe, *per literas honorifice ſcriptas.* And as Ruffinus a man alſo of that time expoundeth thoſe procee-dings vnto vs, this was as the Biſhops willed and di-rected : *ex Sacerdotum ſententia, apud vrbem Nicæ-*
Damaſus in
vit.Sylueſtri
Papæ.
nam Epiſcopale concilium. conuocat. And S. Damaſus an other old writer of the liues of the Popes ſaith expreſſely, it was called by the conſent of Sainct Sylueſter then Pope of Rome. *Huius temporibus factum eſt concilium, cum eius conſenſu, in Nicea Bi-*
Subſcript. in
Concil. Ni-
cæno in fine.
Euſeb. l.3. &
4. de vit.
Conſtantini.
thimiæ. Beſides it is euident in the authenticall ſubſ-cription to that holy Councell, that diuers Biſhops were preſent and ſubſcribed vnto it, out of Perſia, and other Kingdomes and contries where Con-ſtantine had no temporall commaund or dominion, and they which ſo then ruled in them were not Chriſtians at that time. So hath Euſebius & others when they ſay, that aſſembly was frō all Churches in Europe, Afrike, and Aſia, *ex omnibus Eccleſijs quæ frequentes in tota Europa Africa & Aſia extiterunt.*
Euſeb.l.3. de
vit. Conſtan-
tini.cap. 7.
Socrates Ec-
cleſiaſtic.hiſt.
l.1.c.5. Sozo-
men. hiſt. l.2.
c.6.7.8.9.10.
11.12.13.14.
And name diuers in particular, where Conſtantine had then no power by his owne relation, giuing ſtill the moſt he could to that Emperour in all re-ſpects.

This is euident alſo, by the exceeding greate deſire, which all good Biſhops in all places then had, to aſſemble in ſuch a councell, which could not be done at that time, perſecution ſcarcely yet ceaſed by inferiour rulers, and the Biſhops in greate pouerty, and diſtreſſe, by their late perſecu-tion, without the temporall helpe and allowance

of

of the Emperour, which being had, as Eusebius and others write, came together with greatest alacrity, and ioye, as men newly set at liberty out of prison. *Vbi edictum in quaque prouincia diuulgatum erat, omnes summa cum animorum alacritate tanquam è carceribus ad cursum emissi, properè aduolarunt.*

Euseb. l.3.de vit.Constant. cap.6.

This is proued by the greate temporall prouision of Horses, other beasts, and instruments of carriage: *in eare peragenda multum attulit subsidij authoritas Imperatoris, ac nutus, qui nonnullis fecit potestatem, equis publicè ad iter celeriter conficiendum dispositis vtendi: alijs permagnum iumentorum instratorum, quibus veherentur, numerum suppeditauit.* This is manifest by his prouision of the place of their assembly, with Seats, dyet, all necessaries in his owne palace, and he himselfe would not set downe vnlesse entreated, or vrged by the Bishops: *Non prius sedit, quam Episcopi ad id innuissent.* And to put it out of all contradiction, or question, that he onely vsed his temporall power in this busines, referring all spirirituall things to the Bishops, and nothing of that nature to himselfe, he did in open councell protest, and confesse, *that they had power from God to Iudge of Kings, and Emperours, and these no such power at all ouer Bishops.* None but God could Iudge them. They by God were constituted as Gods ouer men, no man could bee their Iudge. *Ait ad Episcopos: Deus vos constituit Sacerdotes, & potestatem vobis; dedit de nobis quoque iudicandi, & ideo nos à vobis, rectè iudicamur. Vos autem non potestis ab omnibus iudicari. Propter quod Dei solius inter vos expectate iudicium. Vos nobis à Deo dati estis dij, & conueniens non est vt homo iudicet Deos, sed ille solus de quo scriptum est. Deus stetit in Synagoga deorum, in medio autem Deos discernit. Mihi*

Euseb.sup. ca. 10. Socrates l. 2.hist.cap.5.

Ruffin. lib. 1. histor. cap. 2. Sozomen. hist.Eccl.l.1. cap. 16.

non

non est fas, cum homo sim, eiusmodi causarum cognitionem arrogare. Theodorit saith, that he would not sit downe vntill he had first asked and obtained leaue of the Bishops. *Paruo in soliolo posito assedit, præfatus veniam prius, & petita concessione ab Episcopis.* Hee did not intermeddle in defining or deecreing the Canons of that councell, but left that to the holy Bishops. And when they had giuen their sentence, and subscribed vnto it, being brought to the Emperour, he reuerenced it as the sentence of God, protesting to bannish whosoeuer should oppose against it, as contradicting the decrees of God. *Defertur ad Constantinum Sacerdotalis concilij sententia. Ille tanquam à Deo prolatam veneratur. Cui si quis tentasset obniti, velut contra diuina statuta venientem, in exilium se protestatur acturum.* Which he performed, to Arius and 6. others, all the rest subscribing. *Sex soli cum Ario se patiuntur expelli: reliqui vndecim, consilio inter se habito, acquiescunt ad subscribendum manu sola; non mente.* So he himselfe writeth in diuers epistles recorded by Eusebius, Socrates, Theodorit, and others neuer taking vpon him to be a Iudge, or commaunder in or ouer Ecclesiasticall men and matters. But wholly leauing such affaires to the councell of Bishops, protesting that in such times of controuersies, as that was, vnity of faith, sincere charity, and true worship in Religion could not be preserued, except either all or the greatest part of the Bishops should assemble together, and euery of them giue his Iudgment in things belonging to most holy Religion. *Vt in Sanctissima Catholicæ Ecclesiæ multitudine, vna fides, sincera charitas, & consentiens erga Deum omnipotentem religionis cultus seruaretur: Istud haud poterat in loco*

tuto

Theodorit.l.
1.hist.Eccl.
cap. 7.

Ruffin. hist.
Eccl. l.1. ca.5.
Sozom.hist.
Eccl.l.1. c 19.

Epist.Const.
apud Euseb. l.
3.de vita c.16.
17.18.Socrat.
lib.1.c.6. hist.
Theod or.
hist.lib.1.cap.
10.
Constant. ep.
ad Ecclesias
de Nic.Synodo apud Euseb.l.3.de vit.
Constant.ca.
16. & alios.

tuto firmoque collocari, nisi vel omnes Episcopi, vel maxima eorum pars in vnum conuenisset, singulique suum iudicium de rebus ad sacratissimam Religionem pertinentibus interposuissent.

And by this it also appeareth to whom the title, right and authoritatiue power of callinge councels, euen generall, which concerne the whole Catholike Church of Christ, belongeth: To no temporall King, Emperour, or Prince, as is manifest before, and in it selfe euident, when hitherto no such man had, or claimed any power spirituall, or temporall, in or ouer those contries and Kingdomes, from which came to many côfessed generall councels, hundreds of Bishops, and so wee should deny there euer was any one lawfull generall councell, when all agree there haue beene 20. or more, and our Protestant of England by publike Parlaments, Canons, statutes, decrees and practise haue receaued many for such. And so the Church of God hath euer from Christ beene destitute of this Soueraigne helpe, and so is now, and euer like to be in that desolate condition, in hauing no remedy to end the Controuersies which now be, and hereafter are to growe to the end of the world. For it is rashe and madde lyeing foolinesse, to affirme, or coniecture, that there either now is, or euer shall be, such an vniuersally ouerruling temporall Prince in the world. No spirituall Patriarke, or potentate of Antioche, Alexandria, Hierusalem, or Constantinople euer claymed this prerogatiue, and if they had, it could not possibly be their due.

Constantinople was not builded, when this first generall Councell was kept, and the Patriarkes

of

of them all haue beene either quite ouerthrowne, or very obſcure and wanting all meanes and power diuers hundreds of yeares, when many confeſſed generall Councels haue beene called and aſſembled. Mutuall aſſent without a Superiours commaunding ability is by experience vnpoſſible, an ordinary or equall Biſhop or Biſhops could not do it, hauing no iuriſdiction the one ouer the other *par in parem non habet authoritatem,* much leſſe ouer Superiours, whoſe preſence is more, and moſt requiſite and needfull in ſuch caſes, places and times. Therefore wee muſt of neceſſity cõfeſſe this power to be the peculiar right of the onely Popes of Rome for the times beeing. They in theſe and ſuch controuerſies, from the dayes of the Apoſtles, and by their order and allowance both claymed and practized; and ſo wee after ſo many hundreds of yeares in times of Controuerſie and contention may not deny it, eſpecially when denying it wee ſhall deny all hope, and meanes to decide and end the moſt daungerous debates in Religion. Pope Iulius in his epiſtle to Biſhops aſſembled at Antioche a patriarchall See, claymeth that Councels could not be called without the Pope of Rome, that the Eccleaſticall Canon was ſo, and decrees otherwiſe made were voyde: *Canon Eccleſiaſticus vetat, ne decreta abſque ſententia Epiſcopi Romani Eccleſijs ſanciantur. Legem eſſe ad Sacerdotij dignitatem ſpectantem, quæ pronunciat acta illa irrita eſſe, quæ præter ſententiam Epiſcopi Romani conſtituuntur.* And thoſe Biſhops themſelues in their common epiſtle acknowledge that the Church of Rome had primacy ouer all, and with all, as being the ſchoole of the Apoſtles and Metropolitaine City of piety, euen from the

Iulius Pap.ep. ad Epiſcopos Antiochiæ. Socrates hiſt. Eccl.l 2.c.13, Sozomen. hiſt. Eccl.l.2. cap. 9.

the beginning. *Literis suis fatebantur Ecclesiam Ro-manam Primas apud omnes ferre, vtpote quæ Apostolorum schola, & pietatis Metropolis (licet authores Religionis Christianæ primum ex oriente eo veniffent) iam ab initio fuiffet. Ecclesia Romana priuilegium præter cæteras obtinet.* And after, the City of Conſtantinople, being made Imperiall claymed the greateſt glory could be giuen vnto it, the Church of Rome was ſtill the cheife and primate euen by the Councell of Conſtantinople it ſelfe. *Decretum fuit, vt Episcopus Conſtantinopolitanus proximè & secundum Episcopum Romanum primas propterea obtinere, quod illa ciuitas noua Roma eſſet appellata.* Our Proteſtants themſelues acknowledge, that Sainct Marcellus Pope decreed longe before any generall Councell, that no Councell should be kept without the peculiar authority of the Pope of Rome. *Ne conciliũ ſine peculiari Pontificis authoritate haberetur ſtatuit.*

But S. Marcellus euen in the place theſe doe cite, deduceth this ſupreame authority to the Church of Rome euer ſince Sainct Peters coming thither, ſo writinge to the Bishops of Antioch yeelding when Sainct Peter was at Antioch, the primacy was there, but Sainct Peter coming from thence to Romè by Chriſts commaũde, *Iubente Domino,* his See and primacy was tranſlated thither. *Eius ſedes Romam tranſlata eſt.* And the See of Antioch at the firſt the cheifeſt thus yeelding to the See of Rome, euery other muſt needs be ſubiect vnto it. So were the decrees of the Apoſtles. Who alſo ordayned that noe Councell might be kept without the authority of that See, nor any Bishop iudged but in Councell called by that authority. *Si veſtra Antiochena, quæ olim prima erat, Romanæ ceſſet ſedi, nulla*

Epiſcopi Antiochiæ conuen. epiſt. ad Iulium Pap. Rom. Sozomen. hiſt. l. 2. cap. 7. Socrat. l. 2. c. 11. Concil. Conſtantin. 1. can. 5. Socrat. hiſt. l. 5. cap. 8.

Rob. Barnes lib. de vit. Pontif. Rom. in Marcello.

S. Marcell. ep. 1. ad Episcop. Antiochiæ Prouinciæ.

I

nulla est, quæ eius non subiecta sit ditioni, ad quam om-
nes quasi ad caput , iuxta Apostolorum eorumque Suc-
cessorum Sanctiones Episcopi, qui voluerint , vel qui-
bus necesse fuerit , suffugere, eamque appellare debent,
vt inde accipiant tuitionem & liberationem. Simulque
ijdem inspirante Domino constituerunt, vt nulla Syno-
dus fieret præter eiusdem sedis authoritatem, nec vllus
Episcopus,nisi in legitima Synodo, suo tempore Aposto-
lica authoritate conuocata, super quibuslibet criminibus
pulsatus audiatur vel iudicetur. Quia Episcoporum
iudicia , & summarum causarum negotia,siue cuncta
dubia, Apostolicæ Sedis authoritate sunt agenda & fi-
nienda. Et omnia comprouincialia negotia,huius sanctæ
vniuersalis Apostolicæ Ecclesiæ sunt retractanda iudi-
cio , si huius Ecclesiæ Pontifex præceperit. Sainct A-
lexander Pope,liuing in this first Apostolike age, is

witnesse, that Christ himselfe gaue this supreame
power to that Apostolike See.*Huic Sanctæ & Apo-*
stolicæ Sedi summarum dispositiones causarum & om-
nium negotia Ecclesiarum ab ipso Domino tradita sunt
*quasi ad caput.*So hath S.Anacletus before him,both
Catholike and Protestants so acknowledging. *Ab*
ipso Domino primatum Romanæ Ecclesiæ super omnes
Ecclesias vniuersumque Christiani nominis populum
concessum esse asseruit. The words of Sainct Anacletus are more large and plaine , then this Protestant
allowance is.

And to come againe, to the first generall Councell held at Nyce: first the Edict of Constantine his
donation and endowing the Romane Church, and
acknowledging therein as greate priuiledges to belonge to that Apostolike See, as any Pope, or
learned Catholike now giueth vnto it , was passed
by all writers before Constantine his seating himselfe

Alexander 1.
epist.1.
Anaclet.epist.
1.Robert.
Barn.l. de vit.
Pontif. Rom.
in Anacleto.
Edict. Conft.
10.1 Concil.
Isodor.Hisp.
in hist.Isod.
Iun.collect.
can.Adrian.1.
epist.ad Cost.
& Iren. 20.
Abrahã leuita
chron.Indiar.
R.Abraham
Aben Esra ad
cap.11. Da-
nielis. Am-
mian. Mar-
cellin.lib.27.

felfe in the eaft, and the callinge of the Nicen Councell.

This is manifeft, not onely by Chriftian antiquaries, too many to be cited, but Iewes and Pagans alfo. By that donation it is euident that neither the Nicen, nor any other fuch Councell, could be called without the allowāce of the Pope of Rome. fecondly in the Councell of Rome confifting of 284. Bifhops all fubfcribeing as Conftantine himfelfe prefent likewife did, by all their harts and hands, as greate primacy is graunted to that See as euer it claymed. *Nemo iudicabit primam* (*Romanam fedem*) *quoniam omnes fedes à prima fede iuftitiam defiderant temperari. Neque ab Augufto, neque ab omni clero, neque à Regibus, neque à Populo Iudex iudicabitur. Et Subfcripferunt 284. Epifcopi, & 45. Prefbyteri, & 5. Diaconi & Auguftus Conftantinus & mater eius Helena.* This was before the Nicen Councell by many arguments. Thirdly the Fathers of the Nicen Coūcell fent it in Latine to Pope Syluefter. *Placuit vt hæc omnia mitterentur ad Epifcopum vrbis Romæ Sylueftrum,* and he therein a Coūcell of 275. Bifhops thus confirmed it. *Syluefter Epifcopus Sanctæ & Apoftolicæ fedis vrbis Romæ dixit: quicquid in Nicæa Bithiniæ conftitutum eft ad robur fanctæ matris Ecclefiæ Catholicæ & Apoftolicæ à fanctis Sacerdotibus trecentis decem & octo, noftro ore conformiter confirmamus: omnes qui aufi fuerint diffoluere definitionem Sancti & magni Concily, quod apud Nicæam congregatum eft, anathematizamus, & dixerunt omnes, placet.* The Pope of Rome, the Imperiall City of the world had his Preifts there which fupplied his place. *Vrbis illius penes quam Imperium eft, Epifcopus ingrauefcente ætate præpeditus, abfuit: eius tamen pre-*

Concil. Rom: fub Syluestro can. 20.

Nicen. Conc: in præfat. ep. Concilij Niceni ad Syluestr. Concil. Rom. 3.

Eufeb. l. 3. de vit. Conftant: c. 7. Socrates. hift. l. 1. cap 5. Theodorit.

I 2   *sbyteri,*

Hift. l.1. ca.7.
Sozomen.
hift.l.1.c.16.

sbyteri, qui aderant, locum eius suppleuerunt. Their names were Vitus and Vincentius , *Vitus & Vincentius eiusdem Ecclesiæ Presbyteri, pro illo adfuere.* What it was for them being but onely Preifts, and not Bishops, to supply the place of the Pope of Rome , and to be present for him among so many Patriarks , Archbishops and Bishops, sufficiently declareth his dignity, and their cheife authority in Councell in that respect. Which these auncient Authours of that time haue proued before, assuring vs,that no Councell might be kept or decree made without the Bishops of Rome their allowance,and consent. This is proued also by the auncient copies and subscriptions of this first generall Councell, where these two Preifts Legats for the Pope of Rome subscribe for him , and by his power before all others Bishops , Archbishops or Patriarks present whatsoeuer *Victor*, or, *Victus* , *& Vincentius, Presbyteri vrbis Romæ, pro venerabili vno Papa & Episcopo nostro Syluestro* , *subscripsimus, ita credentes sicut scriptum est.*

And then after follow the subscriptions of the Bishops of Afrike, Asia, and Europe, The Bishops of Europe, wherein Rome is, beinge the last there in subscription, these Legates of the Pope, onely Preifts subscribeing first of all Europe Asia or Afrike , when of themselues as Preifts they had no place at all, without power, and authority from the Apostolike See of Rome , by which they had, and thus executed the cheifest, in that first cheife, and generall Christian Councell of the world, as it is commonly accompted, and by that title proposed as an example, and presidēt for those that followed. Which hath enforced me to continue my examination

tion of this part of this Proteſtant Article thus longe, in regard this Councell being ſo generally receaued by all, may be a paterne ſquare and rule vnto all in this kinde of Queſtion.

The pretended onely reaſon, which our Proteſtants before haue made, to proue that which followeth in this article, *That generall Councels may erre, & ſometimes haue erred, euen in things pertaining vnto God, being this: foraſmuch as they be an aſſembly of men, whereof all be not gouerned with the ſpirit and word of God*, is vaine, Idle, and to no purpoſe: for ſo wee might diſcredit and deny all thoſe Councels of the Apoſtles, and Diſciples of Chriſt before remembred, eſpecially all after the chooſing of the ſeuen Deacons, Sainct Stephen, and the reſt. For among theſe Nicolas authour of the Nicolaite hereſie, was one, and ſo being ſo vnworthy an heretike, may not be ſaid to haue beene allwayes gouerned with the ſpirit, and word of God. And not finding any other generall Councell from that time vntill the firſt of Nice, which our Proteſtants with generall applauſe receaue, and all the Canons and decrees thereof, being receiued by Parlaments, ſtatutes, communion bookes, Canons, articles before, and all authority they haue, wee may ſtill doubt, or plainely ſay rather that this erred euen in things pertaining vnto God, and the very nature of God himſelfe the bleſſed Trinity. And diuers others: for although, it conſiſted of the cheifeſt Prelates of all noble Churches in all Europe, Afrike, and Aſia, *ex omnibus Eccleſijs quæ frequentes in tota Europa, Africa & Aſia extiterunt, Dei miniſtri, qui facile primas ferre putabantur, in vnum conuocati:* all Patriarkes, either by themſelues or Legats were there, and the

Euſeb. l.3 de vit. Conſtant. cap 7. Socrat. Eccl. hiſt. l.1. cap. 5.

I 3   Em-

Emperour himſelfe, (for ſuch as require his con-ſent) yet they were all but an *aſſembly of men, where-of all were not gouerned with the ſpirit and word of God,* our Proteſtants goodly reaſon, for by all wri-ters there were 17. knowne Arian heretiks amõg them, and for ſuch diuers of them with Arius con-demned and exiled, at that time, and many more were abſent in greate number. And if wee should for this, or any other pretended reaſon, doubt of the truth of this men Councell, it were in vayne euer to labour our ſeeke to haue a true generall, and vn-doubted Councell, for a greater aſſembly and more likely to cõclude the truth, is not morally poſſible to be gathered. For beſides the Emperour, all the Patriarks, and aboue 306. Biſhops, there were learned Cleargy men there without number. *In hoc præſenti choro fuit Epiſcoporum multitudo ad nu-merum trecentorum & amplius: Presbyterorum autem, Diaconorum, acolithorum, & aliorum quiſtos comita-bantur, turba nec munerari quidem poteſt. Atque ex his Dei miniſtris alij prudenter & diſertè dicendo, alij vi-tæ grauitate, & conſtanti rerum arduarum perpeſſione, nonnulli quaſi media inter iſtos interiecta viuendi ra-tione extimij, præclara laudis inſignia adepti ſunt.*

Thus Euſebius there preſent, and others liuing in that time. And if in ciuill and morall bodies, ſuch as the Church, Councels, Diets, Parlaments and ſuch like aſſemblies compoſed of many and diuers perſons and conditions, are, wee should expect an vniuerſall and generall cõſent of men ſo aſſembled, wee shall finde there were or haue beene or can be very few or none ſuch in the world.

That firſt Parlament of Queene Elizabeth which ouerthrewe Catholike Religion, and ſet vp that

new

Ruffin. hiſt.
Eccl. l. 1. ca. 5.
Theodorit.
hiſt. l. 1. Sozo-
men. Eccl.
hiſt. l. 1. c. 19.

Socrates hiſt.
Eccl. l. 1. c. 5.
Euſeb. l. 3. de
vit. Conſtant.
cap. 9.

new profeſſion which profeſſeth and decreed the
articles, had but 4. or 5. voyces and ſuffrages more
for their new Religion, then were for the old, and
yet ſhee made ſo many new Proteſtant Lords for
that purpoſe, and vſed ſuch irreligious practiſes to
encreaſe the number for their new erection, as their
owne hiſtorians aboundantly haue teſtified. The
Roman and Catholike Church neuer proceeded
with ſuch poore ſhifts and ſmall difference of con-
ſents, either in the Councell of Trent againſt proteſtants, or any other former generall Councell, in
ſuppreſſing and condemning other heretiks and
their hereſies, as is euident in this firſt generall
Councell of Nice, where as before ſo many agreed,
and ſo few diſſented.

Cambd. hiſt.
Mar. Regin.
Scot. Stowe
hiſt. an. 1. Eli-
zab.

Conſtantine the great Emperour, if wee would
followe Proteſtants for Princes Supremacy, hath
before made the Iudgment and ſentence of the Nicen Councell, the Infallible Iudgment and ſentence
of God, and giueth the ſame infallibility to all ſuch
Councels, *Quicquid in Sanctis Epiſcoporum concilijs
decernitur, id vniuerſum diuinæ voluntati debet at-
tribui.* If wee will beleeue hundreds of learned Biſhops there aſſembled, ſo they teſtifie: *quæ ritè con-
ſtituta & decreta ſint, ea rata ſtabiliaque permaneant,
Dei Patris omnipotentis, & Domini noſtri Ieſu Chriſti
auxilio, vna cum Spiritus ſancti gratia.* And they A-
nathematized the reſiſters of their decrees: *Quibus
omnibus Sanctum Concilium indicit Anathema. Placuit
Concilio, communibus ſuffragijs Anathema denuntiare.*
It is euident by the 6. and 7. Canon of this Nicen
Councell that the Pope of Rome, Patriarke of Antioch, Alexandria, and by ſome Hieruſalem, had
Iuriſdiction ouer all Biſhops in the world, and they

Conſtant. ep.
ad Eccleſias
apud Socrat.
l. 1. hiſt. Eccl.
c. 6. Ruffin.
hiſt. l. 1. c. 10.
Epiſcopi Ni-
cæni Concil.
epiſt. ad Epiſ-
copos Ægyp-
tum, Libyam
& Pentacol.
incol Socrat.
ſupr. l. 1. ca. 6.
Theodorit. l.
1. hiſt. c. 9.

I 4   all

all aſſented, if they could haue aſſented to er-rour, the whole Church vnder them might haue erred.

Sainct Sylueſter Pope of Rome, as before, with 275. Biſhops confirmed that Councell in all points, anathematizing all gayneſayers vnto it. *Omnes qui auſi fuerint diſſoluere definitionem Sancti & magni Concily , quod apud Nicæam congregatum eſt, anathe-matizamus. Et dixerint omnes , placet.* Things con-cluded and confirmed for the whole Church by ſo many and greate authorities, and their deniall ſo ſeuerely puniſhed , muſt needs be of higheſt and vnfallible truth.

The Apoſtles themſelues in their Councels be-fore haue giuen vndoubted teſtimony to this if they had not by their Councels prefigured and giuen te-ſtimoy to the infallible verity of the decrees of ge-nerall Councels, Their ſo many aſſembles and Councels might haue beene ſpared, for whatſoeuer any one of them did , or ſhould haue decreed, was without queſtion true in matters of faith, other-wiſe wee might call all their ſacred writings & the whole new teſtament into queſtion.

The Apoſtolike men of the firſt age haue giuen like euidence before. And among them S. Ignatius who would haue ſuch councels often kept: *Crebrius celebrentur Conuentus Synodique :* doth make their decrees, and conſtitutions, of ſo greate and vnque-ſtionable power, and authority, that he which doth otherwiſe , *although he is in other things worthy of credit, although he faſteth, although he liueth in virgi-nity, doth miracles and propheſieth is to be accompted for a wolfe , which vnder a sheeps skin bringeth deſtru-ction and bane to the sheepe. Quicunque dixerit quip-*

piam

Ignat. epiſt. ad Polycarp. epiſt. ad Her.

piam præter ea quæ constituta sunt : tametsi fide dignus sit, quamuis ieiunet, quamuis in virginitate degat, quamuis signa edat, quamuis prophetet : pro lupo illum habeas, qui sub ouina pelle exitium, pestemque adfert ouibus. So vnpoſſible he maketh it, that ſuch decrees ſhould be vntrue. And the firſt Nicen Councell declaring, that a generall Councell is the Catholike Church, and reaſon ſo warrantinge, by errour of ſuch a Councell the whole Church might erre in articles of faith. And that article of our Creede, *I beleeue the holy Catholike Church,* euer moſt true, might be falſe at ſometimes : which is a thing moſt prophane, and Antichriſtian to be affirmed. For if a generall Councell repreſenting the whole Church, ruling, gouerning and teaching it in the cheifeſt Biſhops, and Paſtours there preſent, might erre, the whole Church both the Gouernours, and gouerned therein muſt needs be in the ſame deſolate eſtate. And our Proteſtant Biſhops and Doctours with their publike allowance, and approbation doe thus giue warrant vnto vs.

Concil. Nic. in Symbolo, apud Ruffin. l.1.hiſt.Eccl. c.5. Socrat.l.1. hiſt.c.6.

Engl. Proteſt. in Bilſon Suru.p.82. Morton.part. 2.Apolog.p. 340.l.4.c.18. feild p.228.

  The authority of generall Councels is moſt holſome in the Church. A generall Councell is higheſt Iudge. Biſhops aſſembled in a generall Councell haue authority to ſubiect euery man that ſhall diſobey ſuch determinations, as they conſent vpon, to excommunication, and cenſures of like nature. Wee muſt receaue and reſpect the authority of all Catholike Doctours, whoſe doctrine and writings the Church alloweth : wee muſt more regard the authority of Catholike Biſhops : more then theſe the authority of the Apoſtolike Churches: amongſt them more eſpecially the Church of Rome: of a generall Councell, more then all theſe. Falſe it is, that wee admitte no Iudge, but Scriptures, for wee appeale ſtill to a lawfull generall Councell.

L.4.c.5 pag. 202.

Sutcliff ag. D. Kell.pag.40.

This 42.

This being thus generally written with authority, and in the name of all Proteſtants, eſpecially in England, they muſt needs graunt, that generall Councels be of infallible Iudgmēt, in articles of religion, otherwiſe there is no meanes left to finde the truth, but wee might and muſt wander from one falſe & deceitfull rule to an other, without end. And ſeeing euery Court and Conſiſtory;frō which appeales are, or may be made, is inferiour, more vncertaine, and of leſſe authority, then that Seate of Iudgment to whom it is appealed, it is moſt certaine, by theſe Proteſtants themſelues, that they which neuer had, haue, or, as before, can haue hereafter any generall Councell, to which they muſt appeale, as they doe, cannot haue any poſſible title to true religion, for themſelues or the leaſt colour or pretence of Iuſtice or Religion for ſuch monſtrous, and horrible penalties, and cruelties, as are inflicted, to enforce the Catholiks, ſo many generall Councels, conſiſting of diuers hundreds of learned and holy Biſhops, or to perſwade them to embrace their Proteſtant profeſſions which neuer had any lawfull Biſhop according to this ſift Councell. *Illud generaliter clarum eſt, quod ſi quis præter ſententiam Metropolitani fuerit factus Epiſcopus, eum magna Synodus definiuit non eſſe Epiſcopum. That is generally manifeſt, that if any man is made a Biſhop againſt the will or likeing of the Metropolitane, this greate Councell, doth define that he is no Biſhop.* And ſo can make no Biſhop or Preiſt. So by this moſt holy Councell, ſo often and authoritatiuely receaued by our Engliſh Proteſtants, as is before declared, they neither haue nor poſſibly hereafter by their proceedings can haue any one Archbiſhop, Biſhop, Preiſt

Concil.Nic.
can.6.Ruffin.
l.1.hiſt Eccl.
in Concil.
Nicen.

or Cleargy man among them: for if their pretended manner of constitution were true, which wee haue inuincibly proued otherwise, yet they themselues, and all other writers confesse, they had not the assent, but vttermost dissent and disagreement of any domesticall or forreine Metropolitane for their new Religion or consecratio. But this sacred Councell euen in those Canons which our Protestants receaue, doth vtterly condemne the pretended consecration, and ministry of England erected against the Catholike sacrificing Preisthood, assuring vs, that true Preists did offer sacrifice and this Sacrifice was the body of Christ. *Presbyteri offerendi sacrificij habet potestatem. Offerunt corpus Christi.* It maintained the Popes Supremacy as before. It receaued more Scriptures then Protestants doe: *librum Iudith Synodus Nicæna in numero Sanctarum scripturarum legitur computasse.* It approueth Indulgences in 4. Canons: and giueth authority to Bishops in such cases. It forbiddeth Clergy men to keepe any women in their howses, but mother, Sister, grandmother, Aunt. They declared it to be the old tradition of the Church, that Ecclesiasticall men might not marry, and so commaunded. *Qui in clerum ante ascripti erant quàm duxissent, hi secundum veterem Ecclesiæ traditionem, deinceps à nuptijs se abstinerent.* By which the Protestants Church is vtterly disabled, and ouerthrowne, by their owne rule, and article, before, neither hauing the true word preached, Sacraments duely ministred, Church rightly gouerned, nor any one man among them to performe most needfull functions and duties, by their owne definitiue sentence.

Their conclusion of this article, *Things ordained by*

Marginal notes:

Nicen. Conc. can. 14.

Hieron. præf. in librum Iudith. Concil. Nic. can. 11. 13. 14. Can. 3.

Socrates hist. l. 2. c. 2. Sozomen. hist. Ecclef. l. 1. c. 22.

by generall Councels, as necessary vnto saluation haue neither strength, nor authority, vnlesse it may be declared, that they be taken out of holy Scriptures. This is aboundantly before confuted where I entreated of their article of Scriptures. So it is by that is deliuered in this Councell, which they wholy, and without any the least exception, admit. For in denyall of marriage vnto Cleargy men, it hath done it by the old Apostolike tradition of the Church, *secundum veterem Ecclesiæ traditionem.* So they doe in the true gouernment of the Church by the Pope, and Patriarkes. *Antiqua consuetudo. Antiqui mores. Mos antiquus. Seruetur, Seruentur. Consuetudo obtinuit, & antiqua traditio.* Yet true gouernment of the Church, is with them an essentiall property of the true Church, vnseperable, and so necessary to saluation. So is the true Cleargy and consecration as also the holy Sacrifice & Sacrament of the altar, really containing the body of Christ, yet by these men not to be declared by Scriptures, they finding no such thing in them.

And these Protestants themselues with publike allowance write : *Bishops assembled in a generall Councell haue authority, to interpret Scriptures, and by their authority to suppresse all them, that gaine say such interpretation.* Therefore if there were question of truely interpreting Scripture, Protestants must yeeld to generall Councels, and not these to them, particular Churches (if the Protestant was such) must of duty and necessity submit themselues to the vniuersall, and Apostlike Catholike, such as a generall Councell is, as the first Nicen Councell in the Creede thereof, which Protestants receaue, doth declare it selfe, and such generall Councels to

be,

Can. 6.7.

Protest. of Engl. in feild. libr. 4. of the Church pag. 228.

be, and so inflicteth censures. *Anathematizat Ca-*
tholica & Apostolica Ecclesia. Therefore wee are sure
a generall Councell cannot erre in expounding
Scriptures, or any decree of faith. That our Christian Britains were of this minde, opinion and profession, their Bishops with longe and tedious labours present at the greate primitiue Councels of
Arles, Sardice, Ariminum, and others by all witnesses, and with our King and Emperour at Nice,
in most probable Iudgment, also Rome, and the sacred Nicen Councell here then authentically receaued and embraced by all holy writers, giue
aboundant testimony.

Symb. Nicen.
Ruffin. lib. 1.
hist.c.5.Soc.l.
1.hist.c.6.

The X. Chapter.

The 22. Article thus likewise examined,
and condemned.

THE next article the 22. in number is intituled:
of *Purgatory.* And is thus. *The Romish doctrine*
concerning Purgatory, pardons, worshipping, and ado-
ration as well of Images, as of reliques, and also inuoca-
tion of Saincts, is a fond thing, vainely inuented, and
grounded vpon no warranty of Scripture, but rather
repugnant to the word of God. Much matter in few
words, many things peremptorily affirmed, nothing proued. All false, and foolish also, where as
they would haue all thing grounded vpon warranty of Scripture, so many times by thē affirmed,
and as often by me before confuted.

The doctrine
of Purgatory
prayer, and o-
ther satisfa-
ction for the
true faithfull
deceased
practised in
this first age.

And to take their assertions in order beginning
with their first, about the Romish (their phrase)
doctrine concerning Purgatory. This is thus set
downe

downe in the Councels of Florence and Trent : *If men truely penitent depart this life, in the loue of God, before they haue satisfied for their sinnes, their soules are purged with the paines of Purgatory. And that they may be releiued from such paines, the suffrages of the faithfull aliue, to wit, sacrifice of Masse, prayers and almes and other offices of piety, which by the faithfull are vsed for other faithfull people, according to the inſtitutions of the Church, doe profit them.* Definimus ſi verè pœnitentes in Dei charitate deceſſerint, antequam dignis pœnitentiæ fruƈtibus de commiſſis ſatisfecerint & omiſsis, eorum animas pænis Purgatorij purgari. Et vt à pœnis huiuſmodi releuentur, prodeſſe his viuorum fidelium ſuffragia, Miſſarum ſcilicet ſacrificio orationes, & eleemoſynas & pietatis officia, quæ à fidelibus pro alijs fidelibus fieri conſueuerunt, ſecundum Ecclesiæ inſtituta.

Concill. Flor.
Concill. Trid.
Seſsione 4.
can. 30.

Nor is this the Romish onely but alſo the Greekish and Catholike doctrine of the Church of Chriſt. So is affirmed by Gennadius their learned Patriarke in his defence of the recited Councell of Florence: *The doƈtrine of Purgatory, prayer and Sacrifice for the deade was a tradition of the Apoſtles. That which the Latines call purgatorium, purgatory, they of the Greeke Church name catharterion, a purging place. They were onely* Sciſmaticorum Seƈtatores, *followers of Sciſmatikes, which denied it.* This is likewiſe confeſſed by our English Proteſtants, and knowne vnto all trauaylers either into the contries, or writers of the Greekes. Now let vs ſee whether it was the doctrine of the Apoſtolike age, or noe.

Gēnad. Schol.
in defenſ. Cō-
cil. Florent.
def. 5. cap. 3.

Relation of
Relig. c. 53.54.
55.

The Greeke Patriarke hath before affirmed it, So will our Proteſtants hereafter. And the Apoſtolike

ſtolike men of this age affirme and proue it. Sainct
Clement ſaith his Maſter and predeceſſour Sainct Clem. Rom.
Peter among other things did teach, *mortuos ſepe-* Epiſt. 1.
lire, & diligenter eorum exequias peragere, proque eis
orare, & eleemoſynas dare. To bury the deade, and diligently performe their funerals, and pray, and giue almes
for them. He deliuereth further how in their publike Conſtitut. A-
Church ſeruice, and Sacrifice of that time, among poſt. l.8.c.19,
their prayers for other neceſſaries, they prayed for
the faithfull departed out of this world. *Pro ijs, qui*
in fide quieuerunt, oremus.

And from Iames Alphæus named the Brother
of our Lord, *frater Domini*, he ſetteth downe the
manner how the Deacon vſed publikely to giue
warning in the time of the holy Sacrifice, to pray
for the ſoules of the faithfull deceaſed, deliuering
the very prayer commonly vſed in ſuch caſes, directly proueing a place of Purgatory, and prayer for
the deliuery of the faithfull departed from thence,
with a remiſſion of all puniſhment, they had de-
ſerued, and were to ſuffer, vntill they were by ſuch
meanes freed thereof. *Pro defunctis qui in Chriſto re-* L.8.ſupr. cap.
quieuerunt, poſtquam Diaconus edixit, orandum eſſe, 47. iuxt. al.
adiunget etiam hæc: oremus pro fratribus noſtris qui in 40. & 41.
Chriſto requieuerunt, vt Deus ſummæ erga homines
charitatis, qui animam defuncti ſuſcepit, remittat ei
omne peccatum voluntarium, & non voluntarium, &
propitius illi factus, collocet eam in regione piorum qui
laxati ſunt, in ſinu Abrahæ, Iſaac, & Iacob, cum omni-
bus qui à ſæculo condito Deo placuerunt, vnde fugit do-
lor, mæror & gemitus. And againe: *ipſe nunc reſpice*
hunc ſeruum tuum, quem in aliam ſortem elegiſti &
aſſumpſiſti, & condona ei, ſi quid tum volens, tum no-
lens peccauit: & exhibe ei Angelos beneuolos, ac colloca

eum in sinu Patriarcharum, & Prophetarum, atque A-
postolorum. And expresseth plainely, that such holy
prayers, Sacrifice, almes, and the like workes of
piety, did onely helpe and profit such, as the Catholike Councels haue before deliuered, and Catholiks performe such duties for, dying in state of

Cap. 49.   grace, not yet hauing satisfied for their sinnes. *Sed*
hæc de pys dicimus: impios enim tametsi omnia bona ex-
terna pro eis largiaris, nihil iuuare queas. And punctually remembreth diuers solemne times to pray,

Cap. 48.   especially for such. The third day, neenth day,
fourteth day and the yeares day or their deathes,
then vsed. *Exequiæ mortuorum fiant tertio die, die*
nono, quadragesimo, item anno exacto, ad habendam
memoriam ipsius defuncti, & suppeditetur ex bonis eius

Cap. 50.   *pauperibus ad recordationem eiusdem.* The like he
hath in other places. Sainct Denis the Areopagite
speaketh as plainely in this matter, and affirmeth
that this manner of praying for the deade, dying in
state of grace was both an Apostolicall tradition,
and warranted by holy Scriptures. Speaking of the
faithfull deceased, and the ceremonies of the liuing
for them, *he saith the Preists powreth fourth his most*
holy prayer for him that is departed this life. Accedens
diuinus præsul, precem super eo sacratissimam fundit.
And repeating the same againe, he setteth downe,
how all saluted the deade, and prayed for him, or
them, and their prayer was, *that God would remit*
them all their sinnes which by humane frailty they had
committed, and place them in the light and region of the

Dion. Areop.   *liuing, in the bosomes of Abraham, and Isaac, and Ia-*
l.de Ecclef.   *cob, in the place from whence all greefe, sadnesse and*
Hierarch.c.7.   *groneing flyeth away. Accedens diuinus Antistes pre-*
cem suam super mortuum peragit: postquam precem, &
ipse

ipſe eum præſul ſalutat, & ſuo deinceps ordine qui aſtant omnes. Precatur oratio illa, diuinam bonitatem, vt cuncta dimittat per infirmitatem humanam admiſſa peccata defuncto: eumque in luce ſtatuat, & regione vi-uorum, in ſinibus Abrahæ, & Iſaac, & Iacob, in loco vnde aufugit dolor, & triſtitia, & gemitus. And ex-poundeth this Boſome of Abraham, whither the faithfull are tranſlated by the prayers, and other good deeds of the liuing, from the place of puniſh-ment or Purgatory, where they were beforeto the eternall felicity in heauen, as Catholiks now hold and teach. *Sinus autem beatorum Patriarcharum reli-quorumque ſanctorum omnium, vt reor, diuiniſſimæ ac beatiſſimæ ſedes, quæ deiformes omnes ſuſcipiunt, in-ſeneſcibili, & beatiſſima perfectione.* And there hee ſolueth that pretended exception, which our Pro-teſtants make againſt this Apoſtolike doctrine, & practiſe, becauſe they ſuppoſe the ſoules of theſe faithfull deceaſed to be without all hope, to goe to any other place, then that they are receaued in, when they are newly ſeperated from their bodies, and the center of all for euer to be after death as their liues and actions were in this world, and he affirmeth that the prayers of the iuſt doe as well helpe thoſe, that are deade, being worthy of ſuch prayers, in the time of their life, as the liuing, and the true traditions of the Scriptures ſo teach vs. *Ve-rùm, inquies fortaſſis, hæc quidem rectè à nobis dicta eſſe; ſed te dubitare, cur à diuina bonitate poſtulet An-tiſtes mortuo peccatorum remiſſionem, & parem San-ctis ac lucidiſſimam hæreditatem. Si enim vnuſquiſque præmia conſequetur a diuina iuſtitia, eorum bonorum aut malorum quæ in hac vita geßit; perfecit autem is qui defunctus eſt huic vitæ conſentaneas actiones: qua-*

K   *nam*

nam Antistitis orationis in aliam quietis sedem migrabit, præter eam quæ ipso digna, est, & quæ vitæ hic actæ respondet? equidem probe scio, scriptis diuinis insistens, vnumquemque remuneratitiam sortem adepturum. Conclusit enim, inquit, Dominus apud se: & referet vnusquisque ea quæ per corpus gessit, siue bonum siue malum. Quod autem & iustorum preces etiam in hac vita, nedum post mortem, ijs solùm prosint, qui digni sunt sacris precibus, Scripturarum nos edocent veræ traditiones. He teacheth as Sainct Clement hath done before, that this manner of praying and doing other workes of piety, for the deade, was vsed and auayle able for true beleeuing Christians onely, which died in the state of grace. *Prophanis vita functis hæc non precatur: non modo quia in hoc diuinitus acceptum desereret ordinem, & aliquid Hierarchicum contumaciter præsumeret non motus à cæremoniarum conditore, sed quia in execrabili oratione non exaudiretur, atque non immeritò ipse audiret oraculum illud iustitiæ plenum: petitis, & non accipitis, quia malè peti-*

Iacob.c.4.

tis. Wee reade that Sainct Phocas a miraculous Sainct of this time, did acknowledge two lower places, one of the damned, the other must needs be Purgatory, when prophetically foretelling the death of Traian, by whom he was martyred, to fol-

S.Phocus ad Traianum. Walter. Rollwinke fascic. Tempor. in Traian.

lowe, *within three dayes, as it did,* he told him that he *was to goe to the parts of the furthest deepe place, where he should be in perpetuall darkenesse, and burned with cruell fire for euer. Traiane perge ad Vlterioris abissi loca, & ad præparata tibi tormenta festina, vbi nocte perpetua, & sæuo exurendus es incendio.*

This he spake by the spirit of God prophetically, & cõsequẽtly truely: *cui spiritu prophetico dixit.* This was the doctrine, and practise of the whole Church

of

of God expreſſed, and profeſſed in the moſt aunciēt
liturgies, and publike Maſſes, aſcribed to the holy
Apoſtles, then publikely vſed. In the Maſſe of S. *Miſſa S. Ia-*
Iames called the leſſer, Biſhop of Hieruſalem wee *cobi.*
finde this prayer: *pro requie antè defunctorum, & Pa-*
trum, & fratrum, Dominum oremus. Let vs pray to our
Lord for the reſt of them that be already departed this
life, our fathers and brothers.

That God will graunt their *oblation to be acceptable,*
for propitiation of ſinnes, and ignorances, and reſt of the
ſoules of them that be deâde before vs. Fac vt oblatio
noſtra acceptabilis ſit, ſanctificata in Spiritu ſancto, in
propitiationem noſtrorum peccatorum, & ignorantiarum
populi, & in requiem animarum eorum, qui ante nos
dormierunt. Memento Domine Deus ſpirituum & vni-
uerſæ carnis, quorum memoriam egimus, & quorum
memoriam non egimus, orthodoxorum, ab Abeliuſto vſ-
que in hodiernum diem. Ipſe ibi fac eos requieſcere in re-
gione viuentium; in regno tuo, in delicijs Paradiſi in ſi-
nu Abrahæ, & Iſaac, & Iacob, ſanctorum Patrum
noſtrorum, vnde exulat dolor, triſtitia & gemitus, vbi
luſtrat lumen vultus tui, & refulget perpetuo. Pro re-
quie patrum, & fratrum noſtrorum, qui ante nos dor-
mierunt, dicamus omnes toto animo, Domine miſe-
rere.

The like hath the liturgy of Sainct Matthew: *Miſſa S. Mat-*
Memento Domine omnium fidelium dormientium, & in *thæi.*
ſigno rectæ fidei quieſcentium, Domine Deus noſter me-
mento dormientium, & in recta fide quieſcentium. So *Miſſa S. Mar-*
is the Maſſe of Sainct Marke : *animabus patrum &* *ci.*
fratrum noſtrorum, qui antea Chriſti in fide obdormie-
runt, dona requiem Domine Deus noſter. And relating
how it was the vſe to reade the cataloge of ſuch deceaſed, and then to pray thus for all their ſoules. *Ho-*

rum

Chrysostom.
Hom.3.in c.1.
ad Philipp.
Hom.ad pop.
Anthiochen.
Hom.41.in
1.Cor.cap.15.
Epiph. hær.
75. Tertull. l.
de coron. mi-
lit. c.3. cap.4.
Auguſt. En-
chirid. c.100.
de ciuit.Dei l.
21.c.24.
l. de cur. pro
mart. de ver-
bis Apoſtoli
ſerm.32.lſod.
l.1. de offic.
Eccl.c.18.A-
mal.l.1 c.27.
Epiphan. l. de
hæreſ.& c 53.
Philaſtr.l.de
hær. Middlet.
Papiſtom. pa.
49.137.138.
47.64.45.
46.51. feild l.
3.c.19. p.138.
Couel. Exam.
p.114.Middl.
ſupr. pag. 51.
Morton.A-
pol.part .1. p.
329.Caluin.
apud eund.ib.
Perkins pro-
blemat. pag.
178.

rum omnium animabus da requiem , Domine Deus noſter, in ſanctis tuis tabernaculis, in regno tuo , largiens
eis promiſsionum tuarum bona quæ oculus non vidit, &
auris non audiuit , & in cor hominis non aſcenderunt,
quæ præparaſti Deus, diligētibus ſanctum nomen tuum:
eorum, inquam, animabus dona requiem , easque regno
cælorum dignare.

All other auncient publike liturgies and Maſſes
of all natiōs agree herein. The beſt learned Fathers
both of the Greeke and Latine Church doe aſſure
vs, it was a tradition of the Apoſtles , and receaued
and practiſed in the whole Church. Ab Apoſtolis
ſancitum eſt, vt in celebratione venerandorum myſteriorum memoria fiat eorum qui hinc deceſſerunt. Qui
ante nos teſtes fuerunt, habentes ante nos traditionem in
Eccleſia, quique etiam à patribus ſuis traditam acceperunt , quemadmodum etiam hi a ſuis patribus didice-
runt. Pro peccatoribus facimus memoriam, pro peccatoribus miſericordiam Dei implorantes. Eccleſia neceſſa-
riò hoc perficit traditione à patribus accepta. Quis autem
poterit ſtatutum matris diſſoluere, aut legem patris? Sacrificium pro defunctorum fidelium requie offerre , vel
pro eis orare, quia per totum hoc orbem cuſtoditur, credimus quod ab ipſis traditum ſit, hoc enim vbique Catholica tenet Eccleſia.

This was ſo generally receaued, and confeſſed
doctrine, practiſed in all times and places, That vntill Aërius the heretike in the dayes of Conſtantine, no man denied it , and he for his ſingular deniall thereof, was and is condemned of hereſie, with
all his followers. This is a truth ſo euident, that our
Proteſtant writers doe with their publike warrant
thus acknowledge it. The primatiue Church did offer
ſacrifice at the altar for the deade. Sacrifice for the deade

was

was a tradition of the *Apostles*, and the auncient Fathers. *Sainct Chrysostome* taught it to be the *Apostles* ordinance to pray for the deade. *Aerius condemned the custome of the Church in naming the deade at the altare*, and offering the sacrifice of *Eucharist* for them : and for this his rash and inconsiderate boldnesse, and presumption in condemning the vniuersall Church of *Christ*, he was iustly condemned. In the *Masses* or liturgies of *Basile, Chrysostome* and *Epiphanius*, the deade were prayed for. *Ipsi veteres preces fundebant pro defunctis.* The auncient Fathers powred out their prayers for the deade. *Dionysius* (the *Areopagite, Sainct Paules* scholler) taught that sinnes are purged in purgatory. *In purgatorio expiari peccata.*

The prayer made for the departed doth beseech the diuine Clemency, to forgiue the party deceased all sinnes committed by humane infirmity. *Oratio illa precatur diuinam clementiam, vt cuncta dimittat per infirmitatem humanam admissa peccata, defuncto.* If wee should giue any respect to the Iewes, Mahometans and such, to make this a receaued opinion of all the world, they euer held, hold and practise prayer, and such workes for the deade. Coccius tom. 2.l.7.artic.5.

Now wee need not doubt but this so publike and common truth was also brought into Britaine, and here practized and taught by our first Fathers in Religion. Whosoeuer they were the Apostles or their disciples from Hierusalem, Rome or what Apostolike place else they held professed and taught the Apostles doctrine and tradition and vsed their liturgies: if from Hierusalem, that of S. Iames where the deade are so often prayed for, and the sacrifice of Masse offered for them. And where there was a particular Church, in the first dayes of Chri-

K 3 stianity

Bed.libel.de
locis Sanctis
Arnulphus &
Adama. ib. &
l.5.hift.Eccl.

ftianity as S. Bede from antiquity *fequens veterum
monumenta*, with others affureth vs, *in qua fuper altare pro defunctis facrificium folet fieri, pofitis interim
in platea corporibus*, in which Church facrifice was
vfed to be offered for the deade, their bodies in the
meane time remaining in the ftreete. But becaufe
I haue inuincibly proued in my Ecclefiafticall hiftory, and it is not to be denied but our conuerfion
was by S.Peter & his Church of Rome, wee muft

Manufcript.
antiq princip.
ftores.

needs fay with our old Brittish manufcript written
in the Britains time, that his Maffe and the Maffe
of S. Marke his Scholler, came into thefe parts and
were vfed here. And no man, Proteftant or other
finding yet that the prayer in the Romane Maffe

Miffa S. Petri
in Canone.

was added by any, *Memento Domine famulorum famularumque tuarum qui nos præcefferunt cum figno
fidei & dormiunt in fomno pacis. Ipfis Domine & omnibus in Chrifto quiefcentibus, locum refrigerij, locis &
pacis, vt indulgeas deprecamur*, and the Maffe of S.
Marke being fo manifeft as before for this religious doctrine and practife, wee muft needs fay
this was the profeffion and cuftome of our Chriftian Britans from their firft inftruction in the faith
of Chrift. To this old monuments of our moft
auncient and renowned Church of Glaftenbury
giue ample teftimony, when affuring vs, that thou-

Antiquit.
glaft.

fands of Brittish Chriftians *millia dormientium* were
buried there aboue a thoufand yeares fince, they
giue thefe reafons of the religious defires of good
people to be buried there : *quia omnibus hic fepultis
per Sanctorum inibi requiefcentium preces & merita,
creditur magna peccatorum remiffio à Domino conceffa.
Propter Miffas & alias orationes quæ quotidie pro eis
dicuntur*, becaufe thofe that were buried there had
greate

great pardon by the merits of the Saincts, and their praiers resting there, and the Masses and prayers there dayly offered for the dead there buried. Wee finde in the old antiquities of landaffe a Publike Charter of King *Mauricus in S. Dubritius* his time, that it was the old custome and duty of Churches, daily to pray for the soules of the benefactours deceased, and all the faithfull departed out of this life: *oratione quotidiana & Ecclesiastico seruitio pro anima illius & animabus parentum suorum Regum & Principum Britanniæ, & omnium fidelium defunctorum.*

So is the charter of King Arthur to the schoole of Cambredge , *pro remedio animarum antecessorum meorum Regum Britanniæ.* Sainct Gildas our oldest writer, and greate diuine did daily pray for the soule of his brother being slaine. *Orabat pro spiritu fraterno quotidie.* Sainct Patrike prayed for the dead *orauit pro anima eius.* S. Iltutus appointed 50. of his schollers to pray for the soules of the deade continually. *Constituit quinquaginta fratres, qui continuam animarum memoriam haberent.*

And as I haue spoken before , how the first Christians at Hierusalem had a particular Church founded, and employed to that holy vse. So our Christians Britans insisting in the same deuotion from the beginning , had diuers such foundations and Churches especially to offer sacrifice, and pray for the deade. One of them was at london. *Ecclesiam ædificauerunt, in quo pro ipso (Rege) & fidelibus defunctis, diuina celebrantur obsequia.* And this is sufficient for this question.

The next exception, which is taken by our Protestants in this article, is against the Catholike doctrine about pardons, or Indulgences, saying, as they

Manuscript. antiq.de primo statu Landauen.Ecclesię.

Chart.priuileg.Reg. Arthuri apud Caium l.1. antiquit. Cantabrig.pag. 60. 70. Caratoc. hist. M. S. de vita S.Gildel Probus l.2.de vit. S. Patricij. Caius l.1.sup. p 147. 148. l de vit.Sact. Wallię in S. Iltuto.

Galfrid. Monum. hist. Reg.Briton. l. 12 c.13.

The Catholike doctrine of pardons & Indulgences.

they haue done already, of Purgatory, *that the Ro-mish doctrine concerning pardons, is a fonde thing, vai-nely inuented, and grounded vpon no warranty of Scripture, but rather repugnant to the word of God.* The Councell of Trent setteth downe the Catholike doctrine in this point, which these men call the Romish doctrine, that power of graunting indulgences was by Chrift graunted to his Church, and the Church in the most auncient times vsed it, by so great warrant, and therefore declareth the vse of Indulgences to be retained in the Church, as neceffary for Chriftian people, and allowed by the authority of holy Councels, anathematizing them, which affirme them to be vnprofitable, or deny there is power in the Church to graunt them. *Cum poteftas conferendi Indulgentias, à Chrifto Ecclefiæ con-ceffa fit; atque huiufmodi poteftate, diuinitùs tradita antiquifsimis etiam temporibus, illa vfa fuerit: Sacro-fancta Synodus, indulgentiarum vfum Chriftiano po-pulo maximè falutarem, & facrorum conciliorum au-thoritate probatum, in Ecclefia retinendum effe docet, & præcipit: eofque anathemate damnat, qui aut inuti-les effe afferunt, vel eas concedendi, in Ecclefia potefta-tem effe negant.*

Conc. Trid. feff. 9. in dé-creto de In-dulgentijs.

The fame holy Coûcell with all good Catholiks as much côdemneth abufes in pardons or Indulgêces, and as wifely preuenteth them, as any enemy of Indulgences doth, euer did, or can defire.

That there this power of graunting pardons and Indulgences for remitting the temporall punishment, due to finne, is firft euident by that is faid of the paines and punishment of purgatory before. For no man will or can deny but if the Church hath power or meanes to remit paines, to them that be deceafed,

deceased, and out of the state of meriting, in themselues, much rather it hath such power and reme-
dies for the liuing which by themselues may, and
doe merit, and are in all respects parts and subiects
of the militant Church of Christ.

Secondly whereas this Protestant article saith
pardons haue no warranty of Scripture, but rather
repugnant to the word of God. The Apostolike
Fathers of this first age haue taught vs otherwise
before, euen of the paines of Purgatory. And the
Scripture is cleare both that Christ did graunt this
power to his Church, and the Church practized it
in the Apostles time. Of this power of remitting
sinnes, and their punishment, Christ must needs
meane when he said to S. Peter, he would giue   Matth.c.16.
vnto him the keyes of the Kingdome of heauen,
and whatsoeuer he should loose on earth should be
loosed in heauen. *Tibi dabo claues regni cælorum. Et
quodcumque solueris super terram, erit solutum & in
cælis.* So when he said to all his Apostles, *What-*   Matth.18.
*soeuer you shall loose on earth shall be loosed in heauen.
Quæcunque solueritis super terram, erunt soluta & in*   Ioh.cap.20.
*cœlo. And againe, whose sinnes you forgiue they are
forgiuen vnto them. Quorum remiseritis peccata, remittuntur eis.*

And that wee may be assured, these words and
warrants of Christ did carry this construction, and
giue this power, and not onely to the then present
Apostles but their Successours, and Rulers in his
Church for euer, first Sainct Paul who was not an
Apostle, Preist nor Christian then at the giuing of
this commission, nor there present, did thus expounde it, and practise it. For first excommunica-
ting the wicked Corinthian which had committed   1. Cor. 5.
                               sinne

finne with his Fathers wife, his mother in lawe, a finne both in Catholiks and Proteftants Iudgment deferuing greate and longe pennance, and punifhment, he foone after wrote vnto them againe to giue him pardon and indulgéce for the punifhment thereof, *donetis*, or *condonetis*, *cui donaftis*, or *condonaftis & ego*, & *ego donaui* or *condonaui in perfona Chrifti*, S. Paul gaue pardon in the perfon of Chrift, and the Church of Corinth did the fame by the fame warrant and authority.

So the learned holy Fathers after expound it, with the Churches approbation : *cui aliquid donaftis. Pro donaueritis, & ego.* Sicut *vobifcum vindicaui, ita & vobifcum dono. Nam, Et ego quod donaui. Non in mea perfona; fed Chrifti, qui dixit, quæ folueritis in terra, erunt foluta & in cœlo. Si quid donaui propter vos. Ne grauemini. In perfona Chrifti. Quia perfonam gerimus Chrifti.* And both the Greeke and Latine Church euer from the beginning expound thofe words of Chrift in the Ghofpell before cited, as I haue done. And our Proteftants themfelues doe the like making thofe words of Chrift in S. Ihons Ghofpell to be the forme and manner to make their pretended Bifhops and minifters, their pretended cófecratours, faying to all fuch at their admittance, thefe words: *Take the holy Ghoft, whofe finnes you forgiue they are forgiuen vnto them, and whofe you retaine they are retained.* And thereby claime as ample warrant and power as any Prieft, Bifhop, Prelate or Pope doth or euer did, both to abfolue from finnes, and pardon and giue Indulgence, for all paine, and punifhment in any wife due or belonging to any finne, or finnes, how many or enormeous foeuer they be, and by the greateft

au-

2. Cor. 2.

Primafius in c. 2. epift 2. ad Corinth. Aug.l. 2. cótr. epift. parmen. c. 11. Chryf. Homil. 5. de verb. Ifaię vidi Dom. l 3. de Sacerdorio. Eufeb. Emiffen. hom. in dom. 19. poft Pentecoft. Hilar. can. 18. in Matth. Paciá. epiftol. 1. ad Simpronian. Nouatian. Aug l. 50. homil. hom. 40 27. l. 20. ciuit. cap. 9. Engl. prot. Booke of Ordinat.

authority in their Religion presume to practise it
in such manner. For absolution and pardoning of
all sinnes they haue the warrant of as many Parlaments as they haue kept since Queene Maryes
time, all the Reigne of Queene Elizabeth: King
Iames and Charles all their books of articles, Canons, Iniunctions, and generall practise of their
congregation Protestant in England now about
70. yeares allowing and exercising publikely their
communion booke, vtterly and vnder greate penalties forbidding all other Rituals or Church seruice, in this euery minister doth may or is bound
thus to say to men confessing their sinnes vnto
them. *Our Lord Iesus Christ hath left power to his*   Protest. Com-
Church to absolue all sinners which truely repent and be-   muniō booke
leeue in him, and by his authority committed to me, I   Titul. visita-
absolue thee from all thy sinnes, in the name of the Father,   tion of the
and of the sonne and of the holy Ghost, Amen.   Sicke.

King Iames Supreame heade of their Church,
in his Prouinciall Councell, or conference, with
his Protestant Bishops and Doctours thus defineth
or declareth. *The particular and personall absolu-*   King Iames
tion from sinne after confession, is Apostolicall, and a   and Protest.
very godly ordinance. Where wee see, that euery   Bishops at
Parish pretended Preist, or minister with our Pro-   Hampton.
testants (for so their directory is) may, and ought   confer. p. 13.
by their Religion, attempt to giue plenary pardōs,
and Indulgences, in as ample, or rather more ample, and illimited manner then any Pope did. For
by their religion this is to be or may be executed by
any minister to any penitent whomesoeuer without any restriction, and from all sinnes and puni-
shments due to them, which is most manifest by
their last assertion and doctrine of denying purgatory

tory and prayer for the deade, onely conftituting two places for the deceafed, hell and heauen, and teaching that euery penitent fo abfolued, and receauing Indulgence from them, fo dying doth immediately goe to heauen, and fo of neceffity by their doctrine and practife, they muft needs hold, that they giue plenary Indulgence to euery fuch confeffing penitent. This they confirme further, proue, & practife in all their Ecclefiafticall Courts, where they inflict, and continue, or at their pleafure forgiue, pardon and giue Indulgence of all punifhments and paines for finne. This they proteft and declare with their publike authority in their Church feruice, *diuers times in the yeare, their publike direction and commaunde, openly in their Churches thus pronouncing : Brethren in the primatiue Church there was a goodly difcipline, that at the beginning of lent, fuch parfons as were notorious finners were put to ope pennace, & punifhed in this world, that their foules might be faued in the day of the Lord: and that other admonifhed by their example, might be the more afraide to offend: it were much to be wifhed, the faid difcipline may be reftored againe.* And this booke of articles it felfe in the 33. article hath, how after temporall pennance arbitrary by a Iudge hauing authority, who may affigne more or leffe, longer or fhorter, remit and pardon fome or all, the greateft finners euen excommunicated, are to haue Indulgence, pardon, and abfolution. Our Proteftant Parlaments, and Religion doe expreffely receaue the firft Nicen Councell, wherein the doctrine of Indulgences, & practife of them is as expreffely approued, and calleth it the auncient and canonicall law, *antiqua & canonica lex feruabitur,* and to be obferued, and they

leaue

Proteft. Communiō booke Tit. a Commination againft finners.

Proteft. artic. of Relig. art.

Parlament. 1. Elizabeth.
Concil. Nic. 1. c. 12. 11.

leaue it in the power of the Bishop to be Iudge, when and how they are to be vſed, *licebit Epiſcopo humanius aliquid de cis ſtatuere.*

And their priuate writers both in their publike ſermons, and bookes publiſhed with authority, and for which ſome haue beene made Biſhops among them, doe thus confirme it. *As there is a death in ſinne, and a death to ſinne, ſo there is a double reſurrection: the firſt à culpa from ſinne: the ſecond à pœna, from the puniſhment which followeth thereupon. The true Church admitteth and receaueth all, that with ſorrowfull repentance returne, and ſeeke reconciliation, how greate ſoeuer their offences haue beene: not forgetting to vſe due ſeuerity, which yet ſhe ſometime remitteth. The auncient Biſhops were wont to cut of greate parts of enioyned pennance: which remiſsion and relaxation was called an Indulgence.* Theoph higg. ſer. 3. Mart. an. 1610.

Feild bookes of the Church l. 1. c. 17. p. 33.

The like haue others, and among other reaſons and authorities for this old cuſtome, and doctrine they cite and expounde as Catholiks doe, the practiſe and place of S. Paul to the Corinthians before alleadged. Therefore hauing ſo ample and euident teſtimony, and confeſſion of our Proteſtants in this point, wee may be more breife in relating the Fathers of this Apoſtolike age, the doctrine in queſtion being by all euen aduerſaries thus confeſſed to haue beene deliuered by Chriſt, Apoſtolicall and Godly. Firſt to begin with the See of Rome Sainct Clement and many others are worthy witneſſes, that Sainct Peter the Apoſtle left vnto him his Succeſſour in the Roman See this power, in as ample maner as Chriſt communicated it vnto Sainct Peter, and calleth it a rule of the Church, *Ipſi trado à Domino mihi traditam poteſtatem ligandi* Feild ſupr. l. 1. c. 17. 1. Cor. 2. v. 8. 9. 10.

Clem. Rom. epiſt. 1. Leo 2. in epiſt. decret. Marian. Scot. l. 2 ætat. 6. Flor. Wigorniē chron. in Siluan. & Otho. Conſ.

ligandi & soluendi, vt de omnibus quibuscumque de-
creuerit in terris, hoc decretum sit & in cœlis Ligabit
enim, quod oportet ligari, & soluet quod expedit solui,
tanquam qui ad liquidum Ecclesiæ regulam nouerit.

And for all Bishops he setteth downe, from the
Apostles order, that all Bishops should vse mercy

Clem. Conft.
Apoft. lib.2.c.
13. 12.
Cap. 18.

humanity, and indulgence towards penitents. *Pri-*
mum potestate reum iudica, deinde cum misericordia,
humanitate & indulgentia eum concilia, promittens ei
salutem, si morem mutauerit, & ad pænitentiam redie-
rit. Oportet pænitentes libenter admittere, gaudentes il-
lorum causa cum misericordia, & humanitate, iudi-

Cap. 19.

cantes eos, qui deliquerunt. He setteth downe the
manner how Bishops should not suffer sinners to
enter into the Church, vntill they had done pennance as he should thinke fit, and then to forgiue
them. *Cum aliquem peccauisse cognoueris, iube cum fo-*
ras eijci ingressique pro eo rogent. Tunc iubebis illum iu-
uare & expendens an pæniteat, & dignus sit, qui in Ec-
clesiam omnino recipiatur, afflictum illum diebus ieiu-
niorum pro ratione peccati hebdomadas duas, vel tres,
vel quinque, vel septem, dimitte. Where the graunting of pardon, and Indulgence, more or lesse is re-

Cap. 21.

ferred to the Bishops iudgmēt, and discretion. And
further, *omnium curam habeat Episcopus. Pœnitenti-*
bus remissionem concedere oportet. Recognosce ô Epis-
cope, dignitatem tuam, quod sicut ligandi potestatem
accepisti, sic etiam soluendi. Obtinens igitur soluendi
potestatem, recognosce teipsum, & secundum dignita-
tem loci tui, in hac vita versare, sciens quod de pluri-

Luc. 12.

bus rebus ratio abs te requiretur. Cui enim, inquit, de-
positum est multum, abundantius repetetur ab eo. Nam
peccati expers reperitur nemo, excepto eo, qui propter nos

Iob 25.

factus est homo. Quoniam scriptum est nemo mundus à
sor-

fordibus, neque fi vnum diem vixerit. Where pardons and Indulgences are commaunded, and the neceſſity of them among all men ſinners deliuered.

He teacheth the like thus againe, *peccantem caſtiga, & ieiunio afflictum remiſsione releua, & ingemiſcentem recipe.* And leauing all to the Church, to impoſe pennance, to alter chaunge, eaſe or giue, pardon, releaſe, and giue Indulgence of it, he addeth: *nolite pro omni peccato eandem ſententiam ferre, ſed vnicuique propriam pœnam ſtatuite, cum multa prudentia. Alios minis ſubijcies, alijs ſubſidijs pauperum, alios ieiunijs affliges, alios ſegregabis pro delicti magnitudine. Diuerſis delictis diuerſas pœnas imponatis. Si pœnitentem non receperis, inſidiatoribus trades, oblitus Dauid dicentis, ne tradas beſtijs animam confitentem tibi. Si quis Epiſcopus aut presbyter, cum qui à peccato reuertitur, non recipit, ſed reijcit, deponitor, eo quòd Chriſtum offendat, qui dixit, ob vnum peccatorem qui reſipiſcat, gaudium oboriri in cœlo.*

Lib. 2. Conſt. Apoſt. c 21. Cap. 21.

Cap. 52.

Cap. 14.

Pſal. 73. Can. Apoſt. can. 51.

And Sainct Ignatius earneſtly vrgeth to take mercy of, and pardon penitent ſinners, and receaue them with all gentleneſſe, as a meanes to bring them from ſinning to ſaluation. *Obſecro vos, quotquot pænitentia ducti redierint ad vnitatem Eccleſiæ, ſuſcipite illos cum omni manſuetudine, vt per bonitatem & patientiam veſtram reſipiſcentes ex diaboli laqueis, digni iam Chriſto facti, ſalutem conſequantur æternam in regno Chriſti.* And to come home to this our owne contry of Britaine, Giraldus Cambrenſis an old learned Biſhop, and greate antiquary entreating of the firſt faith, and Religion of the Britans, *de antiqua fidei fundatione, Chriſtianitatis amore & deuotione:* ſaith they euer cōtinued in the ſame, &

Ignat. epiſt. ad Philadelp.

This doctrine of Indulgēces vſed in Britaine from the firſt conuerſion thereof, to Chriſt. Girald. Cambren. deſcriptiōne Cambr. cap. 18.

among

among other customes and obseruances kept from the time of their first conuersion, their Churches had farre greater Immunities priuiledges or Indulgences then in other places: *Ecclesiæ istorum longè maiorem quàm alibi pacem habent.*

These Indulgences here did farre exceede them which the Canons graunt, *Longè Canonum Indulgentiam excedente.* An euident argument they were more auncient then the Canons. And being as he teacheth without Innouation or chaunge, euen from the first conuersion of this Kingdome and the Apostles time. Which our oldest antiquities warranted both by Catholike and Protestant historians, and our Protestants themselues will thus proue vnto vs. They testifie with Antiquity that Pope Eleutherius was *bonus paterfamilias*, a good Steward of Gods Church. And King Lucius entreated him to be ioyned to the Christian faith and Church which was then and had beene from the beginning. *Lucius Britanniæ Rex Christiano cætui cum suis subditis adiungi à pontifice petijt, per literas.* And hee so effected it, that the Britãs were cõfirmed and strengthened in the doctrine which they had receaued from the Apostles, and the whole Kingdome here professed it. *Eleutherius vt bonus paterfamilias effecit, vt confirmatis & consolidatis Britannis in susceptaprius ab Apostolis doctrina, totum illud regnum in eius fidei verbum iuraret.* And this Apostolike faith and doctrine was the same, which this good Pope S. Eleutherius and the Romans then, and the Christian Britains here also professed, as these Protestants and all Antiquaries agree, saying that the first preachers to King Lucius were Apostolike men or instructed by them, *per Apostolicos viros.*

Io. Bal. l.x. de vit. Pont. Roman. in Eleut. Robert. Barn. in vit. pont. Rom. in eod.

Bal. lib. de Script. Brit. centur. x. in Eluana & Meduino. Godw. conu. of Brit.

viros in Christo renati, and our King sent for this A-postolike faith to Pope Eleutherius at Rome : *literis suis Rex Lucius, apud Eleutherium Pontificem egit vt apud Romanos Christianorum adscriberetur numero.* And the Apostolike Catholike faith which was here, at Rome and from, thence sent and confirmed here, in this question of Indulgences, was the same which the present Roman Church now profes-seth. For wee reade in the old Acts of those legates which S. Eleutherius sent hither recommended by these Protestants for authenticall, as written by themselues, *Fugatius & Damianus vt apud posteros clariora perdurarent, membranis his dederunt Acta per legatos, inde ad nos peruenerunt,* and many other antiquities. *That these holy Legates procured* 10. *ycares of Indulgence for all visitours of that sacred place of Glastenbury : Sancti Phaganus & Deruianus perquisierunt ab Eleutherio Papa qui eos miserat, decem annos Indulgentiæ.* And these old Acts did testifie, that the same holy Legates obtained 30. yeares of Indulgence for all Bishops ; that should with deuotion visit the chappell there builded, in honour of S. Michael the Archangell. *Dicebat eadem scriptura quod venerandi Phaganus & Deruianus perquisierant triginta annorum Indulgentiam omnibus Episcopis ipsum locum, ob honorem beati Michaelis pia voluntate visitantibus.* The old Manuscript antiquities of Gla-stenbury set downe the names of almost an hun-dred holy and auncient Bishops, which had giuen Indulgences to that holy place. Wee cannot but Iudge the like of other Churches, and places whose monuments haue not beene so happily pre-serued. And this is sufficient for this Question.

The next Protestant exception in this article is

con-

Io. Bal. sup.
Io. Leland.
Assertion.
Arthurij.
Charta S. Pa-tricij. Antiq.
Glastenien.
tab. lign. in
membran. af-fix. Guliel.
Malmesbur. l.
de antiquitat.
Cœnob. Gla-sten. Acta per
legat. Crapgr.
Catal. in S. Pa-tricio. Io. Le-land. in Arth.

The reuerent
vse of holy
Images thus
proued.

concerning Images, and is this: *The Romish doctrine
concerning worship and adoration of images is a fond
thinge, vainely inuented, and grounded vpon no warrant of Scripture, but rather repugnant to the word of
God.* The Councell of Trent for Catholiks thus deliuereth their doctrine, and practise in this point,
which these men terme the Romish doctrine. *Ima-*

Concil. Trid.
Sess. 9.

*gines Christi, Deiparæ Virginis & aliorum Sanctorum,
in templis præsertim habendas & retinendas: eisque debitum honorem & venerationem impertiendam: non
quòd credatur inesse aliqua in ijs diuinitas, vel virtus
propter quam sint colendæ: vel quòd ab eis sit aliquid pe-
tendum: vel quòd fiducia in Imaginibus sit figenda: ve-
luti olim fiebat à gentibus, quæ in idolis spem suam col-
locabant: Sed quoniam honos qui eis exhibetur, refertur
ad prototypa, quæ illæ repræsentant. Ita vt per imagines
quas osculamur, & coram quibus caput aperimus, &
procumbimus, Christum adoremus, & Sanctos, quorum
illæ similitudinem gerunt, veneremur. Id quod conciliorum, præsertim verò, secundæ Nicænæ Synodi decretis
contra imaginum oppugnatores, est sancitum.* That the
Images of Christ, The Mother of God and other Saincts
are to be had and retained especially in Churches: and
due honour and reuerence is to be done vnto them: not
because wee may or doe beleeue, there is any diuinity or
vertue in them, for which they are to be reuerenced: or
that anything is, or may be asked of them, or trust placed
in them, as it was vsed of the gentils, which placed their
hope in Idols. But because the honour which is done to
them is referred to these whose Images they be, and re-
present. So that by the Images which wee kisse, and before which wee put of our hats, and kneele downe, wee
adore Christ, and worship the Saincts, whose similitude
they beare. Which is defined in the decrees of Councels,
espe-

especially of the second Councell of Nice against the op-pugners of Images.

That Nicen generall Councell so defineth, and testifieth it to be the doctrine of the Fathers, and tradition of the Catholike Church in all the world. *Imaginis honor in prototypū resultat,& qui adorat Imaginem, in ea adorat quoque descriptum argumentum. Sic enim Sanctorum nostrorum patrum obtinet disciplina, vel traditio Catholicæ Ecclesiæ, quæ à finibus vsque ad fines Euangelium suscepit.* They say it was the faith of the Apostles, Fathers, and all true beleeuers in the world. And doe anathematize all that alledge the sentences of holy Scripture against Idols, against such sacred Images, or call them Idols, or say the Christians adore Images, as Gods, and those that wittingly communicate with them, that hold opinion against such Images, or abuse them. *Sancta Synodus exclamauit omnes sic credimus, omnes idem sapimus, omnes approbantes subscripsimus. Hæc est fides Apostolorum, hæc est fides patrum, hæc est fides orthodoxorum, hæc fides orbem terrarum confirmauit. Credentes in vnum Deum, in Trinitate laudatum, venerandas Imagines amplexamur. Qui secus agunt, anathemate percelluntur. Quicunque sententias sacræ Scripturæ de Idolis contra venerandas Imagines adducunt, anathema. Qui venerandas Imagines Idola appellant, Anathema. Qui dicunt quòd Christiani Imagines vt Deos adorent, anathema. Qui scientes communicant cum illis, qui contra venerandas Imagines sentiunt, aut eas dehonestant, anathema.* And this being a generall Councell, as our Protestants confesse, and so by their owne allowance before, the greatest authority in the Church of Christ, doth expressely confute all preteded obiections out of Scripture, which

L 2   Pro-

Proteſtants now vſe againſt holy Images being
vrged by the Iconoclaſts Image breakers, heretiks
at that time. And proueth that from the Apoſtles
time, the Catholike doctrine and vſe of them had
euer beene obſerued in the Church.

    And for this firſt Apoſtolike age, Euſebius, So-
zomen, Nicephorus and others teſtifie, that the
woman of phœnicia cured of her infirmity by our
Sauiour in the Ghoſpell, by touching the hemme
of his garment, did make Images of that miracle of
Chriſt healing her, and herſelfe kneeling vnto
him: and that at the Image of our Sauiour there
grew vp an herbe curinge all diſeaſes, to proue the
allowance, and reuerent vſe of ſuch, for the Chriſtians had that Image in greate reuerence, and ſo
it continued at Paneades in phœnicia, vntill Iulian
the Apoſtata pulled it downe, as he did other ſuch
Chriſtian monuments, and ſet vp his owne ſtatua
in the ſame place, which was miraculoſly brokē,
and ouerthrowne by God to make knowne his
wickedneſſe therein. And they were onely Pagan
Idolaters which broke and prophaned the Image
of Chriſt, the Chriſtians gathered the peeces together, placed and reuerently preſerued them in the
Church. *Id temporis gentiles statuam Christi tanta cum
violentia trahebant, vt eam confringerent. At Christiani postea eius fragmenta cum collegissent, in Ecclesia
posuerunt, vbi etiam adhuc custoditur. Nicephorus and
others write. Statuam autem Christi, Christiani tum in
Diæcocinum Ecclesiæ transtulerunt; & honoratiore loco
positam, cultu conuenienti profecuti sunt, locum namque eum libenter frequentantes, & Imaginem ipsam in-
spectantes, desiderium suum & amorem erga statuæ ipsius archetypum, primariumque exemplar declararunt.*

Like

Euſeb. hiſtor.
Eccl.l.7.c.17.
Sozom.hiſt.
Eccl.l.5.c.20.
Niceph. l.10.
c.30. Synod.
Nicæn.2.

Like is the hiſtory of our Sauiours holy Image, miraculouſly made by himſelfe and ſent to King Abgarus, or Abagarus at Edeſſa, in Syria, kept and frequented with great honour and reuerence, as inuincible teſtimonies and authorities of antiquity proue.

Euagrius and others call it *ſanctiſſimam Imaginem diuinitus fabricatam. The moſt holy Image made by God.* The Greeke Church keepeth a yearely feaſte, and ſolemnity of this holy Image on the 17. of the Calends of September. The ſame I ſay, of the holy Image of Chriſt made by himſelfe in wipinge his face, going to his paſſion, with a linnen cloath deliuered to him by S. Veronica, by ſome Berenice, as the traditiō of the Church of Chriſt, Methodius, Marianus, Scotus, Mattheus Weſtmonaſterienſis and others, and the ſame holy Image ſtill with greate reuerence preſerued at Rome inuincibly proue. How much this ſacred Image was honoured preſently in this age, and euer after, wee may informe our ſelues by that hiſtory of Tyberius the Emperour, as it is thus related by our old hiſtorian Matthew of weſtminſter, euen as he is publiſhed by our Proteſtants and others. Tyberius being troubled with a grieuous leproſie, and hearing of the miracles of Chriſt, at and about Hieruſalem ſent Voluſianus thither to entreate Chriſt to come to cure him, but the Iewes hauing put him before Voluſianus coming to Hieruſalem to death, he meeting with S. Veronica, and informed by her & others that this holy Image being deuoutely vſed, (*huius Imaginis aſpectum ſi Dominus tuus deuotè intueatur, continuo ſanitatis beneficio potietur;*) he ſhould preſently be healed. He bringeth S. Veronica with

Tabul. & Archiu. ciuit. Edeſſæ apud Niceph. l. 2. ca. 7. & alios. Euagr. l. 4. c. 26 Damaſc. li. 4. de fid. orth. c. 17. Orthod. c. 17. Conſt. Porph. Imperat. orat. apud Metaphr. 10. Aug. Monol. Græcor. cal. ſeptem. Metaphraſt. 15 Nouemb. & in vit. S. Alexij Niceph. l 2 c. 7. Conc. Nic. 2. Stephan. 1. Pap. apud Adrian. Pap. ep. ad Corol. Mag. Tom. 3. Concil. Tradit. Eccl. de S. Imagine Rom. Meth. in Tyberio. Marian. Scot. in chronic. an. 39. Matth. Weſtmonaſt. chron. an. gratiæ 31. Ranulph. hig. Polychron. l. 4. c. 4.

ſhe

the Image of Christ to Rome, and enformed the Emperour of this matter, whereupon **Tyberius** caused the way to be spredde with silke cloathes, and the Image to be thus presented vnto him. Who presently thus beholding it, obtained his former health.

Cæsar pannis sericis viam sterni fecit, & Imaginem sibi præsentari præcepit: Qui mox vt eam fuit intuitus, pristinam assecutus est sanitatem. This greate honour the greate Emperour by the direction of Christians vsed, as they likewise did, being himselfe either actuall a Christian, or so farre a friend and professour of their faith that as our oldest historian S. Gildas and others write he threatened death to the accusers of Christs Seruants euen against the will of the Senate. *Comminata, Senatu nolente, à Principe morte dilatoribus militum eiusdem Christi.* Wee finde also that the Syndon wherein the sacred body of Christ was wrapped in his holy sepulcher, did receaue and retaine the Image of him, and was preserued with much honour, as still it is so kept *in Ecclesia Tauronensi,* to this day with greate reuerence. So of the Image of Christ in regall attire made by Nicodemus and still honoured at Lucas in Italy. Such was the Image of Christ at Beritum, most miraculous when it was abused by a Iew testified by S. Athanasius, the second Nicen Councell and others, and attributed to S. Nicodemus the maker thereof.

Sainct Epiphanius also maketh mentions of diuers Images of Christ, some of gold, others of siluer, others of other matter preserued from the time of Pontius Pilate before Christs Passion. And those Images must needs be both very auncient, and honoured,

Marginal notes:

Gild. l.de excid.& conq. Brit.c.6.Tertullian. Apol. cont.gent. Antiq.Ecclef. Tauronen. Baron. Aunal. an.34. Athan. Serm. de pass. Imag. Nicen. Conc. 2.act.2.Mat. Westmon. an. 560.Epiph. li 1.Tom.2. contr.heref. c.27. Irenæb. lib. 1. contr.hæref. c.24.Niceph l.4.Eccl.hist.. c.2. Tertull. con. her. & apud Nicep. supr. Epiph. supr.contr. Carpocratiras.

noured, for both S. Ireneus and Tertullian make
mention of Carpocrites and his followers the heretiks of that name, and who began about the yeare
of Chrift 129. whome S. Epiphanius doth charge to
haue exceeded the due Chriftian honour giuen to
Images, and among other their errours to haue offered facrifice, euen fuch as the gentiles vfed to
thefe & other prophane Images of Pagans. *Habent*
Imagines per colores depictos, quidam etiam ex auro &
argento ac reliqua materia, quas fane Imagines Iefu ef-
fe dicunt: & has Iefu Imagines fub Pontio Pilato fa-
Etas effe, quando inter homines verfabatur. Infuperque
philofophorum quorundam, Pythagoræ, Platonis, Ari-
ftotelis, & aliorum. Cum quibus Philofophis etiam alias
Imagines Iefu collocant, collocatasque adorant, & gen-
tium myfteria perficiunt. Erectis enim his Imaginibus
de cætero gentium mores feruant. Qui vero funt gen-
tium mores alij, quàm facrificia atque alia? Nicepho-

Niceph.hift.
Eccl.l.2.c.7.

rus hauing related the hiftory of Chrift his Image,
fent by him to King Abgarus, whom he nameth
Augarus, reigning *vltra Euphratem*, beyond Eu-
phrates, immediatly addeth, that the King of
Perfia alfo fent for, and receaued by a skillfull
painter both the Image of Chrift and his bleffed
Mother: *dicitur quoque Perfarum Rex manu ingenio-*
que promptum pictorem mififfe, & per hunc, feruenti fi-
dei defiderio, fimul & ipfius Chrifti, & quæ eum diui-
no modo genuit, matris, quam celerrimè Imaginem de-
pictam accepiffe. And to affure vs of the certainty of
this hiftory, he immediatly addeth, that it was both
regiftred in the publike records of the then regall
City Edeffa, kept among their publike monuméts
there, contained in the hiftory of King Abgarus,
tranflated out of Syriake, and fo publifhed. *Atque*
hæc

hæc quidem ex Tabularis & archiuis ciuitatis Edeſſæ, quæ tum regia adminiſtrabatur poteſtate, ſunt deſumpta. Fuerant enim in publica librorum monumenta relata. Et libri de Augari rebus conſcripti, hæc quoque complectebantur, ex Syrorum lingua tranſlata. Quæ à me etiam rectè hoc loco opinor eſſe expoſita.

The worshipping of theſe holy Images, eſpecially that which King Abgarus a Chriſtian receaued, is deliuered vnto ys by no leſſe then ſuch publike regall warrant, decree and practiſe. For as the Emperour Conſtantinus porphyrogenitus, Simon Metaphraſtes and others proue vnto vs, King Abgarus being Chriſtened by S. Thaddeus and warranted by that Apoſtle in his Chriſtian proceedings, this King receauing the Image of Chriſt with greate Ioy and honour, whereas there was a Pagan God placed before the common gate of the City, which euery one that was to enter into the City was firſt to adore, and offer vnto it certaine prayers, ſuch as the Pagās ordained for their Gods, and then freely to paſſe into the City. This Idoll the King tooke downe, and ſet in place thereof the Image of Chriſt which Sainct Thaddeus had brought vnto him with theſe words written in letters of gold: *Deus, qui in te ſperat, à ſpe non excidit. O God he that truſteth in thee, ſhall not fayle in his hope.* And withall he gaue commaundment, that whoſoeuer paſſed into the City by that porte, ſhould firſt doe reuerence, and due honour to that Image. And this order was obſerued of all Paſſengers during the Reigne of Abgarus and his ſonne after him.

Arcuulfus an auncient Biſhop of Fraunce and pylgrime to Hieruſalem, *qui locorum gratia SanEto-*

rum

[margin:]
Metaphraſt.
die 10. Aug.
& 15. Nou.
Conſt. Poph.
ſupr. 10. Aug.
Harr. hiſt.
manuſcript. l.
c. 11. hiſt. Miſ.
l. 17.

'Arcuulf. & A-
daman. in re-
lat. locorum
Sanctorū. Beda libello de
locis ſanctis.

rum venerat Hierosolymam lustrata omni terra pro-
missionis, Adamannus an holy Preist and Abbot of
this Britaine, and S. Bede after them is witnesse,
that among the holy memories of Christ at and
about Hierusalem, there was kept a lynnen cloath
about 8. foote longe, made as was thought by the
blessed Virgin, redde on the one side, and greene
on the other, containing the Image of Christ and
his 12. Apostles, and was there worshipped in the
Church. *Aliud quoque aliquanto maius linteum in* Dorotheus
Ecclesia illa veneratur, quod fertur à Sancta Maria con- Synop.de vita
textum, duodecim Apostolorum, & ipsius Domini con- & morte pro-
tinens Imagines, vno latere rubro, & altero viridi. S. Ierem.
Dorotheus writeth, that Ieremy the Prophet pro-
phesying of the coming of Christ, gaue this for a
certaine token and signe, to know the time, because all people then should worship the crosse.
Signum aduentus ipsius erit vobis, quando vniuersæ Pallad. hist.
gentes lignum adorabunt. And gaue an other signe as lauf.in vit. A-
certaine, and notorious, as the other to the Preists pollinis. Soz.
of Egypt, where he prophesied, that when the hist.Eccl.l.5.c.
Messias should be borne of a Virgin, and ly in a c.41.Niceph.
manger, all their Idols should be broken and fall l.10.c.31.Gu-
downe; which the Prophet Esay also thus foretold: liel.
mouebuntur simulachra Ægypti à facie eius. Which all centen.1.part.
writers Greeke and Latine, Catholiks and Prote- 1.distinct.3.
stants confesse and proue to haue beene effected, Volater.cam-
when Christ newly borne with his mother fledde men.l.13 Pet.
into Egypt, the Idols of that nation most Idolatrous 228.
then fallinge downe. And to make euident euen
to blinded men, that Christian Images be not idols,
or forbidden, but allowed, and to be reuerenced, at
that very time when the idols were thus miraculoufly destroyed, the holy Prophet both appointed
the

Dorotheus
supr.

the Egyptians, to make Christian Images namely
of Christ and his blessed mother, and reuerence
them which they did. And this was both publikly,
and by all practized, and by their King as authentically examined and approued. *Ieremias signum dedit Sacerdotibus Ægyptiacis quòd oporteat simulachra
eorum concuti, & decidere per seruatorem puerum ex
virgine nasciturum, & in præsepi iaciturum, propterea
etiam nunc virginem in lecto, & Infantem in præsepio
collocant & adorant. Et cum causam olim Ptolomæus
Rex percontaretur, responderunt mysterium esse ipsis à
maioribus traditum, quod illi a sancto Propheta acce-
perint.*

Sueto.in Aug.
lactant. firm.
Aug. l. de in-
uitat. Mart.
Polon.chron.
in Augusto.
Ran. Highed.
hist.l.4. c.2.3.
Hertin. Sche-
del.ætat.5. fol.
93.
Speed Thea-
ter of greate
Brit. l.6.
Annal.Eccles.
Chart.in Gal-
lia Francisc.
Belleforest
Cosmog.l.2.
p.303. in Iud.
v.druid. &
alij.

This was likewise reuealed to Augustus the Emperour by the apparition of a Virgin with a child
in her armes from heauen. And he fell downe
and worshipped the Image or apparition. And is
commended for it by all writers. *Apertum est cœlum & nimius splendor irruit super eum, & vidit in
cœlo pulcherrimam virginem stantem super altare, &
puerum tenentem in brachijs. Et miratus est nimis, &
vocem dicentem audiuit: Hæc ara filij Dei est. Qui
statim proijciens se in terram, adorauit.* This was the
doctrine and practise of the Druides of this Kingdome and Fraunce, whome our Protestants mer-
ueylouslie commend vnto vs, for hauing a Pro-
phesie among them, that the Sauiour of the world
should be borne of a virgin, they erected Churches
& Images vnto the, namely at Charters in Fraunce.
Where their Prince and they both founded such
a Church with an Image of the blessed virgin with
Christ in her armes, and worshipped it, as the
auncient tradition and Annals of that Church with
others proue.

The

The Image or signe of the Crosse is not so resembling, representatiue of Christ, or his Passiō, as the Images of Christ and his Sainćts be of them, especially that being a common Instrument of death, in the greate Romane Empire at the death of Christ.

And yet in honour of Christ suffering death and redeeming the world by his passion vpon a Crosse, The signe and Image thereof was presently after his death euen by his Apostles, disciples, and first Christians in this age, had, and vsed with greate reuerence, and honour. I may be more breife in this matter seeing our Protestants by their greatest euen regall authority, haue thus declared: *The signe of the Crosse is an Apostolicall constitution and Tradition.* And so they vse in their publike practicall communion booke at the baptisme of euery child, thus prescribing for a rule and law: *The Preist shall make a Crosse, vpon the childes forehead, saying: Wee receaue this child into the congregation of Christs flocke, and doe signe him with the signe of the Crosse, in token that hereafter he shall not be ashamed to confesse the faith of Christ crucified, and manfully to fight vnder his banner, against sinne, the world, and the deuill, and to continue Christs faithfull seruant vnto his liues end. Amen.* Therefore if by so greate a Protestant warrant and profession the signe of the Crosse is so honorable, that it is an Apostolicall constitution, binding and commaunding all, an Apostolicall tradition, to be religiously kept and obserued of all, so honorable and necessary a profession, confession and testimony of our faith, and Religion neuer to be denied, that when wee were infants, and could not doe this of our selues, it was, and ought to be performed by others for vs, as our whole faith

King Iames and his B. B. confer. at Hampt. Co-uel. ag. Burg. p. 139. 124. 125. Communion Booke Tit. publike Baptisme.

was

was so professed for vs in our baptisme, much more ought all Christians coming to yeares of Iudgment, and discretion performe those holy bondes and duties by themselues.

And that our Protestants need not feare they haue herein donne or graunted too much, they shall heare the Apostolike men of this age, from whom they haue in some sorte borrowed this their doctrine, practise, and confession, deliuer the Apostolike doctrine, vse & custome, farre more plainely, amply, and honorably, in this busines.

The old Anonymus writer of the Apostles liues published by the learned Bishop Fredericus of Vienna allmost an hundred yeares since, and then the exemplar exceeding old *characteribus plusque vetustis inscriptum*, writeth, that Sainct Thaddeus cured King Abgarus with the signe of the Crosse, *imposito Regi crucis signaculo, ab omni eum languore sanauit.* An holy Angell engraued in square stones foure Crosses in euery corner of the Church one, *per quatuor angulos circumuolans, digito suo in quadratis saxis sculpsit signum crucis.* And gaue Charge to make the signe of the Crosse on their foreheads. *Quale signum ego sculpsi in his saxis, tale vos digito vestro facite in frontibus vestris, & omnia mala fugient a vobis.* Sainct Ihon the Apostle making the signe of the Crosse ouer poyson drunke it without hurt. *Facto signo Crucis venenum sine læsione bibit.* S. Ephrem in his Sermon intituled of the most holy Crosse of our Lord. *De sanctissima Cruce Domini,* speaking of the glory thereof boldly affirmeth, that the holy Apostles armed therewith, draw all nations to adore it. *Hac Crucis armatura muniti sancti Apostoli omnem inimici potentiam, conculcarunt,*

cun-

Fredic. Nausea ep. Vienn. Prooemen. in vit. Apostol.
Anonym. antiq. in vit. S. Thomæ Apost.
Idem in vit. S. Bartholomæi.

Id. in vit. S. Ioan. Apost.

S. Ephrem Sermon de Sanctissima Cruce Domini.

cunctasque gentes suis sagenis ad huius adorationem attraxerunt, & congregarunt.

S. Basil speaking of traditions of the Apostles, nameth this for one. *Vt signo Crucis eos, qui spem collocarunt in Christum, signemus.* So hath Tertullian, and others, that it was a tradition to vse it in all actions. *Ad omnem progressum, atque promotum, ad omnem aditum & exitum, ad vestitum & calceatum, ad lauachra, ad mensas, ad lumina, ad cubilia, ad sedilia, quacumque nos conuersatio exercet, frontem Crucis signaculo terimus. Traditio tibi pratendetur auctrix, consuetudo confirmatrix, & fides obseruatrix.* He liued soone after this first age, and S. Martiall conuersing with Christ, and his Apostles confirmeth it: *Crucem Domini, semper in mente, in ore, in signo tenete. Crux enim Domini armatura vestra contra Sathanam, galea custodiens caput, lorica protegens pectus, clypeus tela maligni repellens, gladius iniquitatem & Angelicas insidias peruersa potestatis sibi propinquare nullo modo sinens. Hoc solo signo coelestis victoria data est nobis, & per Crucem baptismo Dei sanctificatum est,* The Crosse of Christ is euer to be in our minde, our mouth, and signe. It is an armour against Sathan, a Sallet defending the heade, a breasteplate defending the breast, a sheild repelling the darts of the deuill, a sword keeping vs from his iniquity and deceits. The signe by which celestiall victory is giuen vnto vs, by the Crosse baptisme is sanctified.

Sainct Clement from the Apostles witnesseth, that the Bishops and Preists in the beginning of the sacrifice of Masse armed themselues with this signe on their forehead. *Episcopus splendidam vestem indutus, vnà cum sacerdotibus, & stans ad altare, & facto manu in fronte tropheo Crucis, dicat.* The

history

Basil. l. de Spiritu sancto c. 27.
Tertull. l. de coron. mil. c. 34. Cyrill. Hierosolim. catech. 13. Basil. de Spir. 5. c. 1. Hier. ep. 22. ad Eust. Theod. l. 3. hist. c. 3. Martial. epist. ad Burdegal. c. 8.

Hiſt. S.Petri
Petri aſcript.
S.Lino.

Ignat.epiſt.ad
Philippen.
Vincent.ſpe-
cul.l.10.vit.
S. Andreę per
Presbyter. &
Diacon.A-
chaię. Breuia.
Rom. in feſto
S.Andr.Breu.
Sarisbur.ibid.
Author.l.de
duplici Mart.
inter opera S.
Cypriani.Me-
taphr. in S.
Andrea.S.Iuo
Carnat.ſerm.
de Sacram.
ſer.4. Remig.
Antiſiod. in
pſal.21.& 4.
Bern.ſer.de
S.Andr. Lan-
fran.cont.Be-
rengar. Miſſ.
S.Chryſoſt.
SS. Petri, Ia-
cobi, Marci,
& Dionil.A-
reop.Eccl.
Hierarch.
c.2.c.5.part.2.
part.3.

hiſtory aſcribed to S. Linus Succeſſour to S. Peter,
teſtifieth, that Sainct Peter ſtanding by the Croſſe
wonderfully commended and honoured it for the
miſteries thereof, defending vs, repreſenting our
redemption vnto vs, vſed in the ſacred miſteries,
driuing away the poiſon of the ſerpent. S. Ignatius
ſaith it is a Trophy, or ſigne of victory againſt the
deuill, he trembleth, when he ſeeth it, and feareth
when he heareth of it. *Trophæum eſt contra ipſius po-*
tentiam: quod vbi viderit horret, & audiens timet.

The hiſtory of Sainct Andrew that great Apoſtle written by the Cleargy of Achaia where he
ſuffered martyrdome, then preſent or liuing, and
both confirmed by many other old writers,
and receaued by the Churches authority is wonderfull for his worſhipping of the Image of the
Croſſe. *Adductus Andreas ad locum martyrij, cum*
Crucem vidiſſet, longe exclamare cæpit: ô bona Crux,
quæ decorem ex membris Domini ſuſcepiſti, diu deſide-
rata, ſollicitè amata, ſine interceſſione quæſita, & ali-
quando cupienti animo præparata, accipe me ab homini-
bus, & redde me magiſtro meo. And he is accompted
firſt compoſer of the Maſſe now called S. Chryſo-
ſtomes Maſſe, wherein the ſigne of the Croſſe is
vſed with great honour. So it is diuers times in the
Maſſes of S. Peter, S. Iames, S. Marke, and others,
S. Denis the Areopagite witneſſeth it was honorably vſed in the holy myſteries, Sacraments, and
ceremonies of the Church in this age. *Pontifex*
trino Crucis ſanctæ ſignaculo vnctionem inchoat. Cui-
libet ipſorum à benedicente Pontifice Crucis imprimitur
ſignum. Signi vitalis impreſſio omnium ſimul carna-
lium deſideriorum vacationem, vitamque ad Dei imi-
tationem efficiam ſignat. Prochorus and others write,
that

that S. Ihon the Apoſtle did diuers miracles with this holy ſigne. *Sanctæ Crucis ſignaculo muniuit. Sanctæ Crucis ſigno dixit infirmo: in nomine Domini noſtri Ieſu Chriſti ſurge, & vade in domum tuam ſanus: & continuo ſurrexit æger ſanus.* The like is written of S. Thomas the Apoſtle, and there ſtill remaineth to this day from his time, an Image of the Croſſe engraued in ſtone vpon a tombe, where he preached among the Indians.

The recitall of others in this age committed to writing by credible Authours, would be longe and tedious in ſo manifeſt a truth. Gulielmus Eiſengrenius in his fift Cētenary hath gathered many there to be ſeene. This holy vſe and cuſtome was tranſported euen in this time by all humane Iudgment, euen into the new world, as ſome call America, for both Catholike and Proteſtant Authours and eye witneſſing trauaylers aſſure thus: *In Acuzamil an Ilande neare vnto Iucatan, they founde a Croſſe two fadoms high, to which they of the contry had recourſe as to a celeſtiall and diuine thinge.* Which muſt needs be erected by Chriſtians there, in this primatiue time, this being a plaine and geometricall Image and paterne of the Croſſe of Chriſt, by tradition fifteene foote longe *Crux ſancta quindecim erat longa pedes.*

And to come home to our Britans here, their auncient learned Biſhops and Antiquaries aſſure vs, that from their firſt conuerſion they vſed deuoute reuerence and gaue farre greater honour to the Image and ſigne of the croſſe, and ſuch repreſentatiue holy ſignes, then any other nation Chriſtian did. *Cruci deuotam reuerentiam exhibere longeque magis quam vllam gentem honorem deferre videmus.*

Prochorus in S. Ioa. c. 3. c. 31.
Petr. Maffeus in S. Thoma epiſt. Indic.
Gulielm. Eiſengren. cent. 1. part. 5. diſt. 7.
Gul. Eiſeng. ſupr. fol. 93. 130. 138. 139. 142. 143. 144 147. 149. 149 150. 153. 157. 163. 163. 167. 168.
Authour Coſmogr. diſcript. gent. Edw. Grymſton Booke of Eſtates p. 261.
Tradit. de S. Cruce. Guliel. Eiſengr. cent. 1. diſt 1. f. 42.
The firſt Chriſtian Britans of this profeſſion.
Girald. Cābr. deſcr. Cambr. cap. 18.

mus. And wee finde in the Antiquities of Glaftenbury, that S. Ioseph of Aramathia who buryed
Chrift, and his holy companions which with hym
liued and dyed there, vfed holy Images of the croffe & others, and by thefe founde ther after in King
Lucius time Damianus and Faganus knew that
to haue beene the lyuing and dying place of thofe
Sainēts. *Figuram noftræ redemptionis aliasque figuras
manifeftas repererunt, quibus benè cognoucrunt, quod
Chriftiani prius locum inhabitauerunt*: Where wee
fee the sholy Chriftian Images then to haue beene
a certayne diftinctiue figne, and token, of the firft
Chriftians from other people. For as Baronius,
Spondanus, Seuerinus Binius an others proue by
many auncient old lawes and other authorities, it
was a receaued cuftome euen from the Apoftles, to
erect croffes in the Churches which were founded.
And Sozomen with others affirme, that the gentils
themfelues did freely confeffe, that this was the
Sibyls verfe. *Ipfi gentiles ingenuè fatentur, hoe
effe Sibyllæ carmen.*

　　O lignum fœlix in quo Deus ipfe pependit.

　　O happy croffe whereon God himfelfe did hange.

　　And no man can deny it. *Nemo pernegabit.* And
the Sybils did both Prophefie of the croffe and the
worfhip thereof. *Quare & lignum crucis, & eius
veneratio a Sibylla præfignificata eft.* And this hee
affirmeth from certaine tradition, and vndoubted
true teftimonyes. *Hac ex viris, qui illa accuratè norunt, & ad quos eorum cognitio à patribus ad liberos
fucceffione quadam deriuata peruenit, & qui eadem
ipfa literis prodere, pofterifque relinquere ftuduerunt,
audiuimus.* And thus it was obferued here in Britaine the firft Chriftianitie here in euery age, by S.
　　　　　　　　　　　　　　　　　　　Ioseph

Ioseph and his ossociats in the first age, by S. Damianus Phaganus and their company in the second, and third also. In which we find it was a custome also among Christians, both to carry about
with them the Image of the crosse or crucifixe, and
to giue honour vnto it, as much as Catholichs now
doe. This we proue by S. Amphibalus that blessed
priest, Bishop and martir sent hither from Rome,
and continually carryinge a crucifixe about with
hym in the moste bitter persecution of Dioclesian.
What was the worship hee and others then did
vnto it, wee cannot bee better informed then by
the president and example which S. Albane our
first glorious Martyr by common computation,
left vnto vs penned by a Britan then liuing as he
testifieth in his life, in the presence and with the
allowance of S. Amphibalus, thus related: *sæpe pro-
sternitur ante crucem, & quasi pendentem Dominum
Iesum in cruce cerneret, veniam precatur. Sic pedes,
sic vulneris loca assidua exosculatione demulcet, ac si
ad ipsius quem crucifigi viderat vestigia procumberet
Redemptoris. Sanguine mixtæ per ora voluuntur la-
chrimæ super illud venerabile lignum crucis vbertim
decidentes.* He often falleth downe before the Crosse, and
as he had seene our lord Iesus on the Crosse. The blessed
penitent craueth pardon. So hee did with dayly kissing
embrace the places of his woundes, as if he had fallen
downe at the feete of our redeemer, whom he saw crucified. Teares mixt with bloode do runne. downe his face,
and plentifully fall downe vppon the venerable Crosse.

This is as much as the present Church of Rome
alloweth, or any good Catholike doth, or is allowed to doe. And yet this greate glory of Britayne, so glorious and noble a Saint, & Martyr, giuing

Anonym.
Brit. in vit. S.
Albani. ma-
nusc. ant. Io.
Capgran. Ia-
genuen. & alij
in eodem.

fo greate honour, and reuerence to the Image of
Chriſt crucified, doth by the ſame Authours, as ſtri-
ctly and punctually condemne the Idolatrous gentils for their Idols, as any Chriſtian, Catholike or
proteſtant can doe, and with the ſame cenſors and
authorities which our proteſtants vnlearnedly and
vnaduiſedly vſe, or abuſe rather againſt this Catholike cuſtome and practiſe, he ſtill carryed the crucifixe in his hand to his death, kiſſing, reuerencing
and honoring it, being found prayeinge bare foo-
led before it. *Reperiunt nudis pedibus, ante crucem
Domini, precibus incumbentem. Albanus vt ſe ſeruum crucis oſtenderet, ſignum dominicum in manibus
iugiter præferebat. Crucem Domini quam manu tene-
bat, frequenter deoſculans, & adorans, cauſam ſuam
Domino commendabat.* And thus hee perſeuered
vntill his heade being ſtricken of, his Croſſe em-
brued with his martirs blood fell out of his hands,
and was ſecretly taken vp and preſerued by a Chriſtian there preſent, none but Ghriſts enemyes diſallowed theſe holy Chriſtian ſignes perſecuting
him whome they repreſented. *Crux quam vir ſanctus iugiter in manibus ferre conſueuerat, fælici iam
cruore reſperſa, ſuper herbam decidit, eamque quidam
Chriſtianus occultè rapuit, & ignorantibus Paganis ab-
ſcondit.* Concerning the Images of holy Saincts
I haue ſaid before for Britayne that at Gloſtenbury
beſides the Image of the Croſſe or crucifixe in S.
Ioſeph his tyme, there where other holy Images
there, and the Image of our lady with Chriſt in her
armes, was the auntient armes of that moſt auntient Abbey. For Hieruſalem wee haue hard that
the Images of all the Apoſtles were there worſhipped from their tyme. There was alſo the Image
of our lady paynted by S. Luke the Euangeliſt,

Mat. Weſt.
chron. an. 303.

which is called by Nicephores and others a diuine Image. *Diuinam illius Imaginem quam Lucas Apostolus in Tabula depicta reliquit.* Her Image was also kept with greate honour at Edesse in Syria where Abgarus so much honoured the Image of Christ. There was also an other Image of her miraculously made and doing miracles, which the Emperour Heraclius vsed in his wars against Cosdroas, and thereby preuayled, this was with honour kept at Constantinople Byzantium. *Heraclius ferens secum sanctæ Dei genitricis Iconem, quæ apud Bizantium est, non hominis manu, sed diuino miraculo pictam. Heraclius Iconis Dei genitricis fultus auxilio, omnes aduersarios suos in bello peremit.*

Niceph.hist. Eccl.l.14.c.2. Theod.lect. collect.l.Bar. Annal.an.453 vit.S.Alexij apud Sur. lippom. Bret. Rom & al.Sigebert.chron. an 405 Matt. Westm. an.620. Sigechronic.an. 624.

The Image of this blessed virgyn was honorable and renowned both in Britayne and fraunce from, or before our first Christianitie as I haue proued before. Both Catholick and protestant Antiquaries writing of China where diuers of the Apostles preached, thus testifie of the people there: *They haue the picture of an exceeding fayre woman, holding a child in her armes, whereof they say hee was deliuered a virgin.* And these nations though so remote had also the Images of the 12. Apostles, as these and other Authors thus deliuer vnto vs:

Sebast. Manst. in Typ.orbis. Bilibald.pirckim. in Tob. nou. totius orb.in Claud. Ptol. Ioan. Brun.commen.in Bened. 12.Patriarch. Anonym.ant. in vit. Apost. Auth.of the Booke of E-states in S. Tho.Grimston. p.738.

There bee certayne pictures of the fashion, and with the markes of the twelue Apostles, and being demaunded, what maner of men these twelue Apostles were, they answeare, they were greate Philosophers, which liued vertuously, and therefore they were made Angels in heauen. That God, which they doe the greatest honour vnto, they paint with a body, out of whose shoulders come three heades, which looke one vppon an other, which signifie, as they say that all three haue but one will.

Which

Which no mā can well doubt but that they are true memoryes, though afterward misunderstood in longe tract of tymc, of the holy Trinitie, and Christian Religion preached there by some of the Apostles, whose Images bee so longe honoured there, and that was the maner in that first Apostolicke tyme in all places. At Hierusalem the Images of the 12. Apostles painted vppon the cloath made by our lady before remembred were honoured in the church *in Ecclesia veneratur.* For Greece, Eusebius is wittnesse that the Images of the Apostles namely of S. Peter and S. Paule were paynted as hee had seene them *Apostolorum Imagines, Pauli videlicet & Petri in tabulis coloribus depictas asseruari vidimus.* And the Apostles by them so honoured. *Veteres ad hunc modum honorare soliti fuerunt.*

Arnulf.& Adam.relat.de locis sanct. Beda libell.de loc.Sanctis. Euseb hist. Eccl l.7.c.17

The like or more amply hath Nichephorus & others affirming that S. Luke Euangelist painted their Images as diuers others. It is manifest in the historie of S. Syluester and Constantine, that not onely the Images of S. Peter and S. Paule which appeared vnto Constantine, but of the other Apostles were with reuerence kept, and preserued at Rome amonge so many persecutions.

Nicephor. hist. Eccl. l.6. c.16.l.2. c.43. Petr.de Nat.l. 9.c.79.

I need not to proceed to more particular places and examples, when we haue both vnwritten and written tradition, that euen from the tyme of the Apostles, and Sainct Luke the Euangelist and others then makeinge and reuerently vseinge such sacred Images, the same art and vse was from thence deduced into all the world. *Vnde in omnem deinde habitabilem orbem tam venerandum & pretiosum opus est illatum.* And this Christian manner and custome of makinge reuerencing and honouring holy

Nicephor. hist.l.2.c 43.

holy Images in such sort as is before defined, by the generall Councels, and still vsed by Catholiks, so auntient from the begynninge of Christianitie, so generall in the whole Christian worlde was neuer disallowed or impugned by any man bearing the name of a Christian, vntill about the yeare of Christ 494. Xenaias a prophane, vnbaptized and sacrilegeous Persian vsurping Ecclesiasticall orders, was the first which opposed against it, and therefore is stiled in histories to be a man of an audacious and impudent mouth and placed in the catalogue of damned Heretiks *Xenaias primus, ô audacem animum, os impudens, vocem illam euomuit, Christi & eorum qui illi placuere, Imagines venerandas non esse.* The world hath scarcely seene a more desperate and wicked wretch, then antiquities describe this man to haue beene, & they which haue since followed, and follow hym at this tyme haue hardly hitherto gotten much better fame for their like proceedings, doing therein onely as Iewes, Turkes, Tartars, Pagans, and onely heretiks for that condemned among Christians haue done, and at this tyme where they ouer rule.

The next exception of our Protestants in this Article Against the doctrine & practise of the Church of Rome and Catholiks, is to vse their words concerning their *worshippinge an adoration of Reliques,* termed by them as the others before, *a fonde thinge, vainely inuented, and grounded vpon no warrantie of scripture, but rather repugnant to the worde of God.*

The Councell of Trent for Catholiks thus defineth in this matter. *Sanctorum Martyrum & aliorum cum Christo viuentium sancta corpora quæ viua membra fuerunt Christi; & Templum Spiritus Sancti, à fidelibus*

M 3

Cedren. in compendio Hist. in Xenaia Persa.

Nicephorus hist. Eccl. l. 16 c. 27. Synod. Nic. 2. Ench. hæres. in Xenaia. Baron. an. 485. 486. 487. Spond. ib. & alij.

The Catholick doctrine and practise of reuerence to holy Relikes.

Conc. Trid. sess. 9.

delibus veneranda esse. Affirmantes Sanctorum reli-
quijs venerationem atque honorem non deberi, vel
eas aliaque sacra monumenta à fidelibus inutiliter ho-
norari, omnino damnandos esse, prout iam pridem eos
damnauit, & nunc etiam damnat Ecclesia. The bodyes
of holy Martyrs and others that lyue with Christ are to
be reuerenced. The Church doth now condemne, as longe agoe it hath condemned those which affirme that reliks of Sainsts, or that they and other sacred monuments
ar vnprofitably honoured of the faithfull.

Now lett vs examine what was the doctrine
and practise of the Apostles, and Apostolike men
in this first age, in this question. Moses Bar-cepha
a Syrian many hundreds of yeares since, and Iacobus Orrohaita before hym, and by hym cited, be
wittnesses that the body and Reliks of the first
man Adam a penitent and holy father after his fall,
were honorably preserued by his posteritie, and in
the time of the flood to keepe it from perishing
No carryed it with him into the arke, and left it to
his children. *Noe arcam cum esset cum liberis suis*
conscensurus impendente diluuio, secum in eam intu-
lisse ossa Adami, eaque deinde post diluuium arca
egressum, suis distribuisse. And this was the manner
and custome after the deludge vnto the time of
Christ amonge the faithfull to preserue with honour and reuerence the bodyes and reliks of the
holy Sainets of that Time. And as the scripture
wittnesseth, of the deade body of Elisæus restoring
a mans deade body to life by touching his bones.
Quod cum tetigit ossa Elisæi, reuixit homo & stetit
super pedes suos: So we haue vnquestionable authorities both of Scripture and Fathers, for the honour, and reuerence of the bodies and reliks of
the

Moses Bar-
cepha Syr. E-
pisc.comm.
de Paradis.
part.x.c.14.
Iacob.
Arrohaita a-
pud eund. ib.

4.Reg.c.13.

the reſt of the Prophets, the Iewes themſelues as
the ſcripture teſtifieth adorning and reuerencing
them. *Ædificatis ſepulchra Prophetarum, & ornatis* ·· Matth. 23.
monumenta iuſtorum.

S. Epiphanius and other noble wittneſſes proue, ·· Epiph. l. de
that Daniel the Prophet was buryed and reueren- ·· Prophet. vita
ced with greate honour, and his graue ſo continued ·· & interitu. in
renowned in his time. *Humatus eſt magnis honoribus.* ·· Daniele.
Extat monumentum ipſius vſque ad hoc ſeculum no-
ſtrum in babylone cunctis notiſsimum. The body of ·· Idem ſupr. in
Ezechiel was ſo likewiſe honoured, and had ſuch ·· Ezechiele.
concourſe of people reſorting one pilgrimage vnto
it, to pray there and worſhip it, that the chaldæans
in whoſe contry it was, feared they would carry it
away, and there vpon obſerued and watched them.
In terra Spyrorum vir pius ille ſepultus iacet. Multique
ad monumentum eius corfluunt ad precationem & ob-
ſequium, Sane quando tanta eo frequentia vnà ad
monumentum eius conueniunt, formidant chaldæi ac
metuunt, ne illum auferant, quapropter egredientem
comitantur & deducunt.

The like they teſtifie of Micheas: *eſt monumen-* ·· In Michea
tum ipſius vſque ad hodiernum tempus, nobiliſsimùm. ·· Prophet. in
So of Abacuc: *Magnis honoribus ſepultus eſt.* So of ·· Abac. Proph.
Achias: *poſtremum honorem & monumentum ſortitus* ·· in Achia. in
eſt. Likewiſe of Aggæus: *prope Sacerdotes, cum ho-* ·· Aggeo Reg.
nore & gloria conditus eſt. So of Samuel the Prophet ·· in chron an.
preſerued with greate honour and his reliks in the ·· 350. Hieron.
tme of Arcadius the Emperour. he himſelfe with a ·· l. aduerſ vigil.
greate number of Biſhops, which put his holy re- ·· Theod. lect l.
lks in ſilke and a veſſel of golde being præſent and ·· 2. Nicephor.
tranſlating them from Iury into Thracia with ·· Eccl hiſt. l 10.
ſuch pompe and honour, that the traine continued ·· cap. 13.
rom paleſtina to Chalcedon. *Omnes Epiſcopi in*

M 4 ·· *ſerico*

*ferico & vafe aureo portauerunt; Omnium Ecclefiarum
populi occurrerunt fanctis reliquijs, & tanta lætitia,
quafi præfentem viuentemque Prophetam cernerent,
fufceperunt: vt de palestina vfque Chalcedonem iun-
gerentur populorum examina.*

*Michael Gly-
cas parte 4.
Annal.*

The reliks of the Patriarks were buryed and
honoured with thofe of the Apoftles in our Chriftian altars. *Iftic venerabiles Patriarcharum & Apoftolorum reliquiæ conditæ.* S. Ephrem relateth the

*Ephrem Syr.
l. de Laudibus
Iofeph. Pa-
triarche.*

greate honour and worship, which the holy Patriarke Iofeph, carryed prifoner away by the If-
malites, to whome his Brothers fold him, did to
the graue and Reliks of Rachel his holy mother,
with the lamentable prayer he made in that facred
place, truely tranflated in thefe words.

*O Rachel, Rachel my mother behold Iofeph thy fonne
whome thou haft loued, what is befallen vnto hym.
Beholde he is ledd captyue as a Malefactour. O Rachel
receaue thy fonne: O mother receaue me: ô my mother
heare the mourning and bitter ftriking of my hart: my
eyes can no longer fuftayne teares, neither my life fuffi-
ceth, to fuch lamentations and groanings.*

The honour which was due and done to her
graue at her firft buriall the fcripture recordeth:

Gen. c. 35.

*Erexit Iacob titulum fuper fepulchrum eius: hic eft ti-
tulus Monumenti Rachel, vfque in præfentem diem.*
Thus it was honoured from the time of her death
to the time of Mofes fo longe after. And with his
allowance in holy fcripture. Both the old and new
teftament with other holy writers vnder either
lawe relate vnto vs the greate honour and reuerence were done euen to the figuratiue things of
the lawe of Mofes, the place of the Temple called
holy of holyes Sancta Sanctorum whether none
went,

went but onely the high preist, and onely once in the yeare with sacrifice, the Arke of the Testament, not to bee touched but by sanctified persons.

The reliks which were in it, and made it more honorable were as S. Paul setteth them downe, a golden pitcher with Manna, the Rodd of Aaron, which had budded, and the Tables of the Testament, and aboue it the Cherubim and Images: *in qua vrna aurea habens manna, & virga Aaron quæ fronduerat, & tabulæ Testamenti, superque eam erant Cherubim gloriæ abumbrantia propitiatorium.* And this holy place was there vpon called the propitiatorie or mercy seate or place of mercy, God often mercifully appearing, and shewing mercy there. Where these holy reliks were kept and honoured, all the vessels of the Sanctuary were vayled with greate honour, none but the sonnes of Aaron might touch, or couer them, whosoeuer els touched them vntouerred, or did see them vnueyled, it was death: *non tangant vasa Sanctuarij ne morian-tur. Alij nulla curiositate videant quæ sunt in San-Ctuario prius quam inuoluantur, alioquin morientur.*

The Apostoliks Fathers of this age did also vse and approue this reuerence both in the Iewes and Christians, as also giue the reason thereof. S. Clement giueth this, because they are holy, and the soules of the bodyes honoured were with God. *Eorum qui apud Deum viuunt, ne reliquiæ quidem corporum sunt inhonoratæ. Siquidem Eliseus Propheta, postquam defunctus est, mortuum suscitauit à piratu Syriæ occisum: quod nunquam accidisset nisi Corpus Elisæi Sanctum esset.* And alleadgeth to this purpose and sence that Ioseph embraced the deade body of his Father Iacob, and Moses and Iesus the sonne

of

Hebr. c.9.

Numer. c.4.

Clem. Apost. const.l.6.cap. 29.

of Naue carryed with them the Reliks of Iosephs body. *Castus Ioseph Patrem iam defunctum in lecto iacentem amplexus est : Item Moses & Iesus filius Naue Reliquas Corporis Ioseph ferebant.* And persuadeth all Bishops and others to the like reuerence of such holy things. And deliuereth it so obserued of the Christians then euen going on pilgrimadge (as now it is termed) to visit and honour Reliks, and God miraculously approued it in the graues and Tombes of two holy Christian Saincts euery yeare miraculously without mans helpe whited and adorned quite ouer, and so pacified the Rage

Clem.l.2.Recogn.

of persecutors towards their Reuerencers. *Progressi essemus nos ad Sepulchra duorum fratrum quorumdam quæ sponte sua, per annos singulos dealbabantur . Quo miraculo multorum aduersum nos repressus est furor, videntes haberi nostros in memoria apud Deum.*

Dion: Areop: Ecclef. Hierarch.c.12.

S.Dionyfius the Areopagite setteth downe also this Christian vse and practise, and yeeldeth this reason, because the body was partaker of paines and labours, together with the soule, when they were in this life vnited together it is to be honoured with the soule in such respects. *Si animo & corpore. Deo gratam acceptamque vitam egit is qui decessit, in honore etiam & pretio erit cum sancto animo corpus, quod sacris sudoribus cum eo certauit & dimicauit.*

The same S. Denys, S.Damascen, and others warrated by the receaued tradition of the Church, frome the Apostles time *ex antiqua accepimus traditione,* that all the Apostles, then liuing S. Denys, S.Tymothie first Bishop of Ephesus S.Hierotheus, and many others of Chrifts Difciples, at the death and affumption of the blessed Virgyn Mary, affembled together where shee ended this life at Hierusalem

falem and Gethfemanie to vifit and reuerence her holy body. *Multi ex Sanctis fratribus noftris, corporis quod authorem vitæ Deumque recepiffet videndi caufa conueniffemus, adorat autem, & Iacobus frater Domini, & Petrus maximum antiquiffimumque Theologorum columen.*

The tradition of the Church plainely expoundeth their pilgrimage thither to worshippe that facred body, *corpus quod Deum fufceperat adorare.* And fo then did. And an Angelicall vifion was feene, and an heauenly harmony continued three dayes there. *Vifio apparuit Angelica, & audita eft pfalmodia cælestium potestatum.* Where wee fee, that both the Apoftles, and difciples of Chrift liuing on earth, and the Angels in heauen gaue honour, and reuerence to this holy relike. Greate was the honour and reuerence which the difciples of S. Iohn Baptift did vnto his holy body both as the Scripture and other writers witneffe, when no thing refpecting the rage of his moft potent perfecutours, they honorably buried it, carrying it out of Herodes iurifdiction vnto Sebafte in Samaria to giue it due honour more freely: where alfo the reliks of Elifeas the Prophet were buried, and reuerenced, and fo they continued in honour, vntill the time of Iulian the Apoftata, when the Iewes and Gentiles maligning the great honour the Chriftians did vnto them, tooke them out of their shrines, mixed thē with the bones of beafts burned them together, and fcattered their ashes into the ayre, which antiquities terme the greateft and horrible wickedneffe. *Illud omnium maxime indignum Sebastianæ in Palestina eft admiffum. Offa namque Elifæi Prophetæ, & Ioannis Baptiftæ loculis fuis extracta,*

&

Dionif. Areopagit.l. de diuin. nom. c.3. & apud S.Ioa. Damafc.fer.1. de dormitione Deiparę. Traditio Ecclef.ib Breu. Rom 18.die Aug. die 4. inf. octan. affumpt. B. Mariæ. Dam. fupr.& alij.

Matth.c.14. Ruffin. l. 2. c. 28.Theod.l. 3.c 6.Niceph. l.10. c.13 l.1. c.19. Metaph. 29.Auguft.

& irrationalium animantium oſsibus, ò immanem auda-
ciam, miſta atque igni tradita, in cineres redaƈta, atque
in aerem diſiecta ſunt.

The auncient Fathers, and Antiquities ſay, that
S. Iohn Baptiſt his diſciples buried his body in a famous place, with greate reuerence; *eum diſcipuli*
furt m ſublatum, cum ſolemni veneratione in celebri
quodam apud Sebaſten Paleſtinæ ſepeliere loco. Simon
Metaphraſtes and others write, that S. Luke the E-
uangeliſt with much difficulty, procured his right
hand, and carried it to Antioch his natiue place, and
from that time vntill Iulianus his perſecution, it remained there in greate honour, doing many miracles. *Ab illo tempore ſita eſt manus illa apud Antio-*
chiam in magno honore habita, & iugis quæ in ea habi-
tat gratiæ fidem faciens miraculis, ad Iuliani Imperato-
ris vſque tempora.

Metaphraſt.
de exportat.
man. San. Io.
Bapt. extra
Antiochiam.
Gulielm. Ei
ſeng. centen-
1. part. 5. diſt.
7. Matth.
weſtm. chron.
an. 458.

The auncient learned French Biſhop Gregorius
Turonenſis writeth, that a noble matrone of that
contry brought with greate reuerence, part of the
blood of that greate Martyr, Chriſt yet liuing vnto
the City of Vaſeus, where building a Church in
his honour, ſhee placed it one the Altare. *Concham*
argenteam præparat, truncatique martyris cruorem in
patriam detulit, & apud vaſatenſem vrbem ædificata
in eius honore Eccleſia, in Sancto altari collocauit. His
head though concealed and hidden by his wicked
Murdereſſe, was yet after found and kept with
greate honour. Such reuerence and deuotion was
vſed to the reliks of the Apoſtles, and other Saints
of this age.

Gregor. Tur.
in lib. in glor.
plur. Martyr.
cap. 12.
Mat. Weſt.
chronic. an,
458.

All hyſtories are full of the greate honour done
to the holy bodies of S. Peter and S. Paul at Rome.
And their Tombes reuerenced as Trophies euen in
this

this age prefently vpon their deathes as moft auncient writers are witneffes: *Ego Apostolorum Trophæa oftendere possum. Etenim si ad vaticanum, vel ad viam Oftienfem abire voles, Trophæa inuenies eorum, qui Ecclefiam hanc Romanam, fundarunt.* And pilgrimadges were made thither to reuerece them, and the Reliks of other Martyrs there, from remote parts of the world, as Perfia Afrike and others in the ftorming times of the firft perfecutions, and the pilgrims themfelues, euen whole families all moft, as S. Marius, and S. Martha his wife, with their two holy Sonnes S. Audifar and S. Abachum were Martyred for fuch holy deuotions. *Marius perfa, nobili loco natus, cum Martha coniuge pari nobilitate, & duobus filijs Audiface & Abachum, Romam venerunt, vt Martyrum fepulchra venerarentur.*

So likewife S. Maurus out of Afrik, *ex Africa veniens ad Sepulchra Apoftolorum.* And the Chriftians in the eafte from whence thefe greate Apoftles came to Rome fo much honoured them as the Chriftian Romans likewife did, that they would with greate honour to them, and daunger to themfelues haue tranflated them from Rome into the eaft foone after their death, but that God miraculoufly decided the queftion for the Romans as S. Gregorie and other worthie Authours are witneffes. They were buried by the Chriftians with greate honour, and prefently there was pilgrimadge, waching, praying and reuerence at their graues, as there now is, fo much as the time of perfecution would permitt.

The body of S. Andrew had the honour to be a buryed with greate reuerence euen by *Maximilla,* wife to Ægeas the Proconful of Achaia who put him

Gaius Epift. ad Proclum. Eufeb.lib.2. hift. c.25.

Breuiar.Rom. die 19. Ianua. Martyrolog. Rom. & Bed. Martyrol. 19. Ianuar. Vfuar. die 20. Ianua. Sur. die 14. Febr. Martyr. Roman. 22. Nouemb. Vfuard.eod. die Bed.die 21. Greg.l.3.ep. 30. ad Conft. Aug Abdias. certam. Apoftol.l.1. Marcell. Petri difcipul. in vit. Petri Linus in paft. Petri. Presbyter. & Diacon. Achaiç in Paffion. S. An-

Greg Bed. &
Ado.prid.cal
Dec. Anton.
part. 1.Petr.
de Natal. l.1.
c. 8. Sur. &
& lippel.die
vlt. Nouemb.
in S. Andrea.
Greg. Turon.
l. in glor.
mart. cap. 30.
Anton.part.1.
tit.6.Doroth.
Synop.Theo-
dor.lect.l.2.
Bed.&.vſuar.
Martyr.in S.
Iacob. Anton.
part.1. Tit.6.
c.7. Petr. de
natal.l.6. c.
133. Vincet. l.
8.c.7. Mant.
faſt.l.7. Mar-
tyrol. Rom.
Calliſt.Pap.2.
fer.de tranſ-
lat.S.Iac. Leo
3.de tranſlat.
eius Trithem
l.de vir.Illu-
ſtrib.
Hieron. l.de
Script.Eccl.
in Io.Euang.
Breuiar.Rom.
27.Decembr.
Martyr.Rom.
Bed.& Vſuar.
eod.die Men.
Græc.6.cal.

him to death. *Sacratiſſimum illius corpus inſigni
pudicitiæ & ſanctitate fæmina Maximilla nomine Se-
natrix, ſuorum adiuta ſolatio cum omni reuerentia de
cruce depoſuit, conditumque aromatibus honorificè ſepe-
liuit.* And ſo it continued therein greate honour
with much reſort of pilgrymes vnto it vntill the
quiet time of Conſtantine, when it was, as many
others, tranſlated to the Emperiall citie of Conſtantinople, ſome parte of it into Satland and ſome
to Rome with exceeding glory and reuerence. For
the body of S.Iames the greater, all antiquities ar
witneſſe, how it was ſoone after his Martirdome
at Hieruſalem tranſlated from them into Spayne
where hee had preached, and there at Compoſtella
preſerued with greate honour, and frequented by
deuoute pilgryms from all contryes to this day.
*S.Iacobus Apoſtolus Frater Beati Iohannis Euangeliſtæ
ab Herode Ægryppa decollatus. Eius ſacra oſſa ab
Hieroſolymis ad Hiſpanias tranſlata, & in vltimis
earum finibus apud Galliciam recondita, celeberrima
illarum gentium veneratione, & frequenti Chriſtianorum concurſu religionis & voti cauſa illuc adeuntium,
piè coluntur.*

I cannot ſpeake of this honour to the body of
S. Iohn the Apoſtle and Euangeliſt in this firſt age,
which by common conſent of writers he ouer-
liued. Dying in the ſecond age: *Sexageſimo octauo
poſt Paſſionem Domini anno mortuus.* But as I haue
proued before of him with all other the Apoſtles,
that he honoured the ſacred bodie of the bleſſed
Virgin, and ruling of the Churches of Aſia after
the Martirdome of the other Apoſtles, *totas Aſia
fundauit rexitque Eccleſias,* where diuers of the
Apoſtles & other Saincts of this age were martired,
and

and their bodies honoured, he ruling this Church that gaue such honour vnto them, must needs also giue allowance there vnto and after his death was at the place thereof honoured with greate concourse of pilgryms, that being one of the most frequented in all those parts of the world.

S. Chrysostome writeth that after his death he and his holy Tombe protected Ephesus, where it was, as he did when he liued. *Post mortem tamquam viuus Ephesum curat.* For S. Thomas wee may omitte all others both old and late Antiquaries of other nations, and content our selues with our owne of this Kingdome so farre remote from the Indyes, where he was martired and his body afterward honoured with greate deuotion, testifying vpon knowne experience that the Christians of this nation went so longe and daungerous pilgrimages from hence to visit and reuerence his holy body, and make oblations there. Thus did our best and noblest kings, So our renowned Bishops, with others. So write our renowned Historians Florentius wigorniensis, William of Malmesbury Roger houeden, and others, our Protestant Antiquaries themselues confessing and confirming it. They exemplifie in our most triumphant and holy king S. Edgar Sigelin or Suithelmus Bishop of Shyrburne, and their retinnes.

Edgarus transmare Romam, & ad sanctum Thomam in Indiam multa munera misit. Legatus in hoc miffus Sigelimus Scireburnensis Episcopus cum magna prosperitate, quod quiuis hoc sæculo miretur, Indiam penetrauit. Our Protestāt Antiquaries say Swithelm or Sigelmtrauelled into *India* to the place of S. *Thomas* his *Buriall,* carried thither the almes or offering of King

Al-

Octob.
Celestin.Papâ
epist.ad Syn.
Ephesin.
Chrys.hom.
in laudem 12.
Apost.&hom.
26.in Epist.
Pauli ad Heb.
Anonymus
antiq.in vit.
Apostolorum
in Ioanne.

Flor.Wigorn.
Chron.an
883.Guliel.
Malmesbur.l.
de gest.Reg.
Roger.Houe-
den part.1.
Mat. Westm.
chron.an.883.
Godwin. Ca-
taloge. of
Bishops in
Salesbury 11.
an. 883.

Flor. wigorn.
supr.an. 883.
Henric. Hun-
ting. hist. l. 5.
Martyrolog.
Rom. Bed.
Vsuard. Ado
& alij 3. die
Iulij.

Ruffin. hist.
Eccl. l 2. c. 5
Socrat. hist.
Eccl. l. 4. c. 14
Sozom. hist.
Eccl. l. 6. c. 18.

Hieron. lib. de
Script. Eccl. in
Iacobo. Breu.
Rom. 1. die
Maij in S. Ia-
cobo. Epiph.
hær. 78.
Egesipp. l de-
exnid. Hiero
sol. Euseb.
hist. Eccl. lib.
2. cap 22.
Euseb. hist.
Eccl l 7. c. 18

Alfred, and brought home many pretious stons of greate pryce: Florentius hath the very same of king alfred.

Our Martyrologes and Antiquities sett downe the translation of part of his body out of India to Edessa in Mesopotamia on the third day of Iuly. *Edessæ in Mesopotamia Translatio S. Thomæ Apostoli ex India: cuius reliquiæ Ortonam postea translatæ sunt.*

And Ruffinus Socrates Sozomen and others are auncient witnesses, that the Reliks of S. Thomas were honoured therein a noble Church dedicated to him. *Edessa Mesopotamiæ Vrbs fidelium populorum est Thomæ Apostoli Reliquijs decorata. In ea Ciuitate egregium & magnificum Templum est diuo Thomæ Apostolo dicatum, crebraque hominum multitudo eò propter loci sanctitatem confluit.* So that wheresoeuer in places neuer so distant, Reliks of his body were from the time of his martirdome, wee see them preserued and honoured with greate deuotion.

Like was the cause of S. Iames Bishop of Hie-rusalem, in this kind, his Sanctitie was such, whilest he lyued, that people in multitudes contended to touch the hemme of his garment, *tanta erat Iacobi vitæ Sanctitas, vt fimbriam vestimenti eius certatim homines cuperent attingere;* And being martired, he was with greate honour buryed by the Temple in a piller still standing in the time of Egesippus, and Eusebius after him as they are witnesses: *Columna eius iuxta Templum adhuc manet,* Wee may gather what honour was vsed to his sacred body, if wee consider the greate reuerence was performed to his very chayre wherein he had sit cloathed, being preserued and honoured from his death: *Sedem Iacobi Apostoli ad hoc vsque temporis seruat am, fratres istic qui successione ordinaria subsecuti sunt, ommbus*

ma-

manifestè monstrant, sicut circa sanctos viros, pietatis gratia, cum veteres tum & præsentes competentem honorem seruarunt, & hodie qnoque seruant. Thus hath Eusebius.

So Theodosius Bishop of Hierusalem witnesseth of his stole, which he sent to S. Ignatius Patriarke of Constantinople for an holy Relike with others. His body was honorably preserued by the Christians, and after with greate reuerence tranflated to Rome, where it is buried with the body of S. Philip the Apostle martired at Hierapolis in Phrygia, and honorably there first buryed by S. Bartholomew the Apostle with other Christians, as Nicephorus with others witnesse, *Bartholomeus Philippi sepulturæ honore præstito, & vrbe tota illustrata, was there preserued with honour,* vntill the the honourable translation thereof, and now honoured at Rome with the body of S. Iames in one Church, as the Churh of Christ honoureth them with one festiuall day.

The body of the same Apostle S. Bartholomew was so likewise honoured. First immediately after his martirdome, king Polymius and the Christians of 12. cities buried his body with greate glory. 12. *Ciuitatum populi qui per eum crediderant vná cum Rege Polymi abstulerunt cum hymnis, & cum omni gloria corpus eius.* And when it was afterward tranflated, it was worshipped in all places, with as greate honour and reuerence *eius sacrum corpus primò ad liparam Insulam, deinde Beneuentum postremo Romam ad Insulam Tiberinam translatum, ibi pia fidelium veneratione honoratur.*

Nicephorus writeth that the body of S. Matthew Martired in Æthiopia, was præsently layd on

Theod. Episc. Hier. epist. ad S. Ignat. Syn. 8. act. 1.
Breu. Rom. 1. die Maij martyrol. Rom.
Bed. Vsuar. eod. die Menol. Græc. 13. cal. Iul. Nice. l. 2. hist. c. 39.
Continuat. Sigeb an. 1157
Sigeb. chron. an. 489. Mat. westm. chron. an. 479. 831.
Abdias certa Apost. lib. 8.
Petr. de Nat. l. 7 c. 103 Anton. part. 1. tit. 6 c. 12. Guliel. Eisengr. cent. 1 part. 5, dist. 7. Martyrol. Rom. die 25. Aug.
Bed. Vsuard Ado & alij die 24. Aug.
Nicephorus hist. Eccl. l. 2. c. 41.

N a bedd

a bedde of gold, wrapped in pretious cloathes, and ſo placed in the Princes palace. *Cuius ſacrum tabernaculum in aureo repoſitum lecto, ſplendidiſque inuolutum veſtibus, palatio Fuluianus infert:* It was afterward with greate honour tranſlated into diuers nations, and buried after with much glory at Salernum. *Salerni tranſlatio S. Matthæi Apoſtoli, cuius ſacrum corpus olim ex Æthiopia ad diuerſas regiones: & demum ad eam vrbem delatum, ibidem in Eccleſia eius nomine dedicata ſummo honore conditum fuit.* Wee finde that S. Simon and Iude being martyred in Perſia, King Zerſes, or Xerxes confiſcating the Pagan Prieſts goods which put them to death, did with greate honour within three moneths tranſlate their bodies into his City. *Rex Zerſes confiſcauit omnes Pontifices, corpora autem Sanctorum Apoſtolorum Symonis & Iude ingenti honore ad ſuam tranſtulit ciuitatem.* He erected a moſt ſumptuous Church vnto them, there burying their bodies in a ſyluer shrine. *Sarcophagum corpora beatorum Apoſtolorum portantem ex argento puro inſtituit.*

S. Matthias choſen in the place of Iudas was martyred in Iury, his body was preſerued with greate care and reuerence, and in after times honorably tranſlated to Rome, and Treues in Germany, and there viſited with greate deuotion. And not onely the holy bodies of the Apoſtles, and other Saincts in this age were thus honoured and reuerenced of the Chriſtians, but their cloathes and whatſoeuer touched their ſacred bodies as the auncient learned Fathers and Saincts which alſo were worshippers of them with the whole Chriſtian Catholike world are witneſſes. *Apoſtolorum virtus vſque adeo emicuit, vt in omnem terram eorum ſonus exierit.*

Martyr Rom. die 6. Maij Greg. 7. epiſt. ad Alfanum Epiſc. Salerni. Leo Oſtien. in chron. Caſin. l. 3. c. 44. Anonym. ant in vit. Apoſt. in S. Symone & Iuda. Abd. certâ Apoſt. l 4 Anton. part. 1. titul. 6. cap. 14. Petr. de Nat. l 9. c. 115. Ado Treuer. Bed. & Vſuard 5. Calend. Nou. Rom. Mart. 24. Febr. Ant. part. 1. tit. 6. c. 15. Petr. de Natal. l. 3. cap. 149. Anton. ſupr. Annal. Eccl. Treuer. Sur. & Lippol. die 24 Febr. Petr. Merſſ. Catal Epiſc. Treuer. Iuſt. Martyr queſt. 28. Doroth. in Synopſi. S. Io. Damaſc. hiſt Barlaam c. 12 & alij.

exierit. Horum non verba duntaxat, & opera, sed ipse quoque cruor, & ossa omni sanctitate plena sunt. Dæmones namque in fugam vertunt, atque ijs, qui cum fide accedunt, incurabiles alioqui morbos profligant. Quin vestes quoque ipsæ, & si quid aliud ad pretiosa eorum corpora proprius accessit, omnibus venerationi sunt.

Thus were the chaines of S. Peter both those wherewith he was chained vnder Herod, at Hierusalem, adorned with gold, and pretious stones, *auro gemisque ornata,* & wherewith he was chained at Rome vnder Nero, his chaire and other such reliks of him were honoured by the greatest and holiest Christians. So haue the Latine, so the Greeke antiquities. *Veneratio prætiosæ cathenæ qua beatus Apostolus Petrus, Christi causa Herodis iussu vinctus est.*

So were the nayles with which S. Peter was nayled to his crosse honoured by the holy Fathers: *beati claui qui sancta illa membra penetrarunt.* S. Chrysostome expresseth how they & the sword wherewith S. Paul was be headed had euer beene honoured, when he wished that sword for his crowne, and S. Peters nayles to be set as pretious stones in his diademe. *Sit mihi gladius ille pro corona, & claui Petri pro gemmis infixis in diademate.*

The garment of the blessed Virgin Mary was accompted pretious, preserued with honour in a siluer chest, translated with great reuerence, *in argenteo loculo,* and the very house wherein it was kept and reuerenced, therevpon called the holy Chest: *qua ædes ex eo sacer loculus appellatur.* Part of the garment of S. Iohn Baptist was so kept, and reuerenced: *Venerabilis vestis Ioannis Baptistæ,* as likewise

Breu. Rom. 1 die Aug. Martyr. Rom. Beda. Vsuard. Ado eod. die. Menol. Græc. 17. cal. Frebr. Greg epist. l. 1. epist. 6. lib. 6. epist. 23. Aug. Serm. 29. de Sanctis Arator l. 1. in act. Chrysostom. apud Metaph. Breu. Rom. in octau. SS. A-post. Petri & Pauli. die 6. Iulij.

Io. Zonoras in Leone. Mag. Matth. West. chron. an. 910 Zonor. de Imperio Rom. pueri.

wise

wiſe part of his hayre clotered with blood. *Partem capillorum eiuſdem ſanguine concretam.*

The cloath made by our lady with the pictures of Chriſt and his Apoſtles was honoured at Hieruſalem . *In Eccleſia veneratur.* There is no end in antiquities in ſuch holy reuerence . And not onely of the Reliks of our Lady , S. Iohn Baptiſt, and the Apoſtles, but of all other holy Martirs, and Saincts of this age, S. Stephen, S. Luke, S. Marke, the three Princes of the Eaſt, that offered to our Sauiour new borne, S. Timothie, S. Lazarus, S. Mary Magdalen, S. Martha and others holy men and women to many to be recited.

And this Kingdome of Britaine was as forward as any other in this kinde of worſhip as their renowned Biſhop and Antiquary relateth of his Britans. *Præ omni peregrino labore, Romam peregrè libentiùs eundo, deuotis mentibus Apoſtolorum limina propenſiùs adorant. Sanctorum reliquijs deuotam reuerentiam exhibere, longéque magis quam vllam gentem honorem deferre videmus.* And this he writeth of them from their firſt conuerſion , which was in this age . And doth ſo accordingly intitle that Chapter : *De antiqua fidei fundatione, chriſtianitatis amore & deuotione.*

Pope Bonifacius in an Epiſtle to King Edward the firſt, teſtifieth, that the Further part of Britayne now named Scotland was conuerted by the holy Reliks of S. Peter the Apoſtle. *Regnum Scotiæ per Beati Petri Apoſtoli venerandas Reliquias non ſine ſuperni dono muneris conuerſum extitit ad Fidei Catholicæ vnitatem.* S. Ioſeph of Aramathia coming hither by all aſſent, both of Proteſtant and Catholike Antiquaries, with his Religious company,

---

Beda Arcuulfus & alij de locis Sanctis.

The firſt Chriſtians in Britaine did Profeſſe and practiſe this doctrine.

Girald. Cābr. deſcr. Cambr. c.18.

Bonifacius Pap. epiſt. ad Regē Eduard. The walſingham hiſt. Angl. in Eduard. 1.

pany, was present with the Apostles at the death and Assumption of our blessed lady, and so honoured her sacred body with them, spoken of before, and brought with him hither, and preserued here with greate reuerence all his life two little syluer vessels full of the bloody sweate of Christ, *duo vascula alba argentea cruore Prophetæ Iesu, & sudore per-impleta.*

fix: Io: Cap-grau. in S. Ioseph Ara-mathien:

All histories agree that the body of S. Ioseph was there preserued with greate honour, and reuerenced with great resorte of pilgryms to that, and other Reliks there vntill these times of desolation, and those holy Reliks gaue that glorious denomination to the happy place of their preseruing to be stiled *cœmiterium Sanctum, tumulus Sanctorum, the holy Church-yard, graue of Saincts,* and the like. Vigilantius is remembred in histories to haue beene the first man of note among Christians which denied or impugned this doctrine, and for that, as other his singular assertions condemned for an heretik, so our Protestants thus confesse: *Vigilantius was condemned of heresie for deny all thereof.* He lyued in the fourth hundred of yeares the Church of Christ neuer hearing of this heresie before; and S. Hierome then liuing and writing calleth him for such stramage dreames, rather Dormitantius, a sleepy drowsy fellowe, then Vigilantius, a waking watchfull mã. *Negat sepulchra veneranda, damnatque Sanctorum vigilias. Ex quo fit, vt dormitantius potiùs, quàm vigilantius, vocari debeat.* He calleth him an vnhappy man to be bewayled with floods of teares, a stinking mouth breather of most filthy rotonnesse, a monster to be abandoned to the vthermost part of the world. *Os fœtidum putorem spurcissimum*

Hieronyn. cont. vigilant. & ep. 53. ad Riparium, & Desider. Gennad. in catalog. cap. 53. Willet Antilog pag 13. Wotton def. of part. pag. 9. perkins probl. pag. 81. Iouas Aurelian. l. 1. Sedul. & alij. Hieronym. sup. and Ripar. & desiderium. lib. aduers. vigilant. cap. 2.

proferens. Portentum in terras vltimas deportandum.

Inuocation
and honour
of sain&ts.

The laſt exception which our Proteſtants in this Article make againſt the doctrine of the Church of Rome, is thus regiſtred by them. *The Romish doctrine concerning inuoation of Saincts, is a fonde thing, vainely inuented, and grounded vpon no warrantie of Scripture, but rather repugnant to the worde of God.* This is confuted by that is ſaid before of the holy Reliks and Images of Sain&ts: For if they, as is inuincibly proued by the doctrine and practiſe of this age, may and ought to be reuerenced, their happy and bleſſed ſoules, and Angels in eternall Ioye & bliſſe muſt needs challédge ſuch dutie from them that liue, and prayers may be offered to ſuch

Concil. gan-
gren. epiſt. &
can. 14.15.16.
Socrat. Hi-
ſtor. l. 2. cap.
33. Sozom.
Hiſtor. Eccl.
l. 3. cap. 13.
Epiphan.
Hier. 40.
Nicephor.
Hiſt. l. 9. cap.
16.
Hieron. con-
tra vigilant.

perfe&ted in celeſtiall knowledge, charitie and neuer chaunging bleſſednes.

The firſt among Chriſtians ſuſpe&ted to haue denyed this Catholike doctrine and practiſe of the church of Chriſt was Euſtachius by ſome Euta&tus a Biſhop in Armenia diſallowing the Churches of Martyrs *loca San&torum martyrum vel Baſilicas,* as he is charged in the councell of Gangra wherein he was condemned for that, and other wicked aſſertions, and by other antiquities. Yet Sozomen, Nicephorus and others write, how he ſought to cleare himſelfe from accuſations. And to ſpeake of certaine things, Vigilantius was the firſt knowne and certainely proued impugner of the Inuocation of Sain&ts, as of worſhip to their reliks before ſpoaken of, and was condemned for ſuch a

Socrat. Supr.
l. 2. cap. 33.

monſter as is already declared. And Euſtachius for his ſingular boldnes in ſuch things was degraded, and his errours códemned in publik Councel. *Concilium Gangris in Paphlagonia coa&tum, gradu Epiſco-*
pali

pali dimouit, eiusque dogmata anathemate damnauit.

This is sufficiently proued by our Protestant writers themselues, openly confessing; *all antiquitie taught Inuocation of saincts.* Therefore few testimonies of this first age will be needfull in a confessed doctrine, and practise of all ages with faithfull people. Lesse was the knowledge of the Saincts deceased before the Passion of Christ, then after, when they were by that happy redemption in glory. And yet S. Ephrem produceth the holy Patriarke Ioseph praying to his mother Rachel deceased. *O Rachel, Rachel mater mea, exurge de puluere, & intuere Ioseph filium tuum. Suscipe Rachel filium tuum. Audi mater mea cordis mei gemitum, amarumque eiulatum.*

S. Ignatius in this age, is a worthie witnesse, that not onely the liuing, which were present at the Passion of Christ, did know, behold and see it, but the Angels in heaue & the soules of thê that were vnder the earth, which arose with their bodies at the Resurrection of Christ, did likewise the same. *Crucifixus & mortuus est, videntibus cœlestibus, terrenis, & ijs qui subterra detinebantur: cælestibus quidem inspicientibus, nimirum incorporeis naturis: terrenis verò, vt Iudæis & Romanis, & cæteris qui tunc temporis Crucifixo Domino aderant: subterraneis autem ijs videlicet, qui plurimi cum Domino resurrexerunt.*

If a man on earth and in body, might, though extraordinarily, know the Angels and spirituall things, with their orders in heauen, as S. Ignatius witnesseth of himselfe, *hæc nouerim,* much more do they know the things on earth. *Angelicos ordines, Archangelorum, militiarumque cœlestium discrimina,*

N 4   *vir-*

Morton
Apolog. part.
1. pag. 227.
228. Perk.
probl. pag.
89. 93 Ormer
pict. pap. pag.
26, 27. Middlet. papista.
pag. 129.
Ephrem Syrus lib. de laudibus Ioseph Patriarchæ.

Ignatius epist. ad Trallianos.

Ignat. epist. ad Trallian.

virtutum dominationumque differentias, thronorum,
potestatumque distantias, principatum magnificentias,
Cherubim Seraphimque excellentias, spiritus sublimi-
tatem, & Domini Regnum, & incomparabilem Dei
Patris Omnipotentis diuinitatem, Hæc cum nouerim.

Ignat. epist.
ad Heronem.

And he plainely teacheth in an other place, that
the Angels in heauen, and not onely God know
our affaires on earth and haue regard of them,
and so witnesseth to S. Hieron. *Præcipio tibi coram*
Deo, qui est super omnia, & coram Christo præsente, &

x. Timoth. 5. *Spiritu Sancto, & coram ministrantibus legionibus,*
custodi depositum meum. So S. Paule the Apostle
wrote to S. Timothie: *Testor coram Deo & Christo*
Iesu & electis Angelis vt hæc custodias. Where
botht he Apostle & S. Ignatius acknowledge both
knowledge and care of mens actions on earth to
be in the holy Angels, as in God himselfe, though
with a difference of the Creatour, and excellent
creatures. S. Hierotheus Master of S. Denis the
Areopagite, as he termeth him testifieth and hee
approueth it that all loue not onely of God, *but*

Dionisi
Areopag. l.
diu.nom. cap.
4.

Angels also hath this nature that Superiour things
haue care of the inferiour, and those conforme themselues
to the Superiour. Amorem siue diuinum, siue angelicum,
siue spiritualem, siue (vt ita dicam) animalem, siue
naturalem vim quandam coniungentem miscentemqne
intelligamus, quæ superiora quidem impellit, vt inferio-
ribus prospiciant vt consulant, paria autem, vt inter

Dionyf. l.
cæleft. Hie-
rarch. cap. 9.

se societate iungantur, inferiora verò, vt se conuertant
ad superiora.

And the same S. Denis saith plainely, both that
the Angels are Rulers of nations euen all nations,
Angeli vnicuique nationi præfecti. And that God
hath cōmitted all men to his Angels, for their Saluation,

uation, and this is the prouidence of God. *Vna qui-*
dem de omnibus altißimi prouidentia omnes homines cap. 3. patt. 3.
salutis causa Angelis suis ad se deducendos distri- ante med.
buerit. And he plainely saith that the prayers of
holy people and Saincts both in this world and in
heauen are profitable to them which be worthie
of them. *Iustorum etiam in hac vita, ne dum post mor-*
tem, ijs dumtaxat prosint, qui sacris precibus digni sint,
vere oraculorum traditiones nos edocent.

S. Clement is also witnesse, and citeth it from
S. Peter the Apostle his mouth, that the Angels Clem. Rom.
haue the care and custody of men, and euery nation l. 2. Re-
hath an Angel to whome it is committed by God. cognit.
Est enim vniuscuiusque gentis Angelus, cui credita
est gentis ipsius dispensatio à Deo. And proueth that
not onely God the holy Trinity, but all Saincts and l. 8. Consti-
administring Angels do so and behold our Actions tut. Apo-
on earth, and exemplifieth in the election of stolic. cap. 11.
Bishops. *Coram Iudice Deo & Christo, præsente etiam*
Spiritu sancto, atque omnibus Sanctis, & administra- l. 5. cap 8.
torijs spiritibus. And comaundeth to honour Saints edit. Turr.
and Martirs. *De Martiribus præcipimus vobis, vt in* Græc. & c. 7.
omni honore sint apud vos. And prescribeth diuers Latin. l. 8. c. 33
of their festiuities to be kept holy, with honour.

The short historie of S. Paule ascribed to S. Linus Successour to S. Peter, who by all Antiquitie
wrote the Martyrdome of S. Paule, doth testifie in
the name of S. Plantilla, who ministred to S. Paule,
and was present at his death, that this glorious A-
postle soone after his martyrdome appeared to that
holy woman in glory, with an Innumerable com-
pany of heauenly *creatures innumerabilium candida-* S. Linus hist.
torum caterua comitatus, and sayd vnto her, that as S. Pauli.
shee had done holy offices to him on earth, so he in
heauen

heauen would remember her and shortly returne to bring her thither, and there shew her the glory of God. Which was soone after performed at her Martyr-dome. *Tu mihi Plautilla in terris obsequium prestitisti, ego tibi quam primum ad Regna pergenti officiosissimè obsequar, in proximo namque pro te reuertar, & tibi Regis inuicti gloriam demonstrabo,*

This is proued by the auncient Masses ascribed to the holy Apostles, in which there is expresse prayer, not onely to God to be assisted and helped by the prayers of the blessed Virgin Mary, and other Saincts, *libera nos quesumus Domine, ab omni malo præsente ac futuro, intercessionibus Immaculatæ & Gloriosæ Dominæ nostræ Deiparæ, Semperque Virginis Mariæ.* But to the very Saincts themselues: *commemorationem agamus Sanctissimæ, Immaculatæ Gloriosissimæ, benedictæ Dominæ nostræ Matris Dei & semper Virginis Mariæ, atque omnium Sanctorum & Iustorum, vt precibus & intercessionibus eorum omnes misericordiam consequamur.* It is manifest in histo-ries, that in all places, where Christ was preached, Churches, and Altars were founded and dedicated in honour of Saincts which dyed in this age. And they ther ly and are honoured. S. Martial then liuing and writing so testifieth of S. Stephen. S. Martha with allowance of S. Maximus Bishop there built a Church in honour of the blessed Virgin Mary betwene Arles and Auinion. S. Ma-ternus sent into Germany by S. Peter founded a Church at Bonna in honour of S. Iohn Baptist, and an other at Colē in honour of S. Mathias the Apo-stle. And an other at Tungers in honour of the blessed Virgin. S. Eucharius an other of S. Peters disciples in this time dedicated a Church at Tre-uers

Missa S. Petri Marci, Iacobi Minor. Mat.
Missa S. Iaco-bi Maioris.

Martial. epist. ad Burdegal. c.3.
Petr. de Nat. lib.6. c.151.
Vinc. l 9. c. 99 & seq. Ant. part. 1. Titul. 6. c.20. Petr. Masseus in Ca. Episcop. Colen. Annal. Colonien. Annal.
Tungren in S. Materno.
Annal. Treu.

uers in honour of S. Iohn the Euangelist. S. Saui-
nianus sent by S. Peter into France, builded there
three Churches, one in honour of the blessed Virgin Mary, a second in honour of S. Iohn Baptist,
the third in honour of S. Stephen: *constructis tribus*
Ecclesys in honorem Virginis Mariæ, Iohannis Baptistæ
& S. Stephani. And S. Altinus one in honour of our
lady. The Churches which were thus founded and
dedicated to Saincts in this age in histories, are too
many to recite, confessed to be so in all places
both by Catholik and Protestant Antiquaries. So
it was here in Britayne as the first knowne
Church thereof at Glastenbury witnesseth erected and dedicated to our blessed lady both by
heauenly and earthly warrant. The Angel of God
so directed S. Ioseph and his holy company: And
to make euident to all, that to dedicate Churches
then to the honour of Saincts, was in them to
honour Saincts and pray vnto them, and by them
to be protected, it is so proued of hese our primatiue founders in Religion, of this first age, *that they*
prayed vnto the blessed Virgin and honoured her, and
she protected them, as the most auncient monuments
of that place and other Antiquities clearely proue: præ-
dicti Sancti in eodem deserto conuersantes per Archan-
gelum Gabrielem in visione admoniti sunt, Ecclesiam
in honore Sanctæ Dei Genitricis & perpetuæ Virginis
Mariæ cælitus demonstrato construere, duodecim igitur
Sancti in eodem loco Deo & Beatæ Virgini deuota ex-
hibentes obsequia, vigilijs, Ieiunijs & orationibus
vacantes; eiusdem Virginis Dei Genitricis auxilio in
necessitatibus suis refocillabantur.

These antiquities say this was the first Church
which the Christians builded in this country, and

it

---

in S. Eucha-
rio. Guliel.
Eisengren.
centu. 1. part.
1. dist. 3

The first
Christian
Britans thus
professed, and
practised.

Antiquitat.
glast. manu-
script. Tabul.
ligneis fix.
Gal. Mal-
mesb. l. de
antiquit.
Cænobij gla-
ston. M. S.
Capgrau.
catal. in 6.
Ioseph S.
Patric. in epi-
stol. Historia
apud S. Ed-
mundum.

it was a greate honour vnto it to be dedicated by Christ to his mothers honour. *Et cum hæc Ecclesia in hac Regione prima fuit, ampliori cum dignitate Dei filius insigniuit, ipsum videlicet in honore suæ matris dedicando.* All agree that this Church was builded by S. Ioseph, and his Affociats.

And yet the same antiquities, and other Historians, euen Proteftants who alleadge, the Authoritie of S. Auguftine termed the Apoftle of the English nation, to the fame purpofe are witneffes that there was a Church miraculoufly builded before S. Ioseph and his holy companians came hither, and here founded by them wholly finished and perfected, dedicated alfo to the bleffed Virgin Mary. *Primi Catholicæ legis Neophytæ antiquam Deo dictante repererunt Ecclesiam, nulla hominum arte, vt referunt constructam, immo humanæ saluti à Deo paratam, quam postmodum ipse cælorum fabricator multis miraculorum gestis, multisque virtutum mysterijs, sibi Sanctæque Dei Genitrici Mariæ se consecrasse monstrauit.* This was in the 31. yeare after the Paffion of Chrift, and after the affumption of our lady 15. *Anno post Passionem Domini 31. post Assumptionem Gloriosæ Virginis 15.* When few other Sainéts in the lawe of Chrift were deceafed this life, and then in heauen. Thus were our Two firft Churches dedicated here by greateft warrant to the honour of the bleffed Virgin Mary Mother of God, where shee affifted and protected her Suppliant Seruants and petitioners there. And S. Bede with all Antiquaries, Catholiks & Proteftants confenteth, that the Britans kept their firft faith inuiolate and whole vntill the cruell perfecution of Dioclefian: *suseptam fidem Britanni vsque in tempora Dioclesiani*

Prin-

Antiquitat. glaft. tabulis fix. sup. S. Auguftinus in Ecclefia S. Edmundi. Matth. parker. Antiquit. Britan. c. 2. p. 3. edit. Hanouiç an. 1605.

Bed. hiftor. Eccl. Angl. l. 1. cap. 4.

Principis inuiolatam integramque quieta in pace seruabant: And when this Kingdom was generally, conuerted, which happend in the succeding age all the Temples before founded to false Gods were by common and greatest authoritie in all opinions, euen now whatsoeuer, of the holy pope S. Eleutherius his legats, and our holy kinge S. Lucius, chaunged into Christian Churches, dedicated to God and his Saincts. *Templa quæ in honore plurimorum Deorum fundata fuerant, vni Deo, eiusque Sanctis dedicauerunt.* So they dedicated Churches to the holy Angels namely S. Michael the Archangel, honoured and prayed vnto him and he protected them.

Phaganus & Damianus Oratorium ædificauerunt in honore S. Michaelis Archangeli quatenus ibi ab hominibus haberet honorem qui homines in perpetuos honores iubente Deo est introducturus. So they prayed vnto the Saincts as is euident in the Examples of Sainct Heraclius our Martyr at the death of our fist Martyr S. Alban praying to him and heard, and helped by him. And S. Amphibalus that conuerted Saint Alban, thus prayed vnto him, both to be assisted by him and the holy Angels. *Sancte Albane Deum nostrum depreceris, vt mihi Angelum bonum obuiam mittat, ne mihi prædo truculentus obsistere, nec Iter meum pars iniqua valeat impedire.* So it was in all after times which I am not to speake of in this place, but thus may end this tedious and confused Article stuffed with so many fulshoods, and aunciently condemned heresies. I may be more breife in the rest of their following Articles, not conteyning so many particulars.

Galfrid. histor. Briton. l. 4. c. 19.
Matth. west. an. 185.
Antiquitat. glaston. manuscript. epistol. S. Patricij Capgr. catal. in S. Patric. & Ioseph. Bed. hist. l. 1. c. 7. Matth. westin. An. 303.
Manuscript. Antiq. Iacob. gemen. in vit. S. Amphibali Cap grau. in eod. & in S. Alban. Gradual. antiq. & miss. Sarisb. in festo S. Albani. litan. Angl. antiq. ante bapt. & commend. animæ.

THE

THE IX. CHAPTER.

The 23. article examined.

THeir next Article, the 23. in number, is this. *It is not lawfull for any man to take vpon him, the office of publik preaching or ministring the Sacraments in the Congregation, before he be lawfully called, and sent to execute the same. And those wee ought to Iudge lawfully called and sent, which be chosen and called to this worke by men who haue publik authoritie giuen vnto them in the Congregation, to call and send ministers in the Lords vineyard.* This is the whole Article, wherein there is no controuersie with, or against the Church of Rome neuer allowing any for Preists or publike ministers of the holy Sacraments but such as are duely and truely consecrated in the Sacrament of holy orders, onely ministred by lawfully and Canonically Sacred Bishops, as the doctryne and practise of this Apostolike age was, as I haue proued before and S. Ignatius with others thus proue vnto vs: *Non licet sine Episcopo baptizare neque offerre, neque sacrificium immolare, neque Dochen celebrare, sed quodcumque illi visum fuerit secundum beneplacitum Dei, vt tutum & ratum sit, faciatis.* No Sacrament could be ministred, nothing done in the Church without the Bishops authoritie, and approbation. No man could be a Preist, minister Sacraments, or exercise any Ecclesiasticall order, or function, but onely such as were consecrated thereunto by lawfull Bishops. *Nihil sine Episcopis facito, baptizant, sacrificant, eligunt, manus imponunt.* And these Protestants themselues

both

S. Ignatius epist. ad Smyrnen:

Epistol. ad Heron.

both in their Booke of their pretended confecration and their 36. Article hereafter, intituled, of
Confecration of Bishops, and Minifters, as alfo
their publik gloffe therevpon, and common pra-
&ife do thus teftifie : *The Superioritie and authoritie*
which Bishops and Archbishops do exercife in ordering
and confecrating of Bishops and Ecclefiafticall minifters,
is grounded vpon the word of God. From the Apoftles
dayes hithertothere neuer wanted à Succeffion of Bis-
hops neither in the East, nor wefterne Churches. And
from the firft nurfing of their Religion here in England, they euer by their publik proceedings allowed that confecration, which was in the Romane Church, and moft willingly without any
addition or ceremony allowed fuch as were fo
confecrated to be Preifts, Minifters, and Ecclefiafticall men among them, if they would in wordly refpects, and in externall shew giue any allowance to their Religion. And at this day they
contend to deriue their owne pretended Bishops
and Minifters by Confecration from our Catholik
Roman Bishops.

This Article as their gloffe expoundeth it, feemeth to haue beene made agaynft the *Mancerians,*
Anabaptifts, family of loue, and fuch others rifen vp
in their Proteftat Schoole denying externall Ordination, and calling of cleargie men. But being well
examined, it doth both free the Roman Church, as
is proued and they confeffe, and condemneth all
Proteftants in the world. Firft for forreyne Proteftants none of them take or clayme ordination
true or pretended, from eyther true or pretended
Bishops, and fo by that is already faide, are vtterly
condemned by this Article. And for our English
Pro-

Proteft.Boo-
ke of confe-
crat. pref. &
per tot. artic.
36.infra.prot.
gloffe vpon
the fame. ca-
nons, Iniun-
ctions &c.

Them: Ro-
gers Analif.
vpon the b. of
Articles, art.
23. allowed
by the lawf.
authoritie of
the Church
of Engl.

Proteſtants which pretended a calling, and ordination by Bishops, they are in the ſame caſe by their owne decree in this Article, for therein they ſay that men lawfully called, and ſent, be onely they, *which be choſen and called by men who haue publike authoritie giuen vnto them in the congregation (Churche they meane) to call and ſend miniſters in the Lords vineyard :* But I haue proued before, in particular, and euery of their Articles more then halfe of them in order without excepting any one inuincibly confuted proue the ſame, that theſe men are no part, parcell or congregation of the true Church of Chriſt, and ſo no men among them can pretend to haue authoritie, publike, or other to ſend Miniſters in the Lords vineyard being themſelues no members or parſons, commaundeing or to be commaunded, conſecrating or to be cóſecrated therein, much leſſe to haue ſuch publike authoritie in it, as this Article appointeth for this buſines. Secondly there were no men amonge them at the makinge of theſe Articles, nor at the birth of thir Religion here in the firſt yeare of Queene Elizabeth, which had or poſſibly in their proceedings could haue any ſuch publik authoritie, to call and ſend Mininiſters in the Lords vineyard . For their whole congregation conſiſted of a woman Queene Elizabeth, their pretended cleargie, and others confeſſed meerely temporall men.

Lette vs take all theſe eyther ioyntly togeather as in parlament, or by themſelues ſeuerally, and no ſuch publik authoritie will be founde in them. The Queene a woman by Sexe was neyther men, nor man haueing ſuch authoritie, and their 37. Article denyeth any ſuch prower in her, eyther

for

for herselfe or others. All their pretended Bishops were by all Confiftories Ecclefiafticall & Temporall euen the parlament, and Iudgements in the Temporall lawe, adiudged to haue no fuch authoritie.

The firft parlament of Q. Elizabeth which reuiued their Religion, had not one true or pretended Bishop that had voyce in parlament that confented vnto it, but all the Bishops which had, and onely had, fuch publik authoritie, did difclayme and difagree to that change, the Temporall Lords, knights, and burgeffes neyther had nor could giue which they had not, fuch authoritie. No forreyne Pope, Patriarke, Archbishop or Bishop did or could giue it here, by their owne lawes. For Q. Elizabeth, King Iames and K. Charles by their parlaments and Statutes haue made holy preifthood Treafon. And this new Proteftant Queene Elizabeth her Religion beginning here in the yeare 1558. and 1559. in her firft parlament, neuer had any knowne publike allowed fquare, rule, forme, manner, Order, or fashion whatfoeuer, for any to haue publik authoritie to call, make, fend or fette forth any pretended Minifter vntil the yeare 1562. when their Religion was 4. yeares old, and thefe Articles were made, & in them the booke of King Edward the 6. about 10. or 11. yeares old, when he fette it forth by parlament, was firft called from death werewith it perished in the firft yeare of Queene Mary.

It hath beene pretended from a new borne Regifter of Matthew parker, that hee was made a Bishop by Barlowe, Scorye, and 3. others by vertue of a commiffion from Queene Elizabeth, and

Stow hift. in Q. Mary an. 1. & an. 1. of Q. Elizabeth. Parker. Ant. Brit. in Tho. Cranmar. Godwin. Catal. of Bish. folpe. Hollin. hift. of Engl. in Q. Mary Statutes of Q Eliz. K. Iames and K. Charles make Preifthood treafon.

The new Proteftant booke of Confec. an. 2. Eduardi 6. in Parlam. ftatut. an 1. Marie. Booke of articles an. 1562. art. 36.

O   this

this new worke was acted on the 17. day of December, but alas, they had then no forme our order to do such a busines, if they had beene such publik allowed and authorized men as this Article appointeth, vntill 4. yeares after, this pretended admittance alleadged to haue beene 17. Decemb. an. 1559. And their owne publike confession is, in the Register it selfe as they haue published it in Matthew parker their first pretended protestantly made Archbishope his booke and Register, That none of those pretended Consecratours was admitted for a true or pretended Consecratour vntill after this supposed consecration of Matthew parker. For they say from their pretended Register of Matthew parker *Anno* 1559. *Matth. part. cant. conf.* 17. *Decem. by william Barlowe, Ihon Scory, Miles Couerdale Ihon hodgeskins, by these Matthew parker was consecrated Archbishop of Canterbury, the seuententh day of December, in the yeare* 1559. Their Catalogue of Bishops saith: he was consecrated December. 17. 1559. by W. Barlowe, Io: Scory, and Ihon hodgeskins. This is vtterly false, and vnpossible, by their owne testimonies, and proceedings, to be true. For their owne Register as it is published in Matthew parker his owne writings proueth directly that two of these 4. pretended Consecratouts were neuer allowed for such or Bishops, or any men hauing such publike authoritie in their Protestant Religion, as this their Article requireth of necessitie to call and send Ministers, These were Miles Couerdale, and Ihon Hodgeskings neuer hauing any such power in Q. Elizabeth her time. And for the other two william Barlowe, and Ihon Scory they were not allowed by these Protestants

for

Franc. Mason
l. 3. c. 4. of
conf. p. 127.
ex Regist.
Matth. park.
to: 1. f. 2. &
10. Godw.
catal. of Bish.
in Canterb.
69. Matth.
parker,

for Bishops or such men, vntill Matthew parker
was as they pretend by their Register consecrated
by them william Barlowe stiled before D. of Diuinitie or a preist Regular was allowed for such a
man vpon the 20. day of December 1559. 3. dayes
after matthew parkers pretended ordination, by
him. Will: Barlowe Th. D. Presb. Reg. Conf.
1559. Decem. 20. and the other Ihon Scory then
stiled onely Bachelour of Diuiuitie and preist Regular, was also first allowed the same 20. day of
December. Ioh: Scory Th. Bac. Presb. Regn.
Conf. 1559. Dec. 20. And their owne catalogue of
their pretended Bishops assureth vs further that
this Matthew parker was amóg them Archbishop
of Conterbury in the month of Iuly before. So he
could haue no consecration true or pretended, by
their owne proceeding. I adde further concerning
the pretended Register by which they haue thus
vainely claymed an Inualid Title to Ecclesiasticall
function, and orders, sette out in the booke of
their first pretended Protestant Archbishop, Matthew parker printed at Hanouia 1605. called Antiquitates Britannicæ of the Archbishops of Canterbury, there is no worde our mention at all, of
any such thing, in that old manuscript copie thereof, which I haue seene and diligently examined.

And any man reading the printed booke will
manifestly see it is a meerely foisted and inserted,
thing hauing no connexion correspondence or
affinitie either with that which goeth before, or
followeth it. And conteyneth more things done
after Matthew parker had written that Booke.
But of this their new founde consecration I shall
entreate, more largely hereafter in their 25. and

*Register.
Episcopor.
Protestant.
Angl. apud
Matth. park.
antiquit. Bri-
tanniæ. pag.
39. edit. Ha-
nouiæ an.
1605.*

*Godwyd Ca-
talog. of Bi-
shops in
Durham 58.
Cuthbert Tun-
stall.*

36. Articles, whither it more properly belongeth, and there vtterly difable it, for making, or leauing among them, either true Bishop, Preift, or any other Ecclefiafticall perfon at all.

THE XII. CHAPTER.

The 24. article. Likewife examined and condemned by this firft Apoftolike age, and writers therein.

THe 24. article is this: *It is a thing plainely re-pugnant to the word of God, and the cuftome of the primatiue Church, to haue publike prayer in the Church, or to minifter the Sacraments, in a tongue not vnder-ftood of the people.* What is agreable or repugnant to the word of God, the Church of God, as thofe Proteftants haue confeffed before, is the beft wit-neffe and interpreter, and of neceffity it muft needs be fo in fuch things as be graunted to be agreable or repugnant vnto both, as this queftion is.

The word of God extendeth both to that which is written in Scriptures, and the vnwritten pre-ferued in the Church without fuch canonicall wri-ting, otherwife (which is vnpoffible) God might be contrary to himfelfe, and his word contrary to his word, which is blafphemous to fay or write. And in this queftion of the publike Church feruice, fin-ding no prefcript, forme, order, or office, nor of what language or tongue it is to be vfed, in the written word of God, wee muft needs reforte to vnwritten tradition and the cuftome of the prima-tiue Church to finde it forth. And wee finde in all the publike offices of the Church in this age, afcribed to S. Peter, S. Andrew, S. Matthew, and S.
Iames

Iames Apostles, to S. Marke Euangelist, S. Clement successour to S. Peter at Rome, and whosoeuer in antiquities is taken to be Authour or composer of any liturgy, Masse, or publike seruice or forme of prayers in the Church, in this time, they were all first penned and after practised in all places, wheresoeuer they were vsed in the learned common languages, and no where in any barbarous, or vulgar tongue of any particular Prouince or Contry. All histories, their oldest manuscripts and generally receaued tradition, witnesse they were in the Greeke or Latine tongue. This is so manifestly true that our Protestant writers do thus confesse it: *vntill of late* (since Protestant Religion began) *through out the west part of the world publike prayers were in Latine: in the east part in Greeke, euen among those nations, to whom the languages were no mother tongues.* Thus one of their Bishops with publike allowance.

Doue persuaf. p. 23.24. c. of prayer.

Edw. Sands Relation of Relig. c. 53. or 54.

Their first Protestant Archbishop Matthew Parker writeth, that the publike Church seruice named Masse, *Missa dicta*, did continue 200. yeares and more from Christs institution *à Christi primo instituto*, vntill Pope Zepherine the 16. Pope did change it to a better matter and forme. *Donec eam Zepherinus 16. Romanus Pontifex, quorundam suasionibus ad pulchriorem materiam formamque mutare voluit.* And this Masse was the same which sainct Iames vsed at Hierusalem, and sainct Peter in the easterne Contries. And when this man and other Protestants come to set downe what change S. Zepherine Pope made in the holy Masse, it was not to change it into a Vulgare tongue, but he a Roman *Zepherinus Romanus* kept it still vnchanged

Mat. Parker. Antiq. Brit. in Aug. c. 17. p. 47.

O 3   in

in the Latine tongue, as all his predeceſſours had
done before in the weſt and Latine Church, onely
he tooke away wodden chalices vſed then in ſome
places, ordaining better, and in this all writers Catholikes and Proteſtants agree. *Vitreos calices pro
ligneis ordinauit*. And whereſoeuer there was any
thing changed or added in the Maſſe, it was as
theſe men confeſſe, euer done in the Latine tongue.
*Alexander Romanus ad Adriani tempora peruenit. In
Miſſa, pridiè quam pateretur, vſque ad hæc verba,*HOC
EST CORPVS MEVM,*addidit, ad memoriã paſſionis Chriſti inculcandã. Sixtus Romanus, vt* SANCTVS *in cõmu-
nione Euchariſtiæ ter caneretur, ordinauit. Teleſphorus
Græcus,*GLORIA IN EXCELSIS DEO *eſſe in Miſſa canen-
dum præcepit*. Theſe be all the additions & changes
they finde in the holy Maſſe before S. Zepherines
time, before which S. Eleutherius Pope had publikely ſent it into Britaine, and S.Lucius our King
here publikely receaued it, and all thoſe additions
were taken out of Scripture, not then tranſlated
into any vulgar vnlearned language.So they proue
of all additions after, all euer made in the Latine
tongue, except ſome very few in the Hebrew and
Greeke, in the whole Latine Church. And this is
vnqueſtionably conuinced out of the publike offices of he Church of Chriſt, whether the Sacrifice
of Maſſe, or the reſt, Matins,Laudes,houres, euen-
ſonge, compline or whatſoeuer, to be termed publike prayer of the Church, for the farre greateſt
part of all theſe conſiſteth of the holy pſalmes, and
other parts of Scripture, all bookes thereof publikely reade euery day, and the pſames euery weeke,
yet none of theſe were in any vulgar tongue in this
age, nor many after this time.

The

The rest which is contained in the Catholike Church Creeds, Prefaces, Hymnes, Antiphons, or what else amont not vnto the tenth part of what is taken from Scriptures, and yet these were deliuered to the Church in learned tõgues, in them composed, and not in other. Wee are assured by Scriptures, and good histories that the Apostles 72. disciples and other holy Cleargy men in this first age preached in all nations, they prayed, and had publike prayers, in many contries, and in them founded Churches, and must needs leaue some forme, of such publike seruice for them they conuerted. But wee are assured againe both by Scriptures, and such antiquities, that they all had not the guift of tongues, *numquid omnes linguis loquuntur?* and sainct Paul reckoneth it for a singular guist, and priuiledge in himselfe, to speake in all languages, *gratias ago Deo, quod omnium vestrum linguis loquor.* And our Protestants themselues with other antiquaries confesse, that these renowned men did preach in many places, by interpretours, and diuers Barbarous nations where they preached, had then no vse of letters to write any thing at all in their owne lãguage, much lesse formes and offices of publike prayers, which were, and of necessity, to be vsed in all Churches and by all Preists. And in this condition was this Kingdome of Britaine, all Gallia, now Fraunce, and other parts, where the Druydes ruled, not vsing letters, and writing, because all nations were then accompted, and called by the Romans, Barbarous, in that and such vnciuill respects. Some write the Greeke letters were vsed in Gallia, but if it were so, they were by the same authority, very vnperfect, many added afterward to bringe that

1. Cor. 12.
1. Cor. 14.
Godwin. Conuers. c. 3. p. 36.
Io. Leland. in commentar.
Ant. Brit. v. Britanniæ. Io. Caius hist. Cantabr. p. 19

O 4   wri-

writing to perfection, and no hiftory mentioneth
that euer any forme of publike prayer, or fuch office was fo written or deliuered among, or to that
people, in this, or any after time: but the contrary,
that the firft publike office & Church feruice they
had in this age, was brought thither from Rome,
and fo the Latine tongue.

This is proued by the French Annals, teftifying
that the firft Apoftles of that nation were fent vnto
them by S. Peter, and his fucceffour S. Clement
at Rome. Our old brittish hiftory of the firft inftitution of Church feruice, *prima inftitutio & va-
rietas Ecclefiaftici Seruitij*, as our Peoteftant Antiquaries name it, teftifieth plainely that S. Trophimus Bishop of Arles, and Sainct Photinus Bishop
of Lyons, difciples of S. Peter the Apoftle did deliuer in all Gallia, the Romane order, and forme of

Church feruice. *Beatus Trophimus Epifcopus Arela-
tenfis, & Sanctus Photinus Martyr & Epifcopus Lu-
gdunenfis Difcipulus S. Petri Apoftoli Curfum Romanum in Gallijs tradiderunt*. And it citeth others,
more auncient in this fenfe. And addeth that this
Church feruice was after fent to S. Clement at
Rome, by the Bishops and Martyrs of Gallia, to

be approued by him, and all the Churches of
Fraunce then embraced that Order, that of Arles
being there the cheife Metropolitane Church,
from which, and S. Trophimus, all others there as
Pope Zozimus is an able witneffe, receaued light
and direction. *Metropolitanæ Arelatenfium vrbi
vetus priuilegium minimè derogandum eft, ad quam
primum ex hac fede (Romana) Trophimus Summus
Antiftes, ex cuius fonte tota Gallia fidei Riuulos accepit directus eft.* So hath the old Romane Martyrologe,

rologe, and diuers others. And So it muſt needs be, by all antiquitie conſenting, that all Gallia re-ceaued the water of life from the ſame foûtaine, the Church of Rome, both with their forme and or-der of Church ſeruice and other directions in Re-ligion, all their firſt Apoſtles and paſtours with full inſtruction, and power being directed and ſent from them, as ſainct Martial, ſainct Denys the Areopagite, ſainct Lucianus, ſainct Eutropius, ſainct Eugenius, ſainct Ionius, ſainct Timotheus, ſainct Apollinaris, ſainct Aphrodiſius, ſainct Sa-uianus, ſainct Potentianus, ſainct Altnus, ſainct Totaldus, ſainct Iulianus, ſainct Fronto, ſainct Taurinus, ſainct Paulus Narbonenſis, ſainct Stau-rinnus, ſainct Aſtremonius, ſainct Gratianus, ſainct Firmius, and others ſent from Rome thither in this age, in which time alſo ſainct Peter the Apoſtle ſent into Germany, ſainct Egiſtus, ſainct Clement vncle to ſainct Clement the Pope, ſainct Eucha-rius, ſainct Valerius, ſainct Maternus, ſainct Man-ſuetus, and many others.

The Apoſtles of Spaine were ſent thither alſo from Rome in this Time, namely ſainct Torqua-tus Cteſiphon, Secundus, Indalitius, Cæcilius, ſainct Heſychius, ſainct Euphraſius and others. *In Hiſpania Sanctorum Torquati, Cleſiphontis, Secundi, Indaletij, Cæcilij, Heſichij & Euphraſij, qui Romæ à Sanctis Apoſtolis Epiſcopi ordinati, & ad prædican-dum verbum Dei in Hiſpanias directi ſunt.* And to proue that all nations in this part of the world, cal-led the Latin Church, receaued their firſt Biſhops, preiſts, cleargie men, with their Church ſeruice from Rome S. Peter or his Succeſſour in this age: S. Clement his Succeſſour ſo ſpeaketh from S. Peters

Annal. Galli-can. Ecclef. Martyrolog. Roman. Bed. Adon.vſuard. in his Sant. Matt. weſtm. an. 94. & mult. al. apud Guliel.Eiſen-gren. centen. 1.part. 5. diſt. 3. Henric. Erford. cap. 5. Monſterus in Coſmogr. in German. Antonin. part. 1. petr. de natal. l.10. vincent. l. 9. Annal. Eccl. Treuer. Tungr. meten: Martyrolog. Roman. Beda vſuard. Ado die 15. Maij. Breu. Tole-tan. cal. maij.

Clem. Ro-
man. epist. 1.

ters owne direction and testimonye. *Episcopos per*
singulas Ciuitates quibus ille (S. Petrus) non miserat,
iuxta Domini præceptionem nobis mittere præcepit.
Quod etiam facere inchoauimus, & Domino opem fe-
rente, facturi sumus. Aliquos verò ad Gallias, His-
paniasque mittemus, & quosdam ad Germaniam &
Italiam, atque ad reliquas gentes dirigere cupimus.
And euen to such barbarous and sauage conttyes,
as had not vse of letters and learning *ferociores &*
rebelliores gentes.

This Kingdome of Britayne, excepting, the
Scotts when they came hither, had euer learned
men, and of ciuilitie as the Druids their cheifest
being here, and others. Yet after the coming and
rule of the Romans here, at and after the birth of
Christ & his Religion preached in this contry, the
latin tongue was vsuall to all of qualitie, no man
might beare office but such as vnderstood it, all
publike guifts donations charters, priuiledgs and
Records whatsoeuer, both as old and late Catolike
and Protestant Antiquaries proue, were performed and written in the latin tongue, and onely the
vulgar people vsed their vulgar language, and

Io: Leland. in
commenrar.
antiq. voc.
Britan. v. Bri-
tannin. Cains
histor. Can-
tabrig. p. 19.

yet corruptly without writing. *Coniectura ducor*
eo tempore vulgus Britanorum ineruditissimum fuisse,
ac prorsus non potuisse linguæ suæ voces depingere.
Quamdiu Imperium Britanniæ in Prouinciam reductæ
penes Romanos stabat, tamdiu necesse erat Britannis
Magistratum gerere cupientibus latinè loqui. Prouin-
cialem linguam vulgus cum magna difficultate, & id
quidem corruptè discebat. Tabulæ donationum omnes,
& rationes alicuius momenti latinè siebant. By which
it is euident, that their publike Church seruice,
must needs also be latin, in which onely as S. Bede
with

with others proue all people Inhabitants here, euer
studied, and reade the scriptures, from which it is
taken. *Hæc Insula quinque gentium linguis vnam
eandemque summæ veritatis & vera sublimitatis
scientiam scrutatur & confitetur, Anglorum videlicet, Britonum, Scotorum Pictorum & Latinorum, quæ
meditatione scripturæ cæteris omnibus est facta commu-
nis.* And as S. Gyldas writeth, this Kingdome was
by the reigning of the Romans there so latinized,
and Romanized, that it was rather to be named
Romana then, *Britannia: vt non Britannia, sed Ro-
mania censeretur.* And though the Romans had
many Hands, yet this in antiquities is aboue all,
named the Romane Hand. Greek and latin Catholik and Protestant Antiquaries agree, that S.
Peter the Apostle, who deliuered that latin Church
seruice which the Romans vsed, and brought into
Fraunce by his disciples as is proued before, preached in this Kingdome, stayed here longe time
*longo tempore moratus, founded vs Churches, consecra-
ted for vs Bishops Preists and Deacons: Ecclesias constituit, Episcoposque & Presbyteros & Diaconos ordinauit,* could deliuer vnto them no other Church, seruice, then that latin, which he deliuered at Rome
in Fraunce and other westerne places.

These Bishops Preists and Deacons which were
not Britans, could not vse that brittish tongue, in
their seruice which they did not vnderstand, and
which neither they nor the Britans could write for
them or others to reade. And whosoeuer any man
will say preached here first, S. Peter, S. Paul, S.
Symon, S. Ioseph, or any other, they not vnder-
standing the brittish language, nor any man
writing, they could not possibly vse or deliuer the

seruice

Bed. histor.
ang. l. 1. c. 1.

Gild. epistol.
de excid. &
conquest Bri-
tan. cap. 5.

S. Symeon
Metaphrastes
in S. Petro.
Euseb. apud
eund. ib. Sur.
die 29. Iuuij.
Cambden in
Britannia.
prot. Theater
of greate
Brit. l. 6.

seruice of the Church in that language, our old brittish manuscript mentioned before saith the Church seruice which S. Marke vsed, was also here in vse, *in Scotys ac Britannijs. Cursum qui dicitur præsenti tempore Scotorum beatus Marcus decantauit.* It testifieth further that S. Germanus, S. Lupus S. Patrik and others vsed this seruice here both in Britayne and Scotlands, when our Protestants confesse there was no errour in Religion. *Ipsum cursum decantauerunt Beatus Lupus & Beatus Germanus: & S. Patricius in Scotys ac Britannijs ipsum cursum decantauit.* And after them S. Vuandilocus ad S. Gomogillus who had 3000. monkes in his Monastery, and S. Columban, in whose time this Authour liued, with others, sent with him into Fraunce, vsed euery where in Ireland and Scotland as also Britaine, Fraunce, Germany and Italy the same publik Church seruice in the latin tonge. *Beatus Vuandilocus & Beatus Columbanus partibus Galliarum destinati ipsum decantauerunt.* And he deriueth this Church seruice from S. Marke, shewing where and by whome it was vsed. And it was iustified in open parlament the first of Queene Elizabeth by Abbot Fecknam out of S. Gildas in the prologue of his booke now suppressed by our Protestants, but then extant, that the same publik Church seruice which was vsed here in Queene Maryes time, and now in the Catholike Church, was brought hither and publickly deliuered here in the latin tongue in the generall conuersion of Britaine in King Lucius his time. And that Gildas which Protestants propose vnto vs diuers times citeth the old Church seruice of Britaine in the latin tongue. And the old manuscript antiquities of

Glasten-

Manuscrip. Brit. antiq. de prima Institutione Ecclef. officij.

Gildas in prolog. apud Fecknam orat. public. in 1. parliamento Elizabethæ Reginæ.

Gildas l. de excid. & conquest. Brit,

Glastenbury william of Malmesbury, Capgraue Guliel. Mal-
and others proue as much and more then Doctour mesb. manu-
Fecknam cited from S. Gildas. For they speaking scrip. lib. de
of the Religious men which S. Damianus and S. antiquit. cæ-
Phaganus placed at Glastenbury to be successours nob. glaston.
in place and profession to S. Ioseph of Aramathia, in collego
and his associates there do plainely deliuer, that as S. Benedict.
in other things these professed the same Religion, Cantabrig.
order, Church seruice, and manner of life, which Antiquitat.
glaston: tabu-
S. Ioseph and his companie did, so also as they lis. fix. Cap-
did, they come often euery day together into the grau. in S.
Ioseph & S.
old Church, to say their diuine office which they patric.
brought from Rome, with them, and deliuered Galfrid. mo-
here *in memoriam primorum ex suis socijs 12. elegerunt* num. l. 4.
histor. Brit.
(*S. Damianus & Phaganus) & in præfata Insula Rege* cap. 20. vlt.
Lucio consentiente habitare fecerunt, qui in diuersis locis Matth.
sicut Anachoretæ manserunt ibidem in eisdem lucis Westin.
chron. an.
in quibus prima 12. primitùs habitarunt in vetustam 186.
tamen Ecclesiam ad diuina obsequia deuotiùs complen- Matth. We-
da crebrò conuenerunt quotidiè. stin. an. 187.

And this latin publik Church seruice being the Galfrid. l. 5,
very same which had beene vsed at Rome from cap. 1.
the Apostles time, not changed at that time, as all
Catholiks and Protestants agree, was planted and
deliuered here, not onely by these legates of Pope
Eleutherius, but by himselfe, with the rest which
his legates did here confirme. *restauratis omnibus,*
redierunt Antistites Romani: & quæ fecerant à beatis-
simo Papa côfirmari impetrauerunt. Confirmatione facta
reuersi sunt in Britanniam compluribus alijs comitati.
And if any Protestant will haue the Kings confir-
matiô needfull, our holy King then S. Lucius likewise confirmed this, as the rest. *Gloriosus Britonum.*
Rex Lucius chartis & munimentis omnia communiuit.

THE

THE XIII. CHAPTER.

The 25. Article, intituled, of the Sacraments, *thus examined, and condemned, in all things contrary to Catholike doctrine.*

THEIR next the 25. Proteſtant Article is intitu-led: *of the Sacraments.* And thus beginneth. *Sacraments ordained by Chriſt, be not onely bages or tokens of Chriſtian mens profeſſion, but rather they be certaine ſure witneſſes, and effectuall ſignes of grace, and Gods good will towards vs, by the which he doth worke inuiſibly in vs, and doth not onely quicken but alſo ſtrengthen and confirme our faith in him.*

Hitherto ther appeareth no difference betweene theſe Proteſtants in this article and Catholiks, for they decreeing that Sacraments be effectuall ſignes of grace, that is in all true proper manner of ſpeach, ſignes which doe effect cauſe & worke grace, otherwiſe they be not effectuall ſignes of grace, and that God worketh in vs inuiſibly by them, is as much as Catholiks profeſſe, whē they define a Sacramēt, *Sacramentum eſt viſibile ſignū inuiſibilis gratiæ. A Sacramēt is a viſible or externall ſigne of inuiſible grace giuen thereby.* And theſe Proteſtants declare thēſelues ſo farre, & plainely, in both thoſe they accept for Sacramēts, Baptiſme, & the Euchariſt called by them, the Supper of the Lord. In the firſt, they manifeſtly confeſſe it, and approue and practiſe baptiſme of Infants, who borne by them alſo in originall ſinne, cannot poſſibly haue remiſſion thereof and grace but by their baptiſme, not able to vnderſtand or haue any act of faith, or other vertue. Yet their decree

Proteſt. art. 27. 28. infra.

Art. 27.

decree is: *The baptifme of young children, is in any wife to be retained in the Church, as moft agreable with the inftitution of Chrift.* So they doe or ought to fpeake of their other Sacrament, confeffing it was in the primatiue Church, miniftred fometimes to infants.

The difference betweene vs in this article, is in that, which thus followeth.

There are two Sacraments ordained of Chrift our Lord in the Ghofpell, that is to fay, baptifme, and the fupper of the Lord. Thofe fiue commonly called Sacraments, that is to fay, Confirmation Pennance, Order, Matrimony and extreame Vnction are not to be compted for Sacraments, of the Ghofpell, being fuch as haue growne partly of the corrupt following of the Apoftles, partly are ftates of life allowed in the fcriptures: but yet haue not like nature of Sacraments, with baptifme, and the Lords fupper, for that they haue not any vifible figne or ceremony ordained of God. Hitherto this Proteftant article denying thofe fiue Sacraments which the Catholike Church receaueth for fuch with the two former, baptifme and the moft holy Sacrament of the altar. Now I will proue by this Apoftolike age the doctrine, and practife thereof, that thefe fiue are, and then were vfed, and receaued for Sacraments, and firft of Confirmation the firft which thefe men name and deny.

S. Clement teftifieth this to be a Sacrament, miniftred by Bishops with holy oyle, and giuing the holy Ghoft and grace, all that thefe men doe, or can require to a Sacrament. *Quid dicemus de Epifcopo? per quem Dominus in ordinatione Spiritum fanctum vobis dedit. Per quem confignati eftis oleo exultationis, & chrifmate fapientia: per quem filij lucis facti eftis:*

Confirmatió a true Sacrament.
Clem.Rom. Conftitut. Apoft.l.2.c.36.

per

per quem Dominus illuminatione vestra, Episcopi manus impositionem testimonio suo comprobans, in singulis vestrûm suam sacram vocem emisit. This he further

Clem. Rom. declareth (making a Sacramēt needfull to Christian
epist. ad Iuliū perfectiō, except necessity hindereth, giuing grace)
& Iulian. that Peter and all the Apostles so taught, and pra-
ctised, and Christ so instituted. *Omnibus festinandum est sine mora renasci Deo, & demum consignari ab Episcopo; id est, septiformem gratiam Spiritus sancti percipere, quia incertus est vniuscuiusque exitus vitæ. Quum autem regeneratus fuerit per aquam, & postmodum septiformi spiritus gratia ab Episcopo, (vt memoratum est) confirmatus, quia aliter perfectus esse Christianus nequaquam poterit, nec sedem habere inter perfectos, si non necessitate, sed incuria aut voluntate remanserit, vt a Beato Petro accepimus, & vt cæteri Apostoli, præcipiente Domino docuerunt.*

Dion. Areop.   S. Denis the Areopagite saith, that they which
l. Hierarch. were baptized were brought to the Bishop to be
Eccl. cap. 4. confirmed. *Ducunt ad Hierarcham, is virum vnguen-*
Prope fin. *to quod maximè diuinos efficit, insignit.* And further
In contemp. thus sheweth the Sacramentall power of this holy
Vnction. *Vnguenti illa, quæ perficiendi vim habet, perfusio, eum qui initiatus est, suauitate odoris fragrantem facit.* And plainely calleth it a Sacrament, comparing it in that respect euen with the Sacrament of
the altar, assuring vs, that was the opinion and do-
L. Eccl. Hie- ctrine of his Masters in Religion, the Apostles. *Fi-*
tar. c. 6. *nitimum alterum Sacramentum, quod præcepto-*
In contempl. *res nostri vnguenti mysterium nominant. Est igitur id quod dixi, mysterium quod nunc à nobis laudatur, eius ordinis atque potestatis quæ vim habet perficiendi ea quæ Pontificem attingunt. Itaque ipsum diuini præceptores nostri, vt eiusdem & ordinis & efficacitatis,*
cuius

cuius est Synaxeos Sacramentum, ijsdem sæpe figuris at-
que imaginibus mysticisque descriptionibus ; ac sanctis
verbis descripserunt.

It is the constant opinion, and testimony of the
Fathers, that the Church of Christ receaued and
ministred this Sacrament for a true and properly
named Sacrament, both by Scriptures, and tradition. So both the Latine and Greeke Fathers expound that passage and practise of the Apostles S.
Peter and S. Iohn in the acts of the Apostles, giuing grace to those that were baptized by others,
not Bishops, by imposition of hands. *Imponebant* Act. c. 8.
manus super illos & accipiebant Spiritum sanctum.
And doe thereby proue that Bishops onely may
minister this Sacrament. *Cùm Philippus Diaconus es-* Ephip.l.1.To.
set non habebat potestatem imponendi manus, vt per 2.Contr. hęr.
hoc daret Spiritum sanctum. So hath S. Augustine, c.21.contra
S. Hierome & others prouing this Sacrament both lib.15. Trin.c.
by Scripture and tradition of the vniuersall Church 26.Hieron.
from Christs time. *In actibus Apostolorum scriptum* Dial.aduers.
est. Etiam si scripturæ authoritas non subesset, totius 2.c. 4.
orbis in hanc partem consensus instar præcepti obtineret.
Non abnuo hanc esse Ecclesiarum consuetudinem, vt ad Ambr. c.7.de
eos qui longè in minoribus vrbibus per Presbyteros & ijs qui init.
Diaconos baptizati sunt, Episcopus ad inuocationem mysterijs S.
sancti Spiritus manum impositurus excurrat. This S. Basil. libr. de
Hierome writeth in the name of all, both Catho- Spirit. sancto
liks and others. S. Ambrose, sainct Basile, saint c.27.
Gregory Nazianzen and others haue the like. S. Greg. Naz.
Ambrose, Primasius with others expound those serm.in San-
words in the 6. chapter to the Hebrewes, *impositio-* ctum Iaua-
nis quoque manum, in the very same sense, in these chrum.Ambr.
words. *Impositionem manuum appellat, per quam ple-* in cap. 6. ad
nissimè creditur accipi donum Spiritus sancti, quod post Hebr.Primas.
in cap 6. ad
Hebr.

P   *baptis-*

baptismum ad confirmationem vnitatis in Ecclesia à Pontificibus fieri solet. S. Cyprian and his fellow Bishops in Councell speaking in the name of the Church, calleth it a Sacrament as baptisme is : *si Sacramento vtroque nascuntur.*

Tertullian also doth number it with the other Sacraments, euer vsed in the Church, and giueth both a visible externall signe holy Vnction, and internall grace giuen thereby vnto it. *Caro abluitur, vt anima emaculetur, caro vngitur, vt anima consecretur. Caro signatur, vt & anima muniatur, caro manus impositione adumbratur, vt & anima spiritu illuminetur. Caro corpore & sanguine Christi vescitur, vt & anima de Deo saginetur.*

To come to our Primatiue Christian Britans, their learned old antiquary and Bishop writeth of them, that from their first conuersion, they held this for a Sacrament, giuing grace, that holy Vnction by a Bishop was vsed in it, and all our first Christians in Britaine honoured, and affected this Sacrament, more then any other nation did. *Episcopalem confirmationem, & Chrismatis, qua gratia spiritus datur inunctionem, præ alia gente totus populus magnopere petit.* This wee may easiely learne by the example of their King Cadwalladar, which went to Rome to be confirmed by the Pope there. *Cadwalladrus abiectis mundialibue, propter Deum regnumq; perpetuum, venit Romam, & à Sergio Papa confirmatus.* But wee need not stand vpon particular examples, when wee haue a generall graunt before, that all the Britans, *totus populus*, both by old and new, Catholike and Protestant historians, were so deuoted to this holy Sacrament. And both Theodoret and others do proue that they were onely the

Noua-

Nouatian heretiks, (which by no antiquity euer entered into Britaine) which denied holy Vnction to be vsed in this Sacrament. *Negligant confirmationem habere olei sacri illinitionem.*

And our English Protestants themselues by their owne most authorized and allowed proceedings haue,& doe condemne this their article doctrine in this point. For first in the publike correctiō of their religion at Hampton court, King Iames being present and consenting, they thus decree: *Confirmation is an Apostolicall tradition.* That Confirmation deliuered by the Apostles is a Sacramēt is proued before. Secondly these Protestants confesse and decree, that the order of Bishops hath euer beene in the Church, from the Apostles time, but these men not condemning all forrayne Protestants and in denying to Bishops onely power to make Preists and Clergy men, leaue no act of Order peculiar and proper to them, if they deny confirmation to be a Sacrament, and by them onely to be ministred, for all others are lawfully ministred by Priests, noe Bishops. And these our English Protestāts by the greatest power they haue, haue set fourth, and vse a publike forme, and manner of ministring confirmation by them onely, which they pretend to be Bishops among them. In which they proue it in their proceedings, and by the doctrine of this very article, for supposing their opinion though false, that holy Vnction is not necessary in this practise of Confirmation, they requiring onely two things needfull to a Sacrament, a visible signe, or ceremony ordained of God, and grace giuen thereby thus propose and practise both: first they say and direct. *The Bishop*

Conference at Hampton. p.10,11.

English Prot. Communion booke. Titul. Confirmatiō. Et tit. Catechisme.

P 2   *shall*

shall lay his hand vpon euery childe seuerally. And that

Communion
Booke supr.
§.alliuingly.
in their Iudgment it is a signe, and ceremony, ordained of God, and that grace is thereby giuen,
their pretended Bishops in ministring this to children thus proue: *wee make our humble supplications
for these children, vpon whom after the manner of the
Apostles, wee haue laide our hands, to certifie them, by
this signe of thy fauour, and gratious goodnesse towards
them.* Therefore being a signe vsed by the Apostles,
giuing and certifying grace, by this very article, and
their owne definition of a Sacrament before, this
of Confirmation must needs by their Religion be a
Sacrament in the same degree as they allowe baptisme and the Eucharist to be. This their communion booke is daily practized by them in all their
Churches, vsed both before and after these articles
were ordained, and at this present, and supported
and warranted with the greatest allowance, their
religion, or any, or point therein by their owne
proceedings possibly can haue, Queenes and Kings
supremacy, Parlaments, Iniunctions, Canons,
Conuocations, publike approbation, and practise
of all their pretended Bishops, or named Clergy
men.

THE XII. CHAPTER.

*Pennance, so called in this article, and by Catholikes.
The Sacrament of Pennance, was so iudged
and vsed in this Apostolike age.*

THe next Sacramēt of the Catholike Church,
which this Protestant Article denieth to be
such, is the Sacrament of Pennance. S. Ignatius in
this

this Apostolike age giueth power vnto Pennance,
to bringe sinners both to the vnity of the militant
Church on earth, and inherite euerlasting life in
heauen. *Obsecro vos, quotquot pœnitentia ducti redie-* Ignat.epist.ad
rint ad vnitatem Ecclesiæ, suscipite illos cum omni Philadelph.
mansuetudine, vt per bonitatem & patientiam vestram
resipiscentes ex diaboli laqueis, digni iam Christo facti,
salutem consequantur æternam in regno Christi. And
writeth how Christians were then bound, to ad-
monish and exhort sinners to pennance. *Oportet eos*
commonefacere & ad pœnitentiam cohortari, si forte
manus dent, monitisque cedant. S. Denis the Areopagite deliuereth the manner of penitents, and pennance to haue beene then, as the Catholiks now
vse, the penitent to kneele to the Preist, and with
sorrowe confesse his sinnes, and the Preist by absolution to forgiue them, and so iustifie the penitent
sinner, and greatly reprehendeth one Demophilus for hindering it, saying it was the order of discipline then. *Tu, vt tuæ literæ indicant, procedentem* Dion.epist.ad
Sacerdoti impium, vt ais, & peccatorem nescio quo pa- Demophil.
cto contra disciplinæ ordinem astans calce abiecisti. Ad- ante med.
huc cum ille quidem, quod oportuit, fateretur se ad pec-
catorum remedium quærendum venisse: tu non exhor-
ruisti, sed & bonum Sacerdotem ausus es lacerare con-
uitijs miserabilem eum dicens, quòd pœnitentem & im-
pium iustificasset. S. Ignatius maketh it one of the Ignat.epist.ad
Sacraments ministred by Preists: *Baptizant, sacrifi-* Heronem.
cant, eligunt, manus imponunt. S. Clement setteth it
downe for a tradition of S. Peter and the other A-
postles to confesse all sinnes, vnto the Pastours of
their soules, and to rceaue cure and remedy from
them. *Si forte alicuius cor vel liuor, vel infidelitas,* Clem. Rom.
vel aliquod malum ex his quæ superius memorauimus, ep.st.1.

latenter

latenter irrepserit, non erubescat qui animæ suæ curam gerit, confiteri hæc huic, qui præest, vt ab ipso per verbum Dei, & consilium salubre curetur.

And he addeth afterward, from the mouth of S. Peter: *Instruebat, actus suæ vitæ omni hora custodire, & in omni loco Deum respicere, firmiter scire cogitationes malas cordi suo aduenientes, mox ad Christum allidere, & Sacerdotibus Domini manifestare.* S. Peters instruction was diligently to take knowledge euen of the euill cogitations of the hart, and to confesse them to the Preists of God. He saith in an other place that penance is like vnto baptisme. *Erit ei in locum lauachri impositio manuum.* He setteth downe the verie manner of enioyning penanc, according to the qualitie of the sinnes committed, dayes or weeks in fasting and penance: *Afflictum diebus Ieiuniorum pro ratione peccati hebdomadas duas, vel tres, vel quinque, vel septem, dimitte, dicens ei quæcumque conueniunt ad peccatorem corripiendum.* And he expoundeth those words of Christ in the ghospel, of bynding and loosing of this Sacrament as others after him do. *Pænitentibus remissionem concedere oportet. Recognosce ô Episcope, dignitatem tuam, quod sicut ligandi potestatem accepisti, sic etiam & soluendi. Optinens igitur soluendi potestatem, recognosce teipsum, & secundum dignitatem loci tui, in hac vita versare.* It was so generally a receaued truth here in Britaine, that euen when our Protestant Antiquaries confesse our Christian Britans kept their first faith inuiolate, the contrary was adiudged heresie, and a King himselfe *frequard* summoned and proceeded against for laughing at the Baptisme of Infants, and Confession of sinnes to Preists. *Notatus est aliquando risisse paruulorum Bap-*
tisma,

Clem. Rom. sup. epist. 1.

Constitut. Apost. l. 2. cap. 49.

Cap. 19.

Cap. 21.

Pennancea Sacrament among the Britans.

Hector Boeth. l. 9. Scotor. Hist. fol 179. Georg. Buch.

tiſma, peccatorumque ad Sacerdotis aurem confeſſionem.
Thus it is teſtified both by Catholike, and Proteſtant Hiſtorians.

l. 5. Rer. Sco-
tir. Reg. 52.

And our moſt auncient Brittiſh writers as S.
Gildas ſpeaking of this Sacrament, the practiſe and
vſe thereof here in Britayne deduceth it from
Chriſts words, of bynding & looſteing ſpokē to S.
Peter and the other Apoſtles. *Petro eiuſque Succeſ-
ſoribus dicit Dominus : & tibi dabo claues Regni Cœ-
lorum. Itemque omni ſanƈto Sacerdoti promittitur, &
quæcumque ſolueris ſuper terram, erunt ſoluta & in
cælis: & quæcumque ligaueris ſuper terram, erunt
ligata & in cælis.* Our learned Britan the old Archbiſhop of Orleance, Ionas Aurelienſis, teſtifieth the
auncient deuotion to this Sacrament was ſuch,
that both Preiſts and penitents wept in the miniſtring thereof, and giueth inſtance in S. Euſtachius,
ſo weeping when penitents confeſſed their ſinnes
vnto him, that he cauſed them alſo to weepe. *Quoties illi aliquis ob recipiendam pænitentiam lapſus ſuos
eſſet confeſſus, ita flebat, vt & illum flere compelleret.*
And this is ſo euident a truth, that King Iames,
with his Proteſtant Biſhops and clergie in their
publik examination of their Religion, conclude
this point in theſe words; *That the particular and
perſonall abſolution from ſinne after confeſſion, is Apo-
ſtolical, and a very godly ordinance.*

hollinsh. hiſt.
of Scut. l. pag.
112.

Gild. l. de
excid. cap. 26.

Ionas aurel.
in vit. S. Eu-
ſtachij cap. 1.

King Iames
Confer. at
Hampton
court.

And this is no new thing in their Religion, but
a new approbation of their doctryne herein, againſt
their puritans, for their communion booke elder
then theſe Articles, and at this time the moſt pra-
ƈticall and allowed Rule which they haue, doth
giue direction both for confeſſion of ſyns, and abſolution from them, in the very ſame words, which

Catho-

Engl. Protest.
communion
Booke Titul.
visitation of
the Sike.

Catholik Preist vse in this Sacrament. *The sik per-*
son shall make a speciall confession, if he feele his con-
science troubled with any weightie matter . After
which confession the Preist shall absolue him after this
sort. Our Lord Iesus Christ, who hath left power to his
Church , to absolue all sinners which truely repent, and
beleeue in him, of his greate mercy forgiue thee thyne
offences, and by his authoritie committed to me, I absol-
ue thee from all thy syns, in the name of the father, and
of the Sonne, and of the holy ghost. Amen . Here is all
which this Article requireth to a Sacrament , a visible or externall signe or ceremonie as is Manifest,
and this ordeined of God , both because this communion booke saith, it was left by Christ the sonne of God, to his Church, so to be for euer, as is
Church shall be euer forgiuing sinnes and giueing
grace; which no visible or externall signe or ceremony, but such as is ordained of God, to such end
and purpose can do.

This power is pretented to be giuen to euery
minister among them, when their Protestant Bishop maketh him, by laying his hands vpon him,

Protest.
Booke of
confecration.
Articul. 36.
inf.

saying these words : *receaue the holy ghoste, whose*
sinnes thou forgiuest, they are forgiuen, and whose sin-
nes thou doest retayne, they are retayned. Thus hath
the Protestant manner of confecration in their
booke thereof, approued in these Articles, in as
ample manner, as any thing in their Religion. And
if their confecration were true and lawfull , if they
could not minister this as a Sacrament, they could
do nothing at all, this being the power that is preteded to be be giuen vnto them at that time, and nothing els in playne and expresse termes, at the least
in so manifest true meaning and construction.

T H E

THE XV. CHAPTER.

Holy Orders contrary to this Article, was vsed and held à Sacrament in this first age.

AND by this sufficiently appeareth also, that both by the doctrine, practise and authoritie of this Apostolike age and their owne Proteſtant cheifeſt grownds and proceedings, how vntruely this Article denyeth in the next place, that holie Orders is a Sacramēt;for it is manifeſt before, that both by the Apoſtoſtolik men of this time, and their owne profeſſion and confeſſion, it hath all things needfull to a Sacrament, a viſible externall ſigne, or ceremonie ordained by God giuing grace, and extraordinarie ſpirituall power, and it-ſelfe by that conſecration alſo giueth grace in other Sacraments, which cannot be miniſtred without it, either by Catholike Religion, or our Proteſtants practiſe and profeſſion. Noe terrene and earthly power may or can performe the duties and offices of that gratious and ſpirituall function. This is the plaine and euident teſtimonie of the bleſſed Fathers of this time. S. Clement euen in the words of the Apoſtles maketh preishood more excellent, then the Regall power and dignitie, for that he ruleth ſoules, an this the bodies. And is ſo farre from our Proteſtant courſes in making holie preiſthood treaſon, that he maketh it an offence deſeruing greater puniſhment, to do wrong to Preiſts, then temporall Princes. *Si Reges inuadens ſupplicio dignus iudicatur, quamuis filius vel amicus ſit, quantò magis qui Sacerdotibus inſultat ? Quantò enim*

Clem. Rom.
l.2. conſtitut.
Apoſtol. c. 2.

enim Sacerdotium Regno est excellentius, cùm regendarum animarum officio præsit, tanto grauiori supplicio punitur, qui aduersus id aliquid temerè fecerit quam qui aduersus Regnum.

Ignat. epist. ad Smyrnen.

The like, and more vrgent hath **S.** Ignatius: *Honora Deum, vt omnium Authorem & Dominum: Episcopum verò vt Principem Scaerdotum, Imaginem Dei referentem: Dei quidem propter Principatum:Christi verò propter Sacerdotium . Honorare oportet & Regem: neque enim Rege quisquam præstantior, aut quisquam similis illi in rebus omnibus creatis : neque Episcopo qui Deo consecratus est pro totius mundi salute quicquam maius in Ecclesia . Sacerdotium est omnium bonorum , quæ in hominibus sunt apex , qui aduersus illud facit, non hominem Ignominia afficit , sed Deum & Christum Iesum primogenitum, qui natura solus est summus Sacerdos.*

And they ascribe this extraordinarie dignitie and excellencie of sacred preisthood, to their supernaturall chaunge, and grace bestowed miraculously vpon them in their consecration, and by vertue of that holy Sacrament, no other reason to be giuen of so wonderfull an alteration and preminencie, as both the holy Fathers in the common constructiō of the Church of Christ,and the light of nature assuer vs, that men so lately and euer before their consecratiō, were but as other men, and now nothing externally chaunged , should by Gods decree& ordinance,be eleuated vnto,and endowed with so incomparable honour,power grace, and vnquestionable priuiledges, onely the Sacramentall grace performeth it say these holy Fathers as it doth the like in the holy Eucharist and Baptisme . *Eadem vis etiam Sacerdotem augustum & honorandum*

Gregor. Nyssen. l. de

norandum facit, nouitate benedictionis à comunitate *vulgi segregatum* . *Quàm enim heri ac tempore superiori vnus è multitudine ac plebe esset, repente redditur Præceptor, Præses, Doctor pietatis, mysteriorum latentium Præsul. Eaque contingunt ei, quàm nihil vel corpore vel forma mutatus, sed quòd ad speciem externam attinet, ille sit qui erat, inuisibili quadam vi ac gratia, inuisibilem animam in melius transformatam gerens.* S. Clement, S. Denys the Areopagite S. Ignatius, S. Anacletus made Preist by S. Peter the Apostle, *à quo & præsbyter sum ordinatus,* and others of this Apostolike age, being as they confesse instructed so by S. Peter, and the rest of the Apostles, *vt à Beato Petro Principe Apostolorum sumus instructi,* do plainely testifie and proue holy Orders to be a holy Sacrament, both in Preistly and Episcopall consecration, deliuering both the matter and manner of them, as the Roman Church now vseth. A Bishop to be consecrated by diuers Bishops, by imposition of hands, the holy ghospell, and Inunction with holy Chrisme giuing grace, and the holy ghost. *Ordinationes Episcoporum, authoritate Apostolica ab omnibus qui in eadem fuerint prouincia Episcopis sunt celebrandæ. Qui simul conuenientes, scrutinium diligenter agant, Ieiuniumque cum omnibus celebrent precibus, & manus cum sanctis Euangelijs quæ prædicaturi sunt, imponentes, sacraque vnctione, exemplo Prophetarum & Regum capita eorum, more Apostolorum & Moysis vngentes, quia omnis sanctificatio constat in Spiritu Sancto, cuius virtus inuisibilis sacro Chrismati est permixta.* With this agree S. Clement, S. Ignatius, S. Denys, with the generall custome and practise of their Apostolike age. Not requiring a necessitie of the presence

Bapt. Gregor. Naz. Orat. de S. Athanasio. Cyprian l. de ablut. ped. Tertullian. l. exhort. cast.

Anaclet. epist. 2.

Anaclet. supr. Tom. 1. concil. epist. 2. cited and approued. by protest Matt. parker antiq. Britan. p. 24. Io. Prisens def. histor. Britan. p. 73. Robert. Barnes l. de vit. Pontific. in Anacleto & Alexandro

of

of all Bishops of the prouince, but seeking their consent in so greate, a businnes, *Quòd si simul omnes conuenire minimè poterunt, assensū tamen suis precibus præbeant, vt ab ipsa ordinatione animo non desint.* Onely they require of necessitie three or two Bishops to consecrate a Bishop, and onely one for the consecration of Preists, Deacons, and inferiour Orders. *Episcopum mandamus ordinari à tribus Episcopis, vel ad minus à duobus: non licere autem ab vno vobis constitui. Presbyterum & Diaconum, & reliquorum clerum ab vno Episcopo.* S. Denys the Areopagite Scholler to S. Paule, as he had learned of that his holy Master, and other Apostles and seene it the generall doctrine and practise of that Apostolike time, that great and extraordinary grace and power was giuen by the externall rite, signe and ceremonie thereof, so teacheth, and setteth downe the Order of this consecration, as of Preists and Deacons, euery of them different and distinct from other as their dignities and functions are

with Ecclesiasticall rites and solemnities before the holy altare, as Catholicks vse at this day: *Præsul vbi sacrandus offertur, vtroque genu posito ante altare supra caput habet à Deo tradita Euangelia manumque Pontificis: atque hoc modo à consecrante Pontifice castißimis imprecationibus consummatur. Sacerdos verò coram sancto altari ponens vtrumque genu, in capite habet Pontificis dextram, & in hunc modum à sacrante Præsule sanctißimis inuocationibus consecratur. At verò minister altero tantùm coram sanctis altaribus posito genu, sacrantis se Pontificis dexteram in capite præfert, atque ab eo perficitur precationibus ad eam rem accomodatis, cuilibet autem ipsorum à benedicente Pontifice Crucis imprimitur signum, & per singulos sacra præsi-*

prædicatio nominis, consummansque consalutatio sit.

S. Clement also testifieth, that from the first consecration of Ecclesiasticall men after Christs ascention, when S. Stephen and others were made Deacons, both Bishops and Preists were so consecrated by the Apostles before the Altar, and at Masse, as Christ ordayned. *Nos ablato secundum Christi ordinationem sacrificio puro, & incruento, constituimus Episcopos, Presbyteros & Diaconos numero septem, è quorum numero vnus erat Stephanus Beatus Martyr.* And plainely proueth, that these holy Orders with their particular offices were appointed by Christ himselfe the Bishops to giue Orders, the Preists to offer Sacrifice and receaue grace and power so to do at their consecration, and Deacons to Minister to them both, in their sacred functions. *Nisi propria quædam iura essent, atque ordinum discrimina, satis esset, vt per vnum nomen vniuersa perficerentur. Sed à Domino edocti consequentiam rerum, Episcopis Pontificatus munera assignauimus, presbyteris Sacerdotij, Diaconis ministeria erga vtrosque, vt quæ ad Religionem pertinent, purè perficiantur. Nam nec Diacono fas est offerre sacrisicium, vel baptizare, aut benedictionem paruam vel magnam facere, nec Presbytero ordinationes exercere: impium est enim ordinem peruerti.*

S. Denys recompteth their grace and duties in like manner: *Antistitum ordinem perficientem esse, & perfectionis authorem: Sacerdotum verò illuminantem, atque ad lucem promouentem: porro ministrorum, purgantem atque discernentem. Videlicet Pontificalis ordo non perficere solum, verùm & illuminare & purgare nouit: Sacerdotum verò virtus in se cum illuminante habet purgantem quoque scientiam. Verum quæ infe-*

riaris

Clem. Const. Apost. l. 8. cap. 52. vlt.

Supr. paulò ante.

Dionys. Eccl. Hier. cap. 5.

*rioris sunt ad præstantiora transire nequeant, propterea
quod fas illis non est ad istiusmodi prosilire superbiam.
Porrò sacratiores virtutes vnà cum suis, inferiores
quoque, sua ipsa perfectione scientias sacras nequaquam
ignorant.* S. Ignatius also is witnesse, that these seuerall Orders were ordained by Christ. *Enitimini
charissimi, subiecti esse Episcopo, & Presbyteris, &
Diaconis. Qui enim his obedit, obedit Christo, qui hos
constituit.* And deliuereth their offices seuerall, and
distinct, as the others do. The Episcopall function
he hath before remembred. And saith, all must
obey the Bishop, as our Lord himselfe. *Episcopo
subiecti estote, velut Domino. Episcopus omni principatu & potestate superior est. Decet obedire Episcopo,
& in nullo illi refragari.* He telleth vs, the function
of a Preist, is, to offer Sacrifice, and Minister other
Sacraments, and Deacons are to Minister vnto
them, in such holie mysteries, and so must needs
haue power giuen them accordingly in their consecration, and this was so with the Apostles, and
the first Preists and Deacons. *Sacerdotes sunt, Tu
verò (Diaconus) Sacerdotum Minister. Baptizant
sacrificant, manus imponunt, tu verò illis ministras,
vt Sanctus ille Stephanus Iacobo & presbyteris qui
erant Hierosolymis. Oportet & Diaconos mysteriorum
Chtisti ministris, per omnia placere: nec enim ciborum,
& potuum ministri sunt, sed Ecclesiæ Dei administratores. Ipsi itaque tales sunt, at vos reueremini illos vt
Christum Iesum, cuius vicarij sunt, & Episcopus Ty-
pum Dei Patris omnium gerit: presbyteri verò sunt
consessus quidam & coniunctus Apostolorum chorus.
Sine his Ecclesia electa non est, nulla sine his Sanctorum
congregatio, nulla Sanctorum electio. Quid Sacerdotium aliud est, quam sacer cætus, consiliarij & assesso-*

res

Marginal notes:

Ignat. epist. ad Ephes.

Epistol. ad Trallian.

Epistol. ad Magnes.

Ignat. epistol. ad Heronem Diaconum.

Epistol. ad Trallian.

res Episcopi? Quid verò Diaconi, quàm imitatores Angelicarum virtutum, quæ purum & inculpatum ministerium illi exhibent, vt sanctus Stephanus beato Iacobo, Timotheus & Lnius Paulo, Anacletus & Clemens Petro? Qui igitur his non obedit sine Deo prorsus, & impurus est & Christum contemnit, & constitutionem eius imminuit.

S. Martial deliuereth plainely a cheife and principall cause of the honour and excellencie of this Sacrament of holie Orders, because among other eminencies thereof, Bishops and Preists offer, and Deacon assist them therein, the most holie sacrifice of Christs bodie and blood vpon an holie Altar, the very same which the Iewes did by malice offer, when they crucified Christ. *Sacerdotes honorabatis, qui decipiebant vos sacrificijs suis, qui mutis & surdis statuis offerebant. Nunc autem multò magis Sacerdotes Dei omnipotentis qui vitam vobis tribuunt in calice & viuo pane honorare debetis. Christi corpus & sanguinem iu vitam æternam offerimus. Quod Iudæi per Inuidiam immolauerunt, putantes se nomen eius à terra abolere, nos causa salutis nostræ in ara sanctificata proponimus, scientes hoc solo remedio nobis vitam præstandam, & mortem effugandam, hoc enim ipse Dominus noster iussit nos agere in sui commemorationem.*

This was also the doctrine of our first Christian Britans. Their Preists were consecrated to offer the heauenly Sacrifice at the holie Altar. They consecrated Christs bodie and blood with their mouthes *proprio ore.* And of all the people in the world, as their Antiquities witnes, they most honoured clergie men in such respects. *Ecclesiasticis viris longè magis quàm vlli gentem honorè deferentes.* Their Bishops

Martial. epist. ad Burdegal. cap. 3.

The Britans here so held.

Gildas l. de excid. & conq. Britan. c. 26. manuscript. antiq. de tit. S. Patricij Capg. in eod.
Girald. Camb.

hops were consecrated, with holie Chrisme in ipo-
sition of hands and consecrating words: *in consecra-*
tione Pontificum, capita eorum sacri Chrismatis infu-
sione perungere, cum Inuocatione sancti Spiritus, &
manus impositione. The hands of Preists were consecrated to offer and handle the blessed Sacrifice.
Benedictione initiantur Sacerdotum manus. S. Paule
in diuers places proueth it giueth grace, so making
it a true and proper holie Sacrament. *Noli negli-*
gere gratiam, quæ in te est, quæ data est tibi cum impo-
sitione manuum presbyterij. And, *admoneo te vt re-*
suscites gratiam Dei, quæ est in te per impositionem
manuum mearum.

And Christ himselfe by his owne example, and
testimonie, S. Iohn the Euangelist so recording
affirmeth, that the holie ghost, and power to forgiue sins were giuen in this Sacramentall ceremonie. *Accipe Spiritum sanctum, quorum remiseritis*
peccata, remittuntur eis, And it is the witnesse of
God, that holie Orders is the worke of the holie
ghost. *Dixit Spiritus sanctus: Segregate mihi Saulum*
& Barnabam, in opus ad quod assumpsi eos: Tunc ie-
iunantes & orantes, imponentesque eis manus, dimise-
runt illos. It is confessed by the greatest Protestant
authoritie in England, of King, Protestant Bishops,
and others their best scollers in their publike examen of their Religion. That this power of Orders,
giuen as they pretend by imposition of hands. *Is*
diuinæ Ordinationis, and de iure diuino. The ordinan-
ce of God, and by his diuine lawe. To these persons God
imparted power ouer his mysticall bodie, which is the
societie of soules, and ouer that naturall, which is him-
selfe, which antiquitie doth call the making of Christs
body. The power of the ministry by blessing visible
ele-

in descript.
cambr. c. 18.

Gild. l. de
excid. Britan.
in castigatio-
ne Cleri.

1. Timoth. 4.

2. Timoth. 1.

Io: 20.

Act. 13.

K. Iames and
his protest.
publike con-
ference at
hampton
court
Couell def. of
hooker p. 87.
Mod. exami-
nat. pag. 105,
155. def. of
hooker pag.

clements, it maketh them inuisible grace , & giueth
daily the holy ghost,it hath to dispose of that flesh,which
was giuen for the life of the world: and that blood
which was powred out to redeeme soules . It is a power,
which neither Prince nor potentate, King nor Cæsar on
earth can giue. The Apostles did impart the same
power,to ordayne, which was giuen to them.

And in their publikly authorized Rituall, and
booke of consecration, or making Protestant
Bishops, and Preists, warranted by their parlaments, in these very Articles, and their generall
practise in ordayning all their Church men, it is
diuers times and plainely confessed, both by words
and actions, that the holy ghost, grace, and power
to giue grace, and forgiue sinnes, is infallibly giuen
by the externall signe, or ceremony vsed therein.
And both their publike conference and examen of
their Religion, and the common booke of their
Church seruice do proue and giue warrant, from
hence,from their ministers to forgiue sinns,by such
power committed to them from God in their ordination. Therefore if there be any ground or
warrant for the Protestant Religion of England,
or any one point, or article thereof, though but
such as they pretend for the proposers, and autho-
rizers thereof, whether Protestant Prince, parlament, conuocation, canons, Articles the publik
bookes, and practise thereof, or whatsoeuer els
they can name in this kinde, holie Orders and
preisthood so vehemently persecuted by them, is
by their owne doctrine and Religion an holie Sacrament, in such proper true sense and meaning
as it is vsed in the Romane Church, at this time,
and euer was. They were the Messaliani or Mas-

87. 88. 91.

Protest.
Booke of
Confecrat.
in Order.
Bish. and
Preists.

Protest. conf.
at hampton.
Communion
Booke Titul.
visitat. of the
sike.

Q   saliani

saliani, Euchitæ or Enthusiastæ heretiks about the yeare of Christ 380. which in antiquitie are remembred first to haue denyed the grace of this holie Sacrament, as they did of others, and affirmed that the holie ghost was not receaued therein, & for this as other their Errours were condemned then of heresie. *Messaliani dicunt in clericorum ordinatione Spiritum sanctum non suscipi.* These Protestants Ordination will be spoken of in their. 36. Article, of that Title.

Damascen. de hæresib. hist. tripart. l. 7. Theod. l. 4. c 11. Niceph. hist. Eccl. l. 11. cap. 14.

THE XVI. CHAPTER.

Matrimonie thus proued a Sacrament.

THE next Sacrament which this Protestant Article excepteth against in the same wordes, and phrase of speach, as against the former is that of matrimonie, euer in the Church of Christ, from his, and his Apostles time, receaued, and vsed for an holy Sacrament. The holie scriprures say it is an honorable estate: *honorabile connubium.* God maketh the vnion of husband and wife vnseparable by man. *Quod Deus coniunxit, homo non separet.* The bonde of matrimonie is the greatest, greater then towards father or mother. And a reason is because it is a Sacrament. *Relinquet homo patrem & matrem suam, & adherebit vxori suæ, & erunt duo in carne vna. Sacramentum hoc magnum est: ego autem dico in Christo, & in Ecclesia.*

This supernaturall and Sacramentall Institution in Christian Religion maketh the obligation inuiolable, not admitting separation, to take any other. *Quicumque dimiserit vxorem suam, & aliam duxe-*

Hebr. 13.

Matth. 19.

Ephes. 5.

Matth. 10.

duxerit, adulterium committit super eam . & si vxor dimiserit virum suum & alij nupserit, machatur . Ijs qui matrimonio iuncti sunt, praecipio non ego sed Dominus, vxorem à viro non discedere, quòd si decesserit, manere innuptam, aut viro suo reconciliari, & vir vxorem non dimittat. It was not so, either with the Iewes or gentiles. The Iewes enen in the dayes of Moyses had their diuorces *Moses mandauit dare libellum repudij & dimittere. Moses permisit dimittere vxores.* As they also had pluralitie of wiues then. At the cominge of Christ and after, by their Rabbines allowance. *Rabbini vestri sanè ad hunc vsque diem ; & quatuor , & quinque vestrum quemque vxores habere permittunt.* And yet condemned them not, for other incontinencies. All which as S. Iustine liuing in this age, witnesseth against them, is condemned by the Christian Sacrament of matrimony . *Si quis vestrum venustam inspiciens, eam expetiuerit, nihil iniqui agere asseuerunt, quo quidem etiam miseri & stulti sunt nomine. Nam sicut prius dixi magnorum Sacramentorum œconomiæ & dispositiones in quolibet eius generis facto sunt celebratæ:*

The gentiles though euer without title of true Religion, and therefore needles to be remembred in this busines, were not inferiour to the Iewes in this disorder no more then the later Hereticall Turkes and Mahometans now be . Yet I shall speake of the gentiles by accidentary occasion hereafter . S. Martiall in this age doth say not onely that marriage among Christians, is honest, constituted by God, lawfull, and immaculate, but hath sanctification, and honour of chastitie. *Coniugium honestum; & constitutum à Deo, legitimum & immaculatum, eis qui ex sanctificatione & honore castitatis*

1. Cotinth. 7.

Matth. 19.

Iustinus dial. cum Tryphone.

Martial. epist. ad Tholosan. cap. 9.

Q 2

stitatis nubere volunt. And Christ our Lord himselfe
so approued it . *Dominus & Magister meus Christus*
approbauit.

S. Clement from the Apostles proueth, there
could be no dissolubilitie in Christian mariage , no
taking a second wife, or husband, during the life
of the first. *Si quis Laicus, vxorem propriam pellens,*
alteram, vel ab alio dimissam duxerit communione
priuetur. So S. Euaristus expoundeth S. Paul cited
before, of not parting husband, or wife. So Tertullian prouing that mariage among Christians is
onely dissolued by death , and not diuorce. *Per*
mortem, non per repudium facta solutione, quia repu-
diatis non permitteret nubere Apostolus aduersus
pristinum praeceptum . Manet matrimonium quod
non ritè diremptum est. Manente matrimonio nubere,
adulterium est. He maketh the prayses of matrimonie all most vnspeakeable, the Church maketh
it , sacrifice confirmeth it , the Angels honour it,
God ratifieth it. It is a coniunction of two Faithfull
of one hope, one vowe, one discipline of the same
seruice. To these God sendeth his peace. *Vnde*
sufficiam ad enarrandum felicitatem eius matrimonij,
quod Ecclesia couciliat, & confirmat obligatio, & obsi-
gnatum Angeli renunciant, pater rato habet ? Quale
iugum fidelium duorum vnius spei, vnius voti, vnius
disciplinae, eiusdem seruitutis ? His Deus pacem suam
mittit . He diuers times, and in diuers places calleth it a Sacrament. *Sacramentum, celebrandum*
Sacramentum, diuinum Sacramentum , euen as Baptisme and confirmation. So doth S. Euaristus Pope
liuing in this age, and as other Fathers both greeke
and latin, so expound S. Paul before cited, calling
it a greate Sacrament, *Sacramentum hoc magnum est.*
S. Chri-

Clem. Can.
Apost 48.
Euarist ep, 2.

Tertullian. de
Monogam.
cap. 11. l. 4.
contra Mar-
cion cap. 34.

l. 2. ad vxo-
rem cap. 9.

Tertullian. l.
de Monog.
cap. 5. aduers.
Valentinian.
cap. 30. l. de
praescript.
aduers. heret.
c. Euaristus
Pap. epist. 2.
Ephes. 5.

S. Chrisostome though liueing after this age
yet giueing the custome and practise of thes and
after dayes for his reason, besides S. Paules authoritie so expoundeth him saying it is a Sacrament
and a greate Sacrament as S. Paul did, prouinge
a Sacrament by the Sacramentall grace giuen therein, *for a man or woman to forsake him that begotte*
them nourished and brought them up, her which con-
ceaued them, brought them forth with payne and affli-
ction, who bestowed so many benefites vpon them, as
parents do on children, with whom there was so long
acquaintance, and cohabitation, to adhere to him or her,
that was not seene to them before, and preferr them be-
fore all things, this is verily a Mysterie. And the pa-
rents when these things are done, are not greeued, but
rather if they bee not done, and with Ioy pay money, and
make expences to see them performed. Veriely this is a
greate mistery, hauing a certayne secrette wisedome,
This long since S. Paul Prophesied, saying in Christ and
his Church. But this was not spoken alone for him, but
what? That the husband should cherish his wife, as his
owne flesh. And as Christ doth his Church. Reuera
est mysterium, & magnum mysterium, eo qui procreauit,
qui genuit, qui educauit: ea, quæ concepit, quæ cum
dolore peperit & afflictione, qui tot ac tantis affecerunt
beneficijs, cum quibus diuturnus fuit vsus, & consuetudo, relictis, ei adherere, quæ ne visa quidem fuit,
& cum eo nihil habere commune, & eam omnibus præ-
ferre, reuera est mysterium, & parentes cum hæc fiunt,
non egrè ferunt, sed potiùs ægrè ferunt, si non fiant, &
cum impenduntur pecuniæ, & fiunt sumptus, lætantur.
Reuera magnum est mysterium, arcanam quandam habens sapientiam. Hoc multis retroactis sæculis pro-
phetans dicit: In Christo & Ecclesia. Sed non propter

Chrisostom.
in cap. 5. ad
Ephes. Hom.
20.

Q 3   *ipsum*

ipſum ſolum hoc dictum eſt. Sed quid? Vt ipſam tan-
quam propriam carnem foueat, ſicut & Chriſtus Eccle-
ſiam.

And to inſiſt vpon the graunt of this Proteſtant Article. *That Sacraments be effectuall ſignes of grace,* we haue the teſtimonie of the whole Chriſtian world in this Apoſtolike time, to proue Matrimo-nie, to be ſuch a ſigne, and Sacrament, for all the world at the coming of Chriſt, Iewes, and gentils were giuen to Poligamie and pluralitie of wiues, and yet not ſo contayning themſelues from other incontinencies, but ſuch as receyued this holy Sacrament abſtayned both from the ſinnes of Po-ligamie, and other vnchaſtities, an euident and vn-deniable argument, of the power and ſanctitie of this Chriſtian Inſtitution and holy Sacrament. I will onely exemplifie here in Britayne, infected as the reſt of the vniuerſall world with that generall errour and ſinne, at that time. Iulius Cæſar Empe-rour which inuaded this Kingdome and others after him giue ſuch ſhamefull teſtimonie hereof, modeſtie forbiddeth me to write it in Engliſh: *Vxores habent deni, duodenique inter ſe communes, & maximè fratres cum fratribus, & parentes cum liberis nudi degunt, mulieribus promiſcuè vtuntur.* Their Queene Bandica in her publike ſacrifice to the Britans Goddeſſe Andraſte, or Andaſte, in her ſo-lemne prayer openly pronounced of them: *Qui cum cætera omnia, tum liberos & vxores communes inter ſe putant.* Pagans, Catholiks and Proteſtants write the like of the Picts, The Proteſtants thus ſpeake it in Engliſh: *They liue naked in Tents, their wiues are common.*

The Scots were more barborous in theſe ſinnes, and

Iul. Cæſar belli gallici l. 6. Ioh. Zo-naras in Se-uero. Bandica orat. Solemni apud Ioan. Xephil. in Epitom. Dionis, in Nerone. Dion. ibid. Dion. Hect. Boeth. deſ-cript. Scotiæ. william Har-riſon deſcrip of Scotl. cap. 14.

and their Kings especially Euenus confirmed them
by publike lawes. *Leges tulit improbas omnem olentes*
spurcitiam, vt liceret singulis suæ gentis plures vxo-
res alijs sex, alijs decem pro opibus ducere. Nobilibus
plebeorum vxores communes essent, ac virginis nouæ
nuptæ, loci Dominus primam libandi pudicitiam, pote-
statem haberet. This was the miserable condition
of this Kingdome of greate Britayne, as of other
nations, before it receaued the lawe of Chist, and
the holie Sacrament of Matrimonie, betweene one
man and woman, one husband, and one wife, to
giue infallible demonstration to all people, present
and to come, that great supernaturall assistance,
and grace was giuen by that externall rite or ceremonie, and so consequently ordayned of God, no
other being able to do it all those most horrible
lasciuious incontinencies generally ceased in the
true and due receauers of this Sacrament.

Leges Euan.
Regis Scoto-
rum. Hector
Boeth. Scot.
Hist. l. 3. fol.
36. pag. 1.

And for the barbarous customes and lawes before, these were made, kept, and seuerely executed.
Our Protestants thus translate them. *Any mans*
lemman or concubyne shall suffer the same paynes, that
he doth which offendeth with her. He that rauisheth a
mayde shall dye for it, vnlesse shee require for safe-gard
of his life, to haue him to her husband. If any man be
taken with another mans wife in adulterie, shee con-
senting vnto him therein, they shall both suffer death
for it. But if shee consent not, but beforced against her
will, then he shall dye onely for the same, and shee shall
be released. In such greate seueritie the sinne of
Incontinencie was punished here after this holie
Sacrament, by the grace thereof a preseruatiue
against it was receaued, and few were founde trans-
gressours thereof, all though these lawes were pro-

Veremund.
Hect. Boeth.
hist. Scot. l.
10. fol. 202.
Hollinshed
hist. of Scotl.
pag. 133. cap.
lawes.

Q 4   secuted

secuted with such zeale and deuotion, that we finde, that Princes and Kings found delinquent were neither exempted, nor spared in such cases, as we see in the lamentable example of King Vortigerne testified both by brittish, English, Catholike and Protestant historians who breakeing his Matrimoniall Faith, with his first lawfull wife, and adulterously ioyning himselfe with an other woman, Rowenna Daughter of Engist, was by S. German the Popes legate, with the aduise and consent of the brittish cleargie, cited, Iudged and excomunicated, and by the whole Kingdome deposed. Neyther can the Protestants of England deny Matrimonie to be a Sacrament. For in the manner of celebrating thereof at euery mariage, it termeth it, *holy matrimonie, an honorable estate, instituted of God, signifying vnto vs, the misticall vnion which is betwene Christ and his Church. God instituted it, and did teache, it should neuer be lawfull to put asunder those, whom he by matrimonie had made one. God hath consecrated the stat of matrimonie to such an excellent mistery, that in it is signified and represented the spirituall mariage & vnitie betwixt Christ & his Church.* And this Rituall expresseth, *that God giueth grace, sanctification, and blessing at this externall ceremonie,* so instituted and ordeyned by him. Which euidently ouerthroweth what they haue saide to the contrary in this Article, and proueth by their owne most generall and warranted vse, practise, and profession, that Matrimonie is truely and properly an holie Sacrament.

Nennius hist. Ma manuscript. in Vorthigerno Rege Mat. westm. an. 450. Mat. Park. Antiq. Britan. pag. 7. 8. Protest. annotat. in Mat. westm. an. 454 Stowe and Howes hist. in Vortigern. Hollins hist. of Engl. in cod. Protest. Communion booke Tit. Matrimonie. ʃ. Dearely. 1. ʃ. O God. ʃ. Allmightie God.

THE XVII. CHAPTER.

Extreame Vnction thus proued, to be a Sacrament.

THE Sacrament following being the laſt in number, and order, which this Proteſtant Article deſalloweth, is extreame vnction. But we are moſt aſſured, that in this Apoſtolike age, and by the Apoſtles themſelues it was taught and pra-ctiſed for an holie Sacrament, S. Iames the Apoſtle in his epiſtle maketh it a precept, and matter of neceſſitie, and not arbitrary ſo to vſe it. *Infirmatur* *quis in vobis? inducat Presbyteros Ecclesiæ, & orent* *ſuper eum, vngentes eum oleo in nomine Domini. Etſi* *in peccatis ſit, remittentur ei.* Here we haue all which this Proteſtant Article requireth to a true and properly named Sacrament, teſtified by an Apoſtle in holie ſcripture and tradition of the Church from that time, to be founde in extreame vnction.

Iacob. c. 5.

That it was ordayned of Chriſt, and an effe-ctuall ſigne of grace, the words are playne, as alſo that the viſible ſigne or ceremonie thereof was or-dayned of God, for no power limited and created can ordayne, or inſtitute a ſigne or ceremonie ex-ternall to forgiue ſinnes: *ſi in peccatis ſit remitten-* *tur ei.* The auntient Fathers both of the greeke and Latine Church doe thus expound this place, & deriue this Sacrament from thence, and affirme it euer to haue beene ſo receaued in Chriſts Church and by him inſtituted, propoſed by S. Iames. *ſic* *roges de te, & pro te ſic ri, ſicut dixit Apoſtolus Iacobus,*

Origen. hom. 2. in leuitic. Chriſoſtom. l. 3. de Sacer-dotio. Cirill. Alexandr. l. 6. de adorat.

imino

immo per Apostolum suum Dominus : ipsa videlicet olei sacrati delibutio intelligitur Spiritus sancti typicalis vnctio.

I need not to make repetitions of their testimonies, this veritie being so generally receaued and practized in the first times of Christian Religion, that about the yeare of Christ 279. it was commonly adiudged heresie to deny it, and is so censured, registred, and condemned in the exploded heresies of the Hierarchite Heretiks : *dicebant extrema vnctionis Sacramentum à Deo institutum non esse*. Which being condemned for heresie in the whole Church of Christ, must needs be so also adiudged in this Kingdome, renowned then for true Christian Religion, and the Catholike doctrine, yet we want not particular testimonies hereof, for our Protestants themselues commonly teaching that the Britans neuer chaunged any materiall point in Religion, produce vnto vs a most auntient manuscript as they terme it, written, *ab authore antiquissimo*, and as is euident in the same Antiquitie, when there were yet many Pagans and Idolaters here, in which, commaunde and direction is giuen that all sick persons in daunger of death should both receaue the Sacrament of Christs holie bodie, and this of extreame vnction, sette downe by S. Iames the Apostle and the primatiue Fathers before. *Quotiens aliqua Infirmitas superuenerit, corpus & sanguinem Christi illi qui ægrotant, accipiant: oleum in nomine Domini à presbyteris humiliter petant, & inde corpus suum vngant : vt quod scriptum est, impleatur. Infirmatur aliquis, inducat presbyteros Ecclesiæ, & orent super eum vngentes eum oleo in nomine Domini, & oratio fidei saluabit infirmum*

in spiritu victor Antioch. ad c. 6. marci. Ambros. in missali Hier. ad c. 14. Oseæ August. Serm. 215. de tempor. in Tract. de rectitud. cathol. conuersat. l. 2. de visitat. Infirm. c. 4. Innocent. 1. epistol. ad Decent. Eug. cap. 8. Aug. l. de Hæres. cap. 47. Gabriel Prat. Elench. hæresum in Hierarchitis. Epiph. hæres. 67.
Extreame vnction a Sacrament with the Britans. Manuscript. Brit. Antiquissimi Authoris.

Iacob. 5.

infirmum, & alleuiabit eum Dominus, et si in peccatis sit, dimittentur ei. Videte fratres, quia qui infirmitatem habent, ad Ecclesiam currant, corporis sanitatem recipere, & peccatorum Indulgentiam merebuntur obtinere.

The Proteſtants of England euen the compoſers of theſe Articles, cannot by their owne Religion be of other mind, without groſſe Ignorance and contradiction, for defining a Sacrament, as they haue done in this Article, and in their moſt warranted communion booke thus do define it: *by this word Sacrament I meane an outward and viſible ſigne, of an Inward and ſpirituall grace giuen vnto vs, ordeyned by Chriſt himſelfe, as a meanes whereby we receaue the ſame, and a pledge to aſſuer vs thereof:* They muſt needs graunt that S. Iames in expreſſe words in holie ſcripture, their pretended Rule, hath deliuered as much for this Sacrament as they require, the outward viſible ſigne, the Preiſts prayer and vnction with oyle, and remiſſion of ſinnes, which cannot be without grace, receaued by the ſame.

(margin: Proteſt. commun. booke Tit. catechiſme.)

Thus I haue inuincibly proued by this firſt Apoſtolike age for the doctrine and practiſe of the Catholike Church and againſt this Proteſtant Article, the whole compleat number of 7. Sacraments. And yet if I had onely proued three Sacraments, or any leſſe number then ſeuen, and greater then two I had ſufficiently confuted this Article which onely alloweth two, Baptiſme and the *Euchariſt ſtiled by them, the Supper of the Lord, for ſuch.*

The XVIII. Chapter.

*The rest of this Article repugnant to the Catholike
faith, likewise condemned,*

THE remnant of this Article they deliuer in
these words: *The, Sacraments were not ordeyned of Christ, to be gazed vpon, or to be carryed about:
but that we should duely vse them. And in such onely
as worthyly receaue the same; they haue a wholesome
effect or operation : But they that receaue them vnwor-
thily, purchase to themselues damnation, as Sainct
Paule saith.*

This is the whole content of this Article, and in
this last, if these Protestants desire to speake properly, as they should, and would so be vnderstood:
there is very little or no difference betwene Catholiks and them. For where they say, that Sacraments *haue a wholesome effect* or operation in
their worthie receauers, this agreeth with the
Catholike doctrine, that Sacraments giue grace,
and worke *ex opere operato*, which many Protestants denie. And concerning the vnworthie receauing of them, it is not a thing questioned.
What they meane, by these wordes, *The Sacraments were not ordeyned of Christ to be gazed vppon,
or to be carryed about*, So speaking of Sacraments
in the plurall number, is a straunge speach, excepting one Species of the Sacrament of Eucharist we
reserue none, nor carry any about for any respect
nor can by their doctrine, professing they consist
in their ministration and receauing, as is euident
in Baptisme, Confirmation, Orders, Confession
and

and Abſolution, Matrimony, and Extreame vnction. What they meane by their words, *gazed vpon*, requireth a better gloſſe, then they giue to vnderſtande their meaning, for to take the worde as it is commonly and properly vſed in our language, earneſtly or intenſiuely to beholde, if they forbid ſuch geſture at Sacraments, they forbid publik miniſtration of them, which their practiſe alloweth, warranteth and preſcribeth by their greateſt authoritie.

If they would haue this their termed gating vpon, or carrying about to be vnderſtood any reuerence or reſeruation the Romane Church vſeth towards the bleſſed Sacrament of the Altare, the queſtion with them properly belongeth to their 28. Article, where they expreſſely ſpeake againſt Tranſubſtantiation, or chaunge of breade and wine into the body and blood of Chriſt, and his true and reall preſence in thoſe moſt ſacred miſteries, which being vndeniably confuted, as in that place it ſhall, this errour is thereby clearely ouerthrowne. For whereſoeuer Chriſt is, or howſoeuer he is, he is to be worſhipped and adored, with as greate dutie and reuerence as any Catholike giueth vnto him in this Sacrament. In the meane tyme the Apoſtolike men of this firſt age do thus teſtifie.

S. Clement often teſtifying the reall and true preſence of Chriſt in this moſt holie Sacrament, ſetteth downe the deuotion and honour of all people then, Biſhops, Preiſts, Deacons, Subdeacons, Virgyns, widowes, married, old and young to be as greate or greater then Catholiks now commonly vſe vnto it. When conſecration is ended, and the bleſſed Sacrament was ſhewed vnto the Chriſtians

stians present, the Deacon vsed to say, let vs attend or behold. The Bishop or Preist offering the Sacrifice, said to the people holie things for the holie, and the people answeared one holie one Lord, one Christ in the glorie of God the Father blessed for euer Amen. Glorie to God on highest, and peace to men of good will: Osanna to the sonne of Dauid. Blessed is he that cometh in the name of our Lord, God our Lord, and hath appeared vnto vs, hosanna in the highest. Then all communicate with greate reuerence, acknowledging that which they receaue to be the bodie, and blood of Christ. And that was left, by the Deacons was reuerently carryed into, & kept in the Pastophories.

Clem. Rom.
Const. Apost.
l. 8. cap. 20.
l. 2. cap. 61.

Postquam omnes dixerunt Amen. Diaconus dicat attendamus. Et Episcopus alloquatur populum ijs verbis sancta sanctis, & populus subiungat vnus sanctus, vnus Dominus, vnus Christus in gloria Dei Patris benedictus in saecula Amen. Gloria in altissimis Deo, & in terra pax hominibus bonae voluntatis. Osanna filio Dauid. Benedictus qui venit in nomine domini Deus Dominus & apparuit nobis. Osanna in altissimis. Post hoc sumat Episcopus, deinde Presbiteri, & Diaconi & Hypodiaconi, & Anagnostae, & Cantores, & Ascetae, & ex mulieribus Diaconissae. & Virgines & Viduae, postea pueri & omnis populus cum pudore & reuerentia. Episcopus det oblationem dicens, Corpus Christi, & sumens dicat Amen. Postquam omnes sumpserunt, accipiant Diaconi reliquias, & portent in pastophoria.

Carol. Bou.
Scot. in l. 2.
Clement. de
Const. Apost.
cap. 61.

Thes Pastophories were sacred and religious tabernacles in Churches, wherein the blessed Sacrament, holie and sacred vestments & vessels were kept. And this holie Sacrament was so religiously preser-

preſerued, that as S. Clement witneſſeth, to be
negligent therein in the time of the Apoſtles was
excommunication. *Presbyteri, Diaconi, & miniſtri*
cùm timore & tremore clericorum reliquias fragmen-
torum corporis Domini cuſtodire debent, ne qua putredo
in Sacrario inueniatur, ne quum negligentur agitur
portioni corporis Domini grauis inferatur iniuria. Com-
munio enim Corporis Domini noſtri Ieſu Chriſti ſi ne-
gligentèr erogetur, & presbyter minora non curet ad-
monere officia, graui anathemate, & digna humiliatio-
nis plaga feriatur.

Clem. Rom.
epiſtol. 2.

So greate reuerence, and honour was vſed in
reſeruing this bleſſed Sacrament in that time, that
neither pall, vayle, or any thing that touched it,
might be waſhed out of the Sacrary, ſo named in
reſpect this moſt holie Sacrament was therein with
ſuch deuotion preſerued. And the baſen wherein
they were waſhed was accompted ſo holy, that
nothing but ſuch holy things might be waſhed in
it. *Palla & vela quæ in ſanctuarij ſordidata fuerint*
miniſterio, Diaconi cum humilibus miniſtris iuxta Sa-
crarium lauent, non eijcientes foras à ſacrario velamina
dominicæ menſæ, ne fortè puluis Dominici Corporis
malè decidat à ſindone foris abluto, & erit hæc operanti
peccatum, idcircò, intra ſacrarium miniſtris præcipi-
mus, hæc ſancta cum diligentia cuſtodire: peluis noua
comparetur, & præter hoc nihil aliud tangat. Pallæ
altaris ſolæ in ea lauentur.

S. Ignatius proueth the Euchariſt to be the flesh
of Chriſt our Sauiour, which ſuffered for our ſinnes, and which aroſe agayne, and ſo muſt needs be
honoured. *Panem Dei volo, panem cæleſtem, quæ eſt*
caro Chriſti filij Dei. Euchariſtiam eſſe carnem Salua-
toris noſtri Ieſu Chriſti, quæ pro peccatis noſtris paſſa
eſt,

Ignat. epiſt.
ad Rom.
epiſt. ad
Smyrnent.
apnd Theod.
Dial. 3. & al.

est, quàm Pater sua benignitate suscitauit. And maketh them notorious heretiks which denyed, or called it into question: non confitcantur, which did, not confesse it.

S. Denys the Areopagite deliuereth to vs, how Christ in this Sacrament was honoured, & prayed vnto, setting downe the very prayer itselfe, which that Apostoliketime there vsed vnto him. *O diuinum pignus sacrumque mysterium abducta tibi significantium operimenta signorum dignanter aperiens, nobis palam atque apertè lucesce nostros spirituales oculos singulari & aperto tuæ lucis fulgore imple.* He telleth also, how both the Preist that offered this most holy Sacrifice, worshipped it, and did shew it vnto the people present likewise to be worshipped of them. *Pontifex sacrosancta & augustissima mysteria conficit, & quæ ante laudauerat, venerandis opertas, atque abdita conspectu agit, diuina munera reuerenter ostendens.*

All things belonging to this most holy Sacrament were holy, and honoured both by the writers of this age, and our Protestants testimonie. The Bishops, Preists, Deacons, and others were consecrated as before. And as S. Anacletùs euen by Protestant allowance saith, the Preists might not be Iudged by others, they were honoured as Christ, and their priuiledges were graunted them by Christs commaunde. *Anacletus Christo alienos esse iudicabat, qui Sacerdotes in Ius vocarent. Quia inquit, qui sacerdoti detrahit, Christo detrahit. sacerdotes omnino Christi sunt. priuilegia Ecclesiæ & sacerdotum Apostoli saluatoris iussu inuiolata esse debere iusserunt.* The Altar whereon it was sacrificed, was holy: *Missam non nisi in altari celebrandam esse.* The

cor-

Dion. Areopag. Ecclef. Hierarch. cap. 3.

Dionyf. fupr. cap. 3.

Robert. Barnes l. de vit. Pontif. Rom. in Anacleto. Anaclet.epist. Tom. 1. concil. & alibi. Sixtas Pap. 1. Rob. Barnes fupra in eod.

Corporall whereon it was layed, and the cloathes
of the altare were holy, so were all the vessels vsed
about it, that none but consecrated persons might
touch them . *sacra vasane qui præter sacros minis-*
stros attingerent. The Church vestures both of the
Preist, and other clergymen which assisted him in
this Sacrifice, sacred and holy . *sacerdotem sacrifi-* Anaclet.epist.
caturum, ministros vestibus sacris indutos, seu testes Rob. Barnes
& custodes sibi adhibere ordinauit Anacletus. The in vit. Pontifs.
place named there vpon Sacrarium Sacrary, or Rom. in
holy place, was holy, So was the Tabernacle or Anaclet.
Pastophorium wherein it was religiously kept.
Thus testifie the holy Popes which were liuing in
this first age, Thus testifie our Protestant Antiquaries, whose very words for more iuertie I haue
cited.

And the larned Fathers both greeke and latine Tertullian. l.
in the next ages following testifie this religious & 2. ad vxorem.
reuerent manner of reseruing this blessed Sacra- Ciprian. Ser-
ment: So hath the first generall councell of Nice, mon.delapsis.
and other authorities vndeniable. And that this Basil. in Gor-
was the custome in Britayne is proued before, dio mart.
when I cited from the antiquities thereof, that the Chrisost.
sike receaued this Sacrament reserued, when ex- epist. ad In-
treame vnction was ministred vnto them. And nocent. to. 4.
one of their most auntient antiquities carrying & cit. a Ni-
with it our Protestants approbation, doth witnesse cephor. l. 13.
that the primatiue Christian Britans did publikely cap. 19. con-
at Euery Masse worship and pray vnto Christ pre- cil. nicen. 1.
sent in this Sacrament, this hath our Protestants cau. 14.
translation: *Hereof singe Gods seruants at euery Masse;* A n old
Agnus Dei qui tollis peccata mundi, miserere nobis: manuscript.
That is in our speach : *Thou lambe of God, that takest* British and
away the sinnes of the world, haue mercy vpon vs. dulch Serm.
read in our
old Churches
an. 366. Foxe
Act. and mo-
num. p. 1142.

R   And

And thus I end this their many braunched Article.

The XIX. Chapter.

The 26. and 27. Articles examined and Protestant doctrine in or by them condemned.

THeir next Article being the 26. by their numbring them, is thus intituled. *Of the worthines of the ministers, which hinder not the effect of the sacraments.* The whole Article followeth in these *Allthough in the visible Church the euill be euer mingled with the good, and sometime the euill haue cheife authoritie in the ministration of the worde and sacraments: yet for asmuch as they do not the same in their owne name, but in Christes, and do minister by his commission, and authoritie, we may vse their ministerie, both in hearing the word of God, and in receiuing of the sacraments. Neither is the effect of Christes ordinance taken away by their wikednesse, nor the grace of Gods guifts diminished from such as by faith, and rightly do receiue the sacraments ministred vnto them, which be effectuall, because of Christs institution and promise, allthough they be ministred by euill men. Neuerthelesse, it apperteyneth to the discipline of the Churche, that inquirie be made of euill ministers, and that they be accused by those, that haue knowledge of their offences: and finally, being founde gyltie by iust Iudgment, be deposed.*

Hitherto this Article, in which there it not any one proposition, or sentence, against the doctrine of the Romane Church and Catholike Religion, but rather a graunte and confirmation thereof,

and

and a renowncing of Protestant profession, and
proceedings in diuers particular poyntes, and some
most materiall. As declaring that in the visible
Church the euill be euer mingled with the good,
they confesse the Church to be euer and indefe-
ctible. And so Luther, Caluyn, Cranmar, King
Henry 8. with his daughter Queene Elizabeth, or
whomsoeuer els they will or can make the first
publisher or aduancer of their doctrine, separating
themselues, and being separated and cutt of from
that visible true Church, which was then generally
so held, this their Protestant congregation, and
Religion takeing Originall, & being from thence,
cannot possibly be the true Church and Religion
of Christ.

And in making the true Church euer visible,
they must needs make their association or pretended companie euer inuisible, and so nothing vntill
these dayes, and condemne those their brethren
Protestants, who knowing their new fraternitie
was neuer vntill those late times, haue mathema-
tically framed in their Imagination, a new straung,
chimericall, Inuisible, vnbeeable and vnpossible
Church. Agayne professing that Preists the Ministers of Sacraments do Minister them *in Christes
name, by his commission,* and authoritie, they sufficiently confesse, that if Christ omnipotent could
and did confecrate breade and wyne into his body,
and blood, forgiue sinnes and giue grace in sacraments, truely confecrated Preists haue that power,
and do the same. And affirming, *The sacraments to
be effectuall because of Christes Institution and promise,
neither is the effect of Christes ordinance taken away,
nor the grace of Gods guifts diminished by the wiked-*

R. 2   *nesse*

nesse of ministers, They proue what the Catholiks holde in these things, and Protestants cammonly deny. Their last clause of Discipline in the Church making but one true visible Church, and their congregation being, as before no part thereof, depriueth them of all such discipline, as they haue already spoyled themselues of the pure worde of God preached and Sacraments duely miniſtred vnseparable signes and properties of the true visible Church, by their 19. Article, and thereby want all things which by their owne confession are euer founde in, and belonge vnto the Church of Chriſt.

　　The 27. Article intituled, *of baptisme*, hath nothing contrary to Catholik Religion: But the last clause thereof is againſt their 6. Article before, *that nothing is to be beleeued as an Article of faith or to be thought requisite necessarie to saluation, that is not read in, nor may be proued by scriptures*. And in this place thus they decree: *The Baptisme of yong children, is in any wise to be retayned in the Church, as most agreable with the Instiution of Chriſt*. In this whole Article before they make Baptisme in all requisite necessarie to Saluation, So they do in their communion booke in the administration thereof, and in the reuewe of their Religion at Hampton court, thus they define: *That baptisme to be ministred by priuate parsons, in tyme of necessitie, is an holie tradition*. And so they vse in their common practise, and Baptise Infants both by their ministers, and others men and women, especially my dwiues, instructed how to Baptisme in time of necessitie. Yet with publik consent and allowance thus they write and publish: *Baptisme of Infants is*

named

Prot. Articl. #7.

Proteſt. communion Booke Tit. Baptisme.
Proteſt. Conference at hampton Court.

Engl. Proteſt. in feild Bookes of the Church

named a Tradition, because it is not expressely deliuered *pag.* 239.
in scripture, that the Apostles did baptize Infants, nor and others.
any expresse precept there founde, that they should so do.

That the holy Fathers of the first age held Ba- *Supr. in arti-*
ptisme of Infants for an vnwritten tradition I haue *cul.* 6.
spoken before. And S. Clement doth giue com- *Clem. Rom.*
maund, to haue it obserued: *Baptizate vestros pue-* *lib.* 6. *constit.*
ros infantes. S. Denys the Areopagite affirmeth *Apostolic.*
it was so vsed: *Pueri qui necdum possunt intelligere* *cap.* 15.
diuina, sacri baptismatis participes fiant. And she- *Dionys.*
inge how others answeare and promise for them, *Ecclesiast.*
alij pro ipsis abrenunciant, sanctaque ineunt fædera, *Hierarch.*
calleth it an holy tradition, *sanctam traditionem,* *cap.* 7.
vsed as S. Chrisostome and others testifie generally *concil. mile-*
in the whole Catholik Church in all places, *Præ-* *Chrisostom.*
dicat Ecclesia Catholica vbique diffusa, debere par- *homil. de*
uulos Baptizari propter originale peccatum. And *Adam & Eua.*
they were Nouatian, Pelagian & such condemned *Augustin.*
Heretiks, which at any time called this holy. tra- *l.* 1. *cap.* 23.
dition and custome into question. So it was here *Epiphan.*
in Britayne, which though it was Mother and *Aug. & alij*
Nurse longe time to pelagius the Archeretike, *nocent.* 1.
who among other his damned Errours denyed the *epist. concil.*
Baptisme of Infants, yet it so much detested among *African. cap.*
the rest this his obsurd Inuention, that it spared *77. concil.*
not Princes themselues, that followed him therein, *cap.* 6.
as all Antiquities tell vs, in the case of King Fre- *Hect. Boeth.*
quard, who being noted to haue laught at the *Scot. hist. l.*
Baptisme of Infants, and confession of sinnes to *9. Georg.*
Preists, *Notatus est aliquando risisse paruulorum* *scot. l. 5.*
baptismum peccatorumque ad Sacerdotis aurem confes- *Reg.* 52. *ho-*
sionem, was accused of pelagianisme, cited, con- *linsh. hist. of*
demned, imprisoned and deposed. So testifie both *Scotland. in*
Catholik and Protestant Antiquaries. *pag.* 112.

R 3 THE

THE XX. CHAPTER.

The 28. Article intituled, of the supper of the Lord, examined, and condemned.

THEIR 28. Article being intituled: *of the Lords supper* : is as followeth. *The supper of the Lorde is not onely a signe of the loue, that Christians ought to haue among themselues, on to an other : but rather it is a Sacrament of our redemption, by Christes death : in so much, that to such as rightly, worthily, and with faith receaue the same, the bread which we breake is a partaking of the body of Christ, and likewise the cuppe of blessing is a partaking of the blood of Christe. Transubstantiation (the chaunge of the substance of breade and wine, in the supper of the Lord, cannot be proued by holy writ : it is repugnant to the playne words of scripture, ouerthroweth the nature of a Sacrament, and hath giuen occasion to many superstitions. The body of Christ is giuen, taken, and eaten in the supper, onely after an heauenly, and spirituall manner : And the meane whereby the bodie of Christ is receaued, and eaten in the supper, is faith.*

The Sacrament of the Lords supper was not by Christs ordinaunce reserued, carryed about, lifted vp, or worshipped. Hitherto this 28. Protestant Article. In the first part thereof vntill we come to the word Transubstantiation, or the chaunge of the substance, there is no apparant contradiction to the doctrine of the Catholik Church, And if our Protestants secretly meane otherwise, their Intention is plainely expressed in that which followeth, in denying Transubstantiation or chaunge of the
                                                    substance

substance of breade and wyne. Which I affirme with the Catholike Church, and thus proue against this Article. First by holy writ or scripture, allthough that is not necessarie, as is often made manifest against these men. Where soeuer there is a chaunge or mutation of one thing into an other, as in this case of breade into the body of Christ, and this manifestly expressed and conteyned in holy writ and scripture, there is transubstantiation or chaunge of breade by scripture into Christs body, likewise of wyne into his blood.

This is euident by their *owne exposition and transubstantiation, in this place, declaring it to be a chaunge of the substance of breade and wine*. But the holy writ and scripture in three Euangelists, and S. Paule expressely proue, that before Christ blessed and consecrated the breade and wine, it was noe other but breade and wine, and proue likewise euen from the testimonie of Christ himselfe, that after his blessing and omnipotent worde spoken it was now chaunged into his body and blood, playnely saying this is my body, which is giuen, or shall be giuen for you, and this is my blood which is shedd, or shall be shedd for you. Therefore by these Protestants exposition before there was, and of necescessitie must be transubstantiation, or chaunge of the substance of bread and wine. Thus hath holie writ and scripture in all learned languadges Hebrue Greeke and Latin before consecration it was לֶחֶם lechem, ἄρτος artos, *panis*, breade: after consecration גּוּיה ghenijah σῶμα *soma corpus*, Christs body: likewise of the wine chaunged into his blood, this is the testimony of Christ, S. Matthew, S. Marke, S. Luke, and S. Paule in holie

Matth. cap. 26.
Marc. cap. 14.
Luc. cap. 22.
2 Chorinth. 11.

R 4   writte

Io: cap. 6.

writte and scripture, And S. Iohn is witnesse also,
that Chriſt had taught and promiſed this before.
And yet any one place of ſcripture in ſo playne
words maketh a matter of faith, out of doubt, and
vndeniable. Nothing can be more playne, then
ſuch an affirmatiue propoſition, of a Subiect preſent, in the hands of Chriſt the ſpeaker, and in the
ſight and preſence of the greateſt witneſſes his
Apoſtles, at his laſt ſupper, in the greateſt Sacrament. Chriſt neuer interpreted himſelfe otherwiſe
That his Apoſtles ſo vnderſtood him, beleeued,
practized and left to others, is euidently proued
both by Scriptures and the antiquities of this age.

Io: 6.

Firſt S. Iohn in ſcripture ſpeaketh in Chriſts words,
that breade is made his bodie. *Panis quem ego dabo,
caro mea eſt pro mundi vita.* And were plaine and
often in that his 6. Chapter. And both Catholike
and Proteſtant Antiquaries confeſſe, that hee ſaid
Maſſe wherein this chaunge and tranſubſtantiation is vſed, and confirmed, HOC EST CORPVS
MEVM &c. And aſſuers vs that the Altare on
which he ſaid Maſſe many yeares, before the bleſſed Virgyn, was preſerued in a Church on mount
Syon, miraculouſly brought thither. *Ad occi-
dentalem partem Eccleſiæ, quæ eſt in monte Sion eſt lapis
rubens præ altari, qui lapis portatus erat de monte Sinay per manus Angelorum: ſuper quem celebrabat S.
Ioannes Euangeliſta coram Beatiſſima Virgine Maria
Miſſam per multos Annos poſt aſcenſionem Domini.*

Guliel. way.
Etonem:
presbyter l.
Itinerar. cap.
loc. Sanct.
mont. Sinay.
Hakligts
booke of
Trauailes in
eod.
Matth. cap.
26.

Thus teſtifie holie pilgryms eye witneſſes euen
of this Kingdome ſo remote from Hieruſalem. S.
Matthew in his ghoſpell ſaith in the words of
Chriſt: *This is my bodie* : HOC EST CORPVS MEVM.
This is my blood HIC EST SANGVIS MEVS. In his
litur-

liturgie or Masse deliuered to the Church, and
which he vsed, he directly teacheth transubstantiation and chaunge of breade and wine into
Chrifts bodie and blood: *ò Amator hominum bene-*
dic, sanctifica, munda & transfer panem in carnem
tuam immaculatam, & vinum hoc in sanguinem tuum
pretiosum. And thus hee vsed all his life euen to
his martyrdome at the holie Altare, where he thus
confecrated Chrifts bodie by chaunging breade
into it, as the old hiftorie of his life and death bea-
reth wittnes. *Cum mifteria Domini celebrata fuiffent,*
& miffam fufcepiffet omnis Ecclefia, retinuit fe San-
ctus Matthæus iuxta Altare, vbi corpus fuerat Chrifti
confectum, & illic martyrium expectauit.

S. Paule in holie fcripture faith it was breade
before benediction: *Accepit panem gratias agens,* and
after Chrifts confecrating words, it was his bodie
HOC EST CORPVS MEVM. And promifeth there to
deliuer by tradition, what was to be beleeued and
practifed herein *cætera cum venero difponam.* Which
his moft learned fchöller S. Denys the Areopagite
was moft like to knowe who before hath teftified
it was Chrifts bodie and to be adored. S. Marke
hath affured vs in his ghofpell in the words of
Chrift, that it was breade before the words of Confecration, *accepit Iefus panem:* But after them, the
bodie of Chrift: HOC EST CORPVS MEVM. So he
teftifieth of wine chaunged into his blood. In his
Order of Maffe receaued and vfed here in Britayne, as our old brittish writer of the firft Inftitution of Ecclefiafticall Seruice allowed by our Proteftant Antiquaries, proueth, he calleth it after
confecration, *the holy, moft holy vnfpotted body of*
Chrift, Sanctum, Sanctiffimum Intemeratum Corpus
Chrifti,

S. Matth. in
miffa Æthio-
pum.

Anonym.
antiquiff. in
vit. S. Matth.
edit. per Fre-
deric. Naus.
Epifcopum
Viennen.
Breuiar.
Rom. 21.
Sept.
1. Corinth. 11.

Marc. cap. 14.
Manufcrit.
antiq. de
prima Inftit.
Ecclefiaft.
Seruit.
S. Marcus in
Miffa.

Chriſti, ſo chaunged from breade : likewiſe of his precious blood *pretioſus ſanguis Chriſti,* from wine before.

Luc. cap. 22.

S. Luke in his ghoſpell is moſt playne : H O C E S T C O R P V S M E V M *quod pro vobis datur.* And being ſo inſeparable a companion to S. Paule as he witneſſeth in many places of ſcripture, he could not differ from him in this poynt. Neither from the reſt of the Apoſtles, from whom as he writeth in the beginning of his ghoſpell he receaued what he wrote therein. *Sicut tradiderunt nobis, qui ab initio ipſi viderunt, & miniſtri fuerunt ſermonis.*

Luc. cap. 1.

Iſidor. l. 1. de offic. c. 15. de Miſſa & orat. Albin. l. de diuin. offic. Egbert. Ste. phan. Eduen. l. de Sa, Magdeburg. centur. 1. l. 2. cap. 6. col. 500. Matth. Parker. antiquitat. Britan. cap 17. pag. 47. Paſchaſ. Ratb. lib. de Corp. & Sang. Chriſti. walfrid. Strab l. de obſeruat. cap. 22. Martin. Polon. Supputat. temp. in S. Petro col. 27 Miſſa antiq. S. Petri manuſcript. Brit. antiq. ſupr. cit.

That S. Peter ſaid maſſe, and deliuered a forme and order thereof to the Church of Chriſt we haue more witneſſes, then can eaſely be cited, and their citations more needles, ſeing the principall Proteſtants themſelues confeſſe it and that it remayned without alteration 200. yeares, and more vntill Pope Zepherine added ſome what vnto it. *A Chriſti primo inſtituto ducentis amplius annis in prima Eccleſia durauit.* And this as they and others teach was by S. Peter, *inſtituente Beato Petro.* Yet therein we finde moſt playnely deliuered, that the breade and wine were tranſubſtantiated and chaunged into Chriſts body and blood. *Domine Deus noſter, qui te obtuliſti pro huius mundi vita, reſpice in nos, & ſuper panem iſtum, & calicem hunc, & fac eum immaculatum tuum corpus, & pretioſum ſanguinem.* And in the maſſe ſtill vſed *Corpus & ſanguis fiat dilectiſſimi filij tui.* And often therein repeted, that after conſecration it is ſo chaunged. Our old Brittiſh manuſcript of the firſt Inſtitution of Church ſeruice with others proue, that S. Photinus S. Peters diſciple Biſhop of Lyons, and S. Trophimus Biſhop

hop of Arles in Fraunce brought this Order of S. Peters Maſſe thither, and all Fraunce receaued it from them.

Our old English chronicle in our old language plainely ſaith : *Peter the firſt Pope was a bleſſed man, and glorious Apoſtle of Chriſt, he was heade of the Church, he ſaid Maſſe, he made our Lords bodie.* No men can better witneſſe what was the doctrine and practiſe of this cheife Apoſtle, then his renowned diſciple and Succeſſours, S. Ignatius, and S. Clement, the one at Antioche the other at Rome, both which as I haue before proued from them, and ſhall more hereafter, do directly teach Chriſts reall preſence in this Sacrament, and ſo tranſubſtantiation and ſuch chaunge of breade and wine into Chriſts bodie and blood, as this Article denyeth ; for ſo greate mutation Alteration or whatſoeuer we ſhall name it, cannot poſſibly be otherwiſe.

And our old brittiſh manuſcript ſaith plainely that this Maſſe of S. Peter brought into Fraunce by S. Photinus & S. Trophinus was afterward carryed to S. Clement at Rome to be viewed. *Curſum Romanum quem Beatus Trophinus & Sanctus Photinus in Gallys tradiderunt, ad Beatum Clementem quartum loci Succeſſoris Beati Petri Apoſtoli deportauerunt.* S. Andrew the Apoſtle is thought to be the Author of the Maſſe of the Church of Conſtantinople, named now S. Chriſoſtoms, in which there is manifeſt tranſubſtantiation: *Emitte ſpiritum tuum ſuper nos, & ſuper propoſita dona hæc, & fac panem hunc pretioſum Corpus Chriſti tui: & quod eſt in calice iſto pretioſum ſanguinem Chriſti filij tui, tranſmutans ſpiritu tuo ſancto.* Which he practiſed in his life,

Zozimus ep. 10. 1. concil. Martyrol. Roman. die 29. Decemb. in S. Troph. Magdeburg. cent. t. l 1. in Troph. Old. Engl. chron. an. domini 34. part. 4.

Oniſſa S. Andreæ Eccl. Conſtantin. & Chriſoſt.

life, and at his holie martyrdome openly both before Chriſtians and perſecuting pagans he thus profeſſed. *Ego Omnipotenti Deo immolo quotidie immaculatum agnum in altari, eius carnem poſteaquam omnis populus credentium manducauerit, agnus qui ſacrificatus eſt, integer perſeuerat & viuus.*

Thus teſtified the Preiſt and Deacons liuing at his death, the Church of Rome, ours of England, with others in their publik ſeruice of him, S. Cyprian or whoſoeuer authour of the booke *de duplici martyrio* amonge his workes. The old Anonymus writer of the Apoſtles liues, Symeon Metaphraſtes, S. Iuo, S. Bernard, Algerus Iacobus gemenſis, and others without number. S. Iames brother to S. Iohn was ſoone after Chriſts Aſcenſion martyred by King Herode, as we reade in the Acts of the Apoſtles cap. 12. by reaſon whereof, much memory is not left of him in hiſtories, but being of Chriſts three moſt beloued Apoſtles, brother to S. Iohn, and companion to S. Peter, the two others ſo inuincibly proued to haue beene profeſſours and practiſers of this Catholike doctrine no man can Imagyne hee could be of other minde, eſpecially being martyred in Hieruſalem, where he, S. Peter and S. Iohn profeſſing this doctrine, as before, ordeined the other S. Iames Biſhop, who in his Order of Maſſe writeth: *Rogamus vt Spiritus ſanctus adueniens ſancta bona & glorioſa ſua præſentia ſanctificet, & efficiat hunc panem Corpus ſanctum Chriſti tui, & calicem hunc pretioſum ſanguinem Chriſti tui.* Where tranſubſtantiation, and chaunge of breade and wine into Chriſts bodie, and blood in the bleſſed Sacrament by the omnipotent power of God is moſt playnely deliuered. And ſo muſt needs be
the

the doctrine of this S. Iames as of the other, and S.
Peter and S. Iohn. And this anſweareth alſo for
S. Iames named the brother of our Lord, his Maſſe before cited, being warranted both by Fathers
and conncels, greeke and Latine.

   S. Thomas the Apoſtle who preached not
onely to many eaſterne coñtryes of our continent,
but by many Arguments and authorities in the
new world, as men call America, was of the ſame
faith and practiſe. The Annals of the Indians proue
they had a Chriſtian Church within 10. yeares of
Chriſts Aſcenſion, and the Altare was made of a
Stone brought from mount Syon, and thereby
called the Church of our Ladie of Mount Syon.
And in many places there Chriſtian altars are
founde, and as both Catholike and Proteſtant Antiquaries confeſſe, the Preiſts of theſe Indians conuerted by S. Thomas do in holie Maſſe make, *con-*
ficiunt, the bodie and blood of Chriſt and wine,
behauing themſelues with greateſt attention, reuerence, humilitie, and deuotion. I need not proceede to the other Apoſtles, in particular, they
could not beleeue or teach otherwiſe then theſe
I haue recompted: And both Catholiks and Proteſtants ſo acknowledge. *Sicut Magiſter docuit, Apo-*
ſtoli ſe & alios communicando conſecrationem corporis
& ſanguinis Domini facere cœperunt & fieri per vni-
uerſas Eccleſias prædicando inſtiterunt. And Engliſh
Proteſtants with publik warrant moſt plainely ſay
that Chriſt both ſo did, and ſo gaue power and
commaunde to all his Apoſtles, and they ſo performed: *Panis conſecrationem in corpus Chriſti, &*
vinum in ſanguinem, Ipſe Chriſtus, coram Apoſtolis
fecit: eandem ipſi quoque vt facerent, expreſſè mandauit.

   This

Cenſura
Oriental.
Hier. Patriãr.
Conſtinopol.
ibid. Proclus
S. Michol.
Methon.
Beſſar. apud
Gul. Eiſen.
centen. 1. part.
6. diſt. 6.
concil. gene-
ral. 6. can 52.
Franciſc. Al-
uar. de reb.
Indic. Florin.
Rem. de
Orig. Her. l.
8. c. 8. Grym.
booke of
eſtates pag.
1088. 1089.
201. 203.
Sebaſt. Mun-
ſter. l. 6. cap.
57. Rich.
Hacklints
booke of
Trau. in
Mount Syon.
Mandeu. pag.
36. cap. 14.
Guliel. Eiſen-
gren. centen.
1. fol. 168.
& mult ib.
Steph. Eduen.
l: de Sacram.
Altaris.
Engliſh. Prot.
in Marcus
Anton. l. 2.
c. 4. p. 118.

Tradit. &
Antiquit.
Eccl. Medol.
in Italia.

This was the faith, doctrine, and practise which all the Apostolike men of this age warranted by the example and authoritie of the Apostles followed and vsed. S. Barnabas so neare and deare to S. Peter and S. Paule as scripture and histories assuer vs, and he also called to be an Apostle, with S. Paule is accompted Authour of the Masse of Millane after called S. Ambrose his Masse, famous in these westerne parts, where this doctrine is plainely taught.

Clem. Conft.
Apoftolic.
l. 7. cap. 27.
l. 8. cap. 14.

S. Clement, S. Peters Successour at Rome doth often confirme the same, calling it, *the holie bodie pretious bodie and pretious blood of Christ*, *Sanctum Corpus Saluatoris nostri, pretiosum Corpus, & pretiosus sanguis Iesu Christi*: And teacheth in the forme of Masse deliuered by him, the doctrine *of transubstantiation or chaunge of breade and wyne into Christs bodie and blood*: *Mittas sanctum spiritum tuum super hoc*

l. 8. supr. cap.
17.

sacrificium, testem Passionum Domini Iesu, vt ostendat hunc panem corpus Christi tui, & hunc calicem sanguinem Christi tui. Setting downe the verie words of consecration, by which this miraculous chaunge is made, the words of Christ, as the Euangelists deliuered before: HOC EST CORPVS MEVM *quòd pro multis frangitur in remissionem peccatorum*, HIC EST SANGVIS MEVS, *qui pro multis effunditur in remissionem peccatorum*. S. Alexander Pope lyuing in this Apostolike age, and learning his diuinity then writeth, euen as Protestants confesse, that Christ did giue instruction to offer this Sacrifice, which being at the first but breade and wine, is by consecration made Christs bodie, and blood, being so consecrated, it is the greatest sacrifice, syns are thereby forgiuen, it is to be worshipped of all: and

Alexander
Pap. 1. epist.
1. c. 4. Robert. Banes l.

as

as it is more excellent then all other, so it is more
to be worshipped and reuerenced. *Ipsa veritas nos
instruxit, calicem & panem in Sacramento offerre,
quando ait: accepit Iesus panem &c. crimina atque
peccata oblatis his domino sacrificijs delentur. Talibus
hostijs delectabitur & placabitur Dominus, & peccata
dimittet ingentia, Nihil enim in Sacrificijs maius esse
potest, quàm Corpus & Sanguis Christi: nec vlla oblatio hac potior est, sed hæc omnes præcellit. Quæ pura
conscientia Domino offerenda est, atque ab omnibus veneranda, & sicut potior est cæteris, ita potius excoli &
venerari debet.*

de vit. Pontif. in Alexandro.

S. Ignatius S. Peters Succeſſour at Antioch, the
next and immediate by some, and by all but one S.
Euodius betwene them saith, it is the breade of
God, heauenly breade, the flesh of Christ the sonne of God: *Panem Dei volo, panem cælestem quæ est
caro Christi Filij Dei.* It is the flesh of our Sauiour
Iesus Christ, which suffered for our syns, and was
raised agayne: *Carnem Saluatoris Iesu Christi, quæ
pro peccatis nostris passa est, quam Pater sua benignitate
suscitauit.*

Ignat. epist. ad Roman.

Ignat. epist. ad Smyrnen: cit. Theodor. dialog. 3.

S. Martial, who as he himselfe wittnesseth, had
conuersed with Christ, and was instructed by him,
and by S. Peter sent to preach in Fraunce, saith
plainely that the same bodie of Christ which the
Iewes for enuie did sacrifice, thinking to blott his
name from earth, *the Christians then did offer it on
the holie altar, for saluation knowing that by this reme-
die life is to be giuen, and death auoyded, and Christ
himselfe thus commaunded it to be done in commemoration of him. Vbique offertur Deo oblatio munda, sicut
testatus est cuius corpus & sanguinem in vitam æternam offerimus. Ipse enim corpus habens, & immacu-*
                                                    latum,

Martial epist. ad Tolosan. cap. 3.

Martial. epist. ad Burdegal. cap. 3.

latum, & sine peccato, in ara Crucis ipsum permisit im-
molari. Quod autem Iudæi per inuidiam immolauerunt,
putantes se nomen eius à terra abolere ; nos causa salu-
tis nostræ in ara sanctificata proponimus, scientes hoc
solo remedio nobis vitam præstandam , & mortem effu-
gaudam hoc enim ipse Dominus noster iussit nos agere
in sui commemorationem.

S. Iustinus liued and learned his Religion in this
age, though dying in the next he affirmeth plainely, that as by the word of God Christ our Sauiour became flesh, and had both flesh and blood
for our saluation, *euen so we are taught , that the*
foode on which by prayers of the word which came from
him, thankes be giuen, is the flesh and blood of Iesus in-
carnate. Quemadmodum per verbum Dei Caro factus
est Christus Seruator noster, & canem & sanguinem
salutis nostræ causa habuit : Ad eundem modum etiam
eam, in qua per preces verbi eius ab ipso profecti gratiæ
actæ sunt, alimoniam, incarnati illius Iesu carnem &
sanguinem esse edocti sumus. And besides tradition,
and the cōmon custome & doctrine of the Church,
he doth interprete the Euangelists before cited in
this manner , that Christ so instituted and commaunded, and this in his very next words: *Nam*
Apostoli in commentarijs à se scriptis, quæ Euangelia
vocantur, ita tradiderunt præcepisse sibi Iesum , cum
enim panc accepto gratias egisset, hoc facite in mei
recordationem HOC EST CORPVS MEVM. *& poculo*
similiter accepto, & gratijs actis dixisse: HIC EST
SANGVIS MEVS. And most plainely : *Panem Chri-*
stus conficiendum tradidit , vt Corpus cum factum esse
recordaremur. And, *Dominica caro conscientiam eo-*
rum qui ipsam edunt, ab omni scelere expiat. S. Irenæus also, by our old brittish manuscript, being
made

Iustin apol.
ad Antonium
Pinm.

Iustin. dial.
cum Triph.
post med. &
in quest.
agent propos.
quest. 44.

made Bishop by S. Clement in this first age, *Beatum Irenæum Episcopum Beatus Clemens ordinauit,*
proueth, that none but such Infidels or heretiks as
denyed Christ to be the sonne of God, and so not
omnipotent, did or could deny this transubstantiation or chaunge of breade and wine into his bodie
and blood by his powerfull words in consecration:
*Quomodo constabit eis, eum panem, in quo gratiæ actæ
sint, Corpus esse Domini sui, & calicem sanguinis eius:
si non ipsum fabricatoris mundi filium dicent, id est
verbum eius, per quod lignum fructificat, & defluunt
fontes & terra dat primum quidem fœnum, post deinde
spicam, deinde plenum triticum in spica.*

I haue cited S. Denys the Areopagite to this
purpose before. And shewed also for Britayne
that it had and vsed the Masse of S. Marke as their
old manifcript proueth, where this doctrine and
practise is recorded. And S. Peter preaching here
his Masse brought into these parts both by his,
and S. Paules Disciples, as I haue proued with this
vse and doctrine, Britaine could not be ignorant
thereof. And I haue cited euen from Protestant
Antiquaries, that our first Christian Britans both
worshipped, and prayed vnto Christ present in this
most holie sacrament, when it was shewed vnto
them or they receaued it, at Masse. And our Protestants of England of cheife note among them
with greatest applause and approbation do deduce
this Catholike doctrine and practise in the Church
of Christ from this first age, and in this manner:
*Wee reade in Ignatius this phrase offere and Sacrificium
immolare, to offer and immolate Sacrifice, and like phra-
ses in Irenæus Tertullian and Martialis, who mentioneth also Altares. The auntients when they speake of*

S   *the*

Irenæus con-
tra hær. lib.
4. cap. 34.

This holy
faith euer in
Britaine.

Protest. of
Engl. apud
Sutcliffe
Subuerf. pag.
32.
Perkins probl.
pag. 153. 154.

the *supper*, *haue many formes of speach*, *which shew a conuersion*. *Ambrose vseth the name of conuersion*, *and the name of mutation*. *Cyprian saith it is chaunged not in shape but in nature*, *Origen saith*, *that breade is made the bodie by prayer*. *Gaudentius saith*, *Chrifts bodie is made of bread*, *and his blood of wyne*. *Eusebius Emisfenus saith*, *that the Preist by secrete power doth chaunge the visible creatures into the substance of Chrifts bodie*, *and blood*, *and that the breadedoth passe into the nature of our Lords bodie*. So they deduce it to lower times, wherein they all confesse, the doctrine of transubstantiation to haue beene generally taught and professed.

And with speciall warrant and allowance of King Iames as they themselues testifie, they publikly iustifie, that it was *Religio Regis the Religion of the King and Kingdome*, *that it is Chrifts bodie*, *the same obiect and thing*, *which the Romane Church beleeueth*, *others with publick allowance also write: though breade by nature bee but a prophane and common clement*, *yet by grace it pleaseth the Lord to make it his bodie*. *The omnipotencie of Chrift maketh it his bodie*. *The primatiue Church thought the fructified and consecrated Elements to be the bodie of Chrift*. *To their persons* (*Preists*, *God imparted power ouer his misticall bodie*, *which is societie of soules*, *and ouer that naturall*, *which is himselfe for the knitting of both in one*, *a worke which antiquitie doth call the making of Chrifts body*. *The power of the ministry by blessing visible Elements it maketh the inuisible grace. It giueth daily the holie ghoft*. *It hath to dispose of that flesh which was giuen for the life of the worlde: and that blood which was powred out to redeeme soules*. In their most warranted publick communion booke in the miniftration of this sacrament

Casaubon.
respon. ad
Cardinal.
peron. pag.
50. 51. D. Androwes Prot.
Bish. of Ely.
Midleton
Papiston. p.
106. Copell.
def. of
hooker pag.
276. Feild.
of the
Church pag.
150. Couell.
def. pag. 87.
Couell modeft examinat. pag. 105.

crament after their manner, they deliuer Chrifts inftitution thereof, in fuch fignificant manner of tranfubftantiation, or chaunge, that they muft needs thereby graunte, and affirme it, or deny him to haue fpoken truely, but to haue told an vntruth, a thing moft blafphemous, and vnpoffible, thus they fette it downe as Catholiks do at Maffe: *Ie-fus Chrift who in the night he was betrayed, tooke breade, and when he had giuen thankes he breake it, and gaue it to his difciples, faying, take, eate, this is my bodie which is giuen for you, do this in remembrance of mee. Likewife after fupper he tooke the cuppe, and when he had giuen thankes, he gaue it to them, faying, drinke yee all of this, this is my bloode of the new tefta-ment, which is shedde for you, & for many, for remifsiõ of fyns: do this as oft as yee shall drinke it, in remembrance of mee.* Here Chrift omnipotent that cannot fpeake any vntruth, expreffely teftifieth, it was breade and wyne before, and by his words, his bodie which was giuen, and blood shedd for vs. Therefore fuch tranfubftantiation and chaunge as Catholiks hold. And this thefe Proteftans confirme in their diftribution of this Sacrament to communicants, affuring euery communicant as Catholike Preifts do, and in the very fame words, that it is the bodie of Chrift, which they giue to them, and fo of his blood, in expreffe termes, which should be moft true, if they were true Preifts, as the others be.

And that no teftimonie might be wanting to this Catholike truth, by Proteftants allowance, they haue both publithed & approued with greate warrant, the fentence and opinion of the old Rabbines before Chrift of this miftery, and thus con-

Proteft. commun: booke Tit. communion.

Francifc. Stancar. iu pref... ad etr. Galla. in.

feffe

Prot.Baſilien.
in editione
eiuſd. Thom.
Marton ap-
peale pag.
396. 395.

feſſe of them : *They are more playne and pregnant for
tranſubſtantiation, then are the ſayeings of the tran-
ſubſtantiators themſelues. They make ſo directly for
tranſubſtantiation, that the moſt Romish Doctours for
the ſpace of allmoſt a thowſand yeares after Chriſt, did
not in ſo expreſſe termes publish this miſterie to the
worlde.*

THE XXI. CHAPTER.

*The 29. Article, intituled : of the wicked, which
do not eate the bodie, and blood of Chriſt
in the vſe of the Lords ſupper : examined, and condemned.*

THEIR next 29. Article affirming that the
wicked do not eate the bodie of Chriſt in the
vſe of the Lords ſupper, is confuted iñ the former,
tranſubſtantiation and chaunge of breade and
wine into the bodie and blood of Chriſt by his
omnipotent power and words being therein inuincibly proued both by his owne diuine teſtimonie,
and practiſe, in, and by his Apoſtles, Apoſtolike
men, of that Age, and the allowance of Proteſtants,
the auncient Rabbines and all witneſſes both
Catholiks and Proteſtants, no thing els beſides
the outward formes and ſpecies of breade and wine
there remaining, it is demonſtrated, that whoſoeuer, good or bad receaueth that Sacrament, muſt
needs receaue Chriſts bodie there. And if S. Auguſtine here cited, held the contrarie againſt ſo
great diuine and humane authoritie, he could not
be S. Auguſtine or to be followed, but forſaken, nor
any Article ſo grounded, be true, But to redeeme
S. Au-

S. Auguftines honour I muft leaue the firft age,
and in this come to him . This Article is intituled:
*Of the wicked which do not eate the bodie of Chrift in
the vſe of the Lords Supper.* And thus followeth.

*The wicked and ſuch as be voide of all liuely faith.
allthough they do carnally and viſibly Preſſe with their
teeth (as Sainct Auguftine ſaith , the Sacrament of
the bodie and blood of Chrift, yct in no wiſe are they
partakers of Chrift, but rather to their condemnation, do
eate and drinke the ſigne or Srcrament of ſo greate a
thing .* This is wholly and vnqueftionably condemned before; And if they cite S. Auguftine, as
though he meant the wicked are not partakers of
the grace of Chrift in this Sacrament, that Catholiks confeſſe and it proueth no thing againft them,
& Proteftants makeing the Euchariſt but a ſigne,
and that to godly onely and true beleeuers with a
liuely faith as they ſpeake here can neither ſay that
the wicked and vnbeleeuers do eate or drinke the
ſigne or Sacrament , ſeing by them it is no ſuch
ſigne or Sacrament to ſuch people.

But if they contend from S. Auguftine, that he
meaneth the wicked communicants do not receaue Chrifts bodie : it is manifeftly falſe and contrarie to Sainct Auguftines doctrine, in many places. For no man could be more vnworthie and
wicked, then Iudas , which betrayed Chrift, yet
he witneſſeth with the holie ſcriptures , and Antiquitie, that Indas really & truely receaued Chrifts
bodie and blood, as the other Apoftles did . *Tolerat* Auguftin. ep.
ipſe Dominus Iudam diabolum, furem & venditorem ¹⁶² ep ſt.
ſuum: Sinit accipere inter Innocentes diſcipulos, quod ¹⁶³ Auguft.
fideles nvrunt pretium noſtrum . So he ſpeaketh fur- Euang ioh.
ther both of him, and all wicked communicants in Piaim. ₁o.

that they receaue the same bodie of Christ : *communiter omnibus dedit* . And he maketh his opinion & faith free from all such Protestant construction, saying plainely, that Christ gaue to this Disciples, that bodie, which hanged vpon the Crosse, and that blood, which issued out of his side : *Hoc accipite in pane, quòd pependit in Cruce : Hoc accipite in Calice quod manauit de latere Christi .* And he saith Christ carryed himselfe and his bodie in his owne hands, when he gaue it to this Apostles : *Ferebatur Christus in manibus suis, quando commendans ipsum corpus suum, ait,* HOC EST CORPVS MEVM. *Ferebat enim illud in manibus suis .* And so gaue the same his bodie both to Iudas, whom he calleth a deuill, theise and traytour before, and the rest of his holie Apostles . And so he expoundeth the place of S. Paule, to the Corinthians of worthie and vnworthie communicants, as the other Fathers do, that both of them receaued one and the same holie consecrated bodie. *Et sancta possunt obesse : in bonis enim sancta ad salutem insunt, in malis ad Iudicium, certè enim fratres nouimus quid accipiamus, & vtique sanctum quòd est accipimus, & nemo dicit non est sanctum. Et quid dicit Apostolus ? qui autem manducat & bibit indignè iudicium sibi manducat & bibit . Non ait quia illa res mala est : sed quia ille malus malè accipiendo, ad iudicium accipit, bonum quòd accipit.*

He assureth vs plainely, that communicants receaue the bodie of Christ vnder the forme of breade, and his blood vnder the forme of wine. *Caro Christi est quam forma panis opertam in Sacramento accipimus : & Sanguis eius, quem sub vini specie & sapore potamus. Nos in specie panis & vini quam videmus, carnem, & sanguinem honoramus : Nec similiter*

Augustin.
ad
bytos
Paschaf.
. ad Fra-
d. Iuo
at. 264.

Augustin. in
Psal. 33. conc.
I.

August. tract.
6. in Euang.
Ioh. & tract.
16.

I.Cor. II. 27

August. apud
Prosper. l.
Sentent. cit.
Gratian. dist.
2. de confe-
crat.

militer comprehendimus has duas species, quemadmo-
dum ante consecrationem comprehendebamus, cum fi-
deliter fateamur ante consecrationem panem esse, &
vinum, quod natura formauit: post consecrationem
verò carnem Christi & sanguinem, quod benedictio
consecrauit. The bread ceased to be by consecration: *Panis in accipiendo Sacramento consumitur.*
He affirmeth it was so constantly and commonly
beleeued of all, that Christ was truely and really
present vnder the formes of bread and wine, that
if they had not beene otherwise instructed, and
neuer seene those but in the holie misteries, they
would haue beleeued Christ had not otherwise
appeared in any other shape or forme to the world.
si nunquã discant experimento, vel suo vel aliorum, &
nunquam illam speciem rerum, videant, nisi inter cele-
brationes Sacramentorum, cum offertur & datur, dica-
turque illis authoritate grauißima, cuius corpus &
sanguis sit, nihil aliud credent, nisi omninò in illa spe-
cie dominum oculis hominum mortalium & de latere
tali percusso, liquorem illum omninò fluxisse. He deliuereth, that the omnipotencie of God, is the
meanes to cause this miraculous transubstantiation: *operante inuisibiliter spiritu Dei.*

And againe: *Ante verba Christi, quod offertur*
panis dicitur: vbi Christi verba deprompta fuerint,
iam non prius dicitur, sed Corpus appellatur. So soone
as the Preist hath there pronounced the words of
Christ it is called Christs bodie. *And* he saith plainely, that both Christs Apostles at his last supper did
receaue Christs bodie and blood, and Christians, in all
the world did receaue Christs bodie into their mouthes,
these fasting, the Apostles not fasting. *Liquidò apparet,*
quando primùm acceperunt discipuli Corpus & San-
guinem

S 4

Augustin. l. 3.
Trinitat. c. 10.

l. 3. Trinitat.
cap. 4.

Aug. Ser. 5.
in Appendic.
Tom. 10.

Aug ep. 118.
ad Ianuar. c
6. l 2. re & ct.
c 20. cp. 66.

guinem Domini, non eos accepiße ieiunos. Nunquid tamen propterea calumniandum est vniuerſæ Eccleſiæ, quòd à Ieiunijs ſemper accipitur? & hoc placuit ſpiritui ſanĉto, vt in honorem tanti Sacramenti, in os Chriſtiani prius dominicum corpus intraret, quàm cæteri cibi. Nam ideò per vniuerſum orbem mos iste ſeruatur. And in an other place, that the Christians receaue Chrsts bodie and his blood. *De Agni immaculati corpore partim ſumere, & in poculo ſangui-*

I. 2. contra
Aduerſ. Leg.
& Prophetar.
cap. 9.

nem. He ſaith that all communicants receaue by their mouth, the flesh of Chriſt: *Carnem ſuam ore ſumamus.* Chriſt gaue in this Sacrament, and communicants there receaue that flesh of Chriſt,

In Pſal. 98.

which he tooke of the flesh of his mother, that wherein he walked on earth, and no man eateth that flesh, but he adoreth it before. Chriſtus de carne Mariæ carnem accepit, & quia in ipſa carne hic ambulauit, & ipſam carnem nobis manducandam ad ſalutem dedit: nemo autem illam carnem manducat, niſi prius adorauerit. He ſaith the bread is made Chriſts bodie by con-

I. 20. contra.
fauſtum.

ſecration: *Noster panis & calix, non quilibet, ſed certa conſecratione myſticus, ſit nobis Corpus Chriſti.* He relateth, how his Mother S. Monica deſired

I. 9. confeſſ.
cap. 13.

to be remembred after her death at Maſſe, at the holie Altare, from which that ſacrifice is diſpenſed, which redeemed the world. *Memoriam ſui ad altare fieri deſiderauit, vnde ſciret, diſpenſari victimam, qua deletum est chirographum, quod erat contrarium*

I. 4. Trinitat.
cap. 4.

nobis. He ſaith, it is Made the bodie of Chriſt our high Preiſt. *Corpus effectum Sacerdotis nostri.* The bodie of Chriſt doth enter into the mouthes of Chriſtians: *Ex ore Chriſtianorum, vbi Corpus Chriſti ingreditur.* And in this very place obiected, in this Proteſtant Article.

S. Au-

S. Auguftine faith plainely, that both the good and wicked do receaue Chrifts bodie, and blood, in this Sacrament: *Carnem Chrifti & Sanguinem Chrifti non edamus tantum in Sacramento, quod & multi mali: fed vfque ad fpiritus participationem manducemus & bibamus, vt in Domini Corpore tanquam membra maneamus.* And againe: *de menfa Dominica fumitur, quibufdam ad vitam, quibufdam ad exitium:* And this which both the good and wicked there receaue, is the fame bodie of Chrift, *norunt fideles Corpus Chrifti:* where he fo expoundeth S. Paule as others do: *quam multi de altari accipiunt & moriuntur, & accipiendo moriuntur: vnde dicit Apoftolus, Iudicium fibi manducat & bibit.* And this which bringeth this Iudgment and condemnation to them, is Chrifts bodie which they vnworthely receaue, *carnem fuam dat nobis Chriftus manducare:* and diftinguished a double receauing, the one *foris* externall, which the wicked do as the godly, the other *intus* internall alfo giueing grace to the worthie receauers, which is not fo with the wicked, not participating grace but Iudgment and damnation fo dishonouing Chrift and his holie Inftitution. Yet all, both the good and bade receaue the bodie of Chrift vnder the forme of bread, and his blood vnder the forme of wine. *Caro eius eft, quam forma panis opertam in Sacramento accipimus. Et Sanguis eius quem fub vini fpecie & fapore potamus.*

And in the fame, place thus prophanely cited by this Article, he folueth the obiections vfually made againft this holie Sacrament, firft how Chrift could giue vs his flesh to eate: *Quomodo poteft hic carnem fuam dare nobis ad manducandum.*

That

Aug. Tract. 26 & 67. in Iohan.

I. Sentent. profperi Gratian. Dift 2. de confecrat.

Aug. ſupr.
tract. 26.

That by Chriſts aſcéſion into heauen with his immortall bodie, we ſhould ſee it could not be conſumed, though receaued in theſe myſteries, *non eo modo quo putatis, erogat corpus ſuum. Certe vel tunc intelligetis, quia gratia eius non conſumitur morſibus.* And that, *caro non prodeſt quicquam*, fleſh profiteth nothing, he anſweareth it was onely true in ſuch wicked ſenſe as the prophane capharnites conceaued, as of dead peeces of fleſh, and not of the fleſh of Chriſt as hee gaue it, gyuing life. *O Domine Magiſter bone, quomodo caro non prodeſt quicquam cum tu dixeris, niſi quis manducauerit carnem meam, & biberit ſanguinem meum non habebit in ſe vitam? an vita non prodeſt quicquam? quid eſt ergo, non prodeſt quicquam, ſed quomodo illi intellexerunt: carnem quippe ſic intellexerunt, quomodo in cadauere dilaniatur, aut in macello venditur, non quomodo ſpiritu vegetatur. Spiritus ergo eſt qui viuificat, caro non prodeſt quicquam. Sicut illi intellexerunt carnem, non ſic ego do ad manducandum carnem meam.*

And concerning their cauill that one bodie (naturally they ſhould ſay) cannot be at one time in diuers places, he proueth directly againſt Iewes and others, that this one bodie of Chriſt is that ſacrifice ſpoken of by the Prophet Malachie to be offered in all places, in all the world. *Ipſe de corpore & ſanguine ſuo inſtituit ſacrificium ſecundum ordinem Melchiſedech. Vident tale ſacrificium nunc offerri toto orbe terrarum. Sacrificium quod non à Chriſtianis offertur toto orbe terrarum. Hoc ſacrificium per Sacerdotium Chriſti ſecundum ordinem Melchiſedech in omni loco à ſolis ortu vſque ad occaſum iam videamus offerri. Quid ad hæc reſpondetis? aperite oculos tandem aliquando & videte, ab oriente ſole,*
vſque

Aug. in Pſal.
33. l. 1 cont.
aduerſ legis
& Prophetar.
c. 20. l 16. de
ciuitat. Dei c.
22. l. 18. ciuit. cap. 35.
orat. contra
Iudæos c. 9.

vfque ad occidentem, non in vno, fed in omni loco fa-
crificium Chriftianorum offerri, ei, qui ifta prædixit Deo
Ifrael.

No man can better witneffe, what was S. Auguftines doctrine, or interprete him in this queftion, then Primafius Bishop of vtica his renowned
and learned fcholler, which fetteth downe this
queftion, and the prefent Catholike Religion
therein, as plainely as any prefent Catholike writer doth. *Iftud Sacrificium noftrum cum caufa infirmi-*

tatis fuæ repetitur, quod non pofsit perfectam falutem
conferre: fed in commemorationem Pafsionis Chrifti,
ficut ipfe dixit, hoc facite, inquiens, in meam comme-
morationem, & vna eft hæc hoftia, non multæ, cum à
multis, diuerfiis in locis, diuerfifque temporibus offera-
tur? Aptifsimè ergo aduertendum eft, quia diuinitas
verbi Dei quæ eft vna, & omnia replet, & tota vbique
eft, ipfa facit vt non fint plura facrificia, fed vnum,
licet à multis offeratur: & fit vnum Corpus Chrifti
cum illo quod fufcepit in vtero virginali, non multa
corpora: nec nunc quidem eft aliud magnum, aliud mi-
nus, aliud hodie, aliud cras offerimus, fed femper id-
ipfum æquam magnitudinem habens: proinde vnum
eft hoc facrificium Chrifti, non diuerfa. Nam fi aliter
effet, quoniam multis in locis offertur, multi effent Chri-
fti, quòd obfit. V nus ergo vbique eft, & hic plenus exi-
ftens, & illic: Plenum vnum corpus vbique habens. Et
ficut qui vbique offertur vnum corpus eft, non multa
corpora, ita etiam & vnum facrificium. I haue beene
enforced by this Article forging S. Auguftines authoritie for the grounde thereof, to difcend thus
lowe, to defend him, and shew the feeble and falfe
foundation of our Proteftants in this poynt.

T H E

The XXII. Chapter.

The 30. Article, intituled, of both kindes: examined and where it is contrary to the Romane Church condemned.

THE 30. and next Article being intituled: *of both Kindes: consisteth of these words. The cuppe of the Lord is not to be denyed to the lay people. For both the partes of the Lords Sacrament, by Chrits ordinaunce and commaundement, ought to be ministred to all Christian men alike.* This is all this Article, and it is confuted before, where I haue proued, that both in, and immediately after the Apostles time, and by their order and direction, this blessed Sacrament was both honorably preserued onely vnder the forme of bread, and so often ministred vnto the primatiue Christians, which in no case, or respect might be done, if Christ had ordeyned, and commaunded otherwise, and the contrary as this Protestant Article pretendeth. And so the Apostles themselues, and the Apostolike Church then, the true Church of Christ without all question, both by Catholiks and Protestants, had erred in a thing of necessitie requisite according to Christes ordinance, in so greate a Sacrament, and so by these men and their diuinitie in this Article, the true Church of Christ was not the true Church, and he neuer had a true Church : for in their Article of the Church before they define it to be, *a congregation of faithfull men, in which the pure word of God is preached, and the Sacraments be duely ministred in all those things that of necessitie are*

requi-

Prot. Articl. 19. sup. of sup. of the Church.

requisite to the same : Therefore this Proteſtant Article affirming that *both the partes of the Lords Sacrament by Chriſts ordinaunce and commaundement, ought to be miniſtred to all Chriſtian men alike* , is falſe in itſelfe and contradictorie to their owne moſt allowed proceedings : for not onely diuers of their priuate writers , but the parlament lawe of all our Proteſtant Princes King Edward 6. Queene Elizabeth , King Iames and King Charles their Rule and warrant for this Article, doth confeſſe enact and decree, that in the true primatiue Church this Sacrament was not allwayes miniſtred in both Kindes, but ſometimes in both, ſome times in one onely . Therefore by theſe men the true primatiue Church neuer did nor could adiudge or hold that the miniſtration of this Sacrament allwaies in both Kindes was Chriſts Ordinance, and commaundement , otherwiſe by miniſtring it often in one onely Kinde, as this cheife Proteſtant parlament, and their religion therein, confeſſe it had acknowledged itſelfe to haue erred from Chriſts ordinance, and commaundement in a Sacrament and neceſſitie requiſite , and ſo by theſe Articles not to haue beene Chriſts true Church , and he had by theſe men no true Church at all.

Againe Theſe Proteſtants ſtanding in this Article vpon the Ordinance and commaundement of Chriſt, confeſſe that he inſtituted and ordeyned this Sacrament at his laſte ſupper, and what he commaunded concerning it , he then commaunded it, and they alſo confeſſe the three Euangeliſts S. Matthew , S. Marke and S. Luke to be the Euangelicall Regiſters of that his holie ordination, But all thus do plainely teſtifie, that none but his

twelue

Statute of King Edw. 6. Titul. Sacram. in both Kindes. Stat. in parliam. 1. Elizabeth Iames 1. Charles 1.

Matth. 26.
Marc. 14.
Luc. 22.

twelue Apoſtles were then preſent. *Diſcumbebat cum duodecim diſcipulis eius . Venit cum duodecim. Vnus ex duodecim diſcubuit, & duodecim Apoſtoli cum eo. Et ait illis, deſiderio deſideraui hoc Paſcha manducare vobiſcum.* And our Proteſtants before in their moſt allowed publick communion booke, haue ſo deliuered, ſaying of the Sacrament vnder the forme of bread, *Ieſus gaue it to his Diſciples, ſaying take eate, this is my bodie, which is giuen for you.* And of the other parte, *he gaue it to them ſaying drinke you all of this; for this is my blood of the new teſtament, which is ſhedd for you.*

1. Corinth. 11.

And all theſe witneſſes the Euangeliſts, S. Paule, Catholiks, & Proteſtants do freely acknowledge, that Chriſt then pronounced, and ſpake theſe words, *hoc facite in meam commemorationem,* do this in commemoration of me, vnto them all. Giuing them thereby power and commaunde, to do, what he had done in that miſterie, which was, as is proued before, to tranſubſtantiate and chaunge breade, and wine, into the bleſſed bodie, and blood, giuen and ſhedd for the ſinnes of the world, and this euen our Proteſtants haue before acknowledged, confeſſing that ſupernaturall power to haue beene in Chriſtes Apoſtles then preſent, & Preiſts after them, for there is no other place in ſcripture, the Rule of theſe men, wherein ſuch power was communicated vnto them, or Chriſt a Preiſt after the Order of Melchiſedech exerciſed the office or Act of that preiſhood. So that none but they which were then conſecrated Preiſts, which euer offer this Sacrifice in both Kindes, were preſent to receaue this charge of them both.

And this is directly told vs, not onely by all
Catho-

Catholike writers, but Proteſtants with the greateſt allowance their Religion can giue, the authoritie of the ſupreame of their Church, by the greateſt champion externall which euer it had, the
Archbiſhop of Spalato which with King Iames
and his cheifeſt Proteſtants warrant thus writeth:
*Ad hoc Sacerdotium promoti ſunt Apoſtoli à Chriſto
Domino in vltima cæna, quando eis dixit: hoc facite
in meam commemorationem.*

Marc. Anton.
l. 2. de repub.
Chriſtian. c.
2. pag. 167.

The Apoſtles were promoted to preiſthood by
Chriſt our Lord in his laſt ſupper, when, he ſaid
to them: do this in my commemoration. And
agayne: *Quod conſecrantes panem, orationes fundamus,
eoque fideles paſcamus, Chriſti Iuſſum facimus, qui id
iniunxit, dicens hoc facite in meam commemorationem,
hoc ipſum quod me nunc vidiſtis facere & vos facite,
circa panis & vini benedictionem.* Where the Apoſtles and Preiſts receaued and receaue power and
commaunde to conſecrate bread and wine into the
bodie and blood of Chriſt, as he then did. And
we muſt needs ſo ſay, otherwiſe we haue no warrant in ſcripture, to which onely Proteſtants appeale in ſuch matters as Sacraments be, either to
proue that Preiſts haue any power at all to conſecrate, or miniſter this Sacrament, or that it is a
Sacrament, for beſides S. Paule to the Corinthians,
and in the 6. Chapter of S. Iohns Ghoſpell, there
is no place in the new teſtament that is by any interpreted to ſpeake of the communion vnder both
kyndes. S. Paule plainely referreth himſelfe to
Chriſts Inſtitution ſette downe in the Euangeliſts
cited.

c. 4. p. 219.

And for S. Iohn our Proteſtants deny, that he
ſpeaketh of the Sacramentall and actuall recea-

uing

uing of this misterie. And yet he onely hath words that haue likelynesse of precept to communicate in both Kindes : *Nisi manducaueritis carnem filij hominis & biberitis eius sanguinem non habebitis vitam in vobis*. Except you eate the flesh of the sonne of man, and drinke his blood you shall not haue life in you. And yet this is not so of Sacramentall eating and drinking the bodie and blood of Christ, for the holie scriptures and all expositours of them, Catholiks and Protestants agree, that new baptized infants, and others, martyrs all holie, and iust men shall haue, and haue life in them, though they neuer actually and Sacramentally receaue Chrifts flesh, and blood, and neither Catholiks nor Protestants do communicate young people, though in daunger of death, or dying. S. Paule hath no semblance of a commaundement or necessitie of both Kindes, to be receaued by all. Therefore the precept, commaund and necessitie onely concerning Preifts, at holie Masse, then and there to consecrate and offer as Christ did, and commaunded in both Kindes, *hoc facite*, Catholike Preifts at their sacrifice in all places most dutifully performe it ; at other times, as sicknes, they communicate onely in one Kinde as the lay people doe.

All that is to be founde in scripture of both Kindes, to be receaued or haue beene receaued of all, is in S. Paule to the Christians of Corinthe, arguing that in that Church, and likely some others, both formes were receaued af all: *Quicunque manducauerit panem hunc, & biberit calicem Domini indignè, reus erit Corporis & Sanguinis Domini, probet autem seipsum homo & sic de pane illo edat, & de calice bibat.*

Qui

Qui enim manducat & bibit indignè iudicium sibi manducat & bibit, non dijudicans corpus Domini. Yet here is no præcept. And his words, *non dijudicans corpus Domini*, onely speaking against the abuse towards the bodie of Christ, not mentioning his blood which to dishonour was as greate a sinne, may make questionable, whether he there speaketh of the Sacramentall receauing of both by all persons or no. But if he so did, we finde in diuers other places of scripture, as they be expounded to vs, by the holie Fathers, that communion was then vsed, diuers times and in diuers places in one Kinde onely.

S. Chrisoftome, S. Augustine Isychius S. Bede Theophilact and others so expound that act of Christ taking bread, blessing, breaking & giuing it to his two disciples, at Emaus, registred by S. Luke. *Accepit panem & benedixit ac fregit & porrigebat illis.*

And the scripture, our Protestants Rule, mentioneth not the other Kinde at all. So do the same S. Chrisoftome S. Bede, Ionas Aureliensis with others expound that in the 2. Chapter of the Acts of the Apostles, *erant autem perseuerantes in doctrina Apostolorum, & communicatione fractionis panis & orationibus.* Where no memorie is of the other Kinde. So likewise that in the 20. Chapter of the Acts: *cum conuenissemus ad frangendum panem:* and whereas in the 2. Chapter of the Acts the Latin translation readeth, *in communione & fractione panis,* the Syriak text is, *in fractione Eucharistiæ, in breaking the Eacharist.*

And this was vsed both by the Apostles, and Apostolike Preifts in this firft age to minifter this

Chrif. homil. 16. oper. imperfecti in Mat. Auguft. l. 3. de confenfu Euang. c. 25. Ifych. Hierofol. l. 2. in leuit. c. 9. Bed ad c. 24. Luc. Theophilact. ibid. Luc. 24. Chrif. homil. 17. oper.imp. in Mat. Bed. ad c. 20. Act. Apoft. Ionas Aurelian. lib. 3. de Imag. Act. 2. Act. 20. Text. Syriac. Act. 2.

T

bleffed

Clem. epist.
de reb. gest.
B. Petri.

blessed Sacrament to the Christians onely vnder
the forme of breade. So S. Clement writeth of S.
Peter, he himselfe being one among many others
which so communicated from S. Peters hands:
Petrus panem acceptum actis gratijs consecrauit, fre-
git primoque matri porrexit deinde nobis filijs. The
approued Apostolike Relation of S. Andrew his

Presbyteri &
Diac. Achaiæ
in vit. S. An-
dreæ Breuiar.
Rom. die 30.
Nouemb.
Breuiar. Su-
risbur. & al.
eodem die
Metaphrast.
in S. Andr.
Anonym.
Antiq. in eius
vita Cipr. l.
de 2. Martyr.
Lippom. to
1. Sur. Tom.
6. S. Bernard
Ser. de S. An-
drea Rouig.
Antisiod. in
Psal. 21. & 4.
lausr. cont.
Bereng. Iuo
Sebast. Mun-
ster Cos-
mogr. l. 6. c.
57.
Ignat. epist.
ad Ephes.

martyrdome, written by present wittnesses in this
age, doth wittnesse, that the Christians vnder him
receaued the bodie of Christ vnder the forme of
bread, making no mention of the other Kinde.
Cuius agniimmaculati, carnem posteaque omnis popu-
lus credentium manducauerit, agnus qui sacrificatus est
integer perseucrat & vnius. Here all, *omnis populus,*
so communicated. It was thus preached, and practized by the Apostle or Apostles which preached
to the Abissines, as both they, and others both Catholiks, and Protestants are witnesses, and they
keepe this custome still from the Apostles vpon
the feaste of the Epiphanie. . *cipiunt Corpus Do-*
mini sub exigui specie panis.

S. Ignatius in this age is a sufficient wittnesse, in
diuers places, that it was so vsed in his time. *Nemo*
erret, nisi quis intra altaris septa sit, priuatur pane
Dei. And exorteth often so to communicate. *Date*
operam vt crebriùs congregemini ad Euchariftiam.
And telleth vs such communion bringeth immor-
talitie, is a preseruatiue against death, giueth life
and expelleth all euils. *Frangentes panem, quod*
pharmacum immortalitatis est, mortis Antidotum, vi-
tamque in Deo concilians per Iesum Christum, & me-
dicamentum omnia expellens mala.

Ignat. epist.
ad Phila-
delph.

And allthough in his epistle to the Philadelphians hee speaketh, as if this breade and cup were
giuen

giuen and diſtributed to all. *Vnus panis omnibus*
confractus, & vnus calix qui omnibus diſtributus est,
he ſpeaketh of the giuing and diſtributing of them
by Chriſt to his Apoſtles, vſeing the tenſe and time
paſt, as in Greeke is playne εἷς ἄρτ Θ- τοῖς πᾶσιν θρυ-
θρυφθη , εν ποτηριον τοῖς ὁλοις διενεμηθη, and when
he there ſpeaketh of the preſent vſe and time, he
ſaith, there is one Euchariſt, μια εὐχαριςία, yet entreating of the Inſtitution and as it is offered by
Preiſts at Maſſe, he vſeth the plarall number *Eu-*
chariſts and oblations, Euchariſtias & oblationes non
admittunt, and there nameth the Euchariſt receaued by all the fleſh of our Sauiour Ieſus Chriſt, not
ſpeaking of the other Kinde. *Non confiteantur Eu-*
chariſtiam eſſe carnem Saluatoris noſtri Ieſu Chriſti,
quæ pro peccatis noſtris paſſa est. Calling them Heretiks which denyed that Euchariſt which was
vſually then receaued in the Church in his time,
to be the fleſh of our Sauiour Ieſus Chriſt, that
fleſh of his that ſuffered for our ſinnes.

Ignat. epiſt.
ad Smyrnen.
apud Theo-
doreth. Dia-
log. 3. &
alios.

S. Clement, beſides that he hath teſtified before,
of reſeruing and receauing this bleſſed Sacrament
onely in one Kinde, vnder the forme of bread, he
further wittneſſeth, and preſcribeth by aud from
the warrant of S. Peter, and giueth order that if any
Preiſt ſhould negligently miniſter and giue the
bodie of Chriſt, ſpeaking nothing of the other
Kinde, that he was greuouſly to be puniſhed. *Com-*
munio Corporis Domini noſtri Ieſu Chriſti ſi negligenter
erogetur, & presbyter minora non curet admonere offi-
cia, graui anathemate, & digna humiliationis plaga
feriatur. And in theſe words immediately, that ſo ma-
ny hoſtes ſhould be prepared, as ſhall ſerue the commu-
nicants (not ſpeaking of the other Kind) and if any be

Clem. Rom.
epiſt. 1.

left,

left, they shall be reuerently receaued by some of the clergie. And they which receaue the remnants of the bodie of our Lord, which was left in the Sacrary, shall fast from eating any thing after a good while, tanta in altaria holocausta offerantur, quanta populo sufficere debeant. Quod si remanserint cum timore & tremore clericorum diligentia consumantur. Qui residua corporis Domini, quæ in sacrario relicta sunt, consumunt, non statim ad communes accipiendos cibos conueniant, ne putent sanctæ portioni commiscere cibum. And he giueth most strict charge, for the reuerent keeping of that Kinde alone of this most blessed Sacrament, that is left and to be reserued. Iterum atque Iterum de fragmentis Dominici Corporis demandamus. And they which be the most auncient writers after this age, as Irenæus, Origen, Dionysius Alexandrinus, S. Basile, Amphilochius among the greekes, and the first generall councell of Nice. Tertullian, S. Cyprian, S. Ambrose, S. Hierome, S. Augustine, Paulinus prosper, the 4. councell of Carthage, the second of Towres and others both councels and learned Fathers do not onely testifie, this custome to haue euer beene continued in the Church reuerently to reserue this most honourable Sacrament, in the forme of breade, and so onely to communicate the lay Christians especially pylgryms, straungers, trauailers, persecuted and liuers in desarts, but iustifiie, allowe and honour such practise and custome for holie and religious. And assure vs, as namely Tertullian, S. Ciprian and S. Basile with others, that this reseruation and communion was not onely in Churches, but in priuate howses, where Preists

could

could not be had. *Illud in persecutionis temporibus necessitate cogi quempiam, non præsente Sacerdote aut Ministro, communionem propria manu sumere, nequaquam esse graue, superuacaneum est demonstrare, propterea quod longa consuetudine hoc ipso rerum vsu confirmatum est: omnes enim in eremo solitariam vitam agentes, vbi non est Sacerdos, communione domi seruantes à seipso communicant: in Alexandria vero & Ægypto vnusquisque eorum qui sunt de populo, vt plurimum habet communionem in domo sua. Semel enim Sacerdote sacrificium consecrante, & distribuente, meritò participare & suscipere credere oportet. Etenim & in Ecclesia Sacerdos dat partem, & accipit eam, qui suscipit, cum omni libertate, & ipsam admouet ori propria manu. Idem igitur est virtute siue vnam partem accipiet quisquam à Sacerdote, siue plures partes simul.*

Euagrius relateth it an hold custome in his time, *vetus fuit consuetudo Constantinopoli,* in the Church of Constantinople to make this reseruation, and communion in one Kinde. And in all the greeke Church at this day the sicke do communicate onely in one Kinde, as in the Latin Church. *Ad ægrotos panis dumtaxat species defertur.*

And the Russians when they go to war carry with them this holy Sacrament in one onely Kind, and so receaue it. *Consecrant pro bellantibus panem in Corpus Christi, & laicis & bella præcedentibus tradunt in manus, qui cum sunt cum hoste conflicturi, illic pane illo posito seipsos ordine communicant.* And yet they professe euen in the publike profession of their faith by their Ambassadours that Christs all and whole and the true Sacrament is, receaued in one Kinde. *Fateor sub altera tantùm specie totum*

hom Ser.252. de temp. concil. Carthag. 4. c. 38 Paulin. in vit. S. Ambrosij prosper Aquitan. l 4 c. 6. de promiss. vt prædict. concil. Turonen. 2. c. 3. concil. matisc-con. 2. c. 6. Basil. supr. Ioh. Maschus in prat. spirit. c. 79. Metaphr. in martyr. SS. Indæ & Domne tem: Dioclesiani. Euagrius lib. 4. hist. Eccl, cap. 35.

Gilbert. Genebr. l. de grecor. ritibus.
Ioh. Scraminius in Elucidar.erritus ruthenici cap. 18.
Hypothius Legat. Ruthenor. in fir dei profess. an. 1595.
Ioh. Latif.

T 3   *atque*

cius ad c. YY.
Theol. Mof-
coiticę fol.
115.
Communion
in one Kinde
in Britayne.

atque integrum Chriſtum, verumque Sacramentum ſuum. And ſo they reſerue it conſecrated both for trauailers, and thoſe that die . *Quæ ſuperſunt conſecrata, ea in vſum & peregrè euntium & morientium ſeruantur*. No man can now queſtion but this Catholike doctrine and cuſtome, ſo Apoſtolicall ſo Vniuerſall was alſo receaued, and vſed in Britayne, allwayes ioyning with the Catholike Church.

Sermo antiq.
legiſolit. in
Eccl. Brit.
foxe Act. and
mon. pag.
1142.

And our moſt auncient brittiſh Authours allowed by our Proteſtants doth wittnes, that before the Chriſtians then receaued, they prayed thus to Chriſt in the forme of bread, which they were to receaue . *Agnus Dei qui tollis peccaca mundi miſerere nobis . O lambe of God that takeſt away the ſyns of the world haue mercy vppon vs. And to cite it further as Peoteſtants tranſlate it . The houſell is dealed into ſondry parts, chewed betwene teeth: how be it neuertheleſſe after ghoſtly might, it is all in euery part. Many receaue that holy body, and yet notwithſtanding, it is ſo all in euery part, after ghoſtly miſtery.*

Gildas I. de
excid. & con-
queſt. Brit.

S. Gildas calling the holie Altare, where maſſe was ſaid the Seate of the heauenly ſacrifice, *ſedes cæleſtis ſacrificij*, ſufficiently argueth this part of the ſacrifice was not onely offered, but vpon occaſion kept and reſerued there, for that is properly *ſedes* a ſeate, on which a thing is ſeated and ſometime permanent, longer then the ſhort ſpace betwene conſecration and communion at Maſſe. We finde in the ſecond councell of Tours where were our Biſhops of little Britayne , receauing both norme and Chriſtian Religion, from hence, that Order was therein taken, for the reuerent keeping

Concil. Tu-
ronen. 2. c. 3.

this bleſſed Sacrament in one Kinde, and ſo to be miniſtred . *Vt Corpus Chriſti non in armario, ſed ſub Crucis*

Crucis titulo componatur. Gregorius Turonensis confirmeth, that custome with that people, and exemplifieth how the holie, Bishop S. Gallus, three dayes before his death did communicate all the people in this one Kinde. *Sciens S. Gallus, reuelante Domino, se post triduum migraturum, conuocat populum, & omnibus confracto pane communionem sancta ac pia voluntate largitur.* The like he hath in other places. We read this vse and custome in the life, and in the time of S. Patrik, and among others that so communicated one named Echen, and a King did so receaue. *Accepto Corpore Christi migrauit ad Dominum.*

Gregor. Turon. l. de vit. patrum. cap. 3. l. 1. de glor. patr. cap. 86.

Neuer any order of Religion in the Church of Christ especially in this westerne part of the world was more renowned then our old brittish, I rish and Scottish monkes not onely among the Brittons, Saxons, in Ireland Scotland, Norway Island, but in Fraunce, Germany and Italy itselfe, and none more Religious towards this Sacrament then they, yet by their Rule and vowe they were forbidden to drinke wine, as we finde exemplified by approued Antiquaries in one of their cheifest monasteries, that of Lindisfarne the Nurse of so many Saincts, where King and Saint Ceolnuph entering into Religion about the yeare 733. licence was giuen to that Monastery to drinke wyne or ale, they neuer drunke any before, none but milke or water. *Hoc Rege iam monacho facto efficiente data est Lindisfarnensis Ecclesiæ monachis licentia bibendi vinum vel ceruisiam: antea enim non nisi lac vel aquam bibere solebant, secundum antiquam traditionem Sancti Aidani primi ciusdem Ecclesiæ Antistitis, & monachorum, qui cum illo de Scotia venerunt.* These holy

Roger. Houeden. Annal. parte priore. Mat. Westm. An. 733 continuator Bed. l. 1. cap. 9.

T 4   men

men could neuer drinke the cuppe of Caluyns and
our parlaments Protestants communion but being
made Preists and at Masse transubstantiating wine
into Christs bloode, to receaue this at that time
was neuer denyed vnto them. And this custome
of communicating onely in one Kinde among our
primatiue Christian Britans, Scots and Irish, was
so farr from being an offence, and against Christs
ordinance, that as their auncient learned brittish
Bishop testifieth it was miraculously approued by
him. For a Church of S. Michael the Archangel
in an I land there was euery day in the hollownes
of a stone neare the Church so much wyne miraculously prouided, as would serue all the Preists at
Masse that celebrated there. Yet no prouision for
any communicants spoken of. *In australi Momo-*

Girald.
Cambr. To-
pographie
Hibech c. 9.

*nia, circa partes Corcagiæ, est Insula quædam, Ecclesiam
continens Sancti Michaelis antiqua nimis & authëticæ
religionis. vbi lapis quidam est extra ostium Ecclesiæ
a dexteris, in cuius superiori partis concauitate, quotidie mane per merita Sanctorum illius loci, tantum vini reperitur, quantum ad missarum solemnia, iuxta
numerum Sacerdotum, qui ibi eodem die, celebraturi
fuerint, conuenienter sufficere possit.*

Rabbi Ca-
hanna ad cap.
49 genes.

The reason of this is not onely deliuered by
Catholike Christians, but the Rabbines before
Christ also taught, that whole Christ, bodie and
blood is in either forme, and so wholly receaued
in one onely Kinde, as in both. *In Sacrificio quod fiet
ex pane, non obstante quòd album sit velut lac, conuertetur substantia in substantiam corporis Messiæ; eritque in ipso sacrificio substantia sanguinis Messiæ. Erunt
item in sacrificio vini sanguis & caro Messiæ, &
eadem erunt in pane, quoniam Corpus Messiæ non potest
diuidi:*

diuidi : idque ratio poſtulat . Nam , ſi caro & ſanguis diuiſa eſſent . Diſtinguerentur ab inuicem . Corpus autem Meſſiæ non poteſt diuidi, ſicut ſcriptum eſt Exodi 12. *Et ſubſtantiam non confringetis in eo . Præterea caro ſine ſanguine, & e couuerſo, ſunt res mortuæ. Corpus verò Meſsiæ poſt reſurrectionem quia glorificatum erit ſemper viuet.*

The XXIII. Chapter.

The 31. *Article, being, intituled,* of the one oblation of Chriſt finiſhed vpon the croſſe, *thus examined and condemned.*

THE next their 31. article, being intituled *of the one oblation of Chriſt finiſhed vpon the croſſe:* is this. *The offering of Chriſt once made , is the perfect redemption propitiation and ſatisfaction for all the ſinnes of the whole worlde, both originall and actuall, and there is noe other ſatisfaction for ſinne, but that alone. Wherefore the ſacrifices of Maſſes , in the which it was commonly ſaide that the preiſts did offer Chriſt for the quicke and the the dead , to haue remiſſion of payne , or guilt, were blaſphemous fables and dangerous deceites.* Hitherto this Proteſtant article.

The firſt part being takē in that ſenſe the words doe giue, making Chriſts oblation of himſelfe vpon the Croſſe the perfect redemption, propitiation, & ſatisfaction for all the ſinnes of the world, originall, and actuall, doth euacuate and take away the neceſſity of any Chriſtian act internall, or externall, faith , hope, charity, repentance, Sacraments, and whatſoeuer confeſſed by all to be neceſſary to ſaluation, euen by theſe men themſelues before in diuers articles, as that of originall ſinne that of faith, that

Proteſt. artic. ſupr. artic. 9. art. 11.16 25. 27.

that of good workes, those of sinne after baptisme, of Sacraměts in generall, of Baptisme, of the Lords Supper, and others. And it blaſphemouſly contendeth, that all Infidels, Turkes, Tartars, Iewes, Pagans and whatſoeuer miſbeleeuers, and notorious ſinners ſhall be ſaued by this meanes, and haue as true and certaine Title to Saluation, as the moſt Catholike holy and religious Chriſtians haue, for all ſinnes of the world originall and actuall being thus, as this article ſaith, perfectly redeemed, propitiated and ſatisfied for, no ſinne of hereſie, Infidelity, or any wickedneſſe is excluded, but hath thereby, as the words of this article be, perfect redemption, propitiation and ſatisfaction, and conſequently eternall ſaluation, neyther ſhall the deuills themſelues, by this article be damned but ſaued alſo, for their ſinnes which they haue committed, and all they ſhall or can committ, are comprehended within this generall proteſtant circle and compaſſe of *all the ſinnes of the whole world, both originall and actuall.* All lawes, orders, decrees, rules, gouernement, and principality are needleſſe, all are ſure to be ſaued without them, and the moſt wicked wretch as ſecure as the holyeſt Sainct that euer was, there is noe damnation, there is noe hell at all.

This doctrine putteth downe that beaſtely ſaying of Epicurus, to take all pleaſure in this life, becauſe he thought there was none after death, for this doth Breede all wantonneſſe, and yet promiſeth euerlaſting pleaſures in the world to come. Therefore although wee moſt freely doe, and are ſo bounde to beleeue, and profeſſe, that the paſſion & merits of Chriſt are of infinite cure, validity, worth, and value in themſelues, able to haue beene a perfect redemption propitiation and ſatisfaction for all the ſinnes of the whole worlde, and more then euer were ſhall or can be committed if Chriſt had ſo ordeyned, and ſinners ſo applyed them by ſuch holy Inſtruments, and meanes, as Sacraments and others, as he prouided and Inſtituted, and they which are and ſhall be ſaued, haue and will vſe and apply to that end, and purpoſe, the meanes yet to thoſe that doe not receaue and practiſe, neither Chriſts oblation vpon the Croſſe nor any thing he did or ſuffered can be a perfect redemption, propitiation or ſatisfaction for all or any ſinne.

And among theſe neceſſary Inſtruments, meanes & applications of Chriſts redemption, propitiation and Satisfaction for ſinners, the holy ſacrifice of Maſſe is one, and moſt excellent, eminent, and honorable, wherein the truely and duely conſecrated Preiſts of Chriſts Church by vertue and power giuen them in their conſecration, *doe offer Chriſt for the quicke and the deade to haue remiſſion of paine or guilt,* which this article blaſphemouſly faith, *were blaſphemous fables, and daungerous deceites.*

And firſt our Proteſtants themſelues euen King Iames the heade & cheife interpretour of their Religion and congregation whileſt he liued, with his approued proteſtante writers, Biſhops, Doctours, and others publickly priuiledged, and warranted, by cheife authoritie in their proceedings, thus confeſſe for truth this article to be hereticall. *Neither is the King ignorant, nor denyeth that the Fathers of the primatiue Church did acknowledge one Sacrifice, in the Chriſtian Religion that ſucceeded in the place of the Sacrifices of Moſes lawe.*

The ſacrifice of the Altare and vnbloody ſacrifice were vſed in the primatiue Church, and the auncient Fathers

Caſanbon.
reſp. ad Card.
Per. p. 51. 52.
&c.

Middlet. Papiſt m. pag. 92
113 49. 137
138. 47. 45.

Fathers called the sacrifice of the body & blood of Christ, a sacrifice. The primatiue Church did offer sacrifice at the altare for the deade, sacrifice for the deade was a tradition of the Apostles, and the auncient Fathers. Aërius condemned the custome of the Church, in naming the deade at the altare and offerring, the sacrifice of Eucharist for them : and for this his rashe and inconsiderate boldnesse, and presumption in condemning the vniuersall Church of Christ, he was iustly condemned.

Feild.l.3.pag.
c.29.p.138.
Couel. exam.
pag.114.

Here we see by our Protestants themselues, that vpon a second and better consideration they graúte from our first founders in Christ, that the Catholike doctrine and custome so basely censured in this their Article is Orthodoxall, the Religion and tradition of the Apostles, Iudgment and practise of the vniuersall Church of Christ, and that which this their article concludeth, was iustly condemned for heresie. Therefore I may be more breife in alleadging the Apostolike writers to such propose.

Hebr. c. 8.
Cap 5.

Sainct Paul witnesseth that euery high preist or preist is ordayned to offer Sacrifice to God for the people , omnis Pontifex ad offerendum munera, & hostias constituitur. Omnis namque Pontifex ex hominibus assumptus, pro hominibus constituitur in ijs quæ sunt ad Deum, vt offerat dona & sacrificia pro peccatis. He also with other Scriptures saith both that Christ was a Preist after this Order of Preisthood, and Preists of this Order should be for euer in the lawe of the Ghospell. Tu es Sacerdos in æternum secundum ordinem Melchisedech, necessarium fuit secundum ordinem Melchisedech alium surgere Sacerdotem. Translato Sacerdotio, necesse est , vt & legis translatio fiat sempiternum habet Sacerdotium. But it is also euident, both by Scripture and all A-

Hebr. 7. Ps.
109.

posto-

postolike writers, that neither Christ , nor any
Christian Preist of that Order offered any other sacrifice, hauing resemblance to the Sacrifice of Melchisedech in breade and wine, then when Christ at
his last supper offered, & gaue his blessed bodie and
blood vnder those formes, and gaue then power &
commaunde to his Apostles & other Preists to doe
the same, as I haue aboundantly proued by the Fathers of this age, and our Protestants haue so confessed before.

It was also so certaine among the old Hebrues
before Christ, that Christ the Messias should be
such a Preist, and offer such a sacrifice and his
Preists after him, and all sacrifices in the lawe
should then cease and giue place vnto it, That
Protestants themselues thus confesse it . *Erat apud
Veteres Hebræos dogma receptissimum, in aduentu
Messiæ benedicti cessatura esse omnia legalia sacrificia
tantumque celebrandum sacrificium Thoda, & illud
peragendum pane & vino, sicut Melchizedech Rex
Salem & Sacerdos Dei altissimi temporibus Abrahami
panem & vinum protulit.* And the old Rabbines of
the Iewes before Christ, euen as they are commended vnto vs both by Catholike & Protestant
Antiquaries, do most playnely deliuer vnto vs the
same Catholike truth & as hath beene before confessed by thes Protestāts, that in this holie sacrifice
offered for sinnes, bread and wine are miraculously
chaunged into the bodie and blood of the Messias.

Rabbi Samuel saith vpon the oblation of Melchisedech that he sacrificed, and taught that Sacrifice: *Actus Sacerdotij tradidit: erat ipse Sacrifi-
cans panem & vinum Deo sancto benedicto.* So haue
Rabbi Moses Hadarsan, and Rabbi Enachinam.

Theodor.
Bibliandor
de SS. Trinit.
lib. 2. pag. 89.
vit. l. de test.
Miss. Petr.
Gallat. l. de
arcan. fid. ca.
Franciscus
Stancar: &
Prot. Basil.
in præf. ad
Petr. Gallat.
de Arcan.
Mort. Supr.
& alij.

Rabbi Sa-
muel in Be-
reschit Rabba
ad cap. 14.
Genes.

Melchi-

Melchiſedech proferens panem & vinum, oſtendit quod docuit eum Sacerdotij actum, qui erat panem & vinum ſacrificare. Et hoc eſt quod habetur in Pſalmis: *Iurauit Dominus & non pænitebit cum; tu es Sacerdos in æternum ſecundrm ordinem Melchiſedech.* And Rabbi Phinees ſaith moſt euidétly, that in the time of Meſſias all other Sacrifices ſhould ceaſe, and the Meſſias being a Preiſt after the Order of Melchiſedech ſhould except this alone, and this onely ſhonld be vſed inthis Religion. *Tempore Meſsiæ omnia ſacriſicia ceſſabunt, ſed ſacrificium panis & vini non ceſſauit ſicut dictum eſt Gen. 14. & Melchiſedech Rex Salem protulit panem & vinum: Melchiſedech enim Rex Meſsias excipiet a ceſſatione Sacrificiorum panis & vini, ſicut dicitur pſalmo. Tu es Sacerdos in æternum ſecundum ordinem Melchiſedech.* And they as manifeſtly teſtifie, that this euer continuing Sacrifice vnder the formes of bread and wine ſhould be the bodie andblood ofthe Meſſias, offered by the Preiſts of his lawe. *Panis quem dat omnibus, ipſe eſt caro eius, & dum guſtatur panis conuertitur in carnem, & erit hoc mirabile magnum.*

An other ſaith: *ſacrificium quod fiet ax vino ſolum tranſmutabitur in ſubſtantiam ſanguinis Meſsiæ, ſed etiam conuertetur in ſubſtantiam corporis eius, in ſacrificio quod fiet ex pane, non obſtante quod album ſit velut lac, conuertetur ſubſtantia in ſubſtantiam corporis Meſsiæ: eritque in ipſo ſacrificio ſubſtantia ſanguinis. Erunt item in ſacrificio vini ſanguis & caro Meſsiæ, & eadem erunt in pane.* Rabbi Iudas ſaith: *tranſmutabitur ex ſubſtantia panis, cum ſacrificabitur, in ſubſtantiam corporis Meſsæ, qui diſcendit de cœlis: & idem ipſe erit ſactificium.* An other writeth: *Meſsias erit placenta frumenti in terra.* And Rabbi Salomon wit-

Rabbi Moſes
Hadarſan
com. pſ. 39.

Rabbi Cahana ad ca. 49.
Gen.

Rabbi Barac.
in Ecclesiaſt.
Rabb. Iud. ad
c 28. num.
Rabbi Sim.
Bor. Ioan. l.
Reuel. Secret.

witneffeth that generallie the Rabbineffe, *magiftri noftri expofuerunt*, did fo expounde thefe words in the 72. pfalme. *Erit placenta frumenti in terra, in vertice montium.*

And that this miraculous chaunge in this facrifice should be made by the power of the facrificing Preift words by Gods extraordinary affiftance. *Tunc Deus mifericordia implebitur, & virtute ingenti fanctorum verborum, quæ ab ore Sacerdotium manabunt, illud Sacrificium, quod in vnoquoque altari celebrabitur, in corpus Meffiæ conuertetur.* And accordingly they deliuer how vnfpotted the liues of our Preifts should be, which thus offer Chrifts body, and blood in facrifice. *Qualis debeat effe Sacerdotis* Rabbi Nehu-*vita, hoc facrificium pertractantis, Dominus ipfe infi-* mias epift. *nuat, cum de noftri temporis facrificio, & confecrantis* arcanor.~ *qualitate, ita leuit. 21. capite inquit: & fanctificabis eum, quia Carnem Dei tui ipfe eft vel erit facrificans.*

This auncient Rabbines Teftimonies being fo plaine and pregnant for tranfubftantiation of bread and wine into the body and blood of the Meffias in this holy Sacrifice, as proteftants haue confeffed before, and their words themfelues fo euident, that no Catholike or Romane writer can fet it downe in more manifeft, or expreffe termes, make alfo the contradictory of this Article a clearely and vndeniably true. To take exception to thofe 'authorities would be groffe and foolish rafhneffe, for firft as I haue proued already, and shall hereafter they agree with the Apoftolike doctrine of this firft age, and the vniuerfall Church of Chrift. Secondlie if they had beene counterfaite, being in Hebrewe and extant in the librarics of the Iewes, they were moft like to be counterfaite by them, but this had beene

to

to condemne themselues. Noe Christian coulde inuent and place them in their libraries. There could not be the least suspition, of such Inuention, for they were vulgarly published to the Christian worlde longe before the beginning of the Caluinian Sacramentarie Religion, or other impugners of this most honorable Sacrifice, and so receaued, allowed and approued both by the greatest spirituall and temporall authoritie, euen of the Emperour giuing both power, meanes and allowance for the searching fourth, publishing and receauing those antiquities.

Petr. Gallot. prefat. in l. de Arcanis fid. cath.

And Rabbi Samuel Marochianus in his booke of the coming of the Messias, *de aduentu Messiæ*, receaued by all, and doubted of by none, doth inuincibly proue and demonstrate the same by manie Scriptures, as the Iewes reade and allow them. He proueth it from the 109. psalme and other Scriptures prouing, that the sacrifice of the Messias in the forme of bread and mine and his Preisthood after the order of Melchisedech, being to succeede the sacrifice and Preisthood of Aarō, were promised to endure for euer, and not to cease as those of Aaron, were to cease, and ceased when the euer during sacrifice and Preisthood of the Messias were instituted. *Attende quanta sit differentia inter sacrificium Aaron & Iustiistius Domini. Dixit Dominus Domino meo, tu es Sacerdos in æternum, non ad tempus sicut Aaron. Item sacrificium Aaron fuerunt carnes, & sacrificium illius iusti Domini fuit panis & vinum secundum ordinem Melchisedech. In quibus verbis Dominus per Prophetam ostendit manifeste, quoniam sacrificium Aaron finiretur, quando inciperet sacrificium in pane & vino, æternaliter duraturum, cum Aaron*

Rabbi Samuel Morachian. lib. de Aduentu Messiæ c. 19.

Psal. 109.

non

*nõ fit data æternitas in Sacerdotio, ficuti Sacerdoti Chri-
fto*. He there proueth, that if that promife of eter-
nitie in Sacrifice, and Preifthood, haue beene made
by God to Moyfes, which he made to the Meffias,
or Chrift, the facrifice and Preifthood of Moyfes
lawe had beene eternall, as thofe of Chrifts be,
by that promife. *Si Deus dixiffet noftro Moifi, ficut dixit per os Dauid, Meffiæ, fiue Chrifto : Tu venies Sacerdos in æternum fecũdum legem Myofi & Aaron, fta-
ret illa lex : fed dixit: tu es Sacerdos in æternum fecun-
dum ordinem Melchifedech.*

This he proueth alfo from Moyfes in the 26.
chapter of Leuiticus, that the Sacrifice of the Meffias and his Preiftood after the old Order of Melchifedech being eftablished, and published, thofe of
Aaron were to end. *Ad hoc fonat verbum Moyfi, cum* **Leuit. ca.26.**
*dixit: comedetis vetuftiffima veterum, per quod intel-
ligit facrificium Melchifedech. Et iterum : & nobis fu-
peruenientibus , id eft, nouæ legis facrificio publicato,
vetera, fcilicet veftra, proijcietis.* He proueth it from **Rabbi Sa-**
Leuiticus *cap.23. Exodus cap. 25. & numeri cap. 21.* **myel fupr. C**
Where the facrifice in breade & wine is fet downe, **20.**
and prefigured.

He proueth it from Salomon his words which the **Prouerb. c. 9.**
Apoftle vfeth. *Hoc facrificiũ vini cum aqua mixtum
pulcherrimè & aptè defcribit Salomon Propheta in libro
prouerbiorum cap.9. cum dicit, Sapientia altiffima com-
municauit facrificium fuum, mifcuit vinum fuum &
parauit menfam. Quis eft paruulus, veniat ad me, &
infipientes comedent panem meum, & bibent vinum
meum temperatum aqua. Quid menfa parata fapientiæ
altiffimi, nifi altare? Quid panis & vinum mixtum, nifi
facrificium de pane & vino, & de aqua quod fit in altari? notabiliter dicit. Panem fuum , & vinum fuum,*

V *per*

per id enim innuit hoc Sacrificium gratum esse Deo, & quod ad istud conuiuium tam diuinum & spirituale non vocauit patres nostros, qui erant sapientes in lege, qui

Rabbi Samuel supr. cap. 22.
Prou. c. 17.

erant occupati in sacrificio legis, quod etiam carnale sacrificium non dimisit nobis, sed priuauit nos illa.

He proueth it from the 17. chapter of the same booke, where the Prophet saith : *melior est buccella panis cum charitate, quam vitulus saginatus cum inimicitia:* that a peece of breade, meaning the sacrifice of the Christians, is better, then a fat calfe the sacrifice of the Iewes reiected: otherwise in ciuill valuation it is not so. He proueth it from the Prophets Esay, and Malachie, expressely foretelling that God would reiect, and haue the sacrifices of the Iewes as abomination, and yet haue an euerlasting externall sacrifice among the gentiles. *Completum est, quod Deus dixit de nobis (Iudæis) per hoc Isaiæ, vbi ait: completa est vindemia, & non est de cætero collectio. Et illud Malachiæ, non est mihi voluntas in vobis, & sacrificium non accipiam à vobis. Et illud Isaiæ c. 1. Sabbata vestra, & festiuitates, & sacrificium vestrum non accipiam, quia omnes vos estis in ira mea. Et illud Isaiæ: completum est: Quid mihi multitudo victimarum vestrarum, quid multiplicastis mihi sacrificium de arietibus, & carnibus hircorum, arietum carnes & hircorum. Non offeretis vltra sacrificium, quoniam incensum vestrum, & Sabbata vestra, & solemnitates vestras non recipiam à vobis, quia odit illa anima mea. Omne sacrificium vestrum cadauer fœtidum. Ille qui mihi iugulauerit taurum, sicut qui decollauerit hominem, & ille qui obtulerit in sacrificium hircum, sicut qui obtulit canem, & qui obtulit vinum, sicut qui offert sanguinem porci.* And hereupon inuincibly thus concludeth, that God thus reiecting, & hauing in abomination the*

Isaię 32.

Isa. cap. 1.

the facrifices of the Iewes, it can fignifie nothinge, els, but that he hath chaunged thofe groffe and carnall facrifices into the fpirituall and pure facrifice of Chrift. *Sed abominatio de facrificijs apud Deum nihil aliud fignificat, nifi mutationem facrificij noftri (Iudaici) carnalis & groffi, in facrificium iftius iufti Domini fpirituale & fubtile.*

He proueth it by vnanfwearable reafons, from thefe holie Prophets and the lawe of Moyfes, firft The Sacrifices of the lawe were offered in Hierufalem onely, and the temple there: *Sacrificium noftrum non fuit acceptum, nifi in vno loco fcilicet in domo fancta præcisè* But the Sacrifice of the Meffias among the gentiles conuerted vnto him, was by them to be offered in all nations euen from the rifeing of the fune to the fetting of the fame. *Valde timeo ab illo verbo quod Deus fortis & gloriofus dixit per os Malachiæ cap. 1. vbi fic tangit de facrificio gentium ab ortu folis vfque ad occafum, gentes offerunt facrificium nomini meo mundum:* neuer any fuch generally offered Sacrifice to the true God was in the worlde, but this bleffed Sacrifice of Chrifts bodie and blood, at Maffe, offered and facrificed as that Prophet faid, *in omni loco facrificatur & offertur,* in euery place, and not onely temple, citie, or nation. He proueth it further becaufe the facrifice of the gentiles conuerted to the Meffias was to be receaued, when that of the Iewes was to ceafe, which ceafed with them, foone after their crucifying of Chrift, their citie and temple deftroyed and the Iewes captiues aboue a thowfand yeares, as this Rabbine confeffeth writing 500. yeares ^{Cap. 20. 21.} fynce. *Deus etiam carnale Sacrificium non dimifit nobis, fed priuauit nos illo. Iam funt mille anni com-*

pleti

pleti, quod nobis accidit, propter illum iustum in quem peccauimus. When the conuerted gentiles haue noe other external sacrifice, but this of Christs bodie and blood·

He proueth it, becaufe the Prophet witneſſeth, the ſacrifice of the conuerted gentiles should be *ſacrificium mundum*, a cleane and pure ſacrifice in reſpect of the ſacrifices of the lawe of Moyſes, being ſo vncleane, that they were forced to be waſhed, the bellyes of the beaſts offered were purged, and the places cleanſed with water, when in the Sacrifice of the Meſſias haueing in it nothing but cleane, pure, and vnſpotted things, the pureſt breade, wine and water, chaunged into Chriſts bodie, and blood his humanitie, in a ſpirituall and acceptable manner to God, it muſt needs bee this *ſacrificium mundum* pure and cleane ſacrifice, that was ſo generally to be offered to God. *Deus inſti-tuit offerre panem loco carnium; & aquam mundam loco pinguedinis carnium, & vinum purum loco ſan-guinis: & homo offertur ſpiritualiter & acceptabiliter Deo, non ſicut animalia decollata per nos (Iudæos) quæ per Prophetam comparantur cadaueri putrido. Syna-goga indiget lauare carnes ſacrificiorum, & purgare ventres animalium, quæ in ſacrificio ſacrificabantur, & lauare locum de ſanguine, & pinguedine ſacrificio-rum, aliter eſſet horror tractare & videre. In ſacrifi-cio autem panis & vini & aquæ non apparet aliquid indecens, aut turpe. Timeo de verbis per Malachiam Prophetam dixit Deus Synagogæ: non eſt mihi volun-tas in ſacrificijs veſtris: quia ab ortu ſolis vſque ad occaſum magnum eſt nomen meum inter gentes, quæ offerunt nomini meo ſacrificium mundum. Sicut de na-tura ſua munda ſunt, aqua, vinum, & forma pura de quibus*

Cap. 21. 24.

quibus factum eſt ſacrificium, & non indiget munda-
tione & lotione.

And if any would interpret *mundum Sacrificium,*
the cleane ſacrifice of the Prophet, to be ment as
gratefull and acceptable to God, allthough no
thing in ſacrifice can be more acceptable to him
then the bodie and blood of the Meſſias offered in
this ſacrifice, euen by this and the other Rabbines, **cap. 20.**
yet he moſt clearely expoundeth how in this ſenſe
alſo the Sacrifice of Catholike Chriſtians is the
onely moſt pure and acceptable ſacrifice, and they
iuſtly by the warrant of God auoyde the Iewes
now as the Iewes auoyded the gentils whileſt their
Sacrifice was approued by God. *Apud Deum Sa-*
crificium gentium eſt mundius quam Sacrificium no-
ſtrum:& inſuper, quia Deus priuauit nos omni ſacrificio
mundo, & alias docens Chriſtianos, vt ipſi vitarent
nos, (Iudæos) ne contaminarentur ſicut nos vitaui-
mus gentes omni tempore quo ſacrificium noſtrum fuit
mundum apud Deum & acceptum.

This is proued by the Apoſtolike writers of **Ignat. epiſt.**
this firſt age; S. Ignatius ſpeaketh of this Sacrifice **ad Smyrnen.**
of the Chriſtians, *offerre, ſacrificium immolare,* and
ſpeaking in particular what it is, ſaith it is the bodie of our Lord Ieſu Chriſt which ſuffered for our **Ignat. apud**
ſinnes. *Caro Saluatoris noſtri Ieſu Chriſti, quæ pro* **Theod. Dial.**
peccatis noſtris paſſa eſt. S. Dioniſius the Areopa- **3.**
gite hath told vs before, of the greate honour, and
adoration the Chriſtians in that tyme, gaue to
Chriſt preſent in this holie ſacrifice, and in diuers **Dionyſ. A-**
particulars deliuereth the verie Order and manner **reopag. Eccl.**
thereof. **Hierarc. c. 2.**

S. Clement ſpeaketh of this holie ſacrifice in **c. 3 & epiſt.**
many places, and ſetteth downe at large the whole **ad Demophi-** **lum. Clem.**

order, of offering it for the liuing and deade, and
ſo expreſſely recordeth the cuſtome and vſe in that
Apoſtolike tyme. *Offerimus tibi Regi, & Deo ſe-*
cundum ipſius (Chriſti) ordinationem panem hunc &
calicem hunc, & mittas ſpiritum tuum ſuper hoc ſacri-
ficium , teſtem Paſsionum Domini Ieſu , vt oſtendas
hunc panem Corpus Chriſti tui , & hunc calicem San-
guinem Chriſti, vt qui percipiunt confirmentur in pie-
tate, & remiſsionem peccatorum conſequantur , Chriſto
tuo digni efficiantur , vitam aeternam adipiſcantur.

c. 18. 19. 2 r. And againe : *offerimus tibi pro omnibus qui à ſaeculo*
placuerunt tibi, offerimus pro populo hoc, pro virginibus,
& caſtitatem ſeruantibus , pro viduis Eccleſiae, pro
copulatis honorabilibus nuptijs, pro infantibus populi
tui, vt neminem noſtrum reijcias. Pro ijs qui in fide
quieuerunt rogemus . And he there recited all ſortes
of people for which this moſt holie Sacrifice of
Chriſts bodie and blood is offered, quick or deade,
and that it is for remiſſion of their ſinnes and euerlaſting life . *In ſalutem nobis fiant in vtilitatem ani-*
mae & corporis, in remiſsionem peccatorum , in vitam
futuri ſaeculi.

Iuſtin. Dial.
cum Triph.
Irenęus ad-
uerſ. hęr. l. 4.
cap. 32. S. Iuſtine and S. Irenæus allowed to haue liued
in this age , do expound the propheſy of Malachy,
as the Rabbines haue done before, they ſay Chriſt
inſtituted and taught and deliuered it to be vſed,
and the Church receauing it from the Apoſtles,
offered it in all the world . *Noui teſtamenti nouam*
docuit oblationem, Ieſus Chriſtus fieri tradidit, Eccleſia
ab Apoſtolis accipiens, in vniuerſo mundo offert Deo.

Alexander
Pp. 1. epiſt. 1.
cap. 4. S. Alexander an holie Pope, learning his diuinitie
and offering this bleſſed ſacrifice in this age, doth
moſt clearely ſay , that in this ſacrifice, Chriſts
bodie and blood is conſecrated of bread and wine,
mixed

mixed with water, that it is offered to God, so receaued from the Apoftles, finnes are thereby forgiuen, God is therewith pleafed, and his wrath
pacified, becaufe no facrifice can be greater then
this, which is the bodie and blood of Chrift, and
so with greateft puritie to be offered to be worshipped of all, and aboue all to be reuerenced and
honoured. *Sacramentorum oblationibus, quæ inter
miffarum folemnia Domino offeruntur, Paffio Domini
mifcenda eft, vt eius, cuius corpus & fanguis confici-
tur, pafsio celebretur, panis tantum & vinum aqua
permixtum in facrificio offerantur. Non debet enim, vt
à patribus accepimus, & ipfa ratio docet, in calice domini aut vinum folum, aut aqua fola offerri : fed
vtrumque permixtum : quia vtrumque ex latere eius
in pafsione fua profluxiffe legitur. Ipfa verò veritas
nos inftruit, calicem & panem in Sacramento offerre,
quando ait : accepit Iefus panem &c. crimina enim
atque peccata oblatis his Domino Sacrificijs delentur.
Talibus hoftijs delectabitur, & placabitur dominus,
& peccata dimittet ingentia. Nihil enim in Sacrificijs
maius effe poteft, quam Corpus & Sanguis Chrifti : Nec
vlla oblatio hâc potior eft, fed hæc omnes præcellit. Quæ
pura confcientia domino offerenda eft, & pura mente
fumenda, atque ab omnibus veneranda. Et ficut potior
eft cæteris : ita potiùs excoli, & venerari debet.*

This was the order, vfe, and cuftome of Gods
Church in the publike Maffes thereof, deliuered
by the Apoftles vnto it. In the Maffe of S. Peter
and the Romane Church, thus we finde it : *Me-*
mento Domine feruorum tuorum, qui offerunt hanc
hoftiam pro feipfis, & fuis omnibus, pro redemptione
animarum & corporum, pro fpe falutis & incolumitatis
fuæ. So it was in the Maffe of S. Iames and the

Miffa. S. Pe-
tri & Roman.
Eccl.

Miffa S. Ia-
cobi & Eccl.

V 4 Church

Hieroſolym. Church of Hieruſalem : *Domine conceſſiſti, vt conſidentes accederemus, ad ſanctum altare tuum, & offeremus tibi verendum hoc & incruentum ſacrificium pro peccatis noſtris admitte nos accedentes ad ſanctum tuum altare, vt digni ſimus qui offeramus tibi ſacrificium pro nobis, & pro ijs quæ populus per ignorantiam admiſit. Fac vt oblatio noſtra grata & acceptabilis ſit in propitiationem peccatorum noſtrorum, & eorum quæ populus per ignorantiam admiſit. O Deus reſpice in nos, & ad noſtrum hoc rationale obſequium intuere, vt de manu Apoſtolorum tuorum verum hunc cultum accepiſti.*

Miſſ. S. Marci & Alexandr. Eccleſ.

S. Marke and the Church of Alexandria, our primatiue Church in Britayne here, as before, vſeing it with others haue the like. *Purga cor noſtrum vt corde puro tibi hoc Thimiama offeramus, in remiſsionem peccatorum noſtrorum, & totius populi. Offerimus rationabilem & incruentam oblationem hanc, quam offerunt tibi domine omnes gentes ab ortu ſolis vſque ad occaſum, à Septentrione ad meridiem : quia magnum nomen tuum in omnibus gentibus, & in omni loco inceſſum offertur nomini tuo ſancto, & ſacrificium,*

Miſſ. S. Mat. & Æthiop.

& oblatio . So hath the Maſſe of S. Matthew : *Domine Deus noſter oblationem meam, & omnium famulorum famularumque tuarum, offerentium in nomine ſancto tuo, ſuſcipe, & pro meis & eorum peccatis fiat redemptio .* So hath the Maſſe of S. Barnabas after-

Miſſ. S. Barnab. Ambroſ. & Eccl. Mediolanen.

ward called S. Ambroſe his Maſſe at Millan longe time vſed in many weſt contryes : *Omnipotens ſempiterne Deus, placabilis & acceptabilis ſit tibi hæc oblatio, quam ego indignus pro me miſero peccatore, & pro delictis meis innumerabilibus, tuæ pietati offero. Offerimus pro Eccleſia tua ſancta Catholica .* In the

Miſſ S Andr. Chriſoſtomi

Maſſe of the Church of Conſtantinople aſcribed

first

firft to S. Andrew the Apoftle, and now called S. & Eccl. Con-
Chrifoftomes Maffe, it is offered for all: *pro vni-* ftantinop.
uerfo populo tuo. And it is the bodie and blood of
Chrift therein confecrated by the Preift, Chrift
himfelfe being faid to be offerer, and that is offered. *Propter infinitam clementiam tuam homo factus*
Pontifex nofter extitifti, & myftery huius ac in-
cruentæ hoftiæ Sacramentum nobis tradidifti vt om-
nium Deus. Fac me dignum Sacerdotij gratia indutum
confecrare fanctum corpus tuum, & pretiofum fangui-
nem: concede à me peccatore offerri tibi hæc Sacramenta.
Tu enim es offerens & oblatus, fufcipiens & diftribu-
tus, Chriftus Deus nofter.

These be the moft auncient publike Church
Maffes or liturgies, which Chriftians do, or can
alledge in their Religion, bearing the names of the
Apoftles themfelues, and yet in euery one of them
this moft holie Sacrifice of Chrifts bodie and blood
is, quite contrarie to this article, offered both for
the quicke, as is manifeft, and the deade alfo to
haue remiffion of payne and gilt. *Fac Domine vt*
oblatio noftra accepta fit in propitiationem peccatorum
noftrorum, & in requiem animarum eorum; qui ante
nos dormierunt.

So S. Iames. *Memento Domine famulorum famu-* Miff. S. Iacob.
larumque tuarum qui nos præcefferunt cum figno fidei,
& dormiunt in fomno pacis. Ipfis Domine & omnibus
in Chrifto quiefcentibus locum refrigerij & pacis in-
dulgeas, deprecamur. So S. Peter. *Animabus pa-* Miff. S. Petr.
trum & fratrum noftrorum qui antea in Chrifto fide
dormierunt, dona requiem Domine Deus nofter: horum
omnium animabus Domine Deus nofter dona requiem
in fanctis tabernaculis tuis, in regno tuo, easque cælo-
rum regno dignare. So S. Marke: *Memento Domine* Miff. S. Marc.
om-

omnium fidelium dormientium, & in rectæ fidei quief-

Miſſ. S. Matt. centium. So, and much more S. Matthew. *Memento Domine, Seruorum tuorum, & quæcumque in vita deliquerunt ignoſce. Offerimus tibi rationabile hoc obſequium pro fidelibus dormientibus.* So S. Andrew and S. Chriſoſtome after him with the conſent of the Fathers both of the greeke & Latin Church, teſtifying it was ſo decreed and left by the Apo-

Chriſoſtom. Hom. 69. ad populum Antiochen. ſtles, and practiſed by the Church of Chriſt. *Non temere ab Apoſtolis hæc ſancita fuerunt, vt in tremendis myſterijs defunctorum agatur commemoratio. Sciunt enim illis inde multum contingere lucrum, vtilitatem multam. Cum enim totius conſtiterit populus, Sacerdotalis plenitudo, & tremendum proponatur ſacrificium quomodo Deum non exorabimus pro his deprecantes.*

Oratione 41 in 1. Corinth. And, *neque abs re, is, qui aſtat altari dum veneranda peraguntur myſteria, clamat: pro omnibus, qui in Chriſto dormierunt, & ijs, qui pro ipſis celebrant memorias.*

So in the Maſſes of S. Barnabas and S. Ambroſe, S. Baſile, the Syrians, Mozarabes, Gothes, Muſcouites Armenians and all Chriſtians before theſ

Hilduinus epiſt. ad Loduic Imperat. Berno Augen. Abb. Libell. de reb. ad miſſa ſpectant. r. 2. times. So it was in the old Maſſe vſed in Fraunce Brytaine and all this weſt part of the world from the firſt receauing of Chriſtianitie here, as Hilduinus writing 800. yeares ſince, with others proue, the auncient copies thereof being then ſo old and worne, that they were allmoſt conſumed with age. *Cui adſtipulari videntur antiquiſſimi & nimia vetuſtate pene conſumpti Miſſales libri, continentes Miſſæ ordinem more gallico, qui ab initio receptæ fidei vſus in hac occidentali plaga eſt habitus, vſquequo tenorem, quo nunc vtitur, Romanum ſuſceperit.* Theſe our Miſſals ſo old 800. yeares ſince were no new Inuention. THE

THE XXIV. CHAPTER.

The 32. Article, intituled, of the marriage of Preists thus examined and condemned.

THeir next 23. Article, intituled, *of the marriage of Preists:* is thus. *Bishops, Preists, and Deacons are not commaunded by Gods lawe, either to vowe the estate of single life, or to abstaine from marriage: Therefore it is lawfull also for them, as for all other Christian men, to marry at their owne discretion, as they shall Iudge the same to serue better to godlinesse.*

This is their whole Article, and making the on-ly Scripture, which they meane by Gods lawe, to be the rule of Religion, it is often confuted before. And most false, prophane, and in many cases euen by their owne lawes and proceedings rebellious, trayterous, and tumultuous, to say, or write that no thinge is to be obeyed, and performed, but what is commaunded by Gods lawe or scripture, and euery priuate carnall minister may Iudge herein at his owne discretion. For by this Paradoxe all tem-porall and ciuill lawes of Princes not commaunded in scripture, are voyde, frustrate and not to be o-beyed, and such men and ministers against all pu-blike rule and gouernment, may Iudge & censure, doe and practise against all or any such lawes of his true and lawfull Soueraigne King, though the wi-fest, most Godly, and potent in the world, all com-mon weales are layde open, to manifest, or rather certaine daunger, and destruction.

And no law of England in particular is by this article to be obeyed, except these ministers will interprete

terprete it to be commaunded by Gods laws. And
ſo all humane lawes doe ceaſe, and onely the lawe
of God is in force and to be obeyed.

So wee muſt ſay of all Eccleſiaſticall lawes alſo, if
they be not commaunded in the law of God. all
Courts, Conſiſtories, and Tribunals, muſt be taken
away with their Iudges, Rulers, and Gouernours,
both ciuill and Eccleſiaſticall, except they can proue
to theſe men, that all their proceſſes & proceedings
are commaunded in the lawe of God.

Againe by their owne Religion this Articles doctrine both for the reaſon it maketh, and the con-
cluſion it ſelfe, is falſe: for firſt in their 6. Article before intituled, *of teſtimony of holy ſcriptures for ſalua-*
tiõ. They haue declared *that things read in ſcriptures*
or to be proued thereby are articles of faith, and requiſite
or neceſſary to ſaluation.

And ſo by theſe men it is allowed againſt this
article, that although it is not commaunded by
Gods lawes, or the Scripture, that Biſhops, Preiſts
and Deacons muſt vowe the ſtate of ſingle life, or
abſtaine from Marriage: yet if this is either reade in
holy Scripture, or can be proued thereby, their
Marriage is vnlawfull by their owne confeſſion.
Secondly the iniunctions of Queene Elizabeth nothing inferiour to theſe Articles, doe forbid all their
miniſters to marry, without their Biſhops licence,
and allowance. Therefore this article in their owne
proceedings is vntrue to ſay, they might lawfully
marry *at their owne diſcretion,* as all other Chriſtian
men might doe. And as falſe it is, that all other
Chriſtian men might lawfully Marry euen in theſe
mens doctrine in this article. For if the ſcripture &
Gods lawe did not commaunde Biſhops, Preiſts,

Dea-

Queene Eli-
zabeth her
Iniunctions
an. 1. Regni
eius.

Deacons or any other to vowe the estate of single
life, or to abstaine from Marriage : yet they which
voluntarily doe make such vowes, are commaun-
ded by Gods lawe to keepe them: *redde altissimo vota* Naum 1.psal.
tua. Tibi reddetur votum. Faciamus vota nostra quæ 20. 60. 65.
vouimus. Vouete & reddite Domino. Vota vouebunt 115.Hier.44.
Domino & soluent. If a iust promise of man to man Is. 19.
doth so strickly binde by all lawes , how much
more obligatorie and binding is the promise and
vowe of man to God.

The vowes of *Chastitie, Pouertie*, and *Obedience*
in religious men neither Bishops, Preists, nor Deacons, and of women incapable of such degrees , are
not commaunded in Gods lawe vnto them before
they voluntarilie vowe that holie state, Yet none
but monstrous men doe or can thinke but their
vowes being so made , doe binde then . Thirdly whereas the lawe of God , and these men in
their publike practicall of Religion doe say that
true Marriage *is holy Matrimony , an honorable e-* Protest.com-
state, instituted of God , signifying vnto vs the mysti- munió booke
call vnion, which is betweene Christ and his Church: Tit. Matri-
which holy estate Christ adorned and beatified with his mony.§. dea-
presence and first miracle. The so called Marriage of rely &c.
Protestant Bishops, Preists, and Deacons was not
such in the reigne of Queene Elizabeth , by their
owne lawes, but quite contrarie: the children betweene such men and women, termed their wyues,
were not legitimate, could not inherite either
lands or honour from such a Father, the Father
being a gentleman the sonne could not giue his
Armes but with a bend Sinister a testimony of ba-
stardie, nor inherite anie lands he had. The woman
had not dower by their lawes, giuing it to all lawfull

full wyues, So that in these pretended lawfull Mar-
riages there was nothing by their owne proceedings, which belongeth to the lawfull, holy, & honorable matrimonie, the pretended husbands were
fornicarious concubinaries, their women harlots &
concubines, all their children bastards and illegiti-
mate, and in this opprobrious shamefull condition,
though tolerated without further punishment they

Statute of King Iames for marriage of minist.

continued vntill King Iames after 44. yeares age
of their Religiō, by his Parlament lawe made such
Bargaines, men women and their children legitimate, or not vnlawfull among English Protestants.
4. The Protestant lawes and Religion of England
haue not taken away, or disabled the Canon lawe,
in which they freelie confesse the Marriage of all

**Stat. in Par-
liam. 1. Eliz.
An. 1. Iacobi.**

such men is forbidden, and condemned, further that
it is contrarie to the lawe of God, as in this point it
is not, but most conformable vnto vs, as is euident
before, and shall be made most manifest hereafter.
Therefore these Protestants supplying those places
of Bishops, Preists, and Deacons may not yet law-
fullie, marrie, in their owne Iudgments, and proceedings, nor by the lawe of God in holie Scriptures
themselues, by their exposition of them. For first it

**Matth. 19. 11.
1. Corin. 7. 8.
Apoc. 14. 4.
1. Reg. 21. 15.
25. 1. Cor. 7.
leuit. 20. Luc.
1. exod. 19.
Mat. 8. Marc.
9. Luc. 14.
&c.
Prot. art. 6.**

is euident in Scripture in manie places, that the virginall and chaste life in respect of Religion, is to be
preferred before marriage, and cleargie men by the
same lawe being Pastours, guides, teachers, light,
and example to others, and called to the greatest
perfection, it is most needfull for them, therefore if
the 6. Protestant article decreeth truelie, that things
read in scripture or proued thereby, are articles of
faith, and requisite necessarie to saluation, they may

not

not by Scripture allowe Bishops, Preiſts, and Deacons, or any of them to marrie, either by their owne
diſcretiō, which this Article contendeth, or by their
pretended Bishops allowance, by their Iniunction,
noe Proteſtant Article or Iniuctiō can be of greater
authoritie, then the lawe of God, & Chriſt himſelfe,
our high Preiſt, and Sacrifice, a moſt pure Virgin,
and ſonne according to his humanitie of the moſt
immaculate Virgin, who often in holy Scripture
calleth vpon all Preiſts to followe him. And promi-
ſing to heare the petition of all that duely aske, calleth vpon vs embrace Virginitie. *Sunt eunuchi, qui* **Matth. 19.**
ſeipſos caſtrauerunt propter regnum cælorum. Qui poteſt
capere capiat. He telleth vs by his *Apoſtle*, *virginitie*
and chaſtitie are more pleaſinge to him, and better
for them that ſerue him, eſpecially in ſacred fun-
ctions, then the married life. *Dico non nuptis & vi-* **1. Cor. 7.**
duis: bonum eſt illis, ſi ſic permaneant, ſicut & ego. Qui
ſine vxore eſt, ſolicitus eſt quæ Domini ſunt, quomodo
placeat Deo. Qui non iungit matrimonio virginem ſuam **Apocal. 14.**
melius facit. And theſe virgins, be they which followed Chriſt in this life and doe ſoe in heauen. *Hi*
ſunt qui cum mulieribus non ſunt coinquinati. Vir-
gines enim ſunt. Hi ſequuntur agnum quocunque ierit.

This chaſtitie could not ſoe virginallie and perpetuallie be kept by the Preiſts of Moyſes lawe
being onely of one tribe, the tribe of leui, and ſo
could not be without marriage to keepe a ſucceſſiō
in that tribe, yet although their Sacrifices and ſeruing God were then vnperfect, in reſpect of thoſe
in the lawe of Chriſt, and they ſerued not conti-
nuallie in the temple, and at the altare, as Chriſtian
Preiſts daylie doe, but by their turnes and ſucceeding times, yet when their times and turnes of ſeruing

Leuit. 21. 1.
par. 13. Luc.
1. Exod. 19.

uing in the temple came, they left their wyues at
their contrie howſes in their tribe, and they in Hieruſalem during their time of ſacrifice, and ſeruice
there, performed it in holy chaſtity, euen from their
wyues, And after knowledge of their wyues, before they might ſerue at the altar, were to beſan-
ctified: *& ne appropinquetis vxoribus*, was in ſome
caſes generally commaunded. No Preiſt might
marry a dishoneſt woman. *Scortum & vile proſtibu-
lum non ducet vxorem, nec eam quæ repudiata eſt a ma-
rito, quia conſecratus eſt Deo ſuo, & panis propoſitionis
offert: ſit ergo ſanctus, quia ego ſanctus ſum, Dominus,
qui ſanctifico vos.*

    The high Preiſt might Marrie none but a vir-
gin. *Virginem ducet vxorem.* Neither was it lawfull
in that vnperfect, figuratiue, and marrying lawe
either for Preiſt or other euen in need, not chaſte,
to eate things ſacrificed, as in the raſe of Dauid,
1. Reg. 2.
and his company coming to Abimelech the high
Preiſt for releife and ſuccoour, who hauing nothing to releiue thē with, but the ſacrificed breade,
would not giue it vnto them, but firſt examining
them, whether they had abſtained from women,
ſi mundi ſunt pueri, maximè à mulieribus. And Dauid anſweared they were. *Et reſpondit Dauid Sacerdoti & dixit ei: & quidem ſi de mulieribus agitur,
continuimus nos ab heri & nudius tertius, quando egre-
diebamur, & fuerint vaſa puerorum Sancta.* And
the Preiſts which did eate this ſacrificied breade,
and other oblations were abſent from their wiues
ſeruing in the Tabernacle, and temple, at ſuch times in chaſtitie. And S. Epiphanius ſaith, that
Epiphan.
Hær. 79.
Moyſes himſelfe the giuer of that lawe, did euer
after he was called to be a Profete, abſteyne from
                his

his wife . *Postquam prophetauit moyses, non amplius coniunctus est vxori, non amplius liberos genuit: habet enim vitam domino vacantem, vacare autem domino non potest, qui mariti officio fungitur.*

Therefore seing the Preists of the lawe though marryed, allwayes when they went to serue in the temple were sanctified, and lyued chaste, and the continuall state of Seruing God, especially in a more perfect lawe, doth continually require such puritie, and chastitie, of life, rightly doth S. Ambrose, and other holie learned Fathers, euen from hence conclude by the lawe of God against this Article, that Christian Preists euer conuersant in and executing their sacred offices, must lyue in perpetuall chastitie. *Veteribus idcirco concessum est Leuitis & Sacerdotibus vxores ad vsum habere, quia multum tempus otio vacabant à ministerio, aut Sacerdotio . Multitudo enim erat, Sacerdotum, & magna copia Leuitarum, & vnusquisque certo tempore seruiebat ceremonijs, secundum institutum Dauid . Hic enim viginti & quatuor classes constituit Sacerdotum, vt vicibus deseruirent. Vnde Abia octauam classem habuit, cuius vice Zacharias fungebatur sacerdotio, ita vt tempore quo, non illos contingebat deseruire altari, domorum suarum agerent curam. At vbi tempus imminebat ministerij, purificati aliquantis diebus accedebant ad templum offerre Deo.* Yet these Preists continued a yeare together in this seruing of God, neuer going to their wyues, or howses: *priscis temporibus de templo Dei Sacerdotes anno vicis suæ non discedebant ; sicut de Zacharia legimus, nec domum suam omnino tangebant.*

And the number of them was so greate that seruing but in one place, it euer had thowsands there,

Ambrof. ad c. 3. ep. 1. ad Tim. Euseb., Cæsarien. l. A demonstrat. Euang. c. 9. Innocent. 1. epist. 1. c. 9. Siric. ep. ad Himer Tarrac. Episcop. c 7. Hier. l. 1. contr. Iouinian. c. 14. 19 Apol. ad Pamach. c. 3. 8. ad c. 1. ep. ad Tit. Paralip. cap. 23.

X

as the scripture witnesseth, assuring there were

Paralip. cap. 23.

founde in the time of Dauid 38000. Leuits, aboue the age of 30. yeares appointed by their turns, to serue in the temple. *Numerati sunt Leuitæ à triginta annis, & supra: & inuenta sunt triginta octo millia virorum. Ex his electi sunt, & distributi in ministerium domus Domini viginti quatuor millia: præpositorum autem & Iudicum sex millia. Porro quatuor millia Ianitores: & totidem psaltes canentes Domino in organis. Et distribuit eos Dauid per vices filiorum Leui.*

This persuading these learned Fathers, that chastitie was so generally requisite, exacted by the lawe of God, in so many thowsands of Preists during the execution of their offices so longe time together induring, they conclude from hence by the lawe of God, that the Preists of the lawe of Christ are more perfect, and holie, and being at all times and places bound to the exercise of their sacred functions, not to be borne of one tribe alone, nor to be either the twelueth part of the people, as in that lawe, or the hundreth of true beleeuers

Innocent. 1. Siric. & Ambros. supr.

should lyue in perpetuall chastitie. *Quanto magis hi Sacerdotes & Leuitæ pudicitiam ex die ordinationis suæ seruare debent, quibus vel sacerdotium vel ministerium sine successione est, nec præterijt dies, qua vel à sacrificijs diuinis vel à baptismatis officio vacent?*

The holie Fathers conclude the same necessitie of chastitie in Preists, from the words of S. Paule, how the vnmarryed man is free, and fitte for the

1. Corinth. 7.

seruice of God. *Qui sine vxore est, solicitus est quæ Domini sunt, quomodo placeat Deo.* But the marryed otherwise. *Qui autem cum vxore est, solicitus est quæ sunt mundi, quomodo placeat vxori.* And sheweth

eth the bonde and debt betwene marryed people,
to hinder their seruing of God. *Nolite fraudare in-*
uicem, nisi forte ex consensu ad tempus, vt vacetis
orationi. Therefore they conclude that Preists allwayes bounde to the seruice of God, are allwayes
bounde to chastitie. *Certum est quia impeditur sacri-*
ficium indesinens ijs, qui coniugalibus necessitatibus
seruiunt. Vnde videtur mihi, quòd illius est solius
offerre sacrificium indesinens, qui indesinenti & per-
petuæ se deuouerit castitati.

The perpetuall and neuer ceasing Sacrifice a-
mong Christians requireth perpetuall chastitie in
them, that offer it. And this to be so is ordeined
by the lawe of God. *Diximus nuptias concedi in*
in Euangelio: sed tamen easdem in suo officio perma-
nentes, præmia castitatis capere non posse. Quod si
indignè accipiunt mariti, non mihi irascantur, sed
scripturis sanctis, imò Episcopis, & Presbyteris &
Diaconis, & vniuerso choro sacerdotali & leuitico, qui
se nouerunt hostias offerre non posse, si operi seruiant
coniugali. Neyther need we the consent of Fathers,
and antiquitie, in this exposition of the lawe of
God, but onely to insist vpon the verie words and
letter of the scripture in the new testament, it is
allowed by our Protestants, & both in the Greeke
and Latin text interpreted, and translated by their
owne Greeke and Latin lexicons, and Dictiona-
ryes, and comparing places one with an other,
being their Rules and directions in expounding
scripture, we finde S. Paule to say, *oportet Episco-*
pum esse, A Bishop must be among other necessarie proprieties, and conditions, *continentem* ἐγκρατῆ
which absteineth and keepeth himselfe especially
from haunting women, continent, chaste. So he

X 2 saith

Origen. hom.
23. in numer.
hom. 4. in
leuitic. l. 8.
contra Cel-
sum Euseb.
Cæsar de-
monst. Euãg.
l. 1. c. 9. Si-
ric. ep. 4. ad
Episc. Africæ
c. 9. Hier. ad
c. 1. ep. ad
Tit. l. 1. contr.
Iouinian. c.
19.

epist. ad Tit.

ep.1. ad Tim.
c. 3.

ſaith in an other epiſtle: *oportet Epiſcopum eſſe a* Bishop muſt among other laudable qualities, be *pudicum*, chaſte, shamefaſt, honeſt. Thus our Proteſtant Lexicons and Dictionaries do tranſtate.

And in the ſame place to contradict this Article in all he ſaith likewiſe of Deacons as of Bishops and Preiſts *Diaconos ſimiliter pudicos,* διακόνȣς ὡβαύτως βέμνȣς. Deacons muſt be likewiſe chaſte, as Bishops, and Preiſts. And this he wittneſſeth in both places, allthough the man now called to holie Orders was marryed before. As diuers were in that tyme, the pagan lawe, in the Empire eſpecially, debarring the vnmarryed and wanting children to be heyres, being in force vntill it was taken away by Conſtantine the greate and good Chriſtian Emperour, as hard and wicked. *Dura ſane contra infæcundos lex: quæ illos tanquam ſcelus aliquod admiſiſſent, graui ſupplicio afficiebat.*

Euſeb. l. 4.
de vit. Conſt.
cap. 26.

The Apoſtolicall Fathers of this firſt age are wittneſſes againſt this Article in the canons aſcribed to the Apoſtles, onely ſuch as were in inferiour orders were permitted to marry. *Ex his, qui cælibes ad clerum peruenerunt; Iubemus vt Lectores tantum & Cantores, ſi velint, nuptias contrahant.* S. Ignatius writeth of, and ſaluteth the holie colledge of Preiſts, in this time, in the Church of Antioch as in other places liuing in chaſtitie, as alſo the Deacons did. *Saluto ſanctum præsbyterorum collegium,* and placeth his predeceſſour S. Euodius Bishop there, among the holie Virgins.

Can. Apoſt.
25.

Ignat. epiſt.
ad Anthioch.
ep. ad Epheſ.
ep. ad Philadelphien.

epiſt. ad
Heron.

So did the Deacons alſo liue in perpetuall chaſtitie, as he exemplifieth in S. Heron, Deacon of Antioch to ſucceed him in his Episcopall dignitie there. *Teipſum caſtum cuſtodi, vt Chriſti habita-*
                                                    culam

culum, Templum Christi es, Spiritus es instrumentum. Tu introduces & educas posthac populum Domini qui est Antiochiæ. Saluto *sanctos Condiaconos tuos.* He Epistol. ad Smyrnens. which teacheth that preisthood is the highest dignitie, *Sacerdotium est omnium bonorum quæ in hominibus sunt Apex:* and their Sacrifice, the sacred bodie and blood of Christ, and they which offer it, and performe the other sacred functions, are to be most perfect, in the most holie estate: and virginitie and chastitie, are to be preferred before the married life *vxores maritis subditæ sint in timore Dei,* Epistol ad Philadelph. *Virgines Christo, in puritate, id quod præstantius est amplectentes, vt liberiùs diuinam legem meditentur, virgines solum Christum in precibus vestris ante oculos habete, & patrem illius illuminatæ à spiritu,* must needs so much as he can, ioyne them together in this most holie and sacred calling, as he doth.

S. Clement assigneth such to be admitted to holie orders as are vnmarried, or if married, neuer kept company with their wiues, and if any such shall after his ordination haue knowledge of his wife, though married before, he shall not be admitted to execute his sacred function, but onely the inferiour offices, as of the dorekeeper, and such. *Ad* Clem. Rom. epistol. 2. *Dominica ministeria tales eligantur, qui ante ordinationem suam coniuges suas non nouerint. Quòd si post ordinationem ministro altaris contigerit proprium vxoris cubile inuadere, sacrarij non intret limina, nec sacrificium portet, nec altare contingat, nec ad Dominici Corporis portationem accedat, nec aquam Sacerdotibus ad manus porrigat, nec vrceum siue calicem ad altare ferat; sed ostia forinsecus claudat, & minora sectatur officia.* He ytterly disableth, in the name of the Apostles, that any Bishop, Preist, or Deacon

X 3   vnmar-

vnmarried at their confecration, should marrie
after. *Episcopum & Presbyterum ac Diaconum dici-*
mus vnius vxoris debere constitui, siue viuant eorum
vxores, sine decesserint : non licere autem eis qui post
ordinationem sine vxore fuerint, ad nuptias transire.
Where he expoundeth that saying of S. Paule of a
Bishope or Preifte being husband of one wife, to
be vnderstood of such, before confecration, as Catholiks now doe againft Proteftants, as he also
doth before in the fecond booke of Apoftolike
conftitutions.

And to auoyde all fufpition and occasion of
breach of chaftitie in such persons, no woman
alone without an other, and shee a confecrated
Diaconissa was permitted to come vnto them. *Sine*
Diaconissa nulla mulier accedat ad Diaconum vel Epis-
copum. And this was not onely taught by the Apoftles, and Difciples of Chrift, but practifed also in
themfelues.

Tertullian neare the Apoftles time, writeth,
that he could not finde, that any of them but S. Peter onely, was married. *Petrum solum inuenio mari-*
tum per socrum. Cæteros cum maritos non inuenio, aut
spadones intelligam necesse est, aut continentes. S.
Ignatius in fome copies feemeth to hold that not
onely S. Peter, but S. Paule also and fome others
of the Apoftles were married men, *vt Petri & Pau-*
li & aliorum Apoftolorum, qui nuptijs operam dede-
runt. But in the moft auncient Manufcripts of S.
Ignatius, this is not founde, and by the word *alio-*
rum, he neither doth, nor can meane by any copie
in his owne opinion, that all the other Apoftles
were married, for immediately before he proueth
that S. Iohn both the Euangelift and Baptift, were
perpe-

Lib.conftitut.
Apoft. c. 17.

Lib. 2. conft.
Apoft. cap. 2.

Clem. lib. 2.
conft. Apoft.
cap. 30.

Tertull. l. de
Monogomia.

Ignat.epift.ad
Philadelph.

perpetuall Virgins. *Virgines solum Christum præ oculis habete, sicut Ioannes Baptista, sicut dilectißimus discipulus, qui in castitate de vita exierunt*. And S. 1. Chorinth. 7. Paul for himselfe hath proued before, that he was either vnmarried, or a wydower then liuing in chastitie. *Dico non nuptis & viduis, bonum est illis, si sic permanserint sicut & ego*. And S. Ignatius hath Ignat. epist. ad Philadelphen. supra. sufficiently before proued the chastitie of clergie men, after ther calling, whether Apostles, Bishops Preists, or Deacons, and in this very place deliuereth in particular, that S. Euodius who suceeded S. Peter at Antioch, & S. Clement his Successour at Rome, and S. Timothy and S. Titus to whome S. Paule gaue so strict charge before, of chaste clergy men, lyued and dyed pure Virgins. And neuer denyeth, that either S. Peter or any other Apostle supposed by any man to haue beene married did forsake their wiues, and liued in chastitie, after they were called to be Apostles. Which both holy scriptures & fathers inuincibly proue vnto vs.

S. Peter speaketh in the name of all the Apostles, that they had forsaken all things, & followed Christ: *Ecce nos reliquimus omnia & secuti sumus* Matth. 19. *te*. And expected reward for so doing. *Quid ergo erit nobis?* Among all things forsaken for Christ, wiues the most neare and deare to married men among temporall matters, must needs be comprehended, if they or any of them were Married. And Christ himselfe so expoundeth that speach of S. Peter, putting wife *vxorem* γοναῖκα among the things which S. Peter, and the Apostles had forsaken for his seruice, and were therefore to receaue eternall reward. *Centuplum accipiet & vitam æteruam poßidebit.*

So

Hierom. l. 1.
con. Iouin.
Apolog. ad
Pammach. c.
8. Chrisost.
hom. 33. in
Gen. hom. 2.
in Iob. Basil.
de. ad Amph.
c. 3 Epiphan.
Her. 59. Eu-
seb. prepar.
Euang. l. 9. c.
1. Porphir.
& Herat. ib.
Enseb. l. 1. c.
9. supr. c. 8.
l. 3. c. 8.

So S. Hierome and other fathers expounde this scripture, *assumpti in Apostolatum, relinquunt officium coniugale. Apostoli vel Virgines, vel post nuptias continentes*. The like haue the Greeke Fathers S. Chrisostome, S. Basile, S. Epiphanius, Eusebius, and others: wittnessing not onely that the Apostles liued thus in chastitie, but among the Iewes the Essæi liued in chastitie *vxores non ducunt*. And all that serued in the temple remained in chastitie, *vbi nocte ac die Sacerdotes castè versantur, nunquam in templo vinum bibentes*. All that write of the lyues of the Apostles giue testimonie to this. So it was with the 7. Deacons, except Nicolaus that fell to wantonnesse. So of the Euangelists not Apostles, so of the 72. Disciples of Christ. So with all we finde in Antiquities to haue beene Bishops Preists or Deacons in the vniuersall world in this first Apostolike age, they were all either vnmarried, or absteyning from their wyues, which they had before their conuersion. We finde the names and liues of very many such clergie men, both in Greeke and Latin Authours, we finde not any one but such as liued and died in chastitie, in any approued authour. Their names and number are to greate to be particularly remembred. It will be sufficient for this time and place to make mention onely of them, which ruled in the cheefest Sees, and were a rule to the rest.

Enseb. Cesar
Hist. Eccl. l 4
cap. 5. Epiph
Her. 66. Abd.
l. 6. Ireneus
in S. Io. Euäg.
Hieron. l. de

To begyn with Hierusalé when Christianitie began S. Iames, S. Symeon, S. Iustus, renowned for puritie and chastitie. And after S. Iames and the Apostles death, S. Iohn the Apostle, Euangelist and Virgin, ruled all the Churches of Asia vntill the end of this age, *totus Asia fundauit rexitque Ecclesias.*

The

The Church of Alexandria gouerned by S. Marke the Euangelift directed thither by S. Peter, S. Anizanus or Anianus or by fome Ananus and Abilius in this time is renowned for chaftitie, and all religious conuerfation both by Iewes and Chriftians. In the commaunding See of Antioch after S. Peter, who as before forfooke his wife, & all, for the loue of Chrift, the pure and chafte remembred S. Euodius, and after him that greate and moft continent commender and aduancer of virginitie, and chaftitie S. Ignatius, gouerned vntill the end of this age. He fufficiently, befides that is cited from him before, euidently teftifieth that all Preifts then liued in chaftitie, and fo were bound to doe : *eas quæ in virginitate degunt in pretio habete, velut Chrifti Sacerdotes : viduas in pudicitia permanentes, vt altare Dei*. The See of Rome is confeffed euen by Proteftants to haue beene the higheft Rule in the whole Latin Church, and all this weft part of the world. Yet we finde none but profeffours of chaftitie there, S. Peter, S. Linus, S. Cletus and S. Clement in this time. Of S. Peter I haue faid before, which will alfo teftifie for S. Linus, which was his next Succeffour both in dignitie, and holie chaftitie, as that Church, place, and time then required, and the miraculous fanctitie of his life, cafting out deuils and rayfing the deade proue, with his confecrating of many chafte Preifts and Bifhops, and decreeing, that noe woman might vnuealed enter the Church, fo honouring and maintaining chaftitie, as both Catholiks and Proteftants confeffe *Linus presbyteros* 18. *& Epifcopos* 11. *facris initiauit. Mulierem nifi velato capite ingredi templum prohibuit, mortuos fufcitauit.*

S. Cle-

Script. Eccl.
in S. Ioanne.

Philo. l. de
laude fue
gent. Hieron.
l. de Ecclef.
Scriptor. in
S. Marco
Euangelifta.

Ignat. epift.
ad Tarfen.

Dam. Pontif.
in S. Lin. vita
S. Lini in Breuiar. die 23.
Septemb. Rib.
Barnes l. de
vit. Pont.
Rom. in Lin.

**Damaſ. Rab.
Barnes ſup.
in Cleto vit.
cius in Bre-
uiar. April.
26.**

S. Cletus likewiſe after him liued in the ſame manner, and ordeyned 25. Preiſts in ſuch order as S. Peter had directed to be profeſſours of chaſtitie, as is proued before, this both Catholiks and Proteſtants acknowledge. *Is ex præcepto Principis Apoſtolorum in vrbe viginti quinque presbyteros ordinauit.*

**Ignat. epiſt.
ad Trallian.
epiſt. ad Mar.
Caſſobolit.**

Of S. Clement his chaſtitie I haue ſpoken before from S. Ignatius, putting him in his catalogue of chaſte Virgins, and ſtiling him moſt bleſſed Clement the ſcholler of S. Peter and S. Paule, *Beatiſſimus Clemens Petri & Pauli auditor*, who taught him and all ſuch their ſchollers and Diſciples preiſtly chaſtitie as before, and as S. Clement himſelfe is a wittneſſe from S. Peters owne words, the chaſtitie of S. Clement was one of the motiues

**Clem. epiſt.
1. S. Petrus
ib.**

which cauſed S. Peter to deſigne him to that great paſtorall dignitie. *Quem præ cæteris expertus ſum Deum colentem, homines diligentem, caſtum &c.* This holie chaſte Pope is further wittneſſe, that his Maſter S. Peter did giue him power, and charge to ſend ſuch worthie Biſhops, where S. Peter had not ordeyned the like before. *Episcopos per ſingulas ci-*

**Clem. epiſt.
2. ſupr.**

uitates, quibus ille non miſerat perdoctos & prudentes ſicut ſerpentes, ſimpliceſque ſicut columbas iuxta Domini præceptionem mittere præcepit, quod facere inchoauimus, & domino opem ferente facturi ſumus. And expreſſely nameth Fraunce, Spayne, Germany, Italy, and ſufficiently proueth the ſame of this our greate Britayne, and other contryes in this part of the world. *Aliquos ad Gallias, Hiſpaniaſque mittemus, & quoſdam ad Germaniam & Italiam, atque ad reliquas gentes dirigere cupimus.*

Theſe other nations in theſe parts beſides Italy

Germany

Germany Spayne and Fraunce muſt needs include Britayne alſo. And to omitte other nations here remembred, we finde both in our owne and the hiſtorians and Annals of Gallia now Fraunce, that this virginall Biſhop and Pope, by direction of that his chaſte Maſter and predeceſſour S. Peter ſent very many ſuch chaſte Biſhops with ſuch their Preiſt, and Deacons thither. *Anno gratiæ* 94. *Cle-* *mens Romanæ Sedis Epiſcopus ad locandum in Gallijs fidei fundamentum induſtrios ac magnificos viros de-* *ſtinauit. Pariſienſibus Dionyſium, Siluanectenſibus Ni-* *caſium, Ebroicenſibus Taurinum, Arelatenſibus Tro-* *phinium, Narbonenſibus Paulum, Tholeſenſibus Satur-* *ninum, Aramicis Aſtremonium, Lemouicenſibus Mar-* *tialem, Turonicis Gratianum, Cenomannicis Iulianum,* *Beluacenſibus Lucianum, Ambianenſibus Firmium,* *Lugdunenſibus Photinum. Per quos innumera multi-* *tudo hominum ab Idolorum cultura receſsit.*

Many more holie Biſhops with their Preiſts and Deacons are remembred in the Annals of Fraunce to haue preached there in this time. And not the leaſt ſuſpition left in any antiquitie, but they all liued perpetually in chaſtitie. And they which haue left any thing written behind them, that is ſtill extant, as S. Martial, and S. Diony Gus the A- reopagite conuerted by S. Paul teſtifie ſo much for themſelues and the reſt both in Fraunce or where- ſoeuer in this time S. Martial making the preiſtly life and ſtate moſt excellent of all others, teacheth vs plainely that the viduall life is better then mar- riage, and that of Virgins moſt perfect like to that of Angels. *Vltra hunc (matrimonij) gradum homini licitè conceſſum, viduitatem in præmio maiori conſti-* *tuit Dominus. Sed & tertium excellentem gradum* *honeſta-*

Mat. Weſtm. chron. an. 94. Antiquit. Eccl. mult. in Gallia. Guliel. Eiſen- gren. centen. 1.part.4.diſt. 3. Gregor. Turon. Hiſt. Francorum l. 1. Hincmar. ep. ad Carol. Magn. Imper. Martyrol. Rom. vſuard. Ado. Bed. & alij.

Martial. epiſt. ad Burdegal. cap. 3. Epiſt. ad To- loſ. c. 9. c. 8.

honestatis in virginitate demonstrauit nobis perfectum,
& per omnia similem angelicæ dignitati . And he
thought the chaste life to be so sitte, & requisite for
the more perfect seruing of God, that euen princes
then, & not onely clergy men embraced it to that
holy end. So he writeth of the Queene or Princesse
Valeria, though espoused, how shee had professed
virginitie by his preaching *Virgo Valeria Sponsa Re-*
gis cælestis per meam prædicationem virginitatē mentis
& corporis Deo deuouerat. And of King or Prince Stephen : *pro suauitate præmij futuri illectus , copulam*
carnalium nuptiarum deuitauerit per meam prædica-
tionem : quatenus liberior Deo famulari possit.

Dionys. A-
reopag. Eccl.
Hier. c. 6. ep.
ad Gain. &
alibi,

S. Dionysius is most playne in this matter , and
setteth downe the very manner how chastitie was
professed before the Bishops, in that time, and how
that such in respect of others were cheifly called
Tberapentæ , cultores, the perfect worshippers of
God, euen by the Apostles themselues, *Sancti præ-*
ceptores nostri diuinis eos appellationibus sunt prosecuti.
So both he and they must needs teach , that Bishops, Preists, and Deacons euer conuersant about

Sim. Meta-
phrast.die 19.
Iunij.

most sacred things, were to liue in chastitie . So we
must needs say of Britayne : first because we finde
that S. Peter admitting onely men of chastitie to
thes holie Orders , as before , did first, consecrate
our first Bishops Preists and Deacons here , *A-*
pud Britannos Ecclesias constituit , Episcoposque &
Præsbyteros & Diaconos ordinauit . Secondly if any
were wanting after, they were, as before , sup-
plyed by S. Clement, onely allowing such to
those sacred offices . Thirdly, all those whose names be preserued to haue beene Bishops, in, or of
this nation, as S. Aristobulus, S. Mansuetus, S.

Beatus

Beatus, S. Ioseph sonne of S. Ioseph of Aramathia which buryed Christ, and some others by some writers, are so remebred by the Antiquities where we finde, that there is not the least suspition but they continually liued in virginall or chastelife: If this Aristobulus was the same which Metaphrastes writeth, to haue beene Father in lawe to S. Peter, the scripture wittnesseth his wife remayned in Iury so farre distant from him in Britayne, if shee liued so long.

S. Mansuetus liued a collegiall life with onely Preists, and clergy men, no women with them, and was consecrated by S. Peter the Apostle, hauing before forsaken contrie, kindred verie noble *ex nobili prognatus familia*, men, women and all for the loue of Christ. S. Beatus of noble birth here in Britayne, both by Catholike & Protestant Antiquaries forsooke all, and went to Rome and there with an other Britan whose name is not perfectly remembred, one calleth him Achates, was consecrated, and was so chaste, that except when he preached he seldome or neuer saw women one or other, liuing a solitary single Eremiticall life.

Of S. Ioseph sonne of S. Ioseph said in the oldest monuments and antiquities of that holie company to haue beene miraculously by Christ himselfe consecrated, or at the least elected and desigued a Bishop, and the rest of that sacred company, Preists, Deacons, or whatsoeuer, it is most euident they liued, and died in perpetuall chastitie, in the Iland Aualan, all Antiquaries, Catholiks and Protestants confesse, that King Aruiragus gaue the place onely to those holy men, It was to them onely confirmed by the two next following Kings

Ma-

Metaphrast.
die 26. Iunij.
Mat. 8. Marc.
1. Luc. 4.
Gulielm. Eisengren. cenatenar. 1. part.
1. dist. 3. Petr.
de Natal. l.
11. Anton.
Democh. l. 2.
cont. Caluin.
Arn. Merman.
Theatr. conuers. gent. in metensib.
Martyrolog.
Rom. Bed.
vsuard. &
Molan. die 9.
Maij Guliel.
Eisengren.
centen. 2.
part. 5. Annal
Helueth. Antiquit. Eccl.
Constant.
Baron. an. in
mart. Rom.
9. Maij.
Theater of
great Britaine
l. 6.
Antiquitat.
Glaston. manuscript.

Tab. fix. Gul.
Malmesbur.
l. de Aut.
Cænobij Gla-
ston. Capgr.
Catal. Sanct.
in S. Ioseph
Aramath. &
S. Patricio.
Iacob. Ge-
nuen. in ijs-
dem. Ioh.
Bal. l. de
Script. cent.
1.in S.Ioseph.
Aramathien:
Ioh. Leland.
assertion.
Arthurij.
Godnyn.
Theater of
great Brit. l.
6. Caius l.
antiq. acca-
dem. Canta-
brigien.
Stowe Hist.
Romans
Charta Regis
Hen. 2. &
aliorum Reg.
Socrat. Hist.
Eccl. l. 1.
cap. 8.

Marius and Goillus, celles were made onely for them, there they liued alone, they left no children, or posteritie after them, and the place of habitation was so desart, and desolate, when S. Damianus and Phaganus were sent hither by Pope Eleutherius in King Lucius his time the next age, that their place of dwelling was become a denne for wylde beastes. *Cæpit idem locus esse ferarum latibulum, qui prius fuerat habitatio Sanctorum.*

Therefore we are enforced by the authorities of Scriptnre, tradition, the whole Church, Geeke and Latin, the Apostolike age and writers, and all warrant in religion, to conclude that the doctrine of this article is false: *that Bishops, Preists and Deacons may lawfully marry at their owne discretion.* And verie vainely our Protestants singularily alledge, for their defence from Socrates the historian, that Paphnutius dissuaded the Fathers of the first Nicen councell, not to decree that Bishops, Preists, and Deacons might not keepe companie with their wyues, which they had marryed when they were lay men: *vt qui essent sacris initiati, sicut Episcopi, Presbiteri, Diaconi, cum vxoribus, quas cum erant Laici, in matrimonium duxissent, minimè dormirent.* But it should suffice, that they which were vnmarried when they were called to the clergie, should according to the old tradition of the Church abstayne afterward from marriage: *vt qui in clerum ante ascripti erant, quam duxissent vxores, hi secundum veterem Ecclesiæ traditionem, deinceps à nuptijs seabstinerent.* For here the marriage of such men, and this Article, is plainely condemned by their owne Authour, and the old Apostolike tradition in the Church.

And

And this is confirmed by aboue 200. Later Bishops of the Greeke Church itselfe, testifying it was the doctrine and tradition of the Apostles, that among those of the cleargie none but Lectours and Singers might marrie, and they accordingly decree, that no Subdeacon, Deacon or Preist may marrie, and if he should he must be deposed. *Quoniam in Apostolicis Canonibus dictum est, eorum qui non ductâ vxore, in clerum promouentur, solos lectores & cantores vxorem posse ducere: & nos hoc seruantes, decernimus, vt deinceps nulli penitus Hypodiacono, vel Diacono, vel Presbytero post sui ordinationem, coniugium contrahere liceat : Si autem hoc facere ausus fuerit, deponatur.* And this is their vse and practise to thes dayes.

The other clause of Paphnutius opinion, about Bishops, Preists, and Deacons married before their consecration, not to be barred from such their former wiues, married vnto them when they were lay men, by any expresse lawe to be made by that councell, if it be truely related, nothing concerneth this article, onely speaking of Marriage of such men after holie Orders taken, and not when they were lay men. Yet that citation of Sacrates in this poynt wanteth not suspition of vntruth. For the same Socrates speaking vpon his owne certaine knowledge, affirmeth it was the receaued custome in Thessalia, Macedonia, and other parts of the Greeke Church, that if a clergie man kept companie with his wife, that he had married when he was a lay man, he was to be degraded. *Ipse in Thessalia consuetudinem inualuisse noui, vt ibi qui clericus sit, si cum vxore, quam cum esset Laicus ducebat, postquam clericus factus sit, dormierit, clericatu abdicatus sit.*

Episc. Graec 227. in can. Trullen. can. 6.

Socrat. Hist. Eccl. l. 5. cap. 2l.

fit, eadem consuetudo etiam Thessalonicæ, & in Macedonia, & in Hellade seruatur. And saith, that all the renowned Preists and Bishops also in the easte absteyne from such wiues. Omnes illustres presbyteri in Oriente, & Episcopi etiam, ab vxoribus abstinent.

Socrat. Hift.
Eccl. l. 1. c.
8. supr.

And he confesseth, that the absteyning of clergie men from their formerly married wiues, when they were lay men, was so religious, iust, and necessarie, in the Iudgement of the whole generall councell, that they determined to make a decree and canon thereof: visum erat Episcopis legem in Ecclesiam introducere: vt qui essent sacris initiati, sicut Episcopi, Presbiteri & Diaconi, cum vxoribus, quas cum erant Laici, in matrimonium duxissent, mi-

Concil. Nic.
can. 78. Arabico.

nimè dormirent. And it seemeth by the Arabike copie of that councell, that this or the equiualent lawe and decree was then made: si vxorem duxit, & adhuc vxor viuit, & cum eo habitat, debet imponi duplex pænitentia: Idem seruandum de Diacono.

Concil. Nic.
can. 3.

And the third of those canons of this councell which both Catholiks and Protestants commonly receaue, forbiddeth all Bishops, Preists, Deacons, and clergie men to dwell with any woman, but their mother, sister, grandmother, or Aunt, sister to their father or mother. Nisi fortè mater aut Soror aut auia, aut amita, aut matertera sit. And the second councell of Arles held about the same time, in the dayes of S. Syluester Pope, and Constantine Emperour, plainely forbiddeth all cohabitation or meeting with wiues married before, vnder payne

Concil. Arel.
2. can. 3.

of excommunication. Si quis de clericis à gradu Diaconatus in solatio suo mulierem præter auiam, matrem, sororem, filiam neptem, vel conuersam secum vxorem habere præsumpserit, à communione alienas habeatur.

habeatur. Here the wife marryed before except conuersa professing chastitie as the husband now doth, is forbidden his companie, and he from her, and most plainely in the canon before, a married man is disabled to be a Preist, except promising and professing chastitie. *Assumi ad Sacerdotium non potest, in vinculo coniugy constitutus, nisi fuerit promissa conuersio.* In this councell our Archbishop of Londou *Restitutus*, was present, and subscribed vnto it for this Kingdome, which with Fraunce where this councell was kept, Spayne, Italy, and other contries of the west presently receaued the Nicen councell.

Const Magn. epist. Eccles. Socrat. Hist. Eccl. l. 1. c. 6.

Eusebius Cæsariensis present at the councell of Nice, and writing after it, is plaine that married men receauing holie Orders were bounde to chastitie. *Oportere dicit sermo diuinus, Episcopum vnius vxoris virum esse. Veruntamen eos, qui sacrati sint, atque in Dei ministerio cultuque occupati; continere deinceps seipsos à commercio vxoris decet.* And S. Epiphanius also a grecian and liuing at that time, and writing in that age, testifieth plainely, that the holie Church of God, where the canons were sincerely kept, *did admitt none to be eyther Bishop, Preist, Deacon or Subdeacon but such, as absteyned from their wiues if marryed before, or in single and chaste life. And if it was otherwise vsed in any place wheresoeuer, it was an abuse, this being the custome of the Church directed by the holie ghost euer from the beginning, that Ecclesiasticall men, married, or not married should euer liue in chastitie. Adhuc viuentem & liberos gignentem vnius vxoris virum non suscipit sancta Dei Ecclesia, sed eum qui se ab vna continuit, aut in viduitate vixit, Diaconum & Presbiterum, & Episcopum*

Euseb. demonst. Euang. l. 1. c. 9.

Epiph. Hær. 29. & in compendiar.

Y
&

*& Hypodiaconum : maximè vbi sinceri sunt Canones
Ecclesiastici . At dices mihi, omnino in quibusdam locis
adhuc liberos gignere, & Presbyteros, & Diaconos, &
Hypodiaconos . At hoc non est iuxta Canonem, sed
iuxta hominum mentem, quæ per tempus elanguit. Nam
quod decentius est, id semper Ecclesia per spiritum sanctum bene disposita videns, statuit apparare, vt cultus
diuini indistracti Deo perficerentur .* And he maketh
this a commaundement in scripture. *Si populo præcipit Sanctus Apostolus, dicens, vt ad tempus vacent
orationi : quanto magis Sacerdoti idem præcipit? vt
indistractus sit, inquam, ad vacandum secundum Deum
Sacerdotio, quod in spiritualibus necessitatibus ac vsi-
bus perficitur.*

But if we should allowe, which these holy Fathers both of the Greeke & Latine Church would
not doe, that the chastity of Bishops, Preists, and
Deacons is not commaunded in scriptures, but that
the scriptures onely commend it for the more perfect and better duly to execute those sacred functions, as all both Catholiks and Protestants agree,
it is without question, that the vniuersall Church
of Christ hath euen by these Protestants most religiously decreed, and commaunded Ecclesiasticall
men to liue in chastity. And they contradict and
condemne themselues herein, in their next article
but one in these words: *Whosoeuer through his priuate
Iudgment, willingly and purposely doth openly breake
the traditions and ceremonies of the Church, which be
not repugnant to the word of God, and be ordained and
approued by common authority, ought to be rebuked o-
penly, as hee that offendeth against the common order of
the Church.*

Therefore the continent and chaste life, and profession

1. Cor. 7.

Prot. Artic. 34.

fession of the Cleargie being confessed by all both Catholiks, and Protestants, not to be repugnant to the word of God, but most conformable vnto it: And both commaunded, generally receaued, approued and practised, not onely by all commaunding cheife Churches, but through out the whole Catholike world; must needs be maintained. And our Protestants confessing this, and with priuiledge writing, *the auncient Fathers so receauing it from the, that went before them, taught; That vowes of chastitie, and single life in Preists, is to be obserued by tradition.* The doctrine taught in the article cannot be true, nor the liberty therein allowed, lawfull, but wantonly licentious, and damnable.

Coucl.Exam.
p.64.65.114.
feild pag. 138.
l.3.cap.29.
Middleton.
Papiston. p.
134.

The XXV. Chapter.

The 33. 34. Articles examined, an in whatsoeuer repugnant to the doctrine of the Church of Rome, thus condemned.

THeir 33. next article intituled, *of excommunicate persons, how they are to be auoided*, containeth nothing contrarie to the doctrine or practise of the Church of Rome, as is manifest in these the verie words thereof. *That person, which by open denuntiation of the Church, is rightly cut of from the vnity of the Church, and excommunicate, ought to be taken of the whole multitude of the faithfull, as an heathen and publican, vntill he be openly reconciled by pennance, and receaued into the Church by a Iudge, that hath authority thereto.*

Therefore I passe it ouer, and come to the next 34. article, intituled: *Of the traditions of the Church.*

Y 2

and

and followeth in these words: *It is not necessary, that traditions, and ceremonies be in all places one, or vterly like: for at all times they haue beene diuers, & chaunged according to the diuersity of contries, times, and mens manners, So that nothing be ordained against Gods word. Whosoeuer through his priuate Iudgment, willingly and purposely doth openly breake the traditions, and ceremonies of the Church, which be not repugnant to the word of God, and be ordained and approued by common authority, ought to be rebuked openly, that others may feare to doe the like, as he that offendeth against the common order of the Church, and hurteth the authority of the magistrate, and woundeth the consciences of the weake brethren.*

Hitherto this article seemeth to haue litle or no opposition to the Church of Rome, but it may be passed ouer with silence. The rest of it immediatelie thus followeth. *Euery particular and nationall Church hath authority to ordaine, chaunge, and abolish ceremonies, or rites of the Church ordained onely by mans authority, So that all things be done to edifying.*

This clause is euidentlie false and prophane in it selfe, for making euery particular Church, many thousands such being in the world, to be supreame iudge & sentencer, not onely to ordaine, chauge, & abolish ceremonies, and rites of the vniuersall Catholike Church, but to haue ouerruling authority to decree and commaund, what is fit, or fittest for edification, taketh away all possible hope of edification, and bringeth most certaine destruction, confusion, and desolation, by making so many thousands of Supreame Iudges in these doubts, as there be particular Churches, which is a thinge most foolish and irreligious to affirme, and vnpossible fible to be acted. Further it is directly opposite & repugnant to their owne 19. and 20. articles before of the Church and authoritie thereof. In the 19. article they teach that all particular Churches euen the cheifest haue erred *not onely in their liuing & manner of ceremonies, but also in matters of faith.*

Therefore by these Protestants, wee may neither admit so many, or any one such erring, & false Iudge in such things. Neither by their doctrine may wee stand, to the censure of any particular nationall Church, but onely of the one Catholike militant Church of Christ, which as it is euer by that article of our Creede, *I beleeue the holy Catholike Church,* holy and vnspotted from errour, so by these men in the same article it is thus assigned to be our onely true Iudge in these affaires. *The visible Church of Christ is a congregation of faithfull men, in the which the pure word of God is preached, and the Sacramēts be dayly ministred, according to Christs ordināce, in all those things, that of necessity, are requisite to the same.*   Artic. 19.

And in their next article of the same one onely Church, thus they decree, in these words: *of the authority of the Church. The Church hath power to decree rites, or ceremonies, and authority in Controuersies of faith.* And their best writers haue published with their common and best allowance, this sentence in this Question, *The primatiue Councels haue condemned them as heretikes, onely for being stiffely obstinate in this kinde,* of denying the ceremonies of the Church. They exemplifie thus in Aerius: *Aerius condemned the custome of the Church. For this his rash and inconsiderate boldnesse, in cōdemnig the vniuersall Church of Christ, was iustly condemned.*   Couell. Mod. exam. p.65.

Feild l.3. cap. 29 pag.138.
Couel. exam. pag.

The custome ceremonie and tradition which

this heretike denied, and was therefore by thefe men, iuſtlie condemned, was as they confeſſe, *naming the deade at the altare, and offering the ſacrifice of Euchariſt for them.*

This is but a ceremony by them, becauſe they contend, it is not contained is ſcripture, nor may be proued thereby, as they likewiſe haue pretended for all other things, which their Articles before haue reiected, both in Sacraments and other doctrines, and cuſtomes, which I haue proued againſt them, and doe leaue them as alterable ceremonies, vpon that feeble and vaine pretence. Vnder this pretence they haue taken away all our Miſſals, or orders of holie Maſſe, vſed in all Churches, with their religious ceremonie from the Apoſtles time, as I haue proued before. So they haue done by all rituals, and ceremonials, about the miniſtring the holy Sacraments and brought in their places the childiſh and womanlie deuiſes of a named *communion booke* by yong King Eduard 6. and Queene Elizabeth, *and an other named and ſtiled by them, The forme, and manner, of making and conſecrating Biſhops, Preiſts, and Deacons,* quite omitting all other orders euer vſed in all Churches from Chriſts time, and theſe fashions neuer vſed before by their owne cõfeſſion by anie Chriſtian Britans, Saxõs, French, or others in this Kingdome, or all the world, but, to vſe their owne words, in theſe articles, *lately ſet fourth in the time of Eduard the ſixt, and confirmed at the ſame time by authority of Parlament,* the ſecond yeare of the aforenamed King Edward. He then being about eleuen yeares old, a farre to yonge cenſurer, Iudge, and condemner of all Churches with their holie, vniuerſallie receaued ceremonies,

Communion Booke, and Booke of Conſecrat. of King Edu. 6. Franc. Maſon and the Prot. of their conſecrat. in Mat. Parker. Prot. art. 36. infra. Stat. in parlamento. an. 2. Eduardi 6.

to bring in so straunge and childish an Innouation.
We are assured by the Apostolike men of this first
age, and others, that euen from the Apostles, there
were manie particular ceremonies deliuered to be
immutably vsed in all Churches.

Thus S. Clement, and S. Dionisius the Areopagite, with diuers others deliuer of hallowing oyle
and water to heale diseases, driue away deuils, and
and like effects settinge downe the verie manner
how to sanctifie them. *Domine Deus Sabaoth, Deus
virtutum, qui dedisti aquam ad bibendum, & oleum ad
exhilarandum faciem, in exultationem lætitiæ, ipse
etiam nunc sanctifica per Christum hanc aquā,& oleum,
ex nomine eius qui obtulit, & tribue ei vim sanandi &
depellendi morbum, fugandi dæmones, expellendi insidias, per Christum spem nostram.* And by Apostolike
authority commaunde those ceremonies especially
of holy water, to be perpetuallie vsed by Preists in
all Churches, *aquam sale conspersam populis benedici-
mus, vt ea cuncti aspersi sanctificentur & purificentur,
Quod & omnibus Sacerdotibus faciendum esse mandamus.* So auncient was this holie ceremonie of san-
ctifying water and salt, so cōtinuall generall and inuiolable, which our Protestants themselues thus
acknowledge. *Alexander Romanus aquam admixto
sale precibus bene dicendam, eamque & in templo,& domi ad Satanam propellendum, & ad peccata tollenda,
seruari iussit.*

So it was in hallowing the water of baptisme, S.
Clement and others deliuering the verie manner
thereof: *deprecetur Sacerdos instante baptismo. Et dicet: Aspice è Cœlo & sanctifica hanc aquam; tribue gratiam & vim, & qui baptizatur secundum mandatum
Christi, cum eo crucifixus, commortuus, consepultus &*

*Clem. Rom.
Apost. const.
lib. 8. cap. 29.
Dion. Areop.
Ecclesiastic.
Hierarc. c. 2.*

*Alexander
Pap. 1. epistol.
omnes orth.*

*Robert. Barn.
l. de vit. Pont.
Roman. in A-
lexandro 1.*

*Clem. const.
Apost. l. 7. ca.
43. & l. 8. c. 35.*

Y 4

con-

Cap. 42.

confutatus ſit, in adoptionem, quæ in eo ſit, vt mortuus quidem ſit peccato, viuat autem iuſtitiæ. There he de-liuereth alſo, the forme, and order, of hallowing Chriſme to annoint the baptized. *Benedicitur oleum à Sacerdote in remiſſionem peccatorum.*

Cap. 41.

Cap. 23. ep.3.
conſt. Apoſt.
l.3.c.16.10.
Iuſtinus queſ.
137.
Miſſa. ſs. Mar-
ci. Clem. côſt.
Apoſt. l.8. c.12
Ciprianus ep.
63 Miſſ S. Ia-
cob. Alexand.
i ep.1 Iuſtin.
orar. ad Ant.
pium Ireneus
l.4 c.57. lib.5.
cap. 2
Dion Areop.
l. Eccl. Hier.
c.43. Clem.
conſt. Apoſt.
l.3. c.6. Ignat.
epiſt. ad Eph
Iren. l 4 c.20.
c.34. Euariſt.
apud Burchar.
l i. cap 27.
Pius r. apud
eund l.5. c.47
l.3 c.72. Tom.
1 conç. &c.
Clem. can. A
poſt. 72. ep.2.

There he deliuereth the abrenuntiation which was made beſore baptiſme. *Abrenuntiatio ſathanæ & operibus eius, pompis, cultui, Angelis, & machina-tionibus eius, & omnibus quæ ſubipſo ſunt.* He deli-uereth the annointing of the baptized, *vnges oleo ſanĉto caput eorum, qui baptizantur, ſiue viri ſint, ſiue mulieres.* It was Dominica Traditio, the Tradition euen from Chriſt, that in the chalice water ſhould be mixed with the wine to be offered, *ne quid aliud fiat à nobis, quàm quod pro nobis Dominus Prior fecerit, vt calix qui in commemorationem eius offertur, mixtus vino offeratur.* The Apoſtolike writers of this age aſſure vs, there were altars, and they conſecrated, to conſecrate and offer vpon them, the bleſſed and perpetuall ſacrifice of Chriſts body and blood, and how they were conſecrated as now they are, with holy oyle. *Diuini altaris conſecrationem ſanĉtiſſimo-rum myſteriorum lex ſacratiſſimi vnguenti caſtiſſimis infuſionibus perficit.* And deliuer the verie manner with incenſe and other ceremonies, *Pontifex vbi orationem ſanĉtam ſuper diuinum altare peregit, ex ipſo incenſum adolere inchoans, omnem plani ambitum cir-cuit. Demum ad ſanĉtum altare iterum rediens, pſalmo-rum incipiens melos. Qui verò ipſius ordinis præcipui ſunt, vnà cum Sacerdotibus ſanĉtum panem & bene-dictionis calicem ſanĉtis altaribus imponunt.* So they write of chalices, patens, and veales hallowed: *vas aureum, vel argenteum, vel velum ſanĉtificatum ne-mo amplius in ſuum vſum conuertat hoc enim ſit contra ius, & contra leges.*

So

So of the holie veſtiments of Biſhops, Preiſts, Deacons, Subdeacons, and others of the Cleargie: *Sacris induti veſtimentis.* So our Proteſtants them- ſelues confeſſe : *Anacletus*, *Sacerdotem ſacrificatu- rum, miniſtros veſtibus ſacris indutos, conteſtes & cu- ſtodes ſibi adhibere ordinauit. Epiſcopus verò vt plures miniſtros ſibi in ſacris faciendis adiungat.* I haue ſpo- ken of diuers others before, and ſhall remember more in the 36. *of conſecration of Biſhops, and mini- ſters, hereafter.*

Clem. ep. 2,
Anac. ep. 1.
Robert. Bar-
nes l. de vit.
Pontif Rom.
in Anacleto.

And our auncient monuments are witneſſes, that as other nations', ſo all the Churches of Britaine did in the Britans time, receaue and followe theſe manners, and ceremonies euen by authoritie of the Romane Church. *Omnes Britannicæ Eccleſiæ mo- dum, & regulam Romana authoritate acceperunt.* Therefore moſt certaine it is, that euerie particular and nationall Church, hath not, againſt this ar- ticle, *authority to ordaine, chaunge and aboliſh ſuch ce- remonies or rites of the Churche as the Proteſtants of England haue done.*

Manuſcr. ant.
in vit. S. Da-
uidis. Capgr.
Catal. in eo-
dem.

The XXVI. Chapter.

The 35. 36. articles, intituled, of homilies, and of con- ſecration of Biſhops, and miniſters, thus exa- mined and condemned.

Their next 35. article intituled *of homilies*, doth onely receaue and allowe to be read, in their Proteſtant Church 2. Bookes of homilies, one ſet fourth in the time of King Eduard the ſixt, the other in the beginning of Queene Elizabeth her Reigne. Of which the reader may eaſilie giue cenſure, ac- cording

cording to that is said and proued in the former articles, for whereinsoeuer either of those 2. bookes,
any homilie, in them, on anie part point or doctrine
in anie one of them all doth differ from the first A-
postolike Catholike true doctrine inuinciblie
proued before, those bookes, homilies, parcels, or
assertions of them, are vtterlie to be reiected and
renounced. Which the verie times themselues of
their publication, the condemned erroneous dayes
of that King, and Queene, and their Protestant
composers, and publishers, likewise condemned
for their false teaching, and writing doe manifest
vnto vs.

Their 36. article, *of Consecration of Bishops, and
ministers,* is thus. *The booke of consecration of Archbishops, and Bishops, and ordering of Preists, and Deacons, lately set for the in the time of Edward the sixt, and
confirmed at the same time by authoritie of parliament,
doth conteine all things necessary, to such consecration,
and ordering, neither hath it any thinge, that of it selfe is
superstitious, or vngodly. And therefore whosoeuer
are consecrated or ordered according to the rites of that
booke, since the second yeare of the a forenamed King
Edward, vnto this time, or hereafter shall be consecrated, or ordered according to the same rites, we decree all
such to be rightly, orderly, and lawfully consecrated and
and ordered.* Hitherto this article, which in euery
part thereof is fully confuted before, in my Examination of their 23. *Article intituled of ministring in
the congregation.* Where I haue demonstratiuely
proued, that they neither haue any true lawfull
Iurisdiction, or ordination, among them.

But to do a worke of Supererogation in this so
much concerning the standing or ouerthrowe of
                                                            our

our Proteſtants whole religion quite ouerthrowne by this one diſpute if they haue no rightly, orderly and lawfully conſecrated Biſhops, Preiſts or Deacons I further thus demonſtrate. Firſt then if the decree of this Article, as they terme it, were to be accepted, and receaued for a iuſt and lawfull decree, yet the firſt Proteſtant Biſhops, Preiſts, and Deacons in Queene Elizabeth her time, from which all that now bee in England, or haue beene ſince then, cannot be ſaide to be rightly orderly and lawfully conſecrated and ordered by this verie Article it ſelfe. For that ſuppoſed booke of King Edward the ſixt, being abrogated, and taken away by Queene Maryes lawes, and not afterward receaued by the Proteſtant lawes of Queene Elizabeth, vntill in thes Articles in the yeare of Chriſt 1562. as their date is, Queene Elizabeth beginning her Reigne on the 17. day of Nouember in the yeare 1558. all their firſt pretended Biſhops, Preiſts, and Deacons, muſt needs be vnrightly, vnorderly, and vnlawfully made, though by that booke of King Eduard: becauſe there was no Proteſtant Right, Order, or lawe, to make or admitte any into ſuch places by that booke not approued, or allowed by any Proteſtant Right, Order or lawe, all that time. Againe the firſt Proteſtant conſecration, or admittance of any, to bee a Biſhop by that booke, or order in Queene Elizabeth her Reigne, was on the 17. day of December, in her ſecond yeare, as they pretend from their Regiſter of Matthew Parker. But their owne both priuate and publike Authorities proue, that both Matthew Parker their firſt Proteſtant Archbiſhop, and others were receaued, and allowed for Archbiſhops

Booke of Articl. an. 1562.

Franc. Maſon. of conſecrat. Regiſtr. Matt. Parkeri. Butler ep. de conſecrat. miniſtr. Sutcl. ag. D. Kell. pag. 5.

Franc. God-
win catal. of
Bishops in
Durham 58.
Cutberth
Tunstoll.

hops and Bishops long before that time. Francis
Godwyn a Bishop among them saith, Matthew
Parker was Archbishop of Canterburie in the moneth of Iuly before, about 6. Months before their
first pretended consecration one the 17. of December.

Stow their historian then liuing and writing
testifieth, that the same Matthew Parker, Barlowe, Scorie, and Grindall were allowed and receaued for Bishops in the moneth of August the 9.
day in publik solemnities. The publik Iniunctions
of that Queene stiled, *Iniunctions giuen by the Queenes Maiestie, Anno Domini 1559. the first of the Reigne
of our Soueraigne lady Queene Elizabeth, proue the
same in diuers Iniunctions.* No man can say thes
were onely Bishops Elect, and not perfectly allowed, or admitted for true Bishops. For by the
statute of King Henry 8. an. 25. reuiued by Queene Elizabeth in her first parlament anno 1. cap. 1.
consecration must be within twenty dayes of election. And their common consent in their greate
Theater is, that they were compleately allowed
Bishops, cōsecrated (as they tearme that allowance
many moneths before. *D. Parker was consecrated
Archbishop of Canterbury, and of yorke D. Yong in
steade of Heath, who refused the oath, and so of others.
Then went forth commissioners to suppresse those mo-
nasteryes restored by Queene Mary & to cast out Images
sette vpp in Churches.* So hath Hollinshed, with
others, So in that Queenes pulike Iniunctions.

Thes commissions and commissioners being
thus after those Protestant Bishops made or allowed went out so soone, that as their histories
confesse, the religious howses were suppressed,
Prote-

Stow Histor.
in Queene
Elizab. an.
cius 1.

Iniunction:
Elizab. Regin.
an. 1. Regin.
Iniunct 8. 28.
30. 51 53.

Statut. an. 25
Henr. 8. an. 1.
Elizab. c. 1.

Theater of
great Brit. l.
9. cap. 24.
col. 20.

Hollinsh. hist.
of Engl. an. 1.
Elizabeth. In-
iunct. of Q.
Elizab. In-
iunct. 23.

Proteſtant miniſters were putte into weſtminſter in place of monks, all Church Images were pulled downe and to ſpeake in their owne words, *on the euen of S. Bartholomew, the day and the morrow after were burned in Paules Church yarde, Cheape, and diuers other places of the citie of London, all the Roodes, and other Images of the Churches, in ſome places the coapes, veſtiments, altar cloathes, bookes, banners, Sepulchres, and rood lofts were burned.* The verie Iniunctions teſtifie, that there were compleately receaued for Biſhops diuers moneths before that 17. day of December both in the See of Conterburie, yorke and in the other Dioceſſes, with ample and full Epiſcopall power. Therefore thes pretended Biſhops could not poſſibly bee made but onely by a womanly preſumed vayne, and fruſtrate authoritie, in ſuch things. Neither could any Regiſter called Parkers Regiſter be ſo termed, except he had beene accepted and reputed for Archbiſhop before.

And all the firſt Proteſtant citers of this Regiſter, whether Matthew Parker himſelfe, as it is alleadged in his booke ſtiled *Antiquitates Britannicæ* as Doctour Butler, Doctour Sutcliſſe, their Biſhop Godwyn, and Frauncys Maſon, do differ one from an other, in citing thereof. And whereas the printed Booke of Parkers *Antiquitates Britannicæ* is the firſt that mentioneth any ſuch pretended conſecration of him, and the reſt, and the others ſeeme to borrowe this from thence: In the old manuſcript of that booke which I haue ſeene and diligently examined, there is not any mention or memorie at all, of any ſuch Regiſter, or conſecration of either Matthew Parker or any one of thoſe

preten-

Stowe and howes hiſtor. in an. 1. of Q. Elizab.

Iniunct. 8. 30. 51.

Antiquitat. Brit. Hanouię 1605. Butler ep. ae conſec. miniſt. Sutcliffe contr. Kell. Godw catal. of Biſh. camterbur. in Mat. Parker. & alijs. Franc. Maſō booke of conſ. &c.

pretended Protestant Bishops, as the obtruded Register speaketh of. Neyther was there any one of the pretended consecratours of Matthew Parker, from whome all the rest do clayme ordination, a true and lawfull Bishop, by Protestant pro-ceedings: Thes they name vnto vs: *william Bar-lowe, Iohn Scory, Miles Couerdale, Iohn Hodgeskins, by thefe Matthew Parker was consecrated Archbishop of Canterbury the feuententh day of December, in the yeare 1559.*

Franc. Ma-
fon booke of
confecrat.
Pag. 127.

Two of thes 4. namely Couerdale, and Hod-geskins, were neuer allowed for Bishops in all Queene Elizabeth her time, as the fame pretended Register, the printed *Antiquitates Britannicæ,* God-wyne, Mafon, and others of them confeffe, confef-fing alfo that the other two were but Bishops elect, *Barlowe elect of Chichefter, Scory elect of Hereford.* But all men graunt both Catholiks and Proteftants, that men onely elect Bishops, not confecrated, or admitted, cannot confecrate Bishops much leffe an Archbishop Metropolitan. And Scory had beene adiudged before publickly to be no Bishop. And Barlowe if he had beene a true Bishop, nei-ther would, nor could in his owne Iudgement con-fecrate a Bishop. For as thes men acknowledge both this Barlowe and Couerdale alfo held this horrible opinion againft Epifcopall Order.

Barlowe and
Couerdale
apud Bal. l.
Image of
both Church.

The names of blasphemie againft the Lord, and his Chrift. What els is Pope, Patriarke, Metropolitane, primate Archbishop, Diocefan and fuch like, but very names of blafphemy? Here is not one true confecra-tour. Yet thes men in their pretended ordination of Bishops neceffarily require to the admitting of any fuch Bishop, efpecially an Archbishop, both

the

the preſence & concurrence of a lawfull true Archbiſhop and others ſuch Biſhops as their owne pretended Rite and booke of conſecrating Biſhops
doth thus plainely expreſſe : *Then the Archbiſhop
and Biſhops ſent, ſhall lay their hands, vpon the head
of the elected Biſhop, the Archbiſhop ſaying. Take the
holy ghoſt, &c. And it proueth further in theſe words,
It is euident vnto all men diligently reading holy ſcripture, and auncient Authours , that from the Apoſtles
time, there haue beene thes orders of miniſters in Chriſts
Church, Biſhops, Preiſts, and Deacons. Therefore to
the intent thes Orders ſhould be continued, and reuerently vſed in the Church of England it is requiſite,
that no man, not being at this preſent, Biſhop, Preiſt,
nor Deacon, ſhall execute any of them, except he be called, tryed, examined and admitted, according to the
forme hereafter following.* Which is that booke of
King Edward the ſixt receaued in this article and
approued by their greateſt warrants, parlament,
Princes Supreamacie, and publike practiſe among
them.

And therefore howſoeuer either with, by, or
without this booke, forme, and manner of King
Edward, their firſt Proteſtant pretended Archbishop, Matthew Parker, maker and allower of all
ſuch after, as they freely confeſſe, was made, his
making, and admittance was fruſtrate, inualid,
voide and of noe force by their owne cenſure, and
doome againſt themſelues;& ſo of all others made
by him no Biſhop pretending or clayming that
honour, dignitie and office after by that vaine,
idle, and vnpoſſible Title , to challendge to haue
that, or any other thing, from him, or them, which
neither had it for themſelues, or to giue to others.

And

Prot. forme
and manner
of making
Biſhops
Preiſts and
miniſt. Titul.
conſecrat. of
Biſhops in
præfat.

And this I haue proued before from the Apostolike men of this age and from the Apostles themselues, that a Bishop cannot bee consecrated but
by true and vndoubted Bishops. *Episcopum manda-*
mus ordinari à tribus Episcopis, vel ad minus à duobus:
non licere autem ab vno vobis constitui. And againe:
Episcopus à tribus vel duobus Episcopis ordinetur. Si
quis ab vno ordinetur Episcopo, deponatur ipse, & qui
eum ordinauit. This is sette downe for an Apostolicall decree. Now lette vs come to King Edwards
booke so dignified in this article, and particularily
examine, and disproue the validitie, or sufficiency
of that forme in euery point thereof.

And first whereas it maketh mention onely of
Bishops, Preists, and Deacons to haue beene in the
Church from the Apostles time, This holie time
assureth vs, of all other orders now vsed in the Catholike Church, to haue beene also in those dayes
in vse, and practise, Subdeacons, Acolythists, Exorcists, Lectours and Ostiarij, with their particular
and seuerall offices, duties, consecration, or admittance, to those degrees, and that no man might be
a Bishop Preist or Deacon, except he had first receaued those orders, *nisi prius fuisset lector, deinde*
exorcista, & postea caperet onus Acolithi, vt acciperet
onus Subdiaconi, & deinde ad diaconatus honorem per-
tingeret. By their consecration they were ordeined
to assist and minister at the holie sacrifice of Masse,
a Subdeacon for the holie vessels, calice, paten,
cruetts: *Tribue ei spiritum sanctum vt vasa ad mi-*
nistrandum tibi, Domine Deus, facta dignè attrectet.
An Acolithus to light candels and prepare; and
minister wine for the sacrifice of masse: *accipiat*
ceroferarum cum cereo, vt sciat se ad accendenda Eccle-
                                                    siæ

Clem. const.
Apost. l. 3. c.
20. Anacl. ep.
2. Clem.
const. Apost.
l. 8. c. 33.

Clem. const.
Apost. l. 3. c.
11. l. 8. c. 21.
22. 28. ep. 2.
Ignat. ep. ad
Antioch. ep.
ad Phila-
delphien. ep.
ad Philippen-
ses Anacl. ep.
2. Synod.
Rom. sub
Syluestr. c. 7.
11. Canis ep.
ad fælicem c.
6 Clem.
const. Apost.
l. 2. c. 61.
Clem. Supr.
l. 8. const.
Apost. c. 21.
concil. corth.
4. c. 5. 6. 7.
8. 9.

siæ luminaria mancipari: accipiat & vrceolum va-
cuum, ad suggerendum vinum in Euchariſtiam ſan-
guinis Chriſti. An exorciſt receaued the booke of
Exorciſmes, and power againſt deuils: *accipiat*
de manu Epiſcopi libellum,in quo ſcripti ſunt exorciſmi,
dicente ſibi Epiſcopo: accipe & commenda memoriæ,
& habeto poteſtatem imponendi manus, ſuper energu-
menos. So of Lectour and Oſtiarius. All thes be
wanting in this booke of King Edward, and this
Proteſtant Religion, and all is wanting in it for
which they were ordeined, except deuils and poſ-
ſeſſed perſons. They may well want both them
all Biſhops, Preiſts, and Deacons, alſo, as they do.
For firſt their pretended booke of conſecration
giueth a Deacon onely authoritie to reade the
ghoſpell in their Church, for allthough their pretended Biſhop layeth his hands one the heade of
euerie ſuch parſon, at his admittance to that office,
and ſayeth vnto him: *Take thou authoritie to exe-*
cute the office of a Deacon, in the Church of God com-
mitted vnto thee. Yet they preſently interpret,and
limitte this office, to be onely confined in reading
the ghoſpell in thes words. *Take thou authoritie*
to reade the ghoſpell in the Church of God. And ſuch
is their practiſe, extending a Deacons office no
further.

No true cler-
gie man a-
mong Prote-
ſtants of En-
gland: and
firſt, no Dea-
con.
The Engliſh,
Prot. forme
of making
Biſh. pr. and
Deac Titul,
Deacons.

And they obſtinatelie denie,that he hath power,
or office to aſſiſt either Biſhop,or Preiſt in the holy
Sacrifice of Chriſts bleſſed bodie,and blood,as that
either Preiſt or Biſhop may, or can conſecrate and
offer the ſame. We finde both the doctrine and practiſe of this firſt apoſtolike age,to haue beene o-
therwiſe,and the cheifeſt office of a Deacon, as the
very Greeke name it ſelfe ſtill teſtifieth to be as Ca-

Z   tholiks

tholiks ſtill vſe it, to miniſter vnto, and aſſiſt the Biſhop or Preiſt in his holy Sacrifice.

Miſſ. S. Petri, S. Iacobi, S. Marci. Clem. Conſt. Apoſt. l. 3. c. 20. l. 8. c 28.

So it is plainely witneſſed in the old Maſſes and Miſſals aſcribed to S. Peter, S. Iames, S. Marke, and others. S. Clement from the Apoſtles ſaith : *Diaconus miniſtret Epiſcopo & Presbyteris. oblatione ab Epiſcopo aut Presbytero facta, ipſe Diaconus dat populo, non tanquam Sacerdos, ſed tanquam qui miniſtrat presbyteris.* And expreſſelie teacheth, that it is the office and function of a Deacon thus to miniſter vnto

L. 3. c. 20. ſup.

Biſhops, and Preiſts, this onelie or principally, *Diaconus miniſtret Epiſcopo & Presbyteris, id eſt, agat Diaconum, & reliqua ne faciat.* And ſetting downe the whole forme, and Order of Maſſe, & ſacrifice vſed, and approued by the Apoſtles, Biſhops, and Preiſts in his time, euen from the beginning thereof, vnto the end, he bringeth in Deacons to performe their holie miniſtration and ſeruing therein. Praying to

Clem. ſupr. l. 8. c. 19.

God to accept that Sacrifice. *Deaconus pronunciet. Rogamus Deus. Pro dono oblato Domino Deo, oremus, Vt Deus ſuſcipiat illud in cæleſte altare ſuum, in odorem ſuauitatis.* For all the people of God liuing, and deade. *Pro vniuerſo Eccleſiæ cætu. Pro ijs qui in fide quieuerunt.*

Cap. 15.

They deliuer the breade and wine to be conſecrated, to the Biſhop or Preiſt, that ſaid Maſſe: *Diaconi offerant dona Epiſcopo ad altare.* They attend that nothing falleth into the chalices, *ne in pocula incidant.* At the time of conſecration, they

Cap. 20.

called vpon the people for attention. *Diaconus dicat, attendamus.*

They hold the conſecrated chalice, and confeſſe it to be the blood of Chriſt, the cuppe of life. *Diaconus teneat calicem, & quando tradit dicat, ſanguis Chriſti,*

Christi, calix vitæ. And after all had communicated, they take that which is left, and with reuerence preferue it. *Postquam omnes sumpserunt, accipiant Diaconi reliquias, & portent in pastiphoria.* And they said this prayer, testifying it was the pretious bodie and blood of Christ, which had beene there offered and receaued for remission of sinne and preseruation in pietie. *Diaconus dicat. Percepto pretioso corpore, & pretioso sanguine Christi, gratias agamus ei, qui dignos nos reddidit percipiendi sancta eius mysteria, & rogamus vt non in iudicium sed in salutem nobis fiant, in vtilitatem animæ & corporis, in custodiam pietatis, in remissionem peccatorum in vitam futuri saculi.* And as our Deacons now conclude and end Masse, with. *Ite Missa est.* So did they then with *Ite in pace. Et Diaconus dicat: Ite in pace.*

Cap. 20.21.

Cap. 23.

Thus from S. Clement, and the Apostles, by his relation. S. Denis the Areopagite is witnesse to the like, where testifying of the most holie Sacrifice of Christs bodie, and blood, as is proued from him before, he teacheth that as inferiour orders performed their duties therein, So the Deacons more high in degree, with the Preists more nearelie assisted at the altar about this blessed sacrifice. *Qui ipsius ordinis præcipui sunt, vnà cum Sacerdotibus sanctum panem, & benedictionis calicem sacrosanctis altaribus imponunt.*

Dion Areop. Eccl. Hierar, cap. 3.

So testifieth S. Ignatius writing to S. Hero a Deacon, that such as he being Deacons, did minister vnto Preists at Sacrifice, and that so did S. Stephen to S. Iames, and Preists in Hierusalem. *Sacerdotes sunt, tu Sacerdotem minister. Sacrificant, tu verò illis ministras, vt sanctus ille Stephanus Iacobo, & Presbyteris, qui erant Hierosolymis.* So of all Deacons in other

Ignat. epist. ad Heronem Diaconum.

Ep. ad Trallian. & ad Philadelph.

Z 2 ther

ther places. *Diaconi Imitatores Angelicarum virtu-*
tum, qui purum & inculpatum ministerium illis (Sa-
cerdotibus) exhibent, vt S. Stephanus beato Iacobo. And
for the dignitie of their ministrie in so great misteries ought to be honoured as Christ. *Oportet Dia-*
conis mysteriorum Christi ministris per omnia placere:
nec enim ciborum & potuum ministri sunt, sed Ecclesiæ
Dei administratores. Ipsi itaque tales sunt: at vos reue-
Epist. ad
Heron.
remini illos, vt Christum Iesum, cuius vicarij sunt. So
was saint Stephen, to saint Iames, saint Timothie, and
saint Linus, to saint Paul, saint Anacletus, and Clemens
to saint Peter . He that obeyeth them not, is an enemy
to God, and impure, and contemneth Christ, and diminisheth his ordinance. *Vt sanctus Stephanus beato Iacobo:*
Timotheus & Linus, Paulo: Anacletus & Clemens Pe-
tro. Qui his (Diaconis) non obedit, sine Deo prorsus, &
impurus est, & Christum contemnit, & constitutionem
eius imminuit. And speaking of the dignitie, of the
altare, and Sacrifice of Christians, wherein Dea-
Ignat. epist.
ad Ephesios.
cons with Bishops, and Preists, haue so excellent
ministration, he giueth charge to obey them, assuring vs, he that doth not so, disobeyeth Christ, and
is an abiect. *Enitimini subiecti esse Episcopo & presby-*
teris & Diaconis. Qui enim his obedit, obedit Christo,
qui hos constituit. Qui vero his reluctatur, reluctatur
Christo Iesu, qui autem non obedit filio, non videbit vi-
tam, sed ira Dei manet super eum. Præfractus enim,
contentiosus & superbus est, qui non obtemperat supe-
ribus.

S. Anacletus Deacon to S. Peter, as S. Ignatius
before hath proued, and made Preist by the same
greate Apostle, as he himselfe confesseth, and so perfectly knowing both the doctrine, and practise of
the Apostles did when he came to be Pope ordaine

as

as both Catholiks and Protestants acknowledge, *that Deacons in their holy vestiments should minister vnto Preists and Bishops in the solemne sacrifices. Sacerdotem sacrificaturum, ministros vestibus sacris indutos, adhibere ordinauit. Episcopus verò vt plures ministros in sacris faciendis adiungat.*

Anacletus ep. I. Robert. Barn.l. de vit. Pontif.Rom. in Anacleto.

This is the doctrine of all holie Fathers after, and of the whole Church of Christ, the first generall Councell of Nice receaued in this Kingdome declareth, that this was euer the rule and custome of Christs Church, *Regula & consuetudo,* that Deacons were ministers to Bishops in the holy sacrifice, and vnder Preists to helpe them in their Sacrifice, and not to offer sacrifice, or giue the bodie of Christ to Preists that offer it. *Peruenit ad sanctum concilium, quòd in locis quibusdam & ciuitatibus, presbyteris Sacramenta diaconi porrigant. Hoc neque regula neque consuetudo tradidit, vt hi qui offerendi sacrificij non habent potestatem, his qui offerunt corpus Christi porrigant. Hæc amputentur & maneant Diaconi intra propriam mensuram, scientes quia Episcoporum ministri sunt, Presbyteris autem inferiores sunt.*

Conc. Nicen. cap.14.

This is the cheife office of a Deacon, so his name in Hebrewe, in Greeke & Latine signifie, so his dutie to serue at the altare, to minister there, to the Bishop or Preist, to prepare it, to propose breade and wine to be consecrated, and minister in the whole sacrifice, So write our most auncient writers of these things from the oldest monuments, and authorities. *Diaconus Græcè, Hebraicè leuita, Latinè assumptus vel minister interpretatur, assumptus quia assumitur, id est, eligitur ad seruitium altaris: minister, quia ministrat Presbytero. Ponit linteum in altare, ponit panem & calicem, quæ nec mittendi, nec auferendi*

Albin. flacc. Alcuin.l.de diuin offic. in Diacono.

Z 3   *habet*

habet potestatem Presbyter, si Diaconus adfuerit. Sicut Presbytero officium consecrandi competit, ita Diacono ministrandi. Therefore, howsoeuer wee expounde this pretended Protestant making, or admitting Deacons, that they receaue their power or office, when their pretended Bishop giueth to them the new Testament and saith vnto them, *Take authority to reade the Ghospell in the Church of God; or when he saith, Take thou authority to execute the office of a Deacon in the Church of God committed vnto thee:* or both together, here is no true consecration of a Deacon in their owne proceedings, nor Deacon so made, if their pretended consecrating Bishop were a true & a lawfull Bishop, for first of giuing the new testament and power to reade the ghospell, this cannot be the full and lawfull manner to make Deacons. The first Deacons in the lawe of Christ being made otherwise by the Apostles, as the Scripture witnesseth, and before the new testament or anie part thereof was written, to be giuen to them, or for them to reade the ghospels, then vnwritten, and vnpossible to be read, by them or any at that time, or longe after.

The other of taking authority to execute the office of a Deacon cannot be the manner, for first no man can truely and lawfully execute that, wherein he hath no power, and here is no power of a Deacon giuen in all this their forme, and order. And their owne parlaments and highest authorities in their religion doe not onely disable any man in England, Deacon or other to execute the office of a Deacon, such as the Apostles and Apostolike men of this age haue deliuered, vnto vs, but make it an offence of high treason, for any lawfull Deacon, either

ther

Act. 6.

Statut. in parliament an 27. Elizabethæ Reg. ad 1. Iacobo.

ther to execute that office in any Church, Chappell or other place, or to be in England without executing any such office or function at all, euen reading the ghospell, or any other. And so if we ioyne this Protestant pretended power to execute the offices of a Deacon, and reade the ghospell in the Church together, there is not the least power of a true Deacon thereby either giué, or permitted by them in all England vnto any such Deacon, to doe, or not doe such, or any dutie of that holy function. And thus much of Deacons.

Now it can be no question but the pretended Protestāt Ordination of Preists is altogether vaine, Idle and friuolous; for being so iuuincibly proued, that the cheifest and principall office and function of a Deacon is to assist and minister vnto Preists & Bishops in the holy Sacrifice of Christs blessed body and blood at Masse, such Sacrificing Preists, not heauing any such power before their consecration to holy Preisthood, must needs receaue it at that time, otherwise they should still remaine without it, as they did before. And our Protestants vtterly before denying all such sacrifice, and sacrificing power, and in this their pretended forme, and manner of consecration hauing no thing at all, to receaue or allowe it, but the quite contrary, and by their lawes so straungely persecuting sacrificing Preists, and Preisthood, this their fashió of making or ordering their pretended Preists, must needs be voyde, and frustrate, and they still remaine in that lay state, in this respect, wherein they were before, euen from their first birth into the world. Their Practise in this pretended consecration is this.

The Bishops, the Preists present shall lay their hands

seue-

No true Preist among English Protestants.

Prot. forme
and manner
of making &
consecr. Bish.
Preists and
Deac. Tit.
forme of Or-
der of Preists.

*seuerally vpon the heade of euery one, that receaueth or-
ders: The receauers humbly kneelinge vpon their knees,
and the Bishop saying. Reccaue the holy ghost, whose
sinnes thou docst forgiue they are are forgiuen, and whose
sinnes thou doest retaine, they are retained. The Bishop
shall deliuer to euery one of them, the Bible in his hand
saying. Take thou authority to preach the word of God,
and to minister the holy Sacraments in this congregation,
where thou shalt be so appointed.* Here is all their pretended consecration of Preists, so farre from all
meaning, or intention to conferre any sacrificing
power, or Preisthood, that before they come to
this article, in their 31. Article before they thus defined.

Prot. art. 31.
supr.

*The Sacrifices of Masses in the which it was common-
ly sayde, that the Preists did offer Christ for the quicke
and the deade, to haue remission of paine or guilt, were
blasphemous fables, and dangerous deceites.* In that
place I haue inuincibly proued against them, both
this Sacrifice and sacrificing Preisthood, and Preists
Institution. All his Apostles, and all consecrated
by them and their Successours were massing and
sacrificing Preists, all the Apostolike writers of this
first age gaue testimony to that doctrine and practise. All Masses Missales, or publike liturgies of
all Churches ascribed to the Apostles themselues,
and continued by continuall, neuer interrupted generall tradition beare witnesse vnto it. The holy
Prophets so described the Messias, by a perpetuall
holy Sacrifice to be offered in all places in his time,
that he should be a Preist after the order of Melchisedech teach and establish that Preisthood, neuer to end or ceafe in his Church. Thus taught the
most learned rabbines among the Iewes before
Christ,

Christ; So the Fathers and common practise of both Greeke and Latine Church with the best least learned Protestant writers; euen of England writing, and published by their publike allowance and authority, as I haue vndeniably proued in that article, and there made demonstration by all authothority, that Christ at his last Supper, when he onely did execute the act and office of his Preisthood, according to the order of Melchisedech, did ordaine his Apostles sacrificing massing Preists at that time, in expresse termes, set downe in holy Scripture, *hoc facite in meam commemorationem.*

To offer his consecrated holy body and blood in Sacrifice as he had done. So the Apostolike men of this first age assure vs. *Vbique offertur Deo oblatio munda, sicut testatus est: cuius corpus & sanguinem in vitam æternam offerimus. Quod Iudæi per inuidiam immolauerunt, putantes se nomen eius à terra abolere: nos causa salutis nostræ in ara sanctificata proponimus, scientes hoc solo remedio nobis vitam præstandam, & mortem effugandam. Hoc enim ipse Dominus noster iussit nos agere in mei commemoratione. Domine omnipotens potestatem Apostolis dedisti offerendi tibi sacrificium mundum & incruentum, quod per Christum constituisti, mysterium noui testamenti. Suis discipulis dans consilium primitias Deo offerre, cum, qui ex creatura panis est, accepit, & gratias egit dicens, hoc est corpus meum & calicem similiter, qui est ex ea creatura, quæ est secundum nos, suum sanguinem confessus est, & noui Testamenti nouam docuit oblationem, quam Ecclesia ab Apostolis accipiens in vniuerso mundo offert Deo.* This was the opinion, profession, and practise of the whole Christian worlde, in that generally confessed puer and vnspotted time, both by Catholiks, and Protestants.

Martial. ep. ad Burdegal. cast. 3. Clem. Const. Apost. l. 8. c. 3. Iustin. dialog. cum Triphon. Irenæus adu. hær. l. 4. c. 32 Euseb. l. 1 cap. 10. demon. Euang e-licar. Theodor. in c. 8. ad Hebræos. Alexa. l. ep. 1. cap. 4. Cyprian. l 2. epist. 3. ep. 63. Ambr. in Psal. 38. Gandentius tractat. 2. Aug. lib. 83. q. q. 61.

testants. And these men confessing that Christ did not in any other place of scripture giue this sacrificing Preistly power vnto his Apostles, the cheife founders of his Church, and yet being acknowledged before to be our high Preist, according to that Order of Melchisedech, and both to offer the Sacrifice thereof, and establish it for his perpetuall Preisthood and sacrifice, it cannot be said by any, but his Apostles were by him ordained sacrificing Preists at that time.

The words of the power hee then gaue them, *hoc facite:* do that which he in that preistly act and office, did or had done, being spoken by him, which had both ample power, and intention to giue and continue that preistly order, at and in his place and time of Sacrifice, and now no longer to continue with his disciples, be as significant of that power, as the words of consecrating true Preists, by true and lawfull Bishops, euer vsed in the Church of Christ. *Accipe potestatem offerre Sacrificium Deo, missasque celebrare, tam pro viuis, quàm pro defunctis. Receaue power to offer vpp sacrifice to God & celebrate Masse both for the liuing and deade.* For as I haue proued before, both Christ, and his Apostles so did, and left that preistly power, and practife to posteritie, for euer, to offer Sacrifice both for the liuing, and deade. And our Protestants themselues haue with publike allowance confessed it was the generall custome of the primatiue Church so to do, and such as impugned ordenied it, were iustly condemned for so doing. And they haue with Regall authoritie, and direction from King Iames published, that it was the Religion of the King, and the whole Protestant Church of England, *Hæc est Regis,*

Pont. Rom. in ordinat. Presbyteri.

If. Casaub. resp. ad Card. peron. pag. 51. 52. Middleton

Regis, hæc eſt fides Eccleſiæ Anglicanæ, that the fathers of the primatiue Church did acknowledge one ſacrifice in Chriſtian Religion, that ſucceeded in place of all the ſacrifices, in the lawe of Moſes. And the King with his Proteſtants agreed with the Catholiks in their opinion *de duplici ſacrificio, expiationis nempe, & commemorationis ſiue Religionis. Concerning two Kindes of ſacrifice, the one of expiation, for the world, the other commemoratiue or of Religion.* And this Sacrifice is the bodie of Chriſt in the Euchariſt, as Catholiks hold. *Nobis vobiſcum de obiecto conuenit. De hoc eſt, fide firma tenemus quod ſit. Præſentiam credimus, præſentiam inquam, credimus, nec minus quàm vos veram.*

Therefore to giue Preiſts power to offer this ſacrifice, there muſt needs be ſome conſecratorie words or forme to beſtowe it vpon them, which if we recurre to ſcripture, as thes men muſt do, we can finde nothing there, but thoſe words, of *hoc facite in meam commemorationem*, ſpoken at the ſacrifice time and place by Chriſt to thoſe he then ordeined ſacrificing Preiſts. And this is moſt plainely confeſſed by thes our Engliſh Proteſtants with common and publike warrant, both confeſſing that the order of the preiſthood in the lawe of Chriſt was to offer ſacrifice, this ſacrifice was the bodie and blood of Chriſt, he made his Apoſtles ſuch Preiſts, at his laſt ſupper, when he ſaide thoſe words vnto them: *Hoc facite in meam commemorationem. Do this is my commemoration. Ordinis poteſtatem intelligo ad conficiendam Euchariſtiam, & ſacrificij in cruce per Ieſum Chriſtum peracti memoriam celebrandam: ad quod Sacerdotium quoddam eſt neceſſarium. Ad hoc Sacerdotium promoti ſunt Apoſtoli*

papiſt omaſt. pag. 51, 92. 113. 44. 137. 138. morton appeale l. 3. cap. 13. ſect. 1. pag. 394. & cap. 13.

Marc. Anton. lib. 2. cap. 1. num. 3.

*ſtoli à Chriſto Domino, in vltima cæna, quando eis di-
xit: Hoc facite in meam commemorationem . Quando
Chriſtus Euchariſtiæ conficiendæ Apoſtolis dabat pote-*

cap. 3. pag. *ſtatem, dixit eis: Hoc facite in meam commemoratio-*
193. *nem, nimirum id quod me videtis nunc facere, & vos
facite: Hoc eſt ſumite panem, benedicite, frangite &
porrigite: ſimiliter & vinum, & conſequenter Apoſtoli ex ipſo facto Chriſti inſtructi, certè diuina Chriſti
inſtitutione dabant Euchariſtiam .* And they ſay that
Chiſt in thoſe words gaue power to his Apoſtles to
conſecrate or tranſubſtantiate breade into Chriſts
bodie, and wine into his blood, as he himſelfe had

cap. 4. pag. done. *Accepto pane gratias egit, & fregit, & dedit*
118. *eis dicens.* HOC EST CORPVS MEVM *, quod pro vobis
datur: Hoc facite in meam commemorationem . Panis
conſecrationem in Corpus Chriſti, & vini in ſanguinem, ipſe coram Apoſtolis fecit: eandem ipſi quoque vt,
facerent, frangerent, & darent, expreſſè mandauit.*

Thus haue our Proteſtants publiſhed with their
cheife authoritie . Which I haue inuincibly proued before, And the Apoſtles themſelues beſt witneſſes of their owne conſecration to preiſthood,
and how others are to be conſecrated thereto, ſo
teſtifie and direct as S. Clement their diſciple thus
Clem. conſt. recordeth from their owne words: *Quare vos quo-*
Apoſt. l. 5. *que ſuſcitato Domino offerte Sacrificium veſtrum, de*
cap. 20. *quo vobis præcepit per nos, dicens, hoc facite in meam
commemorationem.*

l. 8. conſt. The like teſtimonie is from them of themſelues
Apoſt. cap. 5. and other Preiſts before: *offerendo Sacrificium mundum & incruentum quod per Chriſtum inſtituiſti, my-
ſterium noui teſtamenti .* So haue others alſo before.
And to followe our Proteſtants Rule in expounding ſcriptures, by comparing places, and the new
teſta.

teſtament to preferre the Greeke Text, S. Paule maketh it plaine vnto vs euen in our Proteſtants proceedings, that thoſe words of Chriſt to his Apoſtles. *Do this in commemoration of mee, were* ſpoken vnto them onely, as Preiſts then conſecrated. For in S. Matthew and S. Marke they are not vſed at all, and in S. Luke, they are onely at the deliuery of Chriſts bodie, vnder the forme of bread, *hoc facite in meam commemorationem,* and not at the calice.

Mat. 26. Mar. 14. Luc. 22.

But S. Paule ſaith plainely, that he had receaued from our Lord, and ſo deliuered vnto others, before he wrote it, *Ego enim accepi à Domino quod & tradidi vobis,* and ſo writeth afterward, that Chriſt ſaid thoſe words to this Apoſtles twice, once at deliuering his bodie, the other time at the calice, yet it is euident before, and our Proteſtants haue ſo graunted, that lay people haue often communicated onely in one Kinde, which had neuer beene lawfull if this commaunde, and power in both had beene giuen to them; therefore it muſt needs be a power and commaunde onely to Preiſts at their holie ſacrifice, who onely in the holie Maſſe haue euer and in all places both conſecrated, offered, and there receaued in both Kindes, and no others ſo euer receaued at all times, and places, nor the Preiſts themſelues, as all writers Catholiks, and Proteſtants confeſſe. And this our Article Proteſtants themſelues in their pretended booke and forme of conſecration receaued in this Article, and other places, do thus acknowledge: *It is euident vnto all men diligently reading holy ſcripture and auncient Authours that from the Apoſtles time, there hath beene thes Orders of Miniſters, in Chriſts Church*

1. Cor. 11.

Prot. forme and Manner of Making Biſh. Preiſts. and Deac. in præf.

Church, Bishops, Preists, and Deacons, which offices were euermore had in such reuerent estimation, that no man by his priuate authoritie might presume to execute any of them, except he were first called, tryed, examined and knowne to haue such qualities, as were requisite for the same, and also by publike prayer, with imposition of hands, approued, and admitted there vnto. Where we finde it thus plainely and authoritatiuely with them confessed, that Bishops, Preists, and Deacons were euer in the Church, and truely and lawfully ordeined by such forme & Order of consecration, as was then vsed, and thes Preists as they haue confessed in thes their Articles before in thes words vsed *the sacrifices of Masses, in which it commonly said was, that the Preists did offer Christ for the quick & the dead, to haue remission of payne or gilt,* they are so farre from disallowing or disabling our Catholikly consecrating Massing Preists of the Roman Church, whom they make Traytours in England, to be truely and duely consecrated Preists, that if any of them for feare or any other wordly respects will ioyne with rhem in their new Church seruice or profession, he is allowed a minister with them without any further pretended order or admittance, and they dignifie their first Catholike ordination so much, that as they haue bestowed their greatest Church liuing vpon such, so they deduce and deriue their owne pretended ordination onely from such men, Matthew Parker, Iohn Scory, and Miles Couerdale, as they freely confesse. And yet all our Catholike Pontificals, or bookes of ordination do plainely proue, & testifie that our Preists being Deacons before, are consecrated Preists by those words of the Bishop: *Accipe potestatem offerre sacri-*

Prot. Artic. 31. supr.

Francis Mason booke of Consecr. Mat. Parker Print. Antiq. Britan. Sutcliff. & alij. Pont. Rom. in ordinat. Presbyteri.

sacrificium. Take power to offer sacrifice to God, and celebrate Masses both for the liuing and dead. And immediately before, he calleth such a parson *ordinandum* and *quem ordinat Episcopus*, a man to be ordered, and to whom the Bishop giueth preistly order, and presently after those words nameth him or them that were thus ordered, *ordinati Sacerdotes, Presbiteri ordinati, Preists that be ordered.* And being thus fully ordered before any other ceremonie vsed by Protestants or not, they celebrate the rest of the Masse euen consecrating the blessed bodie, and blood of Christ, with their consecratour Bishop, and as consecrated Preists. *Presbiteri ordinati post Pontificem in terra genuflexi habeant libros coram se, dicentes. Suscipe Sancte Pater &c. & omnia alia de missa, prout dicit Pontifex : qui tamen bene aduertat, quòd secretas morosè dicat, & aliquantulum altè, ita vt ordinati Sacerdotes possint secum omnia dicere, & præsertim verba consecrationis, quæ dici debent eodem momento per ordinatos, quo dicuntur per Pontificem.*

And to putte all things out of question in this matter. The scripture itselfe is euident witnesse, that the Apostles themselues were ordered Preists by those words of Christ vnto them, Do this in my commemoration, eqyiualent as I haue proued to the forme now vsed in the Roman Church recited, for all writers, Catholiks, and Protestants agree, that all the Apostles S. Thomas and the rest were true and most properly lawfull Preists, all our preisthood claimed and deduced from them, and that they were all present at his last supper, when he said the words, *do this* : vnto them. *Discubuit, & duodecim Apostoli cum eo. Discumbebat cum duo-* Luc. 22. Mat. 26. Marc. 14.

decim

decim discipulis suis . Dedit eis dicens HOC EST COR-
PVS MEVM, *quod pro vobis datur, hoc facite in meam
commemorationem.* But when he said those words to
his Apostles : *receaue the holie ghost, whose sinnes you
forgiue, they are forgiuen, and whose sinnes you reteyne,
they are reteyned.* From and by which thes our Protestants do clayme or pretend ordination . S. Iohn
the Euangelist then and there present doth witnes,
all were not there, and namely S. Thomas was
absent . *Thomas vnus ex duodecim non erat cum eis,
quando venit Iesus .* And so could not possibly be
made Preist then with those words . Yet all agree
he was a Preist as perfectly and fully as any Apostle . Agayne Iudas the Traitour was a Preist, present at the consecration in the last supper, of Christ,

Actor. c. 1.   and as S. Peter saith, *connumeratus erat in nobis , &
sortitus est sortem ministerij huius . Scriptum est in*
Psal. 68.   *libro psalmorum : & Episcopatum eius accipiat alter.
De loco ministerij & Apostolatus præuaricatus est Iudas .* Which is more then our Protestants pretend
for their pretended Preists, or ministers . Yet he
was haged & deade before Christ spooke the other
words, and so could not possibly be eyther made
Preist, or be present then . And S. Paule defining

Hebr. 5.   a Preist, whether of the lawe of Moyses, or Christ,
saith, euery high Preist, or Preist π᾽ᾶς ἀρχιερεὺς *omnis Prontifex, is taken forth of men hauing no such power
ex hominibus assumptus,* to offer sacrifice for sinnes.
Vt offerat dona & sacrificia pro peccatis. ἵνα προσφέρῃ
δῶρα τε ᾗ θοσίας ὑπέρ ἁμαρτιῶν . The Greeke
words and reading which our Protestants followe,
are most proper for sacrifice, and sacrificing Preists,
and so both Catholike & our Protestant linguists,
and lexiconaries, confesse, and translate, Masse and
                                        Masse

Maſſe Preiſt. *Sacrificium* θυσία *à ſacrificio ſacrificulus & ſacrificus* ἱερεὸς. *A Preiſt, à Sacrificer à Maſſe Preiſt*. He ſetteth downe alſo the Sacrificing altar of Chriſtians, as thes our Proteſtants alſo translate θυσιαςήριον *altare*, altar and vnſeparable correlatiue to θυσία ſacrifice as they confeſſe and the word proueth. And the Apoſtle doth ſo appropriate that altare to our Chriſtians at holie Maſſe, and the ſacrifice of Chriſts bodie, that it can be applied to nothing els, ſaying none but Chriſtians may eate of the ſacrifice offered there vpon. *Habemus altare de quo edere non habent poteſtatem, qui tabernaculo deſeruiunt.* When neither Iew, nor gentile is forbidden to beleeue in Chriſt, our Proteſtants eating, but called and exhorted vnto it by all meanes in holie ſcriptures. And the ſame Apoſtle directly affirmeth, that as Chriſt and his Religion remayne for euer, So muſt, this is ſacrificing preiſthood be for euer ἀπαράβατον ἔχει τὴν ἱερωσύνω, *vnchangeable, perpetuall, withont offence, or exception,* as thes Proteſtant lexicons do expound that Greeke adiect.

Therefore we may not giue ſuch power to a ten yeares old Kings booke, a womans, Queene Elizabeths Articles, or any power of Proteſtants, or other one earth to make that mutable, arbitrary & to expire, which Chriſt hath inſtituted to be vnchangeable, perpetuall and neuer to ceaſe. And becauſe we are enforced vpon this Proteſtant exception, eyther to ſay there neuer was conſecration of Preiſts in Chriſts Church vntill the deuiſing of this new Proteſtant forme, and ſo thes men cannot clayme any from them that had it not, for themſelues, or onely ſay thes Proteſtans haue none, & the true Catholike Church as they haue graunted

A a   ted

Thom. Thomas & Scholæ cantabrigien. dictionar. v. v. Sacrificium.
Sacrificulus & altare Morton. Apolog. part. 2. pag. 82. appeal. l. 2. ſect. 1. cap 6. pag. 162.

Hebr. 7. v. 24.

ted before, euer had true Blshops, Preifts, and Deacons we are necessitated by thes mens owne proceedings, and so many vnansweareble proofes and
authorities singularily to exclude thes men from all
true and lawfull preifthood and consecration. And
thes men must needs be the preiftlesse people,
without Preift or sacrifice fore told and prophesied
of, as the famous auncient Fathers, *Hippolitus, Me-*
thodius and others haue recorded. Tolletur honor à Sa-
cerdotibus & supprimetur mysterium Dei, & quiescet
omne sacrificium ab Ecclesijs, & erunt Sacerdotes sicut
populus in eodem tempore Ecclesiarum Ædes tugurij
instar erunt, pretiosumque Corpus & Sanguis Christi
non extabit in diebus tllis.

Method. Pe-
ter. lib. de reb.
quę ab initio
mundi , &
deinceps, Hyp-
polyt. lib. de
consummat.
mund. & An-
tichristo.

And by this not onely these Proteftants forme
and manner of making their pretended Preifts or
minifters, but their pretended Bishops also, is vtterly ouerthrowne. For, holy Preifthood being
giuen by such meanes, and wholly or principally to
such effects, acts and ends as I haue proued, as no
parsons but truely consecrated Preifts can haue
power to forgiue sinnes, or minifter Sacraments,
except onely baptifme a Sacrament of necessity, in
time of necessity, and absence of Preifts, and so all
pretended power of giuing the holy Ghoft to forgiue sinnes, or such pretended authority to Minifter Sacraments, presumed to be conferred to any
others then truely consecrated Preifts is fruftrate
voyde, and to no purpose, So a man not a truely
cōsecrateft Preift cānot possiblely either by Catholike doctrine, or these our Proteftants in this, and
other their articles, and their pretended booke, and
forme of consecration, be truely and lawfully made
a Bishop, these men in these their moft authorifed

No true Bi-
shop among
Proteftants to
make Preifts,
Deacons or
giue orders, or
doe any Epis-
copall or
Preiftly act at
all.

pro-

proceeding in this matter not allowing or permit-
ting any man to be a pretended Preiſt, or miniſter
with them, but ſuch as was allowed for a Deacon
before, nor any to be a preteded Biſhop, with them,
which was not both admitted to be both a Deacon, or Preiſt, at the leaſtby thistheir pretended
forme and faſhion, ſo confuted in both thoſe callings. But fore fullcontent I will particularly alſo &
breifely examine and confute this in like manner
and demõſtrate that it is voyde & inualid, although
the pretended conſecratour, or conſecratours were
true Biſhops, and the pretended conſecrated true
and lawfull both Deacons and Preiſts.

Thus it is ſet downe in this pretended forme of
conſecration. *The Archbiſhop and Biſhops preſent,*
ſhall laytbeir hands vpon the head of the elected Biſhop,
the Archbiſhop ſaying; Take the holy Ghoſt, and re-
member that thou ſtirre vp the grace of God whichis in
thee, by impoſition of hands: for God hath not giuen vs
the ſpirite of feare, but of power, and loue, and ſobernes.
Then the Archbiſhop ſhall deliuer him the Bible, ſay-
ing. Giue heed vnto reading, exhortation, and doctrine.
thinke vpon theſe things contained in this booke. And
the reſt of that exhortation being onely a perſua-
ſion and admonition to doe well, without any pretence of giuing Epiſcopall order or power at all.
And yet theſe men and this their forme and manner
to make Biſhops doe aſſure vs, that the party
whome they pretend to make a Biſhop, is ſo made
by that firſt ceremony of hands, and words then
ſpoken, or not at all. For, as it is cited from thē, they
name and take him to be onely, *elected Biſhop,* at
their laying on of hands. And preſently after that,
which I haue cited is endeed, they call him, *the new*

Prot. forme
and manner
of making &
conſ. Biſh. pr.
and Deacons
in Biſh.

consecrated Bishop, in these termes. *Then the Arch-bishop shall proceed to the communion, with whom the new cosecrated Bishop with others, shall also communicate.* But here is not any one singular, or priuiledged thinge, signe, ceremony, word, or act, that may by probable or possible meanes giue Episcopall order, though the pretended cosecratour or consecratours were the most lawfull and best Bishops in the world; for in their owne proceedings, except in number of Bishops which take not for a matter of necessity, here is noe more done, or said, then was in their making of pretended Preists or ministers, before, for these the same were their ceremony and words, which now. *The Bishop with the Preists present shall lay their hands seuerally vpon the head of euery one that receaueth orders, the Bishop saying. Receaue the holy Ghost.*

Here is no materiall difference, a Bishop is pretended consecratour in both a like, except that they appoint an Archbishop to consecrate a Bishop, and any other Bishop to make a Preist, but this in their owne proceedings is no materiall point, for they graunt their first pretended Archbishops Matthew Parker was made without any, either true or pretended Archbishop. The ceremony of laying on of hands is the same in effect, for if in the consecrating of a Bishop, some Preist or Preists with the consecrating Bishop should lay hands on the elect, though this were a sinne in them, yet it hindereth not consecration, if all essentiall things be vsed. The words spoken doe not differ in substance. For all men knowe, that the words *receaue the holy Ghost.* Spoken to their preteded Preist, be as significant, full, and effectuall, as, *Take the holy Ghost,* spoke spoken to their pretended Bishop. The words, *re-ceaue*, and, *take*, differ not in force, and signification. The other words, *the holy Ghoſt*, and , *the holy Ghoſt*, be the ſame. In both there is the ſame ſentence, and ſenſe in our language in all cõſtruction. If we ſeeke conſtruction from the words, which immediately followe in both places, wee shall rather finde that the words receaue the holy Ghoſt ſpoken to their pretẽded Preiſts are of greater efficacy & meaning, being interpreted with the very ſame words, wherewith Chriſt gaue the higheſt power of binding and lowſing to his higheſt Biſhops, and Apoſtles. In the other pretended ordination of Biſhops, there is no power at all giuen, but the partie onely put in minde or admoniſhed to ſtyrre vp that grace, which was in him before, as they ſuppoſe in their owne words. *Take the holy Ghoſt, and remember* *that thou ſtirre vp the grace of God, which is in thee. by* *impoſition of hands : for God hath not giuen vs the ſpirit* *of feare but of power, and loue and ſobernes.* The very ſame which S. Paul abſent wrote to S. Timothy, longe after he had conſecrated him Preiſt. *Admoneo* *te vt reſuſcites gratiã Dei, quæ eſt in te per impoſitionẽ* *manuum mearum, non enim dedit nobis Deus ſpiritum* *timoris, ſed virtutis , & dilectionis, & ſobrietatis.*

1. Timoth. 1.

So to him in an other place: *Noli negligere gratiam* *quæ in te eſt, quæ data eſt tibi per prophetiam , cum im-* *poſitione manuum presbyterij.* And it muſt needs haue this ſignification and reference to grace giuen before, by impoſition of hands in a precedent conſe-cration, for this act of impoſition of hands being in *fieri* , *doing*, and not acted, cannot poſſibly giue grace in any opinion, though it were in lawfull, and true impoſition, and conſecration, vntill it be acted

1. Timoth. 4.

and

and finiſhed, becauſe it is not an acted and perfect act, nor grace vntill then. And this act ſtill continueth after thoſe words, vntill all theſe *for God hath not giuen vs the ſpirit of feare, but of power and loue and ſobernes,* be pronounced. And grace is ſuppoſed here to be in that party before any mention of impoſition of hands. And both the Greeke, Latine and their owne Engliſh word, ἀναξωπιρεῖν *reſuſcites ſtirre vp the grace, which is in the,* proue there is grace before, if at all, and not then giuen, for none of thoſe words in any language haue a giuing ſignification. So it is in the whole ſentence both in the Greeke, and Latine Text, ἀναμιμυήσκω ἀναζωπορεῖν τὸ χαρισμα τῦ θεῦ, ὅ ἐϛιν ἐν σοὶ. *I doe againe put thee in minde to ſtyrre vp the guift of God which is in thee.* Thus the Greeke. *Adomoneo te, vt reſuſcites gratiam Dei, quæ eſt in te. I admoniſh thee, that thou ſtirre vp the grace of God which is in thee. Thus the Latine.* Here is no grace giuen at that time, but onely a putting in minde and admonition to ſtyrre vp the grace which was before. So in the words tranſlated into Engliſh by our Proteſtants, and here vſed: *remember that thou ſtyrr vp the grace of God which is in thee by impoſition of hands.*

So their words immediatly following : *for God hath not giuen vs, the ſpirit of feare, but of power, and loue, and ſobernes.* All ſpeaking of grace and power giuen before, and not at that time. And there is no ſcripture in any language, no tradition, no Eccleſiaſticall writer, no Pontificall, or booke of Rites, that euer appointed thes words. *Take the holy ghoſt,* and thoſe immediatly ioyned in this Proteſtant forme of pretended conſecration to be vnited and ſpoken together in ſuch manner, nor thoſe from S. Paule to be vſed, either with others, or by

themſelues to be powerable to giue conſecration,
and holie Orders, to Biſhop, Preiſt, or Deacon.
Neither poſſiblely can they cōferre any ſuch grace
or power, being words neyther of giuing or receauing any thing at all from the ſpeaker at that time.
The firſt words, *Take the holie ghoſt*, were not vſed
of our Britans, neyther are in the old Roman Order. Yet our Proteſtans confeſſe they both had
true Biſhops and conſecration, and yet without
them, & the ceremonie of the booke one the head
of the elect. And though the Roman Order now Pontif. Rom.
in conſecrat.
vſeth them, yet it declareth that conſecration is not Electi in
ſo giuen, nor a Biſhop ſo conſecrated, but after Epiſcopum.
them remayneth onely elect, without that holie
Order, as before, and ſo calleth him, *electus*, and
conſecrandus, *elect*, *and to be conſecrated*, but not conſecrated. Further thes Proteſtants haue told vs
before, both in their pretended booke of conſecration, and thes Articles, that, *It is euident vnto all*
men, diligently reading holy ſcripture, and ancient
Authours, that from the Apoſtles time, there hath
beene thes orders, of miniſters in Chriſts Church, Biſ-
hops, Preiſts, and Deacons, which officers were euer-
more had in reuerent eſtimation.

Men ſo euidently knowne to be Biſhops, Preiſts,
and Deacons, and euermore had in ſuch reuerent
eſtimation, muſt euermore be certayne, that they
are truely & effectually admitted to thoſe callings,
and dignities, otherwiſe it would not be euident, Prot. forme
that there be, and who be ſuch men-it would be of Order: in
vncertayne, and doubtfull, who is a Deacon, a Preiſts.
Preiſt, or Biſhop, whether there is any true prea- Prot. Articl.
ching, miniſtring of Sacraments, any Sacraments, Articul. 19.
or Church at all. For thes men allowe none to

preach

preach and minister Sacraments, *but such, they de-*
fine the visible Church to be a congregation of faithfull
men, in the which the pure word of God is preached, and
the Sacraments be duely ministred according to Chrifts
ordinante. *Sacraments be certayne sure witnesses and*
effectuall signes of grace, and Gods good Will toward vs,
by which he doth worke inuifibly in vs. And yet making but two Sacraments, *Baptifme and the Supper*
of the Lord, they thus declare, and decree. *Those*
fyue commonly called Sacraments, that is to say, Confir-
mation, Pennance, Orders, Matrimonie, and Extreame
Vnction, are not to be compted for Sacraments of the
ghospell, for that they haue not any vifible figne, or ce-
remonie ordeyned of God.

Therefore this pretended Proteftant forme, and
manner of confecration, as alfo all their pretended
Bishops, Preifts, and Deacons are vaine and voide
by their owne confeffion, for in all thes they affigne laying one of hands, a knowne and euident
figne and ceremonie, to be the certificate and affu-
rance of fuch admittance, and grace and power giuen as thofe Ecclefiafticall Orders require. But if
God did not ordeine this vifible figne or ceremonie
to fuch a purpofe, to make Epifcopall & other holie
Orders a Sacrament, which thes article, and all
their Religion denie, no created or humane authoritie can giue fuch power and preeminence vnto it,
to be a figne or ceremonie ordeined of God, a certayne and
fure witneffe, and effectuall figne of grace. Which
their Article, and Religion allowe onely to two
Sacraments; and in expreffe terms vtterly denyeth
to all Ecclefiafticall Orders, either in Bishop, Preift,
or Deacon. Hereby falling into fuch defperate
doubts, and proceedings in this cafe, that they are
not

not onely condemned by priuate Catholike writers, but publike cenfures, fentences, and confiftories, of the Catholike Church, and all auncient,
and publikly receaued formes, Pontificals, and
Orders of confecrating Bishops, Preifts, and other
Orders, how old, and generall foeuer from the
Apoftles time, But by our owne temporall lawes
and publike Iudgments, as fpirituall alfo, both in
in Catholike aud Proteftant times, regiftred in
their owne lawes, & Records in their owne courts
and hiftorians to haue neyther Bishop, Preift,
Deacon, or any other true Ecclefiafticall man a-
mong them. They write how Ridley made Preift
by Catholike Order, but Bishop by their new faf-
hion, when he was to be degraded by B. Brooke
Bishop of Glocefter, delegate thereto, in Q. Maryes time, hee did onely then degrade him, concerning preifthood, being iudged to be no Bishop, Foxe tom. 2.
as our Proteftants and Records thereof teftifie in pag. 1604.
thes his words to Ridley: *we muft proceede accor-* Mafon l. 2.
ding to our commißion, to degrading, taking from you pag. 92. Re-
the dignitie of preifthood, for we take you for no Bis- cord. degrad.
hop. Rid.

So it was alfo adiudged by the common lawes Brooke A-
of the land in that time: *Bishops in the time of King* bridg. an.
Edward the fixt were not confecrated, and therefore a 1576. titul.
leafe for yeares, made by fuch, and confirmed by the leafes num.
deane and chapter, shall not binde their Succeßours, 68.
becaufe fuch were neuer Bishops. Of thes pretended
Bishops which were thus by publike Iudgment in
lawe difabled to do teporall offices, for want of true
ordination and power, how much more were they
vnable to performe any fpirituall function, belonging to that higheft holie Order? yet this is published

blished for law euen in Q. Elizabeth her time, longe after thes new Proteſtant Biſhops were ſo allowed, and ſtill remaineth among their receaued
and adiudged lawes. And ſo generall and vniuerſall
a conſent was of all in authoritie, Pope, Prince,
Prelates, and whoſoeuer, that this new Proteſtant
forme gaue no conſecration, that their owne Proteſtant applauded writers thus confeſſe it. *Touching*

Articles of
Q.Mary to
Biſh. Boner.
Conſecrat. l.5.
cap. 12. foxe
Act. & mon.
vol.2. p.1295.

ſuch parſons as were here to fore promoted to any Or-
ders after the new ſorte and faſhion of Orders, they were
not ordered in verie deed.

This was the common and publike ſentence of
Pope, Prince, and Prelates in Queene Mary her
time, of the pretēded Biſhops of King Edward the 6.
when there was more pretence for them, thē theſe,
diuers Catholikely ordained Biſhops then liuing,
and ſome helping in their new ordering; now and
from Q. Elizabeth her time not one at all. And it is

Bracton fol.
401.

contained in our old lawes: *Iudex ſecularis non poteſt*
degradare clericum, magis quàm ad ordines promouere.
A ſecular Iudge can no more degrade a Preiſt, or Clearke,
then he can promote him to orders.

And it was publikly adiudge in lawe: *That the par-*

Temp.Hen-
rici 7.fol.27.
28.

lament could not make the Kinge being a lay parſon, to
haue ſpirituall Iuriſdiction. Then much leſſe could it

Stow an. 1.
Edw.6.Hiſt.

giue to King Edward the ſixt (to ſpeake Proteſtants
words) *proclaimed King of England, and alſo of Ire-*
land, the ſupreame heade immediately in earth, vnder
God, being of the age of nyne yeares, and to Queene E-
lizabeth, a woman by Sexe diſabled in ſuch things,
both to haue ſpirituall Iuriſdiction, and ſupreame
ſpirituall Iuriſdiction, and ſpirituall power Epiſcopall or Pontificall to conferre and giue both ſpirituall higheſt order, and Iuriſdiction, to whom, and
by

by what meanes it pleaſed them, contrary to all
Chriſtians in the world, Catholiks Proteſtants, and
whoſoeuer; none out of England ſo proceeding in
ſuch affaires. And in the time of Queene Elizabeth
both particular writers, records and her parlament
publikely in the 8. yeare of her Reigne aſſure vs,
that their new Biſhops making was by diuers both
doubted of, and denied to be lawfull, The Proteſtant cheife Iuſtice of the common plees Lord dyer
ſetteth downe, that Biſhop Bonner publikely plea-
ded they were no Biſhops, and namely Doctour
Horne, ſo admitted, and it was adiuged by all the
Proteſtant Iudges, that Biſhop Bonner might ſo
pleade. And the Proteſtants would neuer come to
tryall with him therein.

And the next Parlament in her 8. yeare cleared
him and all other Catholikes ſo impugning thoſe
Biſhops offering the oath of ſupremacy vnto them,
in theſe words: *Be it exacted that no perſon or perſons* Statut. in
be empeached, or moleſted in body, lands or good by occa- parliament.
ſion are meane of any certificate by any Archbiſhop, or an 8. Elizab.
Biſhop, heretofore made in the firſt ſeſſion of this parla- cap. 1.
ment, touching or concerning the refuſall of the oathe,
ſet fourth by act of parlament in the firſt yeare of Queene
Elizabeth. And that all tenders of ſuch oath made by
any Archbiſhop, or Biſhop aforeſaid, and all refuſals of
the ſame oath, ſo entered by any Archbiſhop or Biſhop,
ſhall be voyde, and of noe effect or validity in the lawe.
And to helpe afterward, what they could, thus they
enact: *diuers queſtions haue lately growne, vpon the* Statut. in par-
making and conſecrating of Archbiſhops, and Biſhops, liam. an. 8. E-
within this realme, whether the ſame were and be liz. ſupr. c. 1.
duely done according to the lawe, or not: Therefore it is
thought conuenient, hereby partly to touch ſuch authori-
ties,

ties, as doth allowe and approue the making of the same Archbishops, aud Bishops, to be duely and orderly done, according to the lawes of this Realme, her highnesse in her letters patents vnder the greate Seale of England, directed to any Archbishop, Bishop, or others, for the confirming, inuesting, and consecrating of any parson, elected to the office or dignity of an Archbishop, or Bishop, hath not onely vsed such words, and sentences as King Henry, aud King Edward did in their letters patents, diuers other generall words, and sentences whereby her highnesse by her supreame power, and authority, hath dispenced with all causes, or doubts, of any imperfection, or diasbility that can, or may in any wise be obiected, against the same.

These be the onely authorities the statute doth, or could bringe, being all carnall and humane, not one diuine or Ecclesiasticall, vtterly vnable to make a lawfull true Bishop, or confirme any for such, being but meere phantasies, letters patents, the greate Seale of England, of a woman, such words and sentences as King Henry the eight, and King Eduard his child, contrary to the vniuersall Church of Christ vsed, A womans supreame power authority and dispensation in all causes, doubts, Imperfections, or disabilities in any wise to be obiected, and that not onely their pretended Archbishops, and Bishops, but others neither true nor pretended Archbishops or bishops did as their words be plaine, by this most straunge, and infirme feminine commission, confirme, inuest, and consecrate Archbishops, & Bishops, which as they haue confessed before, with all authorities, none but true & lawfull Bishops, in approued & receaued forme, and manner can doe.

And

And yet this parlament doth thus approue & all such, as were thus made, whether by the Queenes letters patent, and men no Bihops true or pretended and without King Edwards forme, or any other remembred, or by King Edwards forme and fashion to be lawfull Bishops in these words: *All,* Statut.an.8. Eliz. supr. *acts, aud things made or done by any person, or persons in,or about any elected to the office of any Archbishop or Bishop by vertue of the Queenes letters patents,shall be by authority of this Parlament be declared good, any matter, or thing, that may be obiected to the contrary thereof, in any wise notwithstanding. All persons that haue beene, or shall be made Archbishops, Bishops, Preists,ministers after the forme and Order prescribed in the order and forme, how Archbishops and should be made,by authority hereof be declared and shall be Archbisbops,Bishops, Preists, Ministers, and rightly made: any statute, lawe, canon, or other thing, to the contrary notwithstanding.* Hitherto this Protestant Parlament, and Queene Elizabeth taking vpon them more then omnipotent and diuine power, for God himselfe euer omnipotent, cannot make that a thing done, is not,or was not done, nor a thing ill done, to haue beene well done, or not ill done. The light of reason, the light of grace, all Philosophers Christians, and others agree, *non est potentia ad præteritum,* there is no power, or possibility, to make a thing that is past not to be past, nor otherwise passed, the it passed. Therefore when it appeareth by so many testimonies before,that men called Bishops by our Protestants, were neuer truely and lawfully made Bishops,and this Protestant parlament it selfe confesseth, *not onely that diuers questiõs had beene whether it were duely, & orderly done according*

ding

ding to the law or not, but declareth their acts and effects done by them, as Bishops, *to be voyde, and of none effect, or validitie in the lawe* : It farre ſurpaſſed a womans power, or her parlament thereby, or any power on earth, or higher, *to make and proue by authoritie of this parlament* (in her 8. yeare) *ſuch men by authoritie hereof be declared, and shall be Archbishops, Bishops, Preiſts, Miniſters, and rightly made, any ſtatute, lawe, canon, or other thing to the contrary notwithſtanding.* Producing no other reaſon, but that, *her highneſſe by her ſupreame power and authoritie hath diſpenced with all cauſes, or doubts of any imperfection, or diſabilitie, that can or may in any wiſe be obiected againſt the ſame.*

If Queene Elizabeth and her Proteſtants would make Epiſcopall Order, and dignity onely an humane inuention, she as a temporall greate Prince might haue had place for her diſpenſation, for time to come. Though not paſt, in aboue 6. yeares, when thouſands, of ſuch Bishops, and miniſters were made among them; But all Proteſtants of England, King, Bishops & whoſoeuer hauing decreed and deliuered before, that it is *diuinæ ordinationis, the ordinance of God, an Apoſtolicall tradition manifeſt to all the world, a canon or conſtitution of the whole Trinitie, enacted for ſucceeding poſteritie:* it is vtterly vnpoſſible, that any Queens, Kings or what diſpenſation ſoeuer on earth, can or euer could make that which was, and is queſtioned, doubtfull, imperfect, and inualide, to be without queſtion, doubt, perfect, and valide, either from the beginning, any time paſt, or to come hereafter. Thus howſoeuer wee examine the making of theſe Proteſtant Biſhops, and miniſters by them, either by holy ſcripture, witneſſing that God placed Bishops in his

Church to gouerne it ; *attendite vobis & vniuerso gregi, in quo vos spiritus sanctus posuit Episcopos, regere Ecclesiam Dei, quam acquisiuit sanguine suo.* And not a woman or child Queene Elizabeth and King Edward the 6. by a new deuised manner: or by the Apostolike Fathers of this first age, tradition of the Apostles, all the old Orders of consecration in Britaine, or what place soeuer, by all Catholike Fathers, or by these Protestants themselues, we finde nothing but a desolation and an vndoubted want of all Episcopall and Ecclesiasticall holy orders among them.

But if we come to the Sacred Bishops, of the Catholike and Romane Church, the holie preisthood and other Orders, we finde by all these testimonies, all things in Order, subordinate, required and necessarie to this highest spirituall dignitie. We haue with the Apostles and the Apostolike Fathers of this time S. Clement, S. Ignatius, and others, Subdeacons, Acolythists, Exorcists, Lectours and all. We haue founde Deacons ministers to Bishops and Preists in the Sacrifice of Masse, we haue founde true massing Sacrificing Preists, and Protestants both by writing and practise so confessing, as also in these words of them all by generall assent : *We thinke that no man possibly haue the Order of a Bishop, which hath not the right Order of preisthood. To the verie being of a Bishop, the Order of preisthood is essentially required.*

Thus they exclude themselues from, and entitle Catholiks to this greatest Order. And plainely confesse the Roman Church not onely to obserue, and vse in the consecration of Bishops, all things whatsoeuer, in any opinion, of Catholiks, or Protestants

Act. c. 20. r.
Timoth. 3. 4.
Tit. 1. 1. Petr.
5. 2. Timoth.
1.

Can. Apost.
43. Clem.
const. Apost.
l. 3. c. 11. l.
8. c. 21. c. 22.
28. epist. 2.
Ignat. epist. ad
Antioch. ad
Philadelph.
Philip.
Engl. Protest.
in Abb. Prot.
Archb. of
canterb. and
Franc. Mas.
Booke of
Consecrat. l.
5. p. 96. 97.
c. 1. p. 207.

teftants, effentiall and neceffarie, but alfo all ceremonies, and ceremonialls therein vfed euer fince, and before England was conuerted to Chrift, plainely confeffing that their firft Proteftant Archbishop Matthew Parker being the 70. from S. Auguftine was the firft of all admitted without them, and otherwife then they were, and their publike continuall practife is fo, euer fince that time.

The ceremonies of paftorall ftaffe, ringe, deliuerie of the booke of Ghofpels to the new confecrated Bishop, by the Confecratour and his Affiftants, taken from the sholders of the newly confecrated, Miter and gloues, we are affured to be ceremoniall onely, all and euerie of them performed, and done after the new Bishop is declared to be confecrated.

And yet thefe were fo aunciently vfed by thefe Proteftants, that all our Bishops of England were confecrated they being vfed. And before S. Auguftine came hither S. Kentegern in the Britans time being confecrated without them going to Rome, *ipfo multoties petente*, with very often fuite and defire, the Pope then miniftred them vnto him. *Sanctus Papa quæ deerunt confecrationi eius fupplens.* The Order of Confecration by which this S. Kentegern was made Bishop, and all the Britans, Scots, and Irish vfed, was more old, then the carions of the ceremonies vfed in confecration, and their old cuftome *mos in Britannia inoleuerat*, when S. Kentegern about 1200. yeares paft was confecrated, was this: *In confecratione Epifcopi tantummodo capita eorum facri chrifmatis infufione perungere. cum inuocatione Sancti Spiritus, & benediCtione,*

ctione, & manus impoſitione. In the conſecration of Biſhops onely to anoynte their heads with holy Chriſme, with inuocation of the holie ghoſt, and benediction, and impoſition of hands. This Order was adiudged by the Popes of Rome, to be auayleable. And all Proteſtants graunt, the Britans haue true conſecration, and Biſhops. Here is neyther the ceremonie of ſaying, *take the holie ghoſt,* nor deliuering the bible to him that is admitted among them, beinge the onely ſignes they vſe except layinge hands one the head of the Elect, which ſigne of itſelfe cannot by any opinion giue this greate dignitie and calling, and as S. Albinus Amalarius and others witneſſe 800. yeares ſince this ceremonie of impoſition of hands was *neither in the old, or new booke of Ordination, or in the Romane tradition: Non reperitur in authoritate veteri, neque noua, ſed neque in Romana traditione.*

So they write of the ceremonie of the booke of the ghoſpels not vſed in any of thoſe authorities, neyther remember that the ceremonie of ſaying, *take the holie ghoſt,* was founde in any of them, and in the old Roman Order it is wanting, as likewiſe in that was vſed in Fraunce, as in that of Britayne Scotland, and Ireland. And yet it is acknowledged freely by all, aſwell Proteſtants as others, that all theſe Kingdomes, contryes, and nations where theſe traditions, Orders, and conſecrations were thus vſed, had true and lawfull Biſhops, Preiſts, and other clergie men, yet omitted all, and vſed none of thoſe Rites to which Proteſtants aſcribe Epiſcopall conſecration.

Therefore it muſt needs be euen in their owne Iudgements that Proteſtants haue no true conſe-

ſecration

cration, or perſons conſecrated in their congregations : But the preſent Catholike and Romane
Church now practiſing all, and euerie Rite, and
ceremonie, which all thoſe Orders, and Ordinations did, in conſecrating Biſhops, & other clergie
men, and vſing, as our Proteſtants alſo confeſſe,
true and lawfull Biſhops, to be conſecratours, muſt
needs haue true and vndoubted conſecration. The
Rites be beſides the remembred which it vſeth
herein. Firſt the Examen of the perſon to be conſecrated ended, which was in all orders of this conſecration, and helpe of the holie ghoſt as the Britans Scots and Iriſh with others vſe *cum inuocatione*
ſancti Spiritus, being called vpon, the conſecratour
telleth him, *the office of a Biſhop to be, to iudge, inter-*
prette, conſecrate, giue Orders, offer ſacrifice, baptiſe
and confirme . Epiſcopum oportet iudicare, interpretari,
conſecrare, ordinare, offerre, baptizare & confirmare.
With this all the cited Orders agree, and the holie
Fathers of this firſt age before, S. Clement, S. Ignatius with others among the greate duties of this
higheſt dignitie haue told vs : *Quid aliud eſt Epiſ-*
copus, quàm qui omni principatu & poteſtate ſuperior
eſt ? Epiſcopi ſunt Sacerdotes, baptizant ſacrificant,
eligunt, manus imponunt. Nemo Epiſcopo honorabilior,
in Eccleſia Sacerdotium Deo gerent pro mundi ſalute.
Sine Epiſcopo nemo quicquam faciat eorum, quæ ad Ec-
cleſiam ſpectant, non licet ſine Epiſcopo baptizare, ne-
que offerre, neque ſacrificium immolare, neque dochen
celebrare. Non ſibi quis ſumit honorem, ſed qui voca-
tur à Deo. Nam per Epiſcopi manus datur hæc digni-
tas.

The benediction remembred in the manner of
the Britans, Scots, Iriſh, and others is performed
with

Pont. Rom.
in conſecrat.
electi in Epiſ-
copum.

S. Ignat. ep.
ad Trall
Antioch.
Phil. Epheſ.
Smyrn. Clem.
3. conſt. c. 10.
11. ep. 4. 1. 3.
conſt. l. 7. 2.
c. 11. 12. 3.
30. 31. 36

with the ſigne of the Croſſe, *vt hunc præſentem electum benedicere & ſanctificare, & conſecrare digneris. Producendo ſemper ſignum Crucis ſuper eum,* thus the Elect kneeling before the altare S. Denys and S. Clement in this firſt age, together with the old Roman Order, thus remember this Rite. *Præful ſacrandus offertur, vtroque genu poſito ante altare, à conſecrante Pontifice caſtiſſimis imprecationibus conſumantur cuilibet ipſorum à benedicente Pontifice crucis imponitur ſignum.* The Rites of laying the booke of ghoſpels one the Elect, with the hands of the conſecratours, and the words, *accipe ſpiritum ſanctum,* I haue ſhewed before, they were not vſed in diuers publike Orders, of conſecration, which by all gaue true Ordination. And both in the Roman Pontificall, and others in which they are vſed, the perſon to be conſecrated is after they be ended, ſtill named onely Elect, and not conſefecrated, vntill the holie vnction of him with holie Chriſme into Epiſcopall Order, thus : *vngatur, & conſecretur caput tuum, cæleſti benedictione, in ordine Pontificali in nomine Patris & Filij & Spiritus ſancti Amen.* And after this vnction, immediately it is declared, both in the Pontificall now vſed, and in the old Roman Order, that Epiſcopall power and calling is giuen vnto him. His hands be alſo anoynted in two Orders. And they call this vnction the ſumme and complement of Ordination, and that vſed the conſecration is ended. *Comple in Sacerdote tuo myſterij tui ſummam, cæleſtis vnguenti flore ſanctifica,* and this ended, *completa benedictione,* they call him conſecrated Biſhop, *conſecratus, Pontifex, and Pontificatus dignitatem ſublimatus,* and before onely *electus, & deſignatus,* Elect & deſigned.

Dioniſ. Areop. Eccl. Hierarch c. ſ. Clem. Rom. conſt. l. 8. c. 122.

The

The Order which the Britans Scots and Irish vſed, vſed onely Anoynting of the head : *tantummodò capita eorum ſacri Chriſmatis infuſione perungere.* So did the old Order which Amalarius Biſhop of Treuers vſed : *additur ad conſecrationem infuſio olei ſuper caput.* So **S.** Auguſtine, ſo S. Gregorie, S. Bede and others, yet all agree, that Epiſcopall Order is hereby conferred and ended. S. Auguſtine ſaith: *vicarius Chriſti Pontifex efficitur: ideo in capite vngitur . Caput noſtrum Chriſtus . Caput noſtrum vnctum eſt oleo inuiſibili: Epiſcopus quia vicarius Chriſti eſt in capite vngitur: ab illo enim ſignificaturſe accipere hanc vnctionis gratiam, qui caput eſt totius Corporis, imitando illum, qui caput eſt totius Eccleſiæ, per vnctionis gratiã ſit & ipſe caput Eccleſiæ, ſibi commiſſæ.* S. Gregorie plainely teacheththis vnction is the Sacrament here. *Qui in culmine ponitur, ſacramenta ſuſcipit vnctionis. Quia vero ipſa vnctio Sacramentum eſt, is qui promouetur, bene foris vngitur, ſed intus virtute Sacramenti roboretur .* And againe: *ſpiritus Domini poſt vnctionem dirigitur: quia foris Sacramenta percipimus. Vt intus ſpiritus ſancti gratia repleamur.* Beſides our brittiſh manner of conſecration before remembred, S. Bede and Amalarius from him, and others witneſſe, how in this Kingdome this was accompted a Rite neceſſarie eſſentiall and giuing grace in this Sacrament: *oleo vnctionis perfunditur, vt per gratiam ſpiritus ſancti conſecratio perficiatur.*

And that this was the tradition of the Church from the Apoſtles, we are aſſured, both becauſe the Fathers of this firſt age, S. Denis, S. Anacletus and others ſo remember it, and the fathers before, and after to be named, euen by Engliſh publike

Prote-

Margin notes:

Auguſt. tract. pſalm. & apud Amalar. l. 3. de offic. Eccl. c. 14.

Gregor. ad cap. 10. lib. 1. Reg.

Bed. l. 3. de Tabernacul. & vaſ. eius. Amalar. fort. l. 3. de Eccl. offic. c. 14.

Engl. Prot. apud Marc.

Proteſtant conſent, ſo proue and deriue it. S. Denis is ſo plaine, that they plainely thus confeſſe it:
*Areopagitæ Dionyſio tributum opuſculum vnctionem
ponit expreſsè.* So they confeſſe of S. Anacletus,
made Preiſt, by S. Peter, the Apoſtle: *addit vnctionem capitis Anacletus, quæ eſt antiquiſſima.*

Anton. l. 2.
de Republ.
Eccl. cap. 2.

The words which he vſeth, deducing his doctrine, and practiſe from the Apoſtles, be theſe:
*Biſhops are to be made by Impoſition of hands of Biſhops,
with the ghoſpels which they are to preach, and holie
vnction by the example of the Apoſtles, becauſe all ſan-
ctification conſiſteth in the holie ghoſt, whoſe inuiſible
power is mixed with holie Chriſme, and by this Rite
ſolemne Ordination is to be celebrated.* Where we
finde by this greate Apoſtolike authoritie, that
the grace of this Sacrament, and power Epiſcopall
is giuen by this Rite.

Anacl. ep. 2.

And theſe Proteſtants, as by this they muſt, and
are enforced, confeſſe ſo of the holie fathers following, both in the Greeke and Latin Church,
that they were conſecrated Biſhops by holie vnction. So of S. Baſile, *vnctione ſacrâ adhibitâ eſt
ordinatus.* So of S. Gregorie Naziancen, *me Pontificem vngis.* So were S. Iohn Chriſoſtome and
S. Seuerus. Of S. Auguſtine, S. Gregorie with
others I haue ſpoken before; To which we may
ioyne S. Iuo, Stephanus Aduenſis and other auntient writers, and expoſitours of holie myſteries,
and all Orders of Conſecration.

Prot. ſupr. in
Marc. Anton.

Gregor.
Naziane.
orat. 20. de
laudib. Baſil.
orat. 5. ad
Baſil. & part.
Sim. Metaph.
in vit. Criſoſt.
Petr. Chriſo-
log. Ser. de S.
Seuero. Iſi-
dor. l. 2. de
offic. Eccl. c.

By this it is euident, how certayne and vndoubted a thing it is, That the conſecration vſed in the
Rômane Church, is moſt true, holie, and honourable, both for Order, and Iuriſdiction, euer, as is
demonſtrated before, both in this and other nations

25. S. Iuo.
Ser. de reb.
Eccl. Steph.
Aduen.
Sacr. alt. c. 9.

tions, from the Apostolike Roman see, and in the old Orders of consecration the Bishop to be consecrated protesteth obedience to the Popes of Rome. And how the case standeth with the Protestants both of England, and all others, it is as lamentable to know their desolate condition.

The XXVII. Chapter.

The 37. article, intituled, of the ciuill Magistrates, thus examined, and whosoeuer against the Roman Church, condemned.

THeir 37. and next Article is intituled : *of the ciuill Magistrates. And thus followeth. The Kings Maiestie hath the cheife power in this Realme of Englād, and other his dominions, vnto whome the cheife gouernment of all estates of this Realme whether they be Ecclesiasticall or ciuill, in all causes doth appertaine, and is not, nor ought to be subiect to any forraine iurisdiction. The Bishop of Rome hath no Iurisdictiō in this Realme of England.*

The rest of this article containeth an excuse of Protestāts that they did not giue to their temporall Prince power to preach and minister Sacraments, as some interpreted their opinion, and other things not questioned betweene Catholiks and English Protestants, but betweene these Protestants and some other new sectaries, among themselues, and be these. *The lawes of the Realme may punish Christian men with death, for heynous and grieuous offences. It is lawfull for Christian men, at the commaundement of the Magistrate, to weare weapons, & serue in the warrs.*

These positions are graunted and allowed by all

Ca-

Catholiks. The firſt part of this article giuing vnto
the King a temporall Gouernour, and Ruler cheife
gouernment ouer all eſtates in all cauſes Eccleſiaſticall or ciuill, as alſo their ſtatute and oath of Princes
Supremacy in ſpirituall things, fighteth with, and
contradicted it ſelfe: for thus it addeth: *we giue not
to our Prince, the miniſtring either of Gods word, or of
the Sacraments: the which the Iniunctions alſo ſometime ſet fourth by Elizabeth our late Queene, doe moſt
plainely teſtifie.* Therefore ſeing Kings be not Teachers, preachers, Doctours, Paſtours, and ſhee-
phards in the Church and fould of Chriſt, to giue
them ſome place therein, members of it, and not to
be quite excluded from the name, and number of
Chriſtians we muſt needs ſay, they be of them
which be taught preached vnto, inſtructed, ſheepe
and ſubiects, fedde, ruled and gouerned by them,
which haue authority, and ſpirituall power in ſuch
things. And theſe our Proteſtants haue accordingly
this defined the Church before in theſe their articles. *The viſible Church of Chriſt, is a congregation of
faithfull men, in the which the pure word of God is preached, and the Sacraments be duely miniſtred, according
to Chriſts ordinance.* Proteſt. art.
19. ſup.

They to whome the word is preached, and Sacraments be miniſtred, and neither haue power to
preach nor miniſter Sacraments, which this Article confeſſeth of their Proteſtant Kings, and temporall Rulers, cannot poſſibly in the reſpect be
cheife Gouernours of the to whome God himſelfe
hath power and preeminence. The holy Scriptures
do in many places commaund obedience both to
temporall & ſpirituall Rulers, but obediece in matters of Religion in feeding and rulingſoules the

flocke

flocke of Chrift, gouerning his Church and such
fpirituall emnencies is onely appropriated in the to
fpirituall gouernours. *Qui bene præfunt Presbyteri*

1. Tim. 5.
1. Petr. 5.
Ioh. 21.
Act. 20.
Hebr. 13.

duplici honore digni funt. Pafcite qui in vobis eft gre-
gem Dei, pafce agnos meos. Pafce oues meas. Attendite
vobis & vniuerfo gregi, in quo vos Spiritus fanctus
pofuit Epifcopos regere Ecclefiam Dei, quam acquifiuit
fanguine fuo. Mementote præpofitorum veftrorum, qui
vobis locuti funt verbũ Dei. Obedite præpofitis veftris
& fubiacete. Ipfi enim peruigilant quafi rationem pro
animabus veftris reddituri. Where we fee neither
king nor Prince, if he will belonge to the Church
of Chrift, haue his foule purchafed with his blood,
a care had of it, and accompt made for it, can be free
from this obedience; much leffe can he clayme it
for himfelfe, from them to whom it fo infallibly belongeth, by the higheft authority.

The Apoftolike men of this firft age, haue

Ignat. epift.
and Antioch
Ep. ad Smyrn.
Epift. ad Phi-
ladelph Ma-
gnefian. Tral-
lian.

teftified this at large before, in the examination of the laft precedent article. S. Ignatius hath
taught vs, a Bishop is aboue all principality and
power. *Epifcopus omni Principatu & poteftate fupe-*
rior eft. No man is more honorable then the Bishop. *Nemo Epifcopo honorabilior.* Preifts and Deacons, all the clergy together with the people, and
Souldiars, and Princes, and the Emperour alfo muft
obey the Bishop. *Cum populo, & militibus atque Prin-*
cipibus, fed & Cæfare obediant Epifcopo. Be fubiect to
the Bishop, euen as to our Lord, for he watcheth
for your foules, and is to make accompt for them.
Therefore it is needfull that you doe nothing without the Bishop. No man may doe any thing that
belongeth to the Church without the Bishop. *Sine*
Epifcopo nemo quicquam faciat eorum quæ ad Ecclefiam
fpectant.   Sainct

Sainct Clement testifieth that Sainct Peter the Apo- Clem. Rom.
stle commaunded præcipiebat Petrus Apostolus, that all epist. 1.
Princes of the earth, omnes Principes terræ, and all men
should obey Bishops. And proued that all which did con-
tradict them were in state of damnation, and imfamy
vntill they made satisfaction; and commaunded them to
be excommunicate except they were conuerted. The Bi- Clem. const.
shop ruleth all Lords, Preists, Kings, Princes, *Re-* Apost lib. 2 c.
gibus, Principibus, Fathers, children Masters, and $\begin{matrix} \text{11.12.} \\ \text{3. 30. 31.} \end{matrix}$
all subiects. *He Iudgeth as God with power. The*
Bishop is mediatour betweene God and men. He is the
next after God our Father, Prince, Ruler, King, Rex,
Gouernour. A Bishop is adorned with the dignitie of
God, he ruleth the clergie and commaundeth all the peo-
ple. Omni populo imperat. Dion. Areop.
The like haue other Apostolike men of this first Hier. Eccl. c.
age. And they are so farre from giuing superiority, $\begin{matrix} \text{2. par. 2. 3. c. 4.} \\ \text{5. Martial. ep.} \end{matrix}$
and commaund to ciuill power ouer Bishops in ad Burdegal.
things of Religion, that in such affaires and causes cap. 3.
they make inferiour all temporall people euen to
Preists and Deacons. Preisthood is the heade or
cheife of all good things in this world, saith S. Igna- Ignat. epist.
tius. *Sacerdotium est omnium bonorum quæ in homini-* ad Smyrnen.
bus sunt, apex. He that rageth against it, doth not igno-
miny to man, but to God . Lay men must be subiect not
onely to Preists but to Deacons. *Laici Diaconis subditi* Polycarpus
sint Subiecti estote Presbyteris & Diaconis sicut Deo $\begin{matrix} \text{epist. ad Phi-} \\ \text{lippen.} \end{matrix}$
& Christo.
And our Protestants themselues acknowledge, Rob. Barnes
that the holy Popes of this time, iudged them no l de vit. Pont.
Christians that called *holy Preists to ciuill consistorys* Roman. in A-
Anacletus Christo alienos esse indicabat qui Sacerdotes $\begin{matrix} \text{nacleto. Ana-} \\ \text{clet. epist. 1.} \end{matrix}$
in ius vocarent. They which tooke away the riches of the
Church were to be adiudged homicidas, because the A-
postles

postles by our Sauiour his commaunde, gaue chardge that the priuiledges of the Church and Preists should be kept inuolate. Christi vel Ecclesiæ pecunias auferentes, homicidas iudicari debere censuit: quia inquit priuilegia Ecclesiæ & Sacerdotum, Apostoli Saluatoris iussu inuiolata esse debere iusserunt. In Ecclesiasticall busines the the greater causes were to be referred to the primates, the lesser to the Metropolitane Bishop, and secular causes to secular Iudges. *In Ecclesiasticis negotys, grauiores causas ad primatem, leuiores ad metropolitanum Episcopum referendas, secularia negotia ad prophanos iudices, agenda esse iussit.* All that were oppressed might appeale to the Ecclesiasticall Court.

And that such causes as could not be composed by the cheifest of the cleargie, should be ended in their councells. *Et causas quæ apud primarios Ecclesiastici ordinis componi non possent, in Concilio siniendas esse.*

To that which followeth in this Article: *The Bishop of Rome hath no iurisdictiō in this Realme of England:* I haue aboundantly answeared, and so proued the weakenesse of such assertion in my Examine of their 19. Article and that which is here said most manifestly conuinceth the same. For if as is proued here, the Bishops in euery Prouince haue the highest and cheifest spirituall power, ouer all others therein whether spirituall or temporall, he which hath the supreame power, and Iurisdiction ouer all, and euery such Bishops, or Bishop, cannot be depriued of that Title, and right, though a farre greater consistory then these Articlers, or their Approuers, and applauders should deny it vnto him? He that hath iurisdiction and power ouer the greater, must needs haue it ouer the lesser and Inferiour in that Kind. S. Ignatius calleth the Church

of

of Rome, *the sanctified and Ruling Church being him-*
selfe Patriarke of Antioch. Ignatius Ecclesiæ sanctifica- Ignat.epist.
tæ quæ præsidet in loco Regionis Romanorum. S.Poly- ad Rom.in in-
carp lyuing in the same age, went from Smyrna in scriptione.
the East, to Rome for decision of Questions about
the day of Easter. *Propter quasdam super die paschæ* Hier l.de. vir.
quæstiones Romam venit. illustrib. in

 S. Dionisius, saith S. Peter liuing and dying Polycarpo.
Bishop of Rome was the supreame glory and head c 3.de diuin.
of diuines. *Petrus supremum decus, & antiquissimum* nominib.
Theologorum columen. S. Clement saith, *S. Peter was* Clem. Rom.
by Christ defined, the foundation of the Church Simon epist.1.Rufino
Petrus fundamentum esse Ecclesiæ definitus est. And as Interpret.
the most worthy commaunded by Christ to con-
uert the westerne parts, and performed that precept. *Qui obscuriorem mundi plagam occidentis, velut*
omnium potentior illuminare præceptus est, quique &
integrè potuit implere præceptum. He liued much, and
dyed at Rome by martyrdome, and committed his
supreame Pastorall charge, and office to S. Clement, which Christ had committed to him, full
power to binde and loose, & whatsoeuer he should
decree on earth should be decreed in heauen. *Cle-*
mentem Episcopum vobis ordino, cui soli meæ prædica-
tionis & doctrinæ cathedram trado.Ipsi trado à Domino
mihi traditam potestatem ligandi & soluendi, vt de
omnibus, quibuscumque decreuerit in terris, hoc decre-
tum sit & in cælis. Among other Pastorall and highest Pontificall duties, he gaue him power, and
chardge to send Bishops into all cyties, whether, or
where S. Peter had not sent, or ordained before. *E-*
piscopos per singulas ciuitates, quibus ille non miserat
nobis mittere præcepit.

 And S. Clement performed it. *Quod facere in-*
choaui-

choauimus, & Domino opem ferente, facturi sumus. A-liquos ad Gallias, Hispaniasque mittimus, & quosdam ad Germaniam, & Italiam atque ad reliquas gentes di-rigere cupimus. Among these Bishops some were primates, or Patriarks, and Archbishops, and the causes of Bishops and greatest Ecclesiasticall Que-stions and busines of the Churches, were to be tried and decided by the primates, and Patriarks, and the Apostles so decreed. *Petrus Episcoporum pri-mates vel Patriarchas ordinauit, qui reliquorum Epis-coporum iudicia, & maiora, quoties necesse foret, negotia in fide agitarent, & secundum Dei voluntatem, sicut constituerunt sancti Apostoli, ita vt ne quis iniu-ste periclitaretur, definirent. Archiepiscopos institui præcepit, qui non tamen primatum, sed & Archiepis-coporum frucrentur nomine. Episcoporum quoque iudi-cia, vt superius memoratum est, & maiora Ecclesiarum negotia, si ipsi reclamauerint, aut aliquem timorem, aut istos vel alios suspectos habuerint, ad iam dictos pri-mates vel Patriarchas, transferri perdocuit. And this* was among the Apostles themselues, one, S. Peter, aboue the rest, *Quoniam nec inter Apostolos par institutio fuit Sed vnus omnibus præfuit.*

Anaclet. ep. decret. Ruffin. interpr. epist. Clem. Leo 2. ep. decret. Marian. Scot. l. 2. ætat. 6. Flor. wigorn. chronic. in Clem. Mart. Polon. Sup-putat. col. 33. in Lino Ro-bert, Barnes.   This is the testimonie of S. Clement, confir-med by S. Anacletus then liuing, Ruffinus, Mar-rianus, Martinus Florentius wigorniensis, Pope Leo the seconde, and many others both Catho-like and Protestant writers. S. Anacletus made Preist by S. Peter, and by him instructed, euen as our Protestants confesse, did teach that Christ gaue to the Church of Rome, primacy ouer all Chur-ches, and all Christian people, neither King nor Cæsar exempted. *Anacletus ab ipso Domino prima-tum Romanæ Ecclesiæ super omnes Ecclesias vniuer-*
                                                          sumque

samque Christiani nominis populum concessum esse asseruit. Thus our Proteſtants, and S. Anacletus is more playne that this ſupreamacie of the Roman Church was not giuen vntoit, by the Apoſtles but Chriſt himſelfe. *Hæc ſacroſancta Romana & Apoſtolica Eccleſia non ab Apoſtolis, ſed ab ipſo Domino Saluatore noſtro primatum obtinuit, & eminentiam poteſtatis, ſuper vniuerſas Eccleſias ac totum Chriſtiani populi gregem aſſecuta eſt.* And both Chriſt commaunded, and his Apoſtles decreed, that great and difficult queſtions ſhould be referred to the Apoſtolike Romane ſee, to be decided, and that Chriſt builded his whole Church vpon it. *Apoſtoli hoc ſtatuerunt, iuſſu Saluatoris, vt maiores & difficiliores quæſtiones ſemper ad ſedem deferantur Apoſtolicam, ſuper quam Chriſtus vniuerſam conſtruxit Eccleſiam.*

So haue alſo S. Euariſtus and S. Alexander, who liued in this firſt age. *Relatum eſt ad huius ſanctæ & Apoſtolicæ ſedis apicem, cui ſummarum diſpoſitiones cauſarum, & omnia negotia Eccleſiarum ab ipſo Domino tradita ſunt, quaſi ad caput.* Our Proteſtants alſo acknowledge thus: *Irenæus ſaith, that euerie Church ought to haue reſpect to the Church of Rome, for her eminent principalitie.*

But S. Irenæus is more cleare, in this manner: *ad hanc (Romanam) Eccleſiam, propter potentiorem principalitatem, neceſſe eſt omnem conuenire Eccleſiam, hoc eſt eos, qui ſunt vndique fideles.* There is a neceſſitie, that euerie Church and all faithfull Chriſtians, whereſoeuer ſhould acknowledge the more powerable principalitie of the Romane Church. No King, contrie, or nation is exempted, from, but all are included in this neceſſitie, of being vnder the Iuriſdiction of

the

---

l. de vit. Pont.
in Lino &
Anacleto.
Anaclet. ep.
decretal. 3.
Barn. ſup. in
Anaclet.
Omerd pict.
Pap. pag. 78.

Anacl. epiſt. r.

Euariſt. ep. r.
Alex. ep. l.

Sutcliffe
ſubu. pag 57.
Iren. l. 3. c. 3.

the Church of Rome. And particularly for this Kingdome of Englaud, which singularly this Article would thus depriue of that honour, and happines from being in the folde & vnder the chardge of the vicar and highest pastour and shephard of Christ one earth.

Godwyn conuers. of Britayne pag. 6.

To begin with a Protestant Bishops censure in these words: *we should accompt it a great glorie to deriue the pedigree of our spirituall linage, from so noble and excellent a father, as S. Peter*. And yet both Greeke and Latin, domesticall and forreyne, Catholike and Protestant Antiquaries, do thus deriue and proue it. *Petrus venit in Britanniam, quo in loco cum longo tempore fuisset moratus, apud Britannos verbo gratiæ multos illuminauit, & Ecclesias constituit, Episcoposque & Presbyteros & Diaconos ordinauit*. S. *Peter came into Britayne, and staying there longe time, did illuminate many with the word of grace, and founded Churches, and ordered Bishops, Priests, and Deacons*. Which more Protestant Doctours and Bishops euen Archbishops with them thus confirme: *Peter preached in no place, bnt he there ordeyned Bishops and teachers and founded Churches*.

Sim. Metaphrast. die 19. Iunij Euseb. & antiq. grec. apud eund. ib. Sur. eod. die. Andr. Chesu. l. 3. histor. Angl. Bucley pag. 171. Cambden in Britan. Sutcliffe Subu. pag. 3. Prot. Archb. whitg. answ. to admo. pag. 65. sect. 1. def. of the answeare pag. 318 Marc. Anton. de Dom. de reb. chr. l. 4. c. 10.

The *Apostle Peter did in euerie prouince appoynt one Archbishop, whome all other Bishops of the same prouince should obey. Est caput Roma, quatenus ab ea diffusum est Euangelium in reliquas totius occidentis Ecclesias. Rome is the heade, in respect that from it, the ghospell was diffused into the rest of the Churches of the west, and into many of the east, and into barbarous nations out of the Romane Empire. Et in multas orientis, atque in barbaras extra Romanum Imperium nationes*. Diuers of the holie Bishops and Apostolike Preists, which S. Peter consecrated for, this

Doroth. l de 72. discip. in Aristob. Ar.

King-

Kingdome are remembred both by Catholike and Proteſtant Hiſtorians, S. Ariſtobulus, S. Manſuetus, S. Beatus and his holie companion, not named in Antiquities. Our Proteſtants make S. Ariſtobulus Archbiſhop here: *Britayne Ariſtobulus, and by their Rule before, The Apoſtle Peter did in euerie prouince appoynt one Archbiſhop*, he muſt needs be ordeined Archbiſhop, by S. Peter.

S. Clement hath ſufficiently proued before, that he ſent Biſhops hither, ſaying he ſent to the other nations of the weſt, *ad reliquas gentes*, beſides Italy, Spayne, Fraunce, and Germany. And both Catholiks and Proteſtants from antiquities affirme, that he ſent to vs S. Nicaſius, who inſtructed the Britons, *Britones inſtruxit formauitque fide S. Nicaſius à S. Clemente delegatus*. Theſe Britans muſt needs be thoſe of this Kingdome, they of little Britayne in Fraunce came not thither vntill aboue 200. yeares after S. Clement, and S. Nicaſius time. Both Brittiſh and Engliſh Catholike and Proteſtant Antiquaries affirme, that the diuiſion of Primates or Patriarkes, Metropolitans, and others with their ſeuerall Iuriſdictions, from the ſee of Rome, being as he ackdowledgeth the decree of his predeceſſour S. Clement and the Apoſtles alſo was receaued in this Kingdome of Britayne, as it comprehendeth England wales and Scotland. Nennius our old brittiſh hiſtorian in his manuſcript antiquities affirmeth that his Succeſſour Pope and S. Euariſtus ſent legates to our Brittiſh King, to receaue the faith of Chriſt, *Miſſa legatione à Papa Romano Euariſto*. Who yet ſaith the generall conuerſion was not vntill the yeare of Chriſt 197. Albertus Krantius well acquainted with our

noſ. merm. Theatr. conu, gent. Antiq. Eccl. Tullen, Gul. Eiſengr. cent. 1. Petr. de Natal 1. 11. Pantal. de vir. Ibl. part. 1. Stumph. 1. 7. de Sanctib. Theater. of great. Brit. 1. 6. Tho. Rogers Anal. in Prot. Articl. ar. 36. whitg. ſupr. Clem. Sup. ep. 1. Arnol. mirm. ſup. Antonin. hiſt. part. 1. will. harriſon. deſcript. Brit. pag. 23. Harris Theatr. l. 1. Girald. Cambr. l. 2. de Iure Metrop. Eccl. Meneu. ad Innocent. 3. Mat. Parker. Antiq Britan. pag. 24. Io. Priſ. defenſ. hiſt. Britan. pag. 73. Nennius hiſt. manuſcript.

Brittiſh

Brittish antiquities, writeth the like of S. and Pope Alexander, next Successour to Pope Euaristus, both of them liuing in this first age, though dying by martyrdome in the seconde, that he sent diuers Apostolike men hither, to preach the faith of Christ, and so they did.

These Popes haue taught vs the supreamacie of the Church of Rome ouer all Churches before. So did the next holie Pope S. Sixtus, euen Prote-

stants so confessing. *Ab Episcopo ad Romanum Pontificem appellandi ius dedit Ecclesiasticis ministris.* So they confesse of all Popes Telesphorus, Higinius, Pius anicetus and Soter, vnto Pope Eleutherius, vnder whome and by whose meanes and authoritie, this Kingdome was wholly conuerted, by all antiquities and testimonies, & made the first Christian Kingdome in the world. This holie Pope as

our Protestants write, did Order, and practise, and as the Apostles and their Successours had defined as he testifieth *sicut ab Apostolis eorumque Successoribus multorum consensu Episcoporum definitum est,* that nothing should be proceeded in, against Bishops, vntil it was defined by the Pope of Rome: *accusationem contra Episcopos, Episcopos audire permisit, sed vt nihil, nisi apud Pontificem definiretur, cauet.*

This highest spirituall Authoritie in the Pope of Rome, was not vnknowne to the Christians and King Lucius in Britayne, which moued that King as both Greeke and Latin, Brittish and Saxon, domesticall and forreyne, Catholike and Protestant Antiquaries informe, to write humble letters *supplices litteras,* to that Pope, entreating him, *obsecrans,* that by his commaundement, he with his

King-

Kingdome might receaue Christianitie, *vt per eius mandatum Christianus efficeretur*. The Pope most willingly assented, and sent his legates with full power to founde the Church of Britayne, to Ordeyne three Archbishops, and 28. Bishops, with their particular Sees, power, and Iurisdiction, who hauing established all things here, returned to Rome, to haue them confirmed by the Pope: the Pope confirmed that they had done, and they with many other preachers and the Popes confirmation, returned agayne into Britayne. *Beati Antistites Romam redierunt, & cuncta quæ fecerant, à Pontifice confirmari impetrarunt: confirmatione facta, cum pluribus alijs redierunt in Britanniam*. Our King craued direction of that Pope also, what lawes he should vse in his Kingdome, and the Pope directed him therein, as his epistle still extant witnesseth, as our Protestants write, and themselues testifie. *We haue scene the Bishop of Romes owne letter to King Lucius*. So witnesse these men.

This Pope went further, in prescribing the limits, bounds, and circuites of the Dominions of this Kingdome, and assigned vnto it all the Ilands to Denmarke, and Norway by his sentence: and by that definition or donation, they were parts of Britayne, as is conteined in our old lawes, many hundreds of yeares since published and approued by our Protestant lawyers, and historians, aswell as others. *Vniuersa terra & tota, & Insulæ omnes vsque Noruegiam, & vsque Daniam pertinent ad coronam Regni, & sunt de appendicijs, & dignitatibus Regis, & vna est monarchia, & vnum est Regnum. Tales enim metas, & fines constituit & imposuit coronæ Regni Dominus Eleutherius Papa sententia sua, qui*

C c   *primo*

de 6. ætat.
Ado Chron.
Marian. Scot.
an. 177 Martin. Pol. Supput. an. 188.
Galfrid. monum. hist. l. 4.
Virun. l. 4.
Radulp. de Dicet. hist. in Lucio. Gul. Mal. l. Antiq. cænob. glaston. Math. West. chron. an. 185. 186. 187. flor. Wigor. chron. an. 162. 184. Antiq Eccl. land. Antiq. Eccl. Wint. Cambd. Brigant. Stowe hist. hollinsh. hist. of Engl. Theatr. of Brit. l 6 Hect. Boeth. l. 5. Parker Godwin. &c. Eleuth. ep. ad Reg. Lucium Lambert. l. de leg. Stowe hist. Godw conu. of Brit. Mat. Parker. Antiq. Brit. Mason. of consecr. foxe

tom. 1. Theat.
of Brit. l. 6.
Bridg. def. of
the gouern. l.
16. pag. 1355.
Iewell ag.
hard. old.
Booke of
Const. Guil.
hall. in lond.
l. Antiq Brut.
t. Caius antiquit. Cantabrig. l. 1. leges Antiq.
Reg. Edward.
cap. 17. Gul.
Lambard. l. 2.
de priscis
Angl. legib.
fol. 130. p.
Hect. Boeth.
Scot. hist. l. 5.
f. 83. Godw.
conuerf. of
Brit. pag. 22.
23
Antiq. Eccl.
Glastonien.
Galfrid monum. l. 5. hist.
Reg. Brit. c.
1. Mat. west.
chron. an.
186.

primo destinauit coronam benedictam Britanniæ, & Christianitatem Deo inspirante, Lucio Regi Britonum. Here also he set first a crowne, or hallowed crowne to our King, being before, as some Catholiks and Protestants write, but a King by courtesie of the Romane Emperour, and authoritie. *Lucus Britonibus Cæsaris beneuolentia & authoritate imperitabat.* He gaue Indulgences to our Churches, namely to the old Church of Glastenbury ten yeares Indulgence, as in the old antiquities of that holie place is recorded. And by his Order and direction, King Lucius endowed the Churches of Britayne with liberties regall, *Lucius Rex Ecclesias Britanniæ libertatibus muniuit. Gloriosus Britonum Rex Lucius cum infra Regnum suum veræ fidei cultum magnificatum esse vidisset, possessiones & territoria Ecclesijs & viris Ecclesiasticis, abundanter conferens, chartis & munimentis omnia communiuit. Ecclesias verò cum suis cæmeterijs, ita constituit esse liberas, vt quicumque malefactor ad illa confugeret, illæsus ab omnibus remaneret.*

Thus reuerent and honourable was the spirituall power, and supreamacie of the Church and Pope of Rome, in Britayne, and all places in these Apostolike dayes. All those Apostolike men, Popes, or others which haue thus taught vs, were glorious Saincts, and King Lucius also, Sainct Lucius, who with all his Kingdome, clergie, and others so embraced it; and though neither he, nor the Romans had then any temporall Rule or dominion in the Kingdome, now called Scotland, yet that glorious Pope by his spirituall supreamacie subiected that contrie to the Archbishop of yorke in the land of an Enemie.

And

And this Papall fupreamacie and Iurifdiction continued here euer after, vntill It was taken away by King Henry the 8. taking firft of all Kings, the title and name of Supreame head of the Church of England, neuer heard of before in any time, as his owne hiftorian Polydor virgill, and all others both Catholike, and Proteftant, English and other hiftorians, acknowledge. *Habetur concilium Londini, in quo Ecclefia Anglicana formam poteftatis nullis ante temporibus vifam induit ; Henricus enim Rex caput ipfius Ecclefia conftituitur.*

And after King Henry the 8. had thus, as he endeuoured, expelled the Papall Authority fpirituall out of England, and affumed it to himfelfe, though he punished with death, as others often fince then haue done, the profeffours thereof, yet both he, and all or Rulers temporall fince, Kings, or Queens, haue retained in their ftile of honour, that title, *Defenfor fidei, defendour of the faith,* which the Pope gaue him for defending before his fall, the Catholike faith againft Martine Luther; though they all, except Queene Mary, impugned it.

And our prefent K. Charles. (whome together with his Queene Mary, God bleffe with all good, and happines) in his late publike declaration to all his louing Subiects, among whome his Catholiks be not in the loweft place of duty, and defert to him, though not in like degree of his fauour to the, thus, and thus vehemently, protefteth : *wee call God to recorde, before whome we ftand, that it is, and alwaies hath beene, our harts defire, to be found worthy of that title, which we accompt the moft glorious in all our Crowne,* DEFENDOVR OF THE FAITH.

But to defend the faith, is not, *to reprint the arti-*

Cc 2   *cles*

Polydor. Virgil Anglic. Hift. l. 27 p. 689 Stowe & Howes hift. an. 1534. ftatut. in Parliament. an. 26, Henr. 8.

cles of Religion, *eſtabliſhed in the time of Queene Eli-*
zabeth, and by a declaration before thoſe articles to ty,
and reſtraine all opinions to the ſenſe of thoſe articles: as
he ſpeaketh immediately before, and to perſecute
Biſhops, Preiſts, and Catholiks as he doth.

That title was giuen by the Pope to King Hēry,
for defence of the true faith, longe before the articles of Queene Elizabeth, or ſhe was borne. Longe
before, hee, K. Edward 6. Queene Elizabeth, King
Iames, and King Charles, perſecuted Catholiks, &
their faith, whereof by their ſtile, they ſhould be
defendours, & longe before their religion, or any of
them (I except King Henry the 8. to whome it
was giuen) receaued beeing. The true faith Catholike, and Apoſtolike, which by that regall ſtile and
title they ſhould defend, againſt theſe articles, I
haue aboundantly by the beſt teſtimonies proued
in euery point, for the two laſt following articles,
the 38. intituled, *of Chriſtian mens goods, which are*
common, and the 39. the laſt, *of a Chriſtian mans oath,*
doe not containe any cōtrouerſie with Catholikes,
but were ordained againſt new Sectaries, among
themſelues. I hope no Proteſtant Parlament will
hereafter glory, that their religion was almoſt 80.
yeares old, though it wanteth 10. of that number,
and ſo extraordinarily contend to perſecute that
which I haue proued to exceed it, aboue 1500.
yeares in time and truth, which they ought to embrace and honour, and not ſo maliciouſly or igno-
rantly, not being the moſt religious, nor learned
diuines, to perſecute it.

F I N I S.

A

TABLE OF

THE CHAPTERS.

A TABLE

Chap.

OF THE CHAPTER.